SUPERSTITION AND FORCE.

ESSAYS ON

THE WAGER OF LAW—THE WAGER OF BATTLE—THE ORDEAL—TORTURE.

BY

HENRY C. LEA.

"Antiquities, or remnants of history, are, as was said, ' tanquam tabula naufragii,' when industrious persons, by an exact and scrupulous diligence and observation, out of monuments, names, words, proverbs, traditions, private records and evidences, passages of books that concern not story, and the like, do save and recover somewhat from the deluge of time."

BACON, *Advancement of Learning*, Book II.

SECOND EDITION, REVISED.

HASKELL HOUSE PUBLISHERS LTD.
Publishers of Scarce Scholarly Books
NEW YORK. N. Y. 10012
1971

First Published 1870

HASKELL HOUSE PUBLISHERS Ltd.
Publishers of Scarce Scholarly Books
280 LAFAYETTE STREET
NEW YORK, N. Y. 10012

Library of Congress Catalog Card Number: 79-148823

Standard Book Number 8383-1228-4

Printed in the United States of America

PREFACE.

THE aim of the following essays is simply to group together facts so that, with a slender thread of commentary, they may present certain phases of human society and progress which are not without interest for the student of history and of man. The authorities for all statements have been scrupulously cited, and it will be seen that, for the most part, they are drawn from the original sources. The conclusions the reader can verify for himself.

In a more condensed form, the first three essays have already appeared in the "North American Review."

In reprinting the work, numerous changes and additions have been introduced, which, it is hoped, may render the volume more worthy of the favor with which it has been received.

PHILADELPHIA, April, 1870.

CONTENTS.

I.

THE WAGER OF LAW.

1*

II.

THE WAGER OF BATTLE.

III.

THE ORDEAL.

IV.

TORTURE.

I.

THE WAGER OF LAW

APART from the exact sciences, there is no subject which more fully repays the student than the history of jurisprudence. To the reflecting mind few popular quotations are so essentially false, or reveal so narrow a view of life as the often cited lines—

> "How small, of all that human hearts endure,
> That part which kings or laws can cause or cure!"

Since the origin of society, each unit of our race has struggled on in his allotted path, through joys and griefs, fashioned, for the most part, by the invisible network of habits, customs, and statutes, which surround him on every side, and silently shape his daily actions. Thus the history of jurisprudence becomes the history of the life of man, and the society of distant ages is more distinctly presented to us in the crabbed sentences of codes than in the flowing rhetoric of the historian. Slender as may be the respect with which we of to-day sometimes regard rotatory assemblymen and partisan judges, still are they none the less noteworthy personages. The parts are more important than the actors, and centuries hence it will be to our statute books and reports that the curious student will resort to find out what manner of men were the restless and energetic race which found self-government a harder task than the founding of a gigantic empire.

The law-giver and the law-dispenser thus are the custodians of all that we hold dear on earth. Save the minister of God, what human being can have interests so vital con-

2

fided to him, or can exercise so momentous an influence over his fellow-men ? Cyrus and Alexander, Tamerlane and Genghis Khan have passed away; their names alone remain, and the world is as though they had never been; while the laws of Confucius and Manu, of Mahomet and Justinian still live, and will sway the destinies of races in the future as they have in the almost illimitable past. When Arogast and Bodogast, Salogast and Windagast assembled to draft into shape the rude customs of a roving and predatory tribe, they little thought that the Salique law which they founded would leave its impress for centuries on nations to which their very names would be unknown. Codes thus endowed with vitality must necessarily reflect the nature and the usages of the races for which they were compiled. The man and his law exercise a mutual reaction, and in the one we may see an image of the other. The stern, resolute brevity of the law of the Twelve Tables furnishes the best corrective commentary on the easy credulity of Livy; in the code of Moses, the Hebrew character and polity are portrayed in the strongest light and shade; and, in general, the historian, who wishes to obtain or to convey a definite impression of a nation or a period, must have recourse to the laws which regulated the daily life of the people, and which epitomize their actions and modes of thought. It may be, therefore, not uninteresting to trace, through the dim light of antiquity, some rude outlines of customs which were the precursors of European civilization.

The idea that crime is an offence against society at large found little place in the conceptions of the barbarian lawgivers. The loosely-knit organizations which overthrew the Roman Empire were based upon two central principles— the independence of the individual citizen and the solidarity of the family; and on the mutual interaction of these organic laws was based the jurisprudence of the period. The criminal was not responsible to the State, but to the injured party; and all that the State professed to do was to provide some definite process by which the latter could assert his rights. Personal chastisement for the freeman was thus unknown, for each man was responsible for his acts not to the law but to those whom he might wrong. All that the law pretended to do was to provide rude courts, before which a plaintiff might urge his case, and settled principles of pecuniary compensation to console him for his injuries.[1] If he disdained this peaceful process he was at liberty to assemble his friends and kindred, and exact what satisfaction he could with sword and axe.

Whether he adopted the one mode or the other, his proceedings were regulated by the other great general principle of the solidarity of the family. All the members of a kindred were indissolubly united. They suffered for the crimes of their kinsmen, and an offence committed against one was committed against all. Together they stood in the court or in the field, in some sort a unit, mutually responsible for each other. Yet the endless warfare of hostile families was for the most part averted by the principle of compensation for injuries, by which every crime was rated at its appropriate price, or *wehr-gild*, which was payable to the injured party; nor could the offender legitimately refuse to appear if summoned to the *mallum* or judicial assembly of his tribe, and claim the right of armed defence if his victim chose to have recourse to peaceable proceedings.

This system of compensation as an alternative for reprisals is expressively condensed in an Anglo-Saxon proverb quoted approvingly in the laws of Edward the Confessor as collected by William the Conqueror—" Bicge spere of side oðer bere"—Buy off the spear from thy side or endure

---

[1] Gradually, however, a portion of the composition-money under the name of *fredum*, was attributed to the king or the judges under guise of readmitting the criminal to public peace.

it[1]—and its results are found in the minute and complex
tariffs of crime which form so large a portion of the barbarian codes.   Every offence against person or property is
rated at its appropriate price, from the theft of a sucking
pig to the armed occupation of an estate, and from a wound
of a little finger to the most atrocious of parricides.   To
what extent this was carried in time may be seen in the
Welsh codes, where every hair of the eyelash is rated at a
penny.[2]

This system introduced into legal proceedings a spirit
of trade which seems strangely at variance with the savage
heroism commonly attributed to our barbarian ancestors.
In the spirited translation by Mr. Dasent of the old Icelandic Saga of Burnt Njal is vividly set forth the complex
code which arose from the development of the principle,
where suits could be sold and assigned by one party to
another, and a plaintiff with a promising claim for damages
would part with it to some speculator who undertook the
chances of the suit; or, if the prospects were not encouraging, he would pay some shrewd lawyer or mighty warrior
to prosecute it in his stead.   As either party in the primitive Icelandic code could at any moment interrupt the
proceedings with a challenge to single combat, or a powerful pleader might collect his friends for a raid on the
Althing and thus break up the court, this transferring of
suits was sometimes a very provident precaution.

In this principle of compensation the solidarity of the
family bore a part as conspicuous as in the alternative of
private warfare.   The kindred of the offender were obliged
to contribute shares proportionate to their degrees of relationship; while those of the man who was wronged received
respective percentages calculated on the same basis.   Thus
the most ancient barbarian code that has reached us—that

---

[1] Ll. Edwardi c. xii. (Thorpe's Ancient Laws, I. 467.)

[2] Gwentian Code, Bk. II. chap. vii. § 8 (Aneurin Owen's Ancient Laws,
&c., of Wales, I. 701).

of the Feini, or ancient Irish—in a fanciful quadripartite enumeration of the principles in force in levying fines, alludes to the responsibility of kindred — "And because there are four things for which it is levied: 'cin' (one's own crime) and 'tobhach' (the crime of a near kinsman) 'saighi' (the crime of a middle kinsman), and the crime of a kinsman in general."[1] A very complete example of the development of this system is to be found in the Icelandic legislation of the twelfth century, where the fines exacted diminish gradually, as far as the relatives in the fifth degree on both sides, each grade of the criminal's family paying its rate to the corresponding grade of the sufferer's kindred.[2] When, however, the next of kin were females, and were thus incompetent to prosecute for murder, the person who undertook that office was rewarded with one-third of the fine.[3] It was not until about 1270 that King Haco, in his unsuccessful attempt to reform the laws, ventured to decree that in cases of murder the blood-money should not be divided among the family of the victim, but should all be paid to the heir.[4] On the other hand, in Denmark, Eric VII., in 1269 relieved the kindred of the murderer from contributing to the *wehr-gild*, although it continued to be divided among the relatives of the slain.[5]

Among the Welsh the provisions for levying and distributing the fines were almost as complex as those of the early Icelandic law; one body of jurisprudence extending the liability even as far as sixth cousins;[6] and perhaps the quaintest expression of the responsibility of the kindred is to be found in the regulation that if any one should draw blood from the abbot of either of the seven great

[1] Senchus Mor, I. 259 (Hancock's ed. Dublin, 1865).
[2] Grágás, Sect. IV. cap. cxiv.　　　　[3] Ibid. Sect. VIII. cap. lv.
[4] Jarnsida, Mannhelge, cap. xxix.
[5] Constit. Eric. Ann. 1269, § vii. (Ludewig, Reliq. MSS. T. XII. p. 204.)
[6] Dimetian Code, Bk. II. ch. i. §§ 17–31—Bk. III. ch. iii. § 4—Anomalous Laws, Bk. IV. ch. iii. § 11.

houses of Dyved, the offender should forfeit seven pounds, while a female of his kindred should become a washer-woman in token of disgrace.[1] The firm hold which this practical solidarity of the family had upon the jurisprudence of the European races is shown by a clause in the statutes of the city of Lille, as late as the fourteenth century, where the malefactor had the right to collect from his relatives a portion of the *wehr-gild* which he had incurred ; and elaborate tables were drawn up, showing the amount payable by each relative in proportion to his degree of kinship, the liability extending as far as to third cousins.[2]

There was one prevailing exception to these rules, however, for ecclesiastical ties dissolved those of the family. By the Carlovingian legislation, when a priest was slain his *wehr-gild* was paid to the church, which was held to be nearer to him than any relative,[3] though this regulation subsequently was modified so as to divide the composition into three parts, of which one was paid to the church of the deceased, one to his bishop, and the third to his kindred.[4] As a general rule, however, the clerk could claim no share of the blood-money collected for the murder of his kinsman, nor be called upon to contribute to that incurred by his family ;[5] though it is true that, by the Welsh laws of Hoel the Good, compiled in the tenth century, children, even prospective, were a link through which the liability might be again incurred. "Neither clerks nor women are to have a share of the *galanas*, since they are not avengers ; however, they are to pay for their children or to make oath that they shall never have any."[6]

In its relations to the community, therefore, each family in the barbaric tribes was a unit, both for attack and de-

---

[1] Dimetian Code, Bk. II. chap. xxiv. § 12.
[2] Roisin, Franchises, etc. de la ville de Lille, pp. 106–7.
[3] Capitul. Lib. IV. cap. 15.   [4] Concil. Tribur. an. 895, can. iv.
[5] Dimetian Code, Bk. II. chap. i. § 32.
[6] Venedotian Code, Bk. III. chap. i. § 21.

fence, whether recourse was had to the jealously preserved
right of private warfare, or whether the injured parties
contented themselves with the more peaceful processes of
the *mallum* or *althing*. This solidarity of the kindred is
the key to much that would otherwise appear singular in
their legislation, and left, as we have seen, its traces late
in the feudal and customary law.

But, between the commission of an offence and its proof
in a court of justice, there lies a wide field for the exercise
or perversion of human ingenuity. The subject of evidence
is one which has taxed man's powers of reasoning to the
utmost; and the subtle distinctions of the Roman law, with
its *probatio, præsumptio juris, præsumptio juris tantum;*
the endless refinements of the glossators, rating evidence
in its different grades, as *probatio optima, evidentissima,
apertissima, legitima, sufficiens, indubitata, dilucida, liqui-
da, evidens, perspicua,* and *semiplena;* and the complicated
rules which bewilder the student of the common law, all
alike show the importance of the subject, and its supreme
difficulty. The semi-barbarian, impatient of such expen-
diture of logic, arrived at results by a shorter and more
direct process.

Some writers have assumed that the unsupported oath
of the accused was originally sufficient to clear him of a
charge, and they present an attractive fancy sketch of the
heroic age, when a lie is cowardice, and the fierce warrior
disdains to shrink from the consequences of his act. All
this is pure invention, for which proof may be vainly sought
in any of the unadulterated " Leges Barbarorum." It was
not, indeed, until long after the Teutonic tribes had declined from the rude virtue of their native forests, that an
unsupported oath was receivable as evidence, and its introduction may be traced to the influence of the Roman law,
in which its importance was overwhelming.[1] The Wisi-

---

[1] The oath may be regarded as the foundation of Roman legal procedure.
" Dato jurejurando non aliud quæritur, quam an juratum sit; remissa

goths, who moulded their laws on the Roman jurisprudence, were the only race of barbarians who permitted the accused, in the absence of definite testimony, to escape on his single oath,[1] and this exception only tends to prove the rule. So great was the abhorrence of the other races for practices of this kind, that at the council of Valence, in 855, the Wisigothic custom was denounced in the strongest terms as an incentive to perjury.[2] It was not until long after the primitive customs of the wild tribes had become essentially modified by contact with the remains of Roman civilization, that such procedures were regarded as admissible; and, indeed, it required the revival of the study of the civil law in the twelfth century to give the practice a position entitled to respect.[3]

---

quæstione an debeatur; quasi satis probatum sit jurejurando." L. 5, § 2, D. XII. ii. The *jusjurandum necessarium* could always be administered by the judge in cases of deficient evidence, and the *jusjurandum in jure* proffered by the plaintiff to the defendant was conclusive : " Manifestæ turpitudinis et confessionis est nolle nec jurare nec jusjurandum referre." Ibid. l. 38.

[1] Ll. Wisigoth. Lib. II. Tit. ii. c. 5.

[2] Concil. Valentin. ann. 855, c. xi.

[3] Thus Alfonso the Wise endeavored to introduce into Spain the mutual challenging of the parties involved in the Roman *jusjurandum in jure*, by his *jura de juicio*. (Las Siete Partidas, P. III. Tit. xi. l. 2.) Oddly enough, the same procedure is found incorporated in the municipal law of Rheims in the fourteenth century, probably introduced by some over-zealous civilian ; " Si alicui deferatur jusjurandum, necesse habet jurare vel referre jusjurandum, et hoc super quovis debito, vel inter quasvis personas." Lib. Pract. de Consuetud. Remens. § 15 (Archives Législat. de Reims, P. I. p. 37). By this time, however, the oaths of parties had assumed great importance. In the legislation of St. Louis, they occupy a position which was a direct incentive to perjury. Thus he provides for the hanging of the owner of a beast which had killed a man, if he was foolish enough not to swear that he was ignorant of its being vicious. "Et si il estoit si fox que il deist que il seust la teche de la beste, il en seroit pendus pour la recoignoissance."— Etablissements, Liv. I. chap. cxxi.

In certain local codes, the purgatorial power of the oath was carried to the most absurd extent. Thus, in the thirteenth century, the municipal law of the Saxons enabled the accused in certain cases to clear himself, however

It is true that occasionally, in the early legislation of the
barbarians, an instance occurs in which certain privileges
in this respect are accorded to some classes in the community, but these are special immunities bestowed on rank,
and are therefore only exceptions, which go to prove the
universality of the rule. Thus in one of the most primitive
of the Anglo-Saxon codes, which dates from the seventh
century, the king and the bishop are permitted to rebut
an accusation with their simple asseveration, and the thane
and the mass-priest with a simple oath, while the great
body both of clerks and laymen are forced to clear themselves by undergoing the regular form of canonical compurgation which will be hereafter described.[1] So, in the
Welsh legislation, exemption from the oath of absolution
was accorded to bishops, lords, the deaf, the dumb, men

notorious the facts of the case, and no evidence was admitted to disprove his
position. " Si quis aliquid agit extra judicium, et hoc maxime est notorium,
id negare possit, præstito juramento, nec admittantur testes contra eum ;
hoc juris est." (Jur. Provin. Saxon. Lib. i. Art. 15, 18.) This irrational
abuse was long in vogue, and was denounced by the Council of Bâle in the
fifteenth century (Schilter. Thesaur. II. 291.) It only prevailed in the
North of Germany ; the Jus Provin. Alaman. (cap. ccclxxxi. § 3) which
regulated Southern Germany, alludes to it as one of the distinguishing features of the Saxon code.

So, also, at the same period a special privilege was claimed by the inhabitants of Franconia, in virtue of which a murderer was allowed to rebut with
his single oath all testimony as to his guilt, unless he chanced to be caught
with the red hand.—Jur. Provin. Alaman. cap. cvi. § 7.

A charter granted to the commune of Lorris, in 1155, by Louis-le-Jeune,
gives to burghers the privilege of rebutting by oath, without conjurators,
an accusation unsupported by testimony.—Chart. Ludovic. junior. ann.
1155, cap. xxxii. (Isambert, Anciennes Lois Françaises I. 157.) And, in
comparatively modern times, in Germany, the same rule was followed.
"Juramento rei, quod purgationis vocatur, sæpe etiam innocentia, utpote
quæ in anima constitit, probatur et indicia diluuntur ;" and this oath was
administered when the evidence was insufficient to justify torture. (Zangeri
Tract. de Quæstionibus cap. iii. No. 46.) In 1592, Zanger wrote an elaborate
essay to prove the evils of the custom.

[1] Laws of Wihtræd, cap. 16–21. Comp. Ll. Henrici I. Tit. lxiv. § 8.

of a different language, and pregnant women.[1] These instances of class privileges are too numerous throughout
the whole period of the dark ages to afford any basis for
general deductions.[2]

So far, indeed, were the barbarians from confiding in the
integrity of their fellows that, as they emerge into the light
of history, their earliest records show how eagerly they
endeavored to obtain some additional guarantee for the
oaths of litigants. What these guarantees were during
the prevalence of paganism we can only guess. After their
conversion to Christianity, as soon as written documents
afford us the means of tracing their customs, we find many
expedients adopted. As the practice of invoking objects
of affection or veneration in witness of an oath has been
common to mankind in all ages,[3] so the forms of religion

---

[1] Anomalous Laws, Book IV. chap. i. § 11.—(Owen's Laws and Institutes
of Wales, II. 5.)

[2] Thus, by the law of Southern Germany in the thirteenth century, the
unsupported oath of the claimant was sufficient if he was a personage of sub-
stance and repute, while, if otherwise, he was obliged to provide two conjurators. (Jur. Provin. Aleman. cap. ccxliv. §§ 7, 8.) So in Castile, until the
middle of the fourteenth century, the fijodalgo or noble could rebut a claim
in civil cases by taking three solemn oaths, in which he invoked the vengeance of God in this world and the next.—"Nuestro Señor Dios, a quien lo
jurades, vos lo demande en estro mundo al cuerpo, e en il otro al animo."
(Fuero Viejo, Lib. III. Tit. ii.)

[3] Thus, in the Roman law, oaths were frequently taken on the head of the
litigant, or on those of his children. (Ll. 3, 4, D. XII. ii.) The code of
Manu, which regards oaths as a satisfactory mode of proof, endeavors to
secure their veracity by selecting for invocation those objects most likely to
impress the different castes into which society was divided.

"And in cases where there is no testimony, and the judge cannot decide
upon which side lies the truth, he can determine it fully by administering
the oath."

"Oaths were sworn by the seven great Richis, and by the gods, to make
doubtful things manifest, and even Vasichtha sware an oath before the
king Soudâmâ, son of Piyavana, when Viswâmitra accused him of eating
a hundred children.

"Let not the wise man take an oath in vain, even for things of little
weight; for he who takes an oath in vain is lost in this world and the next.

were speedily called in to lend sanctity to the imprecation, by ingenious devices which were thought to give additional solemnity to the awful ceremony. In the middle of the sixth century, Pope Pelagius I. did not disdain to absolve himself from the charge of having been concerned in the troubles which drove his predecessor Vigilius into exile, by taking a disculpatory oath in the pulpit, holding over his head a crucifix and the Gospels.[1] About the same period, when the holy Gregory of Tours was accused of reproachful words truly spoken of the infamous Fredegonda, a council of bishops decided that he should clear himself of the charge by oaths on three altars, after celebrating mass on each, which he duly performed, doubtless more to his corporeal than his spiritual benefit.[2] This plan of reduplicating oaths on different altars was an established practice among the Anglo-Saxons, who, in certain cases, allowed the plaintiff to substantiate his assertion by swearing in four churches, while the defendant could rebut the charge by taking an oath of negation in twelve.[3] Seven altars are similarly specified in the ancient Welsh laws in cases where a surety desired to deny his suretyship.[4]

"Let the judge swear the Brahmin by his truth; the Kchatriya by his horses, his elephants, or his arms; the Vaisya by his cows, his corn, and his gold; the Soûdra by all crimes."—Book VII. v. 109–113. (After Delongchamps' translation.)

A curious exception to this general principle is found in the legislation of the ancient Egyptians, where the laws of Bocchoris received as conclusive the simple oath of a debtor denying his indebtedness, in cases where there were no writings.—(Diod. Sicul. L. I. cap. lxxix.) It was thence, probably, that Moses adopted the same rule in cases where there was no evidence (Exod. XXII. 11.)

[1] Anastas. Biblioth. No. LXII.

[2] Gregor. Turon. Hist. Lib. v. cap. xlix. Gregory complains that this was contrary to the canons, of which more hereafter.

[3] Dooms of Alfred, cap. 33.

[4] Dimetian Code, Bk. II. chap. vi. § 17 (Owen, I. 431.) According to the *Fleta*, as late as the thirteenth century, a custom was current among merchants, of proving the payment of a debt by swearing in nine churches, the abuse of which led to its abrogation (Fleta, Lib. II. cap. lxiii. § 12). The

The intense veneration with which relics were regarded, however, caused them to be generally adopted as the most effective means of adding security to oaths, and so little respect was felt for the simple oath that, ere long, the adjuncts came to be looked upon as the essential feature, and the imprecation itself to be divested of binding force without them.   Thus, in 680, when Ebroin, mayor of the palace of Burgundy, had defeated Martin, Duke of Austrasia, and desired to entice him from his refuge in the stronghold of Laon, two bishops were sent to him bearing the royal reliquaries, on which they swore that his life should be safe. Ebroin, however, had astutely removed the holy remains from their cases in advance, and when he thus got his enemy in his power, he held it but a venial indiscretion to expose Martin to a shameful death.[1] How thoroughly this was in accordance with the ideas of the age is shown by the incorporation, in the canons of the church, of the doctrine that an oath was to be estimated by its externals and not by itself. The penitential of St. David, dating from the latter half of the sixth century, provides that perjury committed in a church shall be punished by a fine of four times the value of that for which the false oath was taken,[2] but no penalty is provided for false swearing elsewhere.   As the theory developed itself this tacit condoning of such perjury was boldly declared to be good ecclesiastical law, and the venerable code of morality which passes under the name of Theodore Archbishop of Can-

Moslem jurisprudence has a somewhat similar provision for accusatorial oaths in the Iesamé by which a murderer can be convicted, in the absence of testimony or confession, by fifty oaths sworn by relatives of the victim. Of these there must be at least two, and the fifty oaths are divided between them in proportion to their respective legal shares in the Dié, or blood-money for the murder.—Du Boys, Droit Criminel des Peuples Modernes, I. 269.

[1] Fredegarii Chron. cap. xcvii.

[2] Excerpt. de Libro Davidis No. xvi. (Haddan and Stubbs's Councils of Great Britain, I. 120.)

terbury assumes that a perjury committed on a consecrated
cross requires, for absolution, three times the penance necessary in cases where the oath had been taken on an
unconsecrated one, while, if the ministration of a priest
had not been employed, the oath was void, and no penalty
was inflicted for its violation.[1] In a similar mood the pene-
tential of Gregory III. provides that three years' penance
will absolve for perjury committed on a consecrated cross
or on the hand of a bishop or priest, while seven years are
requisite if the oath has been taken on the gospels or on
an altar with relics.[2]

These principles were adopted as the fundamental basis
of all legal procedures in Wales. Every prosecution and
defence required relics to give validity to the oaths of
both parties, and even in the fifteenth century a collection
of laws declares that a plaintiff coming into court without
a relic on which to make his oath, not only lost his cause
but incurred a fine of nine-score pence. The same tendency is shown in the rule by which a man who suspected
another of theft could go to him with a relic and in the
presence of witnesses demand an oath of negation, a failure in which was a conviction of the crime imputed, without further trial.[3] In the same spirit, ecclesiastical authority was even found to admit that a powerful motive
might extenuate the sin of perjury. If committed voluntarily, seven years of penitence were enjoined for its absolution ; if involuntarily, sixteen months, while if to pre-

---

[1] Si in manu episcopi . . . aut in cruce consecrata perjurat III. annos pœniteat. Si vero in cruce non consecrata, perjurat I. annum pœniteat ; si autem
in manu hominis laici juraverit, nihil est.—Theodori Cantuar. Pœnit. cap.
xxiv. § 2. (Thorpe, Ancient Laws, vol. II. p. 29.)

[2] Gregor. PP. III. de Criminibus et Remediis cap. vii.

[3] Anomalous Laws, Book ix. chap. v. § 3, chap. xxxviii. § 1. (Owen, II.
233, 303.) The definition of relics, however, was somewhat vague—"There
are three relics to swear by : the staff of a priest; the name of God ; and
hand to hand with the one sworn to."—Bk. xiii. ch. ii. § 219. (Ibid. II.
557.)

3

serve life or limb, the offence could be washed out with four months.[1] When such doctrines were received and acted upon, we can hardly wonder at the ingenious device which the sensitive charity of King Robert the Pious imitated from the duplicity of Ebroin, to save the souls of his friends. He provided two reliquaries on which to receive their oaths —one for his magnates, splendidly fabricated of crystal and gold, but entirely empty, the other for the common herd, plainer and enshrining a bird's egg. Knowing in advance that his lieges would be forsworn, he thus piously sought to save them from sin in spite of themselves, and his monkish panegyrist is delighted in recounting this holy deceit.[2]

It was easy, from a belief such as this, to draw the deduction that when an oath was sworn, on relics of peculiar sanctity, immediate punishment would follow perjury; and thus it followed that some shrines obtained a reputation which caused them to be resorted to in the settlement of disputed judicial questions. Even as early as St. Augustine there are traces of such practices, which that Father of the Church not only records, but imitated,[3] and at a later period the legends are numerous which record how the perjured sinner was stricken down senseless or rendered rigid and motionless in the act of swearing falsely.[4] The profit which the church derived from thus administering

---

[1] Regino. de Eccles. Discip. Lib. i. cap. ccc. See also Gregor. PP. III. de Crimin. loc. cit. Notwithstanding the shocking laxity of these doctrines, it is not to be supposed that the true theory of the oath was altogether lost. St. Isidor of Seville, who was but little anterior to Theodore of Canterbury, well expresses it : " Quacunque arte verborum quisque juret, Deus tamen, qui conscientiæ testis est, ita hoc accipit, sicut ille cui juratur intelligit," and this, being adopted in successive collections of canons, coexisted with the above as a maxim of ecclesiastical law (Ivon. Decret P. xii. c. 36.— Gratian. caus. xxii. q. 2 can. 13).

[2] Helgaldi Vit. Roberti Regis.

[3] Augustin. Epist. 78 §§ 2, 3.   (Ed. Benedict.)

[4] Gregor. Turon. de Gloria Martyr. cap. 58, 103.

oaths on relics affords an easy explanation of her teachings, and of the extension of these practices. Their resultant advantages are well illustrated by the example of the holy taper of Cardigan, in Wales. A miraculous image of the Virgin was cast ashore, bearing this taper burning in her hand. A church was built for it, and the taper " contynued styll burnynge the space of nyne yeres, without wastynge, until the tyme that one forsware himselfe thereon, so then it extincted, and never burned after." At the suppression of the house under Henry VIII., the prior, Thomas Hore, testified : " Item, that since the ceasynge of burnynge of the sayd taper, it was enclosed and taken for a greate re- lyque, and so worshipped and kyssed of pylgremes, and used of men to sweare by in difficill and harde matters, whereof the advauntage admounted to great sommes of money in tymes passed, payenge yerely to the same XXti nobles for a pencion unto thabbott of Chersey."[1]

Notwithstanding the earnestness with which these teach- ings were enforced, it may readily be believed that the wild barbarian, who was clamoring for the restoration of stolen cattle, or the angry relatives, eager to share the wehrgild of some murdered kinsman, would scarcely sub- mit to be balked of their rights at the cost of simple perjury on the part of the criminal. While their Christianity was yet new, they would not attach much value to the addi- tional security afforded by religious ceremonies or super- stitious observances, and, as we have seen, before they became old in the faith, craft and trickery defiled the most

---

[1] Suppression of Monasteries, p. 186. (Camden Soc. Pub.) The Priory of Cardigan was dependent upon the Abbey of Chertsey, and the sum named was apparently the abbot's share of the annual spoils.

Perhaps the most suggestive illustration of the reverence for relics is a passage in the ancient Welsh laws limiting the protection legally afforded by them—" If a person have relics upon him and does an illegal act under the relics, he is not to have protection or defence through those relics, for he has not deserved it."—Venedotian Code, Bk. i. chap. x. § 7.

sacred solemnities. It was therefore natural that they should still have recourse to an ancestral custom, which had arisen from the structure of their society, and which derived its guarantee from the solidarity of families alluded to above. This was the remarkable custom which was subsequently known as canonical compurgation, and which long remained a part of English jurisprudence, under the name of the Wager of Law. The defendant, when denying the allegation under oath, appeared surrounded by a number of companions—*juratores, conjuratores, sacramentales, collaudantes, compurgatores,* as they were variously termed—who swore, not to their knowledge of the facts, but as shares and partakers in the oath of denial.

This curious form of procedure derives importance from the fact that it is an expression of the character, not of an isolated sept, but of nearly all the races that have moulded the destinies of Europe. The Ostrogoths in Italy, and the Wisigoths of the South of France and Spain were the only nations in whose codes it occupies no place, and they, as has already been remarked, at an early period yielded themselves completely to the influence of the Roman civilization. On the other hand, the Salians, the Ripuarians, the Alamanni, the Baioarians, the Lombards, the Frisians, the Saxons, the Angli and Werini, the Anglo-Saxons, and the Welsh, races springing from origins widely diverse, all gave to this form of purgation a prominent position in their jurisprudence, and it may be said to have reigned from Southern Italy to Scotland.

That the custom was anterior to the settlement of the barbarians in the Roman provinces is susceptible of reasonable proof. The earliest text of the Salique law presents us with the usages of the Franks unaltered by any allusions to Christianity, and it may therefore be presumed to date from a period not later than the conversion of Clovis. In this primæval code there are directions for the employment of conjurators, which show that the pro-

cedure was a settled and established form at that period.[1]
So in the Frisian law, which although compiled in the
eighth century, still reveals pagan customs and the primitive condition of society, the practice of compurgation
evidently forms the basis of judicial proceedings. The
other codes have only reached us in revisions subsequent
to the conversion of the several tribes, and their authority
on this point is, therefore, not so absolute. The universality of the practice, however, at a period when intercom-
munication was rare, and ancestral habits not easily infringed upon, is a strong corroborative evidence that its
origin with all is traceable to prehistoric times.[2]

---

[1] First Text of Pardessus, Tit. xxxix. § 2, and Tit. xlii. § 5 (Loi Salique,
Paris, 1843, pp. 21, 23). It is somewhat singular that in the subsequent recensions of the code the provision is omitted in these passages. One cannot
without hesitation accuse Montesquieu of ignorance, and yet it is difficult
under any other supposition to account for his assertion that canonical compurgation was unknown to the Salique law (Esprit des Loix, Lib. xxviii.
chap. 13), an assumption from which he proceeds to draw the most extensive
deductions. Although compurgation is referred to but twice in the *Lex
Emendata* of Charlemagne (Tit. l., lv.), still those references are of a
nature to show that it was habitually practised; while the earlier texts, of
which that of Herold and the Wolfenbuttel MS. were accessible to him in
the well-known edition of Eckhardt, contain precise directions for its use,
designating the conjurator under the title of *Thalapta*. Even without
these, however, the Merovingian and Carlovingian Capitularies, the Formulary of Marculfus, and the history of Gregory of Tours should have preserved him from so gross an error.

[2] Among the Anglo-Saxons, for instance, the earliest written code is the
Dooms of Æthelbirht (Bedæ Hist. Angl. II. 5), compiled shortly after his
conversion by Augustine in 597. It is scarcely more than a list of fines and
punishments, containing no instructions for judicial procedures, and therefore its silence on the subject of compurgation affords no indication on the
subject. The next in point of date, however, the Dooms of Hlothhære and
Eadric, promulgated about A. D 680, alludes to conjurators under the name
of *æwdas* (cap. 2, 4, 5, &c.), after which they form a prominent feature in
Anglo-Saxon jurisprudence.

It is somewhat remarkable that the custom should not have been indigenous among the inhabitants of Iceland, when it was universal among their
parent Scandinavian races. Their earliest code, the Grágás, which dates
from the twelfth century, contains no allusion to it (Schlegel, Comment. ad

The church, with the tact which distinguished her deal-
ings with her new converts, was not long in adopting a
system which was admirably suited for her defence in an
age of brute force. As holy orders sundered all other ties,
and as the church was regarded as one vast family, ecclesiastics speedily arrogated to themselves and obtained the
privilege of having men of their own class as compurgators, and, thus fortified for mutual support, they were aided
in resisting the oppressors who invaded their rights on
every hand. How completely the custom became part and
parcel of ecclesiastical law is shown by Gregory II. in the
early part of the eighth century, when he ordered its employment in cases where husband and wife desired to deny
the consummation of marriage.[1] At last the final seal of
approbation was bestowed when Charlemagne, in the year
800, went to Rome for the purpose of trying Pope Leo III.
on a grave charge, and in that august presence the Pontiff, whom no witnesses dared to accuse, cleared himself of
the crimes imputed to him by solemnly taking the oath of
denial in company with twelve priests as compurgators.[2]
Three years afterwards, the Emperor decreed that, in all
doubtful cases, priests should defend themselves with three,
five, or seven ecclesiastical compurgators, and he announced
that this decision had been reached by the common consent

Grágás p. lxxxiv.). It was, however, introduced in the *Jarnsida*, the code
which Haco of Norway endeavored, with indifferent success, to impose upon
them towards the close of the thirteenth century.

[1] Can. Requisisti, caus. xxxiii. q. 1.

[2] Eginhart. Annal. ann. 800.—The monkish chroniclers have endeavored
to conceal the fact that Leo underwent the form of trial like a common
criminal, but the evidence is indubitable. Charlemagne alludes to it in the
Capitularium Aquisgranense ann. 803, in a manner which admits of no dispute.

The monk of St. Gall (De Gestis B. Carol. Mag. Lib. I. cap. 28), whose
work is rather legendary in its character, describes the Pope as swearing to
his innocence by his share at the day of judgment in the promises of the
Gospels, which he had placed upon his head.

of Pope, patriarchs, bishops, and all the faithful.[1] It is
true that a few months later, on being shown a decretal of
Gregory II.[2] ordering the clergy to rebut all accusations

[1] Capit. Aquisgran. ann. 803, cap. vii.

[2] De presbytero vero vel quolibet sacerdote a populo accusato, si certi
non fuerint testes, qui crimini illato approbent veritatem, jurejurando erit
in medio, et illum testem proferat de innocentiæ suæ puritate, cui nuda et
aperta sunt omnia, sicque maneat in proprio gradu.—Bonifacii Epist. cxxvi.

The subject of the oaths of priests was one of considerable perplexity
during the dark ages. Among the numerous privileges assumed by the sacerdotal body was exemption from the necessity of swearing, and their efforts
to obtain the recognition of this claim date from an early period. That it
was a disputed question even in the time of St. Augustine is shown by his
arguing that the responsibility properly attaches to him who requires the
oath, not to the oath-taker himself. " Non est contra Dei præceptum jura-
tio, quæ a malo est non jurantis sed incredulitatis ejus a quo jurare cogitur.
. . . Quantum ad me pertinet, juro, sed quantum mihi videtur, magna necessitate compulsus" (apud Ivon. Decret. P. xii. c. 3, 8). At the Council of Ephesus in 431, St. Cyril, in calling upon Theodotus Bishop of Ancyra
and Acacius Bishop of Melitene to give evidence as to the heterodox opinions
of Nestorius, caused them to be sworn, in view of the importance of the
questions involved (Concil. Ephesin. Act. I.—Harduin. I. 1398). On
the other hand, in 449, in the second synod held in Constantinople for
the condemnation of Eutyches, when the imperial officers called upon the
bishops to swear to the correctness of the records of the prior synod,
Basilius Bishop of Seleucia declared the demand to be unprecedented " Hac-
tenus juramentum episcopis nescimus oblatum," and the protest was
effectual (Concil. Chalced. Act. I.—Harduin. II. 178). Shortly after this,
the force of law was given to the claim, for in 456, the Emperor Marcian
admitted that ecclesiastics were forbidden by the canons to swear—" quia
ecclesiasticis regulis, et canone a beatissimis episcopis antiquitus instituto,
clerici jurare prohibentur," a provision which was retained by Justinian.
(Const. 25 C. i. 3.) Yet when the latter was eagerly engaged in obtaining
the condemnation of Theodore of Mopsuestia, and a synod was held at
Mopsuestia, under his auspices, to investigate the removal of Theodore's
name from the diptychs, all the ecclesiastics of the church were formally
examined under oath (Concil. Constantinop. II. Collat. V.—Harduin. III.
126). The Rule of St. Benedict contained a clause " Non jurare, ne forte
perjuret," on which his commentator Smaragdus, in the ninth century,
observes "non est contra Dei præceptum jurare," but out of abundant caution
he adds "necesse est ergo ut nunquam juret, qui perjurare timet" (Comment. in Reg. S. Ben. cap. iv. § 27). Even Charlemagne in 801 yielded
his assent to the rule, and forbade the clergy from taking formal oaths—
" ut nullus sacerdos quicquam cum juramento juret" (Capit. ann. 801) ;

with their single oaths, he modified his previous command,
and left the matter to the discretion of his prelates;[1] but

and the manufacturers of the False Decretals sought to support it by the
authority of the primitive church (Pseudo-Cornelii Epist. II. cap. i).

This, however, had no permanent effect. The bishops of Neustria, who
in 858 claimed exemption from taking oaths of allegiance, admitted that
judicial oaths could properly be exacted of them (Cap. Car. Calvi. Tit. xxvii.
c. 15). As the line of demarcation between the clergy and the laity grew
wider and deeper, the effort was renewed, and the oath was regarded as a
degradation to those engaged in the sacred ministry of the altar—"Manus
enim per quam Corpus Christi conficitur juramento polluetur? Absit !"
(Concil. Tribur. ann. 895 can. xxi.) The Emperor Lothair, in his additions to the Lombard Law gave to bishops, abbots, and abbesses the right to
have two advocates, one to conduct their cases and the other to take the
necessary oaths (Ll. Langobard. Lothar. XV.—Canciani, I. 196) ; and this
swearing by proxy seemed to be so satisfactory a solution of the difficulty
that in both civil and criminal proceedings it was proclaimed as a general
rule, more than two centuries afterwards, by the Emperor Henry II. in 1020
(Constit. Ariminen. S. Henrici—Migne's Patrolog. T. 140, p. 232). This
law probably was not long respected, for about the year 1125 it was disin-
terred and re-enacted with much emphasis by Honorius II. (Honor. PP.
II. Epist. 90).

Where legislation was so variable and conflicting, it is not easy to ascertain positive results; but in the eleventh century it would seem that ecclesiastics summoned as witnesses before lay judges could not be forced to the
oath, but that when they themselves were parties it could be administered,
at the option of their superior, with the proviso that it should be employed
only in important cases. (Cf. Ivon. Panorm. Lib. v. c. 9, 10, 11.) Ivo of
Chartres, whose authority as a canonist was undoubted, classes the prohibition among the "præceptiones mobiles," explaining that a necessary oath
is no sin, but that he who can avoid swearing is in less danger of committing perjury than he who takes an oath. (Prolog. in Decretum.) The
struggle between the secular and ecclesiastical authorities on this subject
is well exemplified in a case which occurred in 1269. The Archbishop of
Rheims sued a burgher of Chaudardre. When each party had to take the
oath, the prelate demanded that his should be taken by his attorney. The
defendant demurred to this, alleging that the archbishop had in person presented the complaint. Appeal was made to the Parlement of Paris, which
decided that the defendant's logic was correct, and that the personal oath of
the prelate was requisite. (Olim, I. 765.)

In Spain, a bishop appearing in a secular court, either as plaintiff or
defendant, was not exempt from the oath, but had the singular privilege
of not being compelled to touch the Gospels on which he swore.—Siete Partidas, P. III. Tit. xl. l. 24.

[1] Capit. de Purgat. Sacerd. ann. 803.

this had no practical result. In 823, Pope Pascal I. was
more than suspected of complicity in the murder of Theodore and Leo, two high dignitaries of the papal court.
Desirous to avoid an investigation by the commissioners
sent by Louis-le-Débonnaire, he hastily purged himself of
the crime in anticipation of their arrival, by an oath taken
with a number of bishops as his compurgators;[1] and it is
a striking example of the weight accorded to the procedure,
that although the assumed fault of the victims had been
their devotion to the imperial party, and though the Pope
had by force of arms prevented any pursuit of the murderers, the Emperor was powerless to exact satisfaction, and
there was nothing further to be done. Pope Pascal stood
before the world an innocent man.

It is true that, in the tenth century, Atto of Vercelli
complains bitterly that a perverse generation refused to be
satisfied with the single oath of an accused priest, and required him to be surrounded by compurgators of his class,[2]
which that indignant sacerdotalist regarded as a grievous
wrong. As the priesthood, however, failed in obtaining
the entire immunity for which they strove during those
turbulent times, the unquestioned advantages which compurgation afforded recommended it to them with constantly
increasing force. Forbidden at length to employ the duel in
settling their differences, and endeavoring, in the eleventh
and twelfth centuries, to obtain exemption from the ordeal,
they finally accepted compurgation as the special mode of
trial adapted to members of the church, and for a long
period we find it recognized as such in all the collections
of canons and writings of ecclesiastical jurists.[3] From this

[1] Eginhard. Annal. ann. 823.

[2] Satisfactionem igitur accusati sacerdotis sub jurejurando minime dicunt
valere nisi plures etiam sacerdotes secum compellat jurare.—Atton. de Pressuris Ecclesiast. P. I.

[2] Burchardus, Ivo, Gratianus, *passim.*—Ivon. Epist. 74.

fact it obtained its appellation of "purgatio canonica," or canonical compurgation.

As already remarked, the origin of the custom is to be traced to the principle of the unity of families. As the offender could summon his kindred around him to resist an armed attack of the injured party, so he took them with him to the court, to defend him with their oaths. Accordingly, we find that the service was usually performed by the kindred, and in some codes this is even prescribed by law, though not universally.[1] This is well illustrated in

---

[1] L. Longobard. Lib. II. Tit. xxi. § 9 ; Tit. lv. § 12.—L. Burgund. Tit. viii.—Laws of Ethelred, Tit. ix. §§ 23, 24.—L. Henrici I. cap. lxxiv. § 1.— See also the decretal of Gregory II. alluded to above.

This point affords an illustration of the divergent customs of the Latin and Teutonic races. The Roman law exercised great discrimination in admitting the evidence of a relative to either party in an action (Pauli Sentent. Lib. v. Tit. xv.—Ll. 4, 5, 6, 9. Dig. XXII. v.). The Wisigoths not only adopted this principle, but carried it so far as to exclude the evidence of a kinsman in a cause between his relative and a stranger (L. Wisigoth. Lib. II. Tit. iv. c. 12, which was adopted into the Carlovingian legislation (Benedict. Levit. Capitul. Lib. VI. c. 348) under the strong Romanizing influence which then prevailed. The rule, once established, retained its place through the vicissitudes of the feudal and customary law (Beaumanoir, Coutumes du Beauvoisis, cap. xxxix. § 38.—Cout. de Bretagne, Tit. viii. art. 161, 162).

On the other hand, the Teutonic custom is shown as still influential in the eleventh century, by a law in which the Emperor Henry II. directs the employment of twelve of the nearest relations as conjurators, in default of three peers of the accused—"cum tribus paribus se expurget ; si autem pares habere non potuerit, cum duodecim propinquioribus parentibus se defendat" (Feudorum Lib. v. Tit. ii.). It was a settled principle in the Danish law to a later period. A code of the thirteenth century directs "Factum autem si negat, cognatorum jurejurando se tueatur" (Leg. Cimbric. Lib. II. c 9); and in another of the thirteenth and fourteenth centuries it is even more strongly developed : "Si juramento cognatorum, quod dicitur neffn i kyn se non defenderit, solvat bondoni XL. marcas, et regi tantum" (Constit. Woldemari Regis, § ix., also §§ 52, 56, etc.). He who had no relatives was obliged to take an oath to that effect, and then he was permitted to produce twelve other men of proper character, *lag feste men*. (Ibid. § 86.) A relic of the same principle is shown at the same period in a provision of the municipal law of Southern Germany, by which a child under fourteen years of age, when accused of any crime, could be cleared by the purgatorial oath of the father (Jur. Provin. Alaman. cap. clxix. § 1).

the Welsh laws, where the " raith," or compurgation, was the basis of almost all procedure, and where consequently the system was brought to its fullest perfection. Complicated rules existed as to the proportion of paternal and maternal kindred required in various cases, and the connection between the *wehr-gild* and the obligation of swearing in defence of a kinsman was fully recognized—" Because the law adjudges the men nearest in worth in every case, excepting where there shall be men under vows to deny murder," therefore the compurgators were required to be those " nearest to obtain his worth if killed."[1] Under these circumstances, the raith-man could be objected to on the score of not being of kin, when the oaths of himself and his principal were received as sufficient proof of relationship ;[2] and the " alltud," or foreigner, was not entitled to the raith unless he had kindred to serve on it.[3] How the custom sometimes worked in practice among the untameable barbarians is fairly illustrated by a case recounted by Aimoin as occurring under Chilperic I. in the latter half of the sixth century. A wife suspected by her husband offered the oath of purgation on the altar of St. Denis with her relatives, who were persuaded of her innocence ; the husband not yet satisfied, accused the compurgators of perjury, and the fierce passions of both parties becoming excited, weapons were speedily drawn, and the sanctity of the venerable church was profaned with blood.[4]

It was manifestly impossible, however, to enforce the rule of kinship in all cases, for the number of compurgators varied in the different codes, and in all of them a great number were required when the matter at stake was large, or the crime or criminal important. Thus when Chilperic

---

[1] Anomalous Laws, Bk. ix. chap. ii. § 4 ; chap. v. § 2. (Owen II. 225, 233.) This collection of laws is posterior to the year 1430.

[2] Anomalous Laws, Bk. v. chap. ii. § 117 (Ibid. II. p. 85).

[3] Ibid. § 144 (p. 95).

[4] Aimoini Lib. iii. c. 29.

I. was assassinated in 584, doubts were entertained as to
the legitimacy of his son Clotair, an infant of four months
—doubts which neither the character of Queen Fredegonda
nor the manner of Chilperic's death had any tendency to
lessen; and Gontran, brother of the murdered king, did not
hesitate to express his belief that the royal child's paternity
was traceable to some one of the minions of the court—
a belief doubtless stimulated by the promise it afforded
him of another crown.   Fredegonda, however, repaired her
somewhat questionable reputation and secured the throne
to her offspring, by appearing at the altar with three bishops
and three hundred nobles, who all swore with her as to
the legitimacy of the little prince, and no further doubts
were ventured on the delicate subject.[1]   A similar case
occurred in Germany in 899, when Queen Uta cleared herself of an accusation of infidelity, by taking a purgatorial
oath with eighty-two nobles.[2]   So in 824, a dispute between
Hubert, Bishop of Worcester, and the Abbey of Berkeley,
concerning the monastery of Westbury, was settled by the
oath of the bishop, supported by those of fifty mass-priests,
ten deacons, and a hundred and fifty other ecclesiastics.[3]
These were, perhaps, exceptional instances, but in Wales,
the law required, as a regular matter, enormous numbers of
compurgators in many cases.   Privity to homicide, for instance, was divided into three triads, or nine classes of
various degrees of guilt.   Of these, the first triad called
for one hundred raithmen to establish the denial; the
second triad, 200, and the third, 300;[4] while, to rebut an
accusation of killing with savage violence or poisoning, the

[1] Greg. Turon. Lib. VIII. c. 9.
[2] Herman. Contract. ann. 899.
[3] Spelman. Concil. I. 335.
[4] Venedotian Code, Book III. chap. i. §§ 1–10.—Dimetian and Gwentian
Codes, Book II. chap. i. §§ 10–12. (Owen I. 219–21, 407, 689.)—There is
very great confusion in these laws as to the numbers requisite for many
crimes, but with respect to the accessories of "galanas" or homicide the
rule appears to have been absolute.—Cf. Spelman, Glossary s. v. *Assath*.

enormous number of six hundred compurgators was considered necessary.[1] Even these armies of oath-takers did
not widen the circle from which selection was allowed, for
the law absolutely specifies that " the oaths of three hundred men of a kindred are required to deny murder, blood,
and wound,"[2] and the possibility of finding them is only
explicable by the system of tribes or clans in which all
were legally related one to another.   This is illustrated by a
further regulation, according to which, under the Gwentian
code, in an accusation of theft, with positive evidence, the
thief was directed to clear himself with twenty-four raith-
men of his own *cantrev* or district, in equal number from
each *cymwd* or sub-district.[3]

Under a different social organization, it is evidently
impossible that a kindred sufficiently large could have
been assembled in the most numerous families, and even
when the requirements were more reasonable, the same
difficulty must frequently have occurred.   Among such
tribes, therefore, the aid of those not connected by ties of
blood must often have been necessary, and as it was a service not without danger, as we shall see hereafter, it is not
easy to understand how the requisite number was reached.
In certain cases, no doubt, the possibility of obtaining
those not bound by kindred to undertake the office is traceable to the liability which in some instances rested upon a
township for crime committed within its borders.[4]

---

[1] Venedotian Code, Book III. chap i. § 18. Anomalous Laws, Book IV.
chap. iii. §§ 12, 13 (Ibid. I. 231, II. 23).

[2] Ibid. § 17 (p. 231) ; cf. Book II. chap. viii. § 4 (p. 137).

[3] Gwentian Code, Book II. chap. iii. § 11. (Ibid. I. 691).

[4] This has been denied by those who assume that the *frithborgs* of Edward
the Confessor are the earliest instance of such institutions, but traces of com-
munal societies are to be found in the earliest text of the Salique law (First
text of Pardessus, Tit. XLV.), and both Childebert and Clotair II., in edicts
promulgated near the close of the sixth century, hold the hundreds or

4

It would be endless to specify all the variations in the numbers required by the different codes in all imaginable cases of quarrel between every class of society. A few generalizations may, however, be deduced from among the chaotic and conflicting mass of regulations which are to be found in the laws of the numerous races who adhered to the custom for so many centuries. Numerous elements entered into this; the nature of the crime or claim, the station of the parties, the rank of the compurgators, and the mode by which they were selected. Thus, in the simplest and most ancient form, the Salique law merely specifies twenty-five compurgators to be equally chosen by both parties.[1] Some formulas of Marculfus specify three freeholders and twelve friends of the accused.[2] A Merovingian edict of 593 directs the employment of three peers of the defendant, with three others chosen for the purpose, probably by the court.[3] Alternative numbers, however, soon make their appearance,

---

townships responsible for robberies committed within their limits (Decret. Childeberti ann. 595, c. 10—Decret. Chlotarii II. c. 1).

It is not improbable that, as among all the barbarian races, the family was liable for the misdeeds of its members, so the tribe or clan of the offender was held responsible when the offence was committed upon a member of another tribe, and such edicts as those of Childebert and Clotair were merely adaptations of the rule to the existing condition of society. The most perfect early code that has reached us, that of the ancient Irish, expresses in detail the responsibility of each sept for the actions not only of its members, but of those also who were in any way connected with it. "And because the four nearest tribes bear the crimes of each kinsman of their stock. . . . And because there are four who have an interest in every one who sues and is sued : the tribe of the father, the chief, the church, the tribe of the mother or foster-father. . . . Every tribe is liable after the absconding of a member of it, after notice, after warning, and after lawful waiting."—Senchus Mor, I. 263–5.

So in the earliest Russian law, the Rouskaïa Prawda, promulgated by Yaroslaf Vladimirovitch in the eleventh century (Art. 2), the district where a murder was committed in a quarrel or through drunkenness, was responsible for it, if the murderer escaped.

[1] First text of Pardessus, Tit. XLII. § 5.

[2] Marculf. App. xxxii. ; Ibid. xxix.

[3] Pact. pro Tenore Pacis cap. vi.

depending upon the manner in which they were chosen.
Thus among the Alamanni, on a trial for murder, the
accused was obliged to secure the support of twenty chosen
men, or, if he brought such as he had selected himself, the
number was increased to eighty.[1] So in a capitulary of
803 Charlemagne prescribes seven chosen conjurators, or
twelve if taken at random,[2] a rule which is virtually the
same as that laid down by the Emperor Henry III. in the
middle of the eleventh century.[3] In Bigorre the law thus
discriminated against the *cagots*—a wandering race of uncertain origin—for cases in which the oaths of seven conjurators ordinarily sufficed required thirty *cagots*, when the
latter were called upon to act.[4]

Variations likewise occur arising from the nature of the
case and the character of the plaintiff. Thus in the Scottish
law of the twelfth century, in a criminal charge, a man could
defend himself against his lord with eleven men of good
character, but if the king were the accuser, twenty-four
were requisite, who were all to be his peers,[5] while in a civil
case twelve were sufficient.[6] So in the burgher laws of
David I., ordinary cases between citizens were settled with
ten conjurators, but eleven were necessary if the king were
a party, or if the matter involved the life, limb, or lands of
one of the contestants.[7] In the complicated rules for com-

---

[1] L. Alaman. Tit. lxxvi. So in 922 the Council of Coblentz directed that
accusations of sacrilege could be rebutted with " XXIV totis nominatis atque
electis viris . . . aut aliis non nominatis tamen ingenuis LXXII." (Hartzheim Concil. German. II. 600.)

[2] Capit. Car. Mag. IV. ann. 803, cap. x.

[3] Goldast. Constit. Imp. I. 231.

[4] Lagrèze, Hist. du Droit dans les Pyrénées, p. 47, Paris, 1867.

[5] Quoniam Attachiamenta cap. xxiv. §§ 1, 4. In another code of nearly
the same period, in simple cases of theft, when the accuser had no testimony
to substantiate his claim, thirty conjurators were necessary, of whom three
must be nobles.—Regiam Majestatem Lib. IV. c. 21.

[6] Quoniam Attachiamenta cap. lxxv. §§ 1, 4.

[7] Leg. Burgorum cap. xxiv. § 3. In cases occurring between a citizen
and a countryman, each party had to provide conjurators of his own class.—
Ibid. § 1.

purgation which form the basis of the Welsh jurisprudence, there are innumerable details of this nature. We have seen that for some crimes many hundred *raith-men* were required, while similar numbers were enjoined in some civil suits respecting real property.[1] From this the number diminishes in proportion to the gravity of the case, as is well illustrated by the provisions for denying the infliction of a bruise. If the mark remained until the ninth day, the accused could deny it with "two persons of the same privilege as himself;" if it remained until the eighteenth day, the oaths of three conjurators were necessary; if till the twenty-seventh day, four *raith-men* were required.[2]

The character of the *raith-men* also affected the number demanded. Thus, in a collection of Welsh laws of the fifteenth century there is an explanation of the apparent anomaly that privity to theft or homicide required for its defence a vastly greater number of compurgators than the commission of the crime itself. The large bodies prescribed for the former consisted simply of any men that could be had—of course within the recognized grades of kindred—while, for the latter, rules of varying complexity were laid down. Thus of the twenty-four required for theft, in some texts it is prescribed that two-thirds are to be of the nearest paternal kin, and one-third of the nearest maternal; or, again, one-half *nod-men*.[3] So, in accusations of homicide, the same proportions of paternal and maternal kindred

---

[1] Anomalous Laws, Book XIII. chap. ii. § 94 (Owen II. 521).

[2] Gwentian Code, Bk. II. chap. vii. § 10 (Ibid. I. 701).

[3] Anomalous Laws, Bk. IX chap. ii. § 4; chap. xx. § 12; chap. xxi. § 3.— Book. XIV. chap. xxxviii. § 16.—Book V. chap. ii. § 112 (Ibid. II. 225, 261, 709, 83).

Under the primitive Venedotian Code (Book III. chap. i. §§ 13, 19) only twelve men were required, one-half to be *nod-men*, two thirds of paternal, and one-third of maternal kin; while in the Gwentian Code (Book II. chap. ii. § 10) and in the Dimetian Code (Book II. chap. iii. § 10, Book III. chap. i. § 24), fifty are prescribed.

The *nod-men*, as will be seen hereafter, were conjurators, who took a special form of oath.

were required, all were to be proprietors in the country of the *raith*, and three, moreover, were to be men under vows of abstinence from linen, horses, and women, besides a proper proportion of *nod-men*.[1]

Instances also occur in which the character of the defendant regulated the number required. Among the Welsh, the laws of Hoel Dha provide that a wife accused of infidelity could disprove a first charge with seven women; if her conduct provoked a second investigation, she had to procure fourteen; while, on a third trial, fifty female conjurators were requisite for her escape.[2] Another application of the same principle is found in the provision that when a man confessed a portion of the crime imputed to him and denied the remainder, an augmented *raith* was required to support his denial, because it is more difficult to believe a man who has admitted his participation in a criminal act. Thus when only fifty men were requisite to rebut a charge of homicide, and the accused admitted one of the accessaries to homicide, his denial of the main charge had to be substantiated by one hundred, two hundred, or three hundred men, according to the nature of the case. On the other hand, where no criminal act was concerned, confession of a portion diminished the *raith* for the remainder. Thus in a claim of suretyship, six compurgators were necessary to the defendant; but if he admitted part

---

[1] Anomalous Laws, Book XIV. chap. xxxviii. § 16; Book IX. chap. xx. § 12, chap xxi. § 1.

[2] Leges Wallice, Lib. II. cap. xxiii. § 17 (Owen II. 848). It is worthy of remark that one of the few directions for legal procedures contained in the Korán relates to cases of this kind. Chapter xxiv. 6–9 directs that a husband accusing his wife of infidelity, and having no witnesses to prove it, shall substantiate his assertion by swearing five times to the truth of the charge, invoking upon himself the malediction of God; while the wife was able to rebut the accusation by the same process. As this chapter, however, was revealed to the Prophet after he had writhed for a month under a charge brought against his favorite wife Ayesha, which he could not disregard and did not wish to entertain, the law is rather to be looked upon as *ex post facto* than as indicating any peculiar tendency of the age or race.

of the suretyship, his unsupported oath was sufficient to
rebut the remainder, as the admission of a portion rendered
him worthy of belief.[1] In the Anglo-Saxon jurisprudence,
the *frangens jusjurandum*, as it was called, also grew to be
an exceedingly complex system in the rules by which the
number and quality of the conjurators were regulated according to the nature of the crime and the rank of the
accused. In cases of peculiar atrocity, such as violation
of the sanctity of the grave, only thanes were esteemed
competent to appear.[2] In fact, among the Anglo-Saxons,
the value of a man's oath was rated according to his rank,
that of a thane, for instance, being equal to those of seven
yeomen.[3] The same peculiarity is observable among the
Frisians, whose laws required that compurgators should
be of the same class as their principal, and the lower his
position in the State, the larger was the number requisite.[4]

Equally various were the modes adopted for the selection
of compurgators. Among the untutored barbarians, doubtless, the custom was originally universal that the defendant
procured the requisite number of his friends, whose oaths
were sufficient for his discharge. Even to a comparatively
late period this prevailed extensively, and its evils were

---

[1] Anomalous Laws, Book XI. chap. v. §§ 40, 41 (Ibid. II. 445).

[2] Wealreaf, *i. e.* mortuum refere, est opus nithingi; si quis hoc negare
velit, faciat hoc cum xlviii. taynis plene nobilibus.—Leg. Æthelstani, de
Ordalio.

[3] Sacramentum liberalis hominis, quem quidem vocant *tvelfhendeman,*
debet stare et valere juramentum septem villanorum. (Cnuti Secular. cap.
127.) The *twelfhendeman* meant a thane (Twelfhindus est homo plene nobilis
i. Thainus.—Leg. Henrici I. Tit. lxxvi. § 4), whose price was 1200 solidi. So
thoroughly did the structure of jurisprudence depend upon the system of
wehrgild or composition, that the various classes of society were named
according to the value of their heads. Thus the villein or *cherleman* was
also called *twyhindus* or *twylindeman*, his wehrgild being 200 solidi; the
radcnicht (road-knight, or mounted follower) was a *sexhendeman;* and the
comparative judicial weight of their oaths followed a similar scale of valuation, which was in force even subsequently to the Conquest. (Leg. Henrici I.
Tit. lxiv. § 2.)

[4] L. Frision. Tit. I.

forcibly pointed out by Hincmar in the ninth century. In objecting to admit the purgation of an offending priest with ecclesiastics of his own choice, he states that evil-minded men combined together to defeat justice and secure immunity for their crimes by serving each other in turn, so that when the accused insisted on offering his companions to the oath, it was necessary to make them undergo the ordeal to prove their sincerity.[1] His expressions show that the question of selection at that time was undecided in France, and the alternative numbers alluded to above prove that efforts had been made to remove the difficulty without success. Other nations, however, met the question more decidedly. The original Lombard law of King Rotharis gave to the plaintiff the privilege of naming a majority of the compurgators, the remainder being chosen by the defendant,[2] but even in this the solidarity of the family was recognized, since it was the duty of the plaintiff to select the nearest relatives of his adversary.[3] This same spirit is shown even so late as 1116 when Baldwin VII. of Flanders gratified the citizens of Ypres by substituting among them the process of compurgation for the ordeal and battle trial. According to this charter the accuser selected four of the relatives of the accused to take the purgatorial oath; if they refused through known enmity, he was bound to select four other of the kindred, and if none such were to be found then four legal men sufficed.[4] The English law was the first to educe a rational mode of trial from the absurdity of the barbaric traditions, and there it finally assumed a form which occasionally bears a striking resemblance to trial by jury—in fact, it insensibly

[1] Hincmari Epist. xxxiv. So also in his Capit. Synod. ann. 852, ii. xxv.
[2] L. Longobard. Lib. ii. Tit. lv. § 5.
[3] Ibid. Tit. xxi. § 9. The plaintiff, however, was prohibited from nominating any of the family who were personally hostile to the defendant.
[4] Proost, Récherches sur la Législation des Jugements de Dieu, Bruxelles, 1868, p. 96.

runs into this latter, to which it probably gave rise. By
the laws of Canute, in some cases, fourteen men were named
to the defendant, among whom he was obliged to find eleven
willing to take the purgatorial oath with him.[1] The selection of these virtual jurors was probably made by the
gerefa, or sheriff;[2] they could be challenged for suspicion
of partiality or other competent cause,[3] and were liable to
rejection unless unexceptionable in every particular.[4] Very
similar to this was the *stockneffn* of the ancient Danish
law, by which, in cases where the relatives were not called
upon, thirteen men were chosen, a majority of whom could
clear the accused by taking the oath with him. They were
nominated by a person appointed for the purpose, and if
the court neglected this duty, the privilege enured to the
plaintiff.[5]

The Northern nations were evidently less disposed to
favor the accused than the Southern. In Sweden and
Denmark, another regulation provides that although the
defendant had a right to demand this mode of purgation,
yet the plaintiff had the selection of the twelve men who
served as conjurators; three of these the accused could
challenge for enmity, but their places were supplied by the
plaintiff.[6] The evanescent code compiled for Norway and
Iceland by Haco Haconsen towards the close of the thir-

[1] Nominentur ei XIV., et adquirat XI., et ipse sit duodecimus.—L. Cnuti
c. lxvi. Horne, who probably lived in the reign of Edward II., attributes
to Glanville the introduction of the jury-trial.—"Car, pur les grandes ma-
lices que lon soloit procurer en testmonage et les grandes delaies qui se fie-
rent en les examinements, exceptions et attestations, ordeina Randulph de
Glanvile celle certeine Assise ou recognitions et jurées se feissent per XII
jurors, les procheins vicines, et issint est cest establissement appelé assise."—
Myrror of Justice, cap. II. sect. xxv.

[2] Laws of Ethelred, Tit. III. c. xiii.

[3] L. Henrici I. Tit. xxxi. § 8.

[4] Ibid. Tit. lxvi. § 10.

[5] Constit. Woldemari Regis, §§ lii. lxxii.

[6] L. Scaniæ Lib. vii. c. 8.—Chart. Woldemari Regis, ann. 1163. (Du
Cange s. v. *Juramentum*.)

teenth century is more equitable in its provisions. Though it leaves the nomination of the conjurators to the defendant, the choice is subject to limitations which placed it virtually in the power of the court. They were required to be men of the vicinage, of good repute, peers of the accused, and in no way connected with him by blood or other ties.[1]

Such care in the selection of those on whom duties so responsible devolved did not prevail among the more Southern races at an earlier age. Among the Lombards slaves and women in tutelage were often employed.[2] The Burgundians required that the wife and children, or, in their absence, the father and mother of the accused should assist in making up the number of twelve,[3] the object being evidently to increase the responsibility of the family for the actions of its head. The abuses of this custom, however, caused its prohibition under Charlemagne for the reason that it led to the swearing of children of tender and irresponsible age.[4] That legislator, however, contented himself with forbidding those who had once been convicted of perjury from again appearing either as witnesses or conjurators;[5] and the little care that was deemed necessary in their selection under the Carlovingian jurisprudence is shown by a law of Louis-le-Débonnaire ordering that landless freemen should be allowed to serve as conjurators, though ineligible as witnesses.[6] A truer conception of the course of justice is manifested, some centuries later, by the Béarnese legislation, which required that the *seguidors* or conjurators should be men able to pay the amount at stake, together with the fine incurred by the losing party,[7]

---

[1] Jarnsida, Thiofa-Balkr, cap. ix. x.

[2] L. Longobard. i. xxxiii. 1, 3.

[3] L. Burgund. Tit. viii.

[4] Capit. Car. Mag. i. ann. 789 c. lxii.

[5] Ibid.

[6] Capit. Ludov. Pii ann. 829 Tit. iii. § vi.

[7] For de Morlaas, Rubr. xli. art. 146-7. The same capacity was required of the *testimonis* or witnesses.

or that they should be fair and loyal men, not swayed by enmity.[1]

Variations are likewise observable in the form of administering the oath. Among the Alamanni, for instance, the compurgators laid their hands upon the altar, and the principal placed his hand over the others, repeating the oath alone;[2] while among the Lombards, a law of the Emperor Lothair directs that each shall take the oath separately.[3] It was always, however, administered in a consecrated place, before delegates appointed by the judges trying the cause, sometimes on the altar and sometimes on relics. In the Welsh laws of the fifteenth century it is specified that all raiths shall be administered in the parish church of the defendant, before the priest shall have disrobed or distributed the sacramental bread.[4] At an earlier period a formula of Marculfus specifies the Capella S. Martini, or cope of St. Martin,[5] one of the most venerated relics of the royal chapel, whence we may perhaps conclude that it was habitually used for that purpose in the business of the royal Court of Appeals.

There has been much discussion as to the conditions under which resort was had to this mode of establishing innocence or vindicating disputed rights. Some authors assume that in the early period, before the ferocious purity of the German character had become adulterated with the remains of Roman civilization, it was used in all descriptions of cases, at the option of the defendant, and was in itself a full and satisfactory proof, received on all hands as equal to any other.[6] The only indication that I have

---

[1] Que sien boos et loyaus, et que no sien enemicxs.—Fors de Béarn, Rubr. xxx.

[2] L. Alaman. Tit. vi.   [3] L. Longobard. Lib. ii. Tit. lv. § 28.

[4] Anomalous Laws, Book ix. chap. vi. § 4 ; chap. xvii. § 5.—cf. Book vi. chap. i. § 50 (Owen. II. 235, 255, 113).

[5] Marculf. Lib. i. Formul. xxxviii.

[6] Königswarter, Études Historiques, p. 167.

met with, among the races of Teutonic stock, tending to
the support of such a conjecture, occurs in the Lombard
code, where Rotharis, the earliest compiler of written laws,
abolishes a previously existing privilege of denying under
oath a crime after it had been confessed.[1] A much more
powerful argument on the other side, however, is derivable
from the earliest text of the Salique law, to which reference
has already been made. In this, the formula shows clearly
that conjurators were only employed in default of other
testimony;[2] and what lends additional force to the conclusion is that this direction disappears in subsequent
revisions of the law, wherein the influences of Christianity
and of Roman civilization are fully apparent. No safe
deductions, indeed, can be drawn from mere omissions to
specify that the absence of witnesses was necessary, for
these ancient codes are drawn up in the rudest possible
manner, and regulations which might safely be presumed
to be familiar to every one would not, in their curt and barbarous sentences, be repeated with the careful redundancy
of verbiage which marks our modern statutes. Thus there
is a passage in the code of the Alamanni which declares in
the most absolute form that if a man commits a murder
and desires to deny it, he can clear himself with twelve
conjurators.[3] This, by itself, would authorize the assumption that compurgation was allowed to override the clearest
and most convincing testimony, yet it is merely a careless

[1] Nam nulli liceat, postquam manifestaverit, postea per sacramentum
negare, quod non sit culpabilis, postquam ille se culpabilem assignavit.
Quia multos cognovimus in regno nostro tales pravas opponentes intentiones,
et hæc moverunt nos præsentem corrigere legem, et ad meliorem statum
revocare.—L. Longobard. Lib. II. Tit. lv. § 8.

[2] Si quis hominem ingenuo plagiaverit et probatio certa non fuit, sicut pro
occiso juratore donet. Si juratores non potuerit invenire, VIII M dinarios,
qui faciunt solidos CC, culpabilis judicetur.—Tit. xxxix. § 2. A similar
provision—"si tamen probatio certa non fuerit"—occurs in Tit. xlii. § 5.

[3] Si quis hominem occiderit et negare voluerit, cum duodecim nominatis
juret.—L. Alaman. Tit. LXXXIX.

form of expression, for another section of the same code expressly provides that where a fact is proved by competent witnesses the defendant shall not have the privilege of producing compurgators.[1]

It therefore seems to me evident that, even in the earliest times, this mode of proof was only an expedient resorted to in cases of doubt, and on the necessity of its use the *rachinborgs* or judges probably decided. That it was so in subsequent times is generally admitted. It is scarcely worth while to multiply proof; but a few references will show the light in which the custom was regarded.[2]

---

[1] L. Alaman. Tit. XLII.

[2] For instance, in the Baioarian law—"Nec facile ad sacramenta veniatur. . . . In his vero causis sacramenta præstentur in quibus nullam probationem discussio judicantis invenerit." (L. Baioar. Tit. VIII. c. 16.) In a Capitulary of Louis-le-Débonnaire—"Si hujus facti testes non habuerit cum duodecim conjuratoribus legitimis per sacramentum adfirmet." (Capit. Ludov. Pii ann. 819, § 1.) In one of the Emperor Lothair—"Si testes habere non poterit, concedimus ut cum XII. juratoribus juret." (L. Longobard. Lib. I. Tit. IX. § 37.) So Louis II., in 854, ordered that a man accused of harboring robbers, if taken in the act, was to be immediately punished; but if merely cited on popular rumor, he was at liberty to clear himself with twelve compurgators. (Recess. Ticinen. Tit. II. cap. 3.)

It was the same in subsequent periods. The Scottish law of the twelfth century alludes to the absence of testimony as a necessary preliminary, but when an acquittal was once obtained in this manner, the accused seems to have been free from all subsequent proceedings, when inconvenient witnesses might perhaps turn up—"Et si hoc modo purgatus fuerit, absolvetur a petitione Regis in posterum." (Regiam Majestatem, Lib. IV. c. 21.) So, in the laws of Nieuport, granted by Philip of Alsace, Count of Flanders, in 1163. "Et si hoc scabini vel opidani non cognoverint, conquerens cum juramento querelam suam sequetur, et alter se excusabit juramento quinque hominum." (Leg. secundæ Noviportus.) The legislation of Norway and Iceland in the next century is even more positive. "Iis tantum concessis quæ legum codices sanciunt, juramenta nempe purgatoria et accusatoria, ubi legitimi defuerint testes." (Jarnsida, Mannhelge, cap. xxxvii.)

On the other hand, an exception to this general principle is apparently found in a constitution of the Emperor Henry III., issued about the middle of the eleventh century. "Si quem ex his dominus suus accusaverit de quacunque re, licet illi juramento se cum suis coæqualibus absolvere, exceptis tribus: hoc est si in vitam domini sui, aut in cameram ejus consilium habuisse

The Welsh, however, were exceptional in this respect. The *raith* was the corner-stone of their system of jurisprudence. It was applied to almost all actions, whether of civil or criminal law, and even cases of doubtful paternity were settled by it, no woman, except one "of bush and brake" who had no legal kindred, being allowed to give testimony or take an oath with respect to the paternity of her illegitimate child.[1] It excluded and superseded all other procedures. If the accused declined to take the oath of denial, then testimony on both sides could be introduced, and the case be settled on the evidence adduced;[2] but where he chose to abide by the *raith*, the Book of Cynog formally declares that "Evidences are not to be brought as to *galanas* [homicide], nor *saraad* [insults], nor blood, nor wound, nor ferocious acts, nor waylaying, nor burning buildings, nor theft, nor surety, nor open assault, nor adultery, nor violence, nor in a case where guardians should be, nor in a case where an established raith is appointed by law; because evidences are not to extinguish a raith."[3] Indeed, the only case which I have found wherein it was refused is where a priest of the same parish as one accused of theft testifies to have seen him in open daylight with the article stolen in his possession, when apparently the sacred character of the witness precludes a denial on the part of the defendant.[4]

Among other races confidence in its ability to supplement absent or deficient testimony was manifested in a

---

arguitur, aut in munitiones ejus. Cæteris vero hominibus de quacunque objectione, absque advocato, cum suis coæqualibus juramento se poterit absolvere." (Goldast. Constit. Imp. I. 231.)

[1] Gwentian Code, Book II. chap. xxxix. § 40 (Owen, I. 787). So, in disowning a child, if the reputed father were dead, the oaths of the chief of the kindred, with seven of the kinsmen, were decisive, or, in default of the chief, the oaths of fifty kinsmen (Ibid. § 41).

[2] Anomalous Laws, Book IX. chap. ii. § 9 (Ibid. II. 227).

[3] Ibid. Book VIII. chap. xi. § 31 (Ibid. II. 209).

[4] Ibid. Book IX. chap. ii. § 6 (Ibid II. 227).

singular form—the *juramentum supermortuum*—which was employed by various races, at wide intervals of time. Thus, in the earliest legislation of the Anglo-Saxons, we find that when the defendant or an important witness was dead, the oath which he would have taken or the deposition which he would have made was obtained by proceeding to his tomb, where a certain number of conjurators swore as to what he could or would have done if alive.[1] Two centuries later, the same custom is alluded to in the Welsh laws of Hoel Dda,[2] and even as late as the thirteenth century it was still in force in Southern Germany.[3]

The employment of compurgators, however, depended frequently upon the degree of crime alleged, or the amount at stake. Thus, in many codes, trivial offences or small claims were disposed of by the single oath of the defendant, while more important cases required compurgators, whose numbers increased with the magnitude of the matter in question. This principle is fairly illustrated in a charter granted to the Venetians in the year 1111 by Henry V. In suits which involved only the value of a silver pound, the oath of the party was sufficient; but if the claim amounted to twelve pounds or more, then twelve chosen men were requisite to substantiate the oath of negation.[4]

In later times, compurgation was also sometimes used as an alternative when circumstances prevented the employment of other popular modes of deciding doubtful cases. Those, for instance, who would ordinarily be required to defend themselves by the wager of battle, were permitted by some codes to substitute the oaths of a certain number of conjurators, when precluded by advanced age from ap-

---

[1] Dooms of Ine, cap. liii.

[2] Leg. Wallice, Lib. ii. cap. xix. § 2 (Owen II. 842).

[3] Ea autem debita de quibus non constat, super mortuum probari debent, septima manu.—Jur. Provin. Alaman. cap. vii. § 2. (Ed. Schilter.)

[4] Lünig Cod. Ital. Diplom. II. 1955.

pearing in the arena. The burgher law of Scotland affords
an example of this,[1] though elsewhere such cases were
usually settled by the substitution of champions.

The primitive law-givers were too chary of words in their
skeleton codes to embody the formula usually employed
for the compurgatorial oath. We have therefore no positive evidence of its nature in the earliest times; but as the
forms made use of by several races at a somewhat later
period have been preserved, and as they resemble each
other in all essential respects, we may reasonably assume
that little variation had previously occurred. The most
ancient that I have met with occurs in an Anglo-Saxon
formulary which is supposed to date from about A.D. 900:
" By the Lord, the oath is clean and unperjured which N.
has sworn."[2]   A century later, in a compilation of the
Lombard law, it appears: " That which the accused has
sworn is true, so help me God."[3]   The form specified in
Béarn, at a period somewhat subsequent, is curt and decisive: " By these saints, he tells the truth;"[4] while the code
in force in Normandy until the sixteenth century directs
an oath identical in spirit: " The oath which William has
sworn is true, so help me God and his saints."[5]   It will be
observed that all these, while essentially distinct from the
oath of a witness, are still unqualified assertions of the
truth of the principal, and not mere asseverations of belief

[1] Si burgensis calumniatus præteriit ætatem pugnandi, et hoc essoniaverit
in sua responsione, non pugnabit. Sed juramento duodecim talium qualis
ipse fuerit, se purgabit.—L. Burgorum cap. 24 §§ 1, 2.

[2] On þone Drihten se að is clæne and unmæne þe N. swor.—Thorpe's Ancient Laws, I. 180–1.

[3] Hoc quod appellatus juravit, verum juravit. Sic Deus, etc.—Formul.
Vet. in L. Longobard. (Georgisch, 1275.)

[4] Per aquetz santz ver dits.—Fors de Béarn, Rubr. LI. art. 165.

[5] Du serment que Guillaume a juré, sauf serment a juré, ainsi m'aist Dieu
et ses Sainctz.—Ancienne Cout. de Normandie, chap. lxxxv. (Bourdot de
Richebourg, IV. 54.)

or protestations of confidence. The earliest departure from this positive affirmation, in secular jurisprudence, occurs in the unsuccessful attempt at legislation for Norway and Iceland by Haco Haconsen in the thirteenth century. In this, the impropriety of such oaths is pointed out, and it is directed that in future the compurgator shall swear only, in confirmation of his principal, that he knows nothing to the contrary.[1]

We shall see that before the custom fell into total disuse, the change which Haco vainly attempted for his subjects came to be generally adopted, in consequence, principally, of the example set by the church. Even before this was formally promulgated by the Popes, however, ecclesiastics occasionally showed that they were more careful as to what they swore, and at a comparatively early period they introduced the form of merely asserting their belief in the oath taken by their principal. Thus, in 1101, we find two bishops endeavoring to relieve a brother prelate from a charge of simony, and their compurgatorial oath ventures no further than " I believe that Norgaud, Bishop of Autun, has sworn the truth. So help me God."[2]

In the form of oath, however, as well as in so many other particulars, the Welsh had a more complicated system, peculiar to themselves. The ordinary *raith-man* only was required to take an oath "that it appears most likely to him that what he swears to is true." In many aggra-

---

[1] Nobis adhæc Deo coram periculosum esse videtur, ejus, cujus interest, jusjurandum purgatorium edendo præeunte, omnes (ab eo productos testes) iisdem ac ille conceptis verbis jurare, incerti quamvis fuerint, vera ne an falsa jurent. Nos legibus illatum volumus ut ille, cujus interest, jusjurandum conceptis verbis solum præstet, cæteri vero ejus firment juramentum adjicientes se nequid verius, Deo coram, scire, quam jurassent.—Jarnsida, Mannhelge, cap. xxxvii.—The passage is curious, as showing how little confidence was really felt in the purgation, notwithstanding the weight attaching to it by law.

[2] Credo Norigaudum istum Eduensem episcopum vera jurasse, sicut me Deus adjuvet.—Hugo. Flaviniac. Lib. ii.

vated crimes, however, a certain proportion, generally one-half, had to be *nod-men* who were bound to a more stringent form, as the law specifies that "the oath of a nod-man is, to be in accordance with what is sworn by the criminal."[1] The difference, as we have seen, in the numbers required when a portion were *nod-men* shows how much more difficult it was to find men willing to swear to an absolute denial, and how much more weight was attached to such a declaration than to the lax expression of opinion contained in the ordinary oath of the raith-man.

Notwithstanding the universality of the custom, and the absolute character of the decisions reached by the process, it is easy to discern that the confidence reposed in it was of a very qualified character, even at an early period. The primitive law of the Frisians describes some whimsical proceedings, prescribed for the purpose of determining the responsibility for a homicide committed in a crowd. The accuser was at liberty to select seven from among the participants of the brawl, and each of these was obliged to deny the crime with twelve conjurators. This did not absolve them, however, for each of them was also individually subjected to the ordeal, which finally decided as to his guilt or innocence. In this, the value of the compurgation was reduced to that of the merest technical ceremony, and yet a failure to procure the requisite number of supporters was tantamount to a conviction, while, to crown the absurdity of the whole, if any one succumbed in the ordeal, his conjurators were punished as perjurers.[2] A similar want of confidence in the principle involved is shown by a reference in the Anglo-Saxon laws to the conjurators of an accused party being outsworn (*overcythed*), when recourse was likewise had to the ordeal.[3] As regards the

---

[1] Anomalous Laws, Book VII. chap. i. § 18 (Owen, II. 135).

[2] L. Frisionum Tit. xiv.

[3] Dooms of King Edward, cap. iii.

church, although the authoritative use of compurgation among ecclesiastics would seem to demand for it among them implicit faith in its results, yet we have already seen that in the ninth century, Hincmar did not hesitate to require that in certain cases it should be confirmed by the ordeal; and two centuries later, a remark of Ivo of Chartres implies a strong degree of doubt as to its efficacy. In relating that Sanctio, Bishop-elect of Orleans, when accused of simony by a disappointed rival, took the oath of negation with seven compurgators, he adds that the accused thus cleared himself as far as he could in the eyes of man.[1]   That the advantages it offered to the accused were duly appreciated, both by criminals and judges, is evident from the case of Manasses, Archbishop of Rheims. Charged with simony and other offences, after numerous tergiversations he was finally summoned for trial before the Council of Lyons, in 1080.   As a last effort to escape the impending doom, he secretly offered to Bishop Hugh, the Papal legate, the enormous sum of two hundred ounces of gold and other presents in hand, besides equally liberal prospective payments, if he could obtain the privilege of compurgation with six suffragan bishops.   Gregory VII. was then waging too uncompromising a war with the corroding abuse of simony for his lieutenant to yield to any bribe, however dazzling; the proffer was spurned, Manasses confessed his guilt by absence, and was accordingly deposed.[2]   Instances like this, however, did not destroy confidence in the system, for, some sixty years later, we find Innocent II. ordering the Bishop of Trent, when similarly accused of simony, to clear himself with the oaths of two bishops and three abbots or monks.[3]

The comparative value attached to the oaths of conjurators is illustrated by the provisions which are occasionally

---

[1] Quantum in conspectu hominum purgari poterat.—Ivón. Epist. liv.
[2] Hugo. Flaviniac. Lib. ii.   [3] Jaffé, Regesta, p. 596.

met with, regulating the cases in which they were employed in default of witnesses, or in opposition to them. Thus, in the Baioarian law, the oath of one competent witness is considered to outweigh those of six conjurators;[1] and among the Lombards, an accusation of murder which could be met with three witnesses required twelve conjurators as a substitute.[2]

It is thus evident that conjurators were in no sense witnesses, that they were not expected to give testimony, and that they merely expressed their confidence in the veracity of their principal. It therefore at first sight appears somewhat unreasonable that they should have been held guilty of perjury and subject to its penalties in case of unluckily sustaining the wrong side of a cause. It is probably owing to this inconsistency that some writers have denied that they were involved in the guilt of their principal, and among others the learned Meyer has fallen into this error.[3] The proof, however, is too clear for dispute. We have already seen that the oath was an unqualified assertion of the justice of the side espoused, without reservation that would enable the compurgator to escape the charge of false swearing, and one or two allusions have been made to the punishments inflicted on them when subsequently convicted of mistake. The code of the Alamanni recognized the guilt involved in such cases when it denied the privilege of compurgation to any one who had previously been more than once convicted of crime, giving as a reason the desire to save innocent persons from incurring the sin of perjury.[4] Similar evidence is derived from a regulation promulgated by King Luitprand in the Lombard law, by which a man nominated as a conjurator, and declining to

---

[1] L. Baioar. Tit. xiv. cap. i. § 2.

[2] L. Longobard. Lib. i. Tit. ix. § 37.

[3] Institutions Judiciaires, I. 308.

[4] Ut propter suam nequitiam alii qui volunt Dei esse non se perjurent, nec propter culpam alienam semetipsos perdant.—L. Alaman. Tit. xlii. § 1.

serve, was obliged to swear that he dared not take the oath for fear of his soul.[1] A case in point occurs in the life of St. Boniface, whose fellow-laborer Adalger in dying left his property to the church. The graceless brothers of the deceased disputed the bequest, and offered to make good their claim to the estate by the requisite number of oaths. The holy man ordered them to swear alone, in order not to be concerned in the destruction of their conjurators, and on their unsupported oaths gave up the property.[2]

The law had no hesitation in visiting such cases with the penalties reserved for perjury. By the Salique code unlucky compurgators were heavily fined.[3] Among the Frisians, they had to buy themselves off from punishment by the amount of their wehr-gild—the value set upon their heads.[4] A slight relaxation of this severity is manifested in a constitution of Pepin, King of Italy, by which they were punished with the loss of a hand—the immemorial penalty of perjury—unless they could establish, by undergoing the ordeal, that they had taken the oath in ignorance of the facts.[5] This regulation is a tacit disavowal of the fundamental idea upon which the whole system was erected, but it was only a temporary edict, and had no permanent effect. Even as late as the close of the twelfth century, we find Celestin III. ordering the employment of conjurators in a class of cases about the facts of which they could not possibly know anything, and decreeing that if the event

[1] Quod pro anima sua timendo, non praesumat sacramentalis esse.—L. Longobard. Lib. ii. Tit. lv. § 14.

[2] Othlon. Vit. S. Bonif. Lib. ii. c. xxi.—"Vos soli juratis, si vultis : nolo ut omnes hos congregatos perdatis."—Boniface, however, did not weakly abandon the cause of the church. He freely invoked curses on the greedy brethren, which being fulfilled on the elder, the terror-stricken survivor gladly relinquished the dangerous inheritance.

[3] L. Salic. Tit. i. §§ 3, 4.

[4] L. Frisionum Tit. x.

[5] Capit. Pippini ann. 793, § 15.—Capit. Car. Mag. incert. anni c. x. (Hartzheim Concil. German I. 426.)

proved them to be in error, they were to be punished for perjury.[1] That such liability was fully recognized at this period is shown by the argument of Aliprandus of Milan, a celebrated contemporary legist, who, in maintaining the position that an ordinary witness committing perjury must always lose his hand, without the privilege of redeeming it, adds that no witness can perjure himself unintentionally; but that conjurators may do so either knowingly or unknowingly, that they are therefore entitled to the benefit of the doubt, and if not wittingly guilty, that they should have the privilege of redeeming their hands.[2]

All this seems in the highest degree irrational, yet in criticizing the hardships to which innocent conjurators were thus exposed, it should be borne in mind that the whole system was a solecism. In its origin, it was simply summoning the kinsmen together to bear the brunt of the court, as they were bound to bear that of battle; and as they were liable for a portion of the fine which was the penalty of all crimes—personal punishments for freemen being unknown—they could well afford to incur the risk of paying for perjury in order to avoid the assessment to be levied upon them in case of the conviction of their relative. In subsequent periods, when this family responsibility became weakened or disused, and the progress of civilization rendered the interests of society more complex, the custom could only be retained by making the office one not to be lightly undertaken. A man who was endeavoring to defend himself from a probable charge of murder, or who desired to confirm his possession of an estate against a competitor with a fair show of title, was expected to produce guarantees that would carry conviction to the minds of impartial men. As long as the practice existed, it was therefore necessary

---

[1] Celest. PP. III. ad Brugnam Episc. (Baluz. et Mansi, III. 382.)

[2] Cod. Vatican. No. 3845, Gloss. ad L. 2 Lombard. II. 51, apud Savigny, Geschichte d. Rom. Recht. B. iv.—I owe this reference to the kindness of my friend J. G. Rosengarten, Esq.

to invest it with every solemnity, and to guard it with penalties that would obviate some of its disadvantages.

Accordingly, we find that it was not always a matter of course for a man to clear himself in this manner. The ancient codes have frequent provisions for the fine incurred by those unable to procure the requisite number of compurgators, showing that it was an occurrence constantly kept in mind by legislators. Nor was it only landless and friendless men who were exposed to such failures. In 794, a certain Bishop Peter was condemned by the Synod of Frankfort to clear himself, with two or three conjurators, of the suspicion of being involved in a conspiracy against Charlemagne, and, small as was the number, he was unable to procure them.[1] So, in the year 1100, when the canons of Autun, at the Council of Poitiers, accused their bishop, Norgaud, of simony and other irregular practices, and he proposed to absolve himself with the compurgatorial oaths of the Archbishop of Tours and the Bishop of Rédon, the canons went privately to those prelates and threatened that in such event they would bring an accusation of perjury and prove it by the ordeal of fire, whereupon the would-be conjurators wisely abandoned their intention, and Norgaud was suspended.[2] The most rigid compliance with the requisitions of the law was exacted. Thus the statutes of Nieuport, in 1163, provide a heavy penalty, and in addition pronounce condemnation, when a single one of the conjurators declines the oath.[3]

No regulations, however, could be more than a slight palliation of a system so vicious in its fundamental principles, and efforts were made for its abrogation or limitation

[1] Capit. Car. Mag. ann. 794, § 7.

[2] Hugo. Flaviniac. Lib. II. ann. 1100. Norgaud, however, was reinstated next year by quietly procuring, as we have already seen, two brother prelates to take the oath with him, in the absence of his antagonists.

[3] Et si quis de quinque juvantibus defecerit, accusatus debet tres libras, et percusso decem solidos.—Leg. Secund. Noviportus (Oudegherst).

at a comparatively early period.   In 983, a constitution of
Otho II. abolished it in cases of contested estates, and
substituted the wager of battle, on account of the enormous
perjury which it occasioned.[1]   In England, a more sweeping
denunciation, declaring its abolition and replacing it with
the vulgar ordeal, is found in the confused and contradictory compilation known as the laws of Henry I.[2]

   We have already seen, from instances of later date, how
little influence these efforts had in eradicating a custom
so deeply rooted in the ancestral prejudices of all the European races.   The hold which it continued to enjoy on the
popular confidence is well illustrated in a little ballad by
Audefroi-le-Bâtard, a renowned *trouvère* of the twelfth
century.

LA BELLE EREMBORS.[3]

"Quand vient en mai, que l'on dit as lous jors," etc.

In the long bright days of spring-time,
   In the month of blooming May,
The Franks from royal council-field
   All homeward wend their way.
Rinaldo leads them onward
   Past Erembors' gray tower,
But turns away, nor deigns to look
   Up to the maiden's bower.
               Ah, dear Rinaldo !

---

   [1] L. Longobard. Lib. ii. Tit. iv. § 34.—Qua ex re mos detestabilis in
Italia, improbusque non imitandus inolevit, ut sub legum specie jurejurando
acquireret, qui Deum non timendo minime formidaret perjurare.

   [2] L. Henrici I. cap. lxiv. § 1.   " Malorum autem infestacionibus et perju-
rancium conspiracione, depositum est frangens juramentum, ut magis Dei
judicium ab accusatis eligatur ; et unde accusatus cum una decima se pur-
garet per eleccionem et sortem, si ad judicium ferri calidi vadat." This
cannot be considered, however, as having abrogated it even temporarily in
England, since it is contradicted by many other laws in the same code,
which prescribe the use of compurgators.

   [3] Le Roux de Lincy, Chants Historiques Français, I. 15.

Full in her turret window
   Fair Erembors is sitting,
The lovelorn tales of knights and dames
   In many a color knitting.
She sees the Franks pass onward,
   Rinaldo at their head,
And fain would clear the slanderous tale
   That evil tongues have spread.
                Ah, dear Rinaldo !

"Sir knight, I well remember
   When you had grieved to see
The castle of old Erembors
   Without a smile from me."
"Your vows are broken, princess,
   Your faith is light as air,
Your love another's, and of mine
   You have nor reck nor care."
                Ah, dear Rinaldo !

"Sir knight, my faith unbroken,
   On relics I will swear ;
A hundred maids and thirty dames
   With me the oath shall share.
I 've never loved another,
   From stain my vows are free.
If this content your doubts and fears,
   You shall have kisses three."
                Ah, dear Rinaldo !

Rinaldo mounts the staircase,
   A goodly knight, I ween,
With shoulders broad, and slender waist,
   Fair hair and blue eyes keen.
Earth holds no youth more gifted
   In every knightly measure ;
When Erembors beholds him,
   She weeps with very pleasure.
                Ah, dear Rinaldo !

Rinaldo in the turret
   Upon a couch reposes,
Where deftly limned are mimic wreaths
   Of violets and of roses.

Fair Erembors beside him
   Sits clasped in loving hold,
And in their eyes and lips they find
   The love they vowed of old !
        Ah, dear Rinaldo !

In England, owing probably to the influence of the jury-trial, the custom seems to have lost its importance earlier than elsewhere. Towards the close of the twelfth century, Glanville compiled his excellent little treatise "De legibus Angliæ," the first satisfactory body of legal procedure which the history of mediæval jurisprudence affords. Complete as this is in all the forms of prosecution and defence, the allusions to conjurators are so slight as ·to show that already they constituted an infinitesimal part of legal machinery, and that they were employed rather on collateral points than on main questions. Thus a defendant who desired to deny the serving of a writ could swear to its non-reception with twelve conjurators;[1] and a party to a suit, who had made an unfortunate statement or admission in court, could deny it by bringing forward two to swear with him against the united recollections and records of the whole court.[2] The custom, however, still continued in use.

---

[1] Glanville, Lib. i. cap. ix. Also, Lib. i. c. xvi., Lib. ix. c. i., Lib. x. c. v.

[2] " In aliis enim curiis si quis aliquid dixerit unde eum pœnituerit, poterit id negare contra totam curiam tertia manu cum sacramento, id se non dixisse affirmando."—(Ibid. Lib. viii. c. ix.)—In some other systems of jurisprudence, this unsophisticated mode of avoiding justice was obtained by insisting on the employment of lawyers, whose assertions would not be binding on their clients. Thus in the Assises de Jerusalem (Baisse Court, cap. 133): " Et por ce il deit estre lavantparlier, car se lavantparlier dit parole quil ne doie dire por celuy cui il parole, celui por qui il parle et son conceau ÿ pueent bien amender ains que le iugement soit dit. Mais se celuy de cui est li plais diseit parole qui li deust torner a damage, il ne la peut torner arieres puis quil la dite." The same caution is recommended in the German procedure of the fourteenth century—" verbis procuratoris non eris adstrictus, et sic vitabis damnum."—(Richstich Landrecht, cap. ii.) The same abuse existed in France, but was restricted by St. Louis, who made the assertion of the advocate binding on the principal, unless contradicted on the spot.—(Établissements, Liv. ii. chap. xiv.)

6

In 1194, when Richard I. undertook, after his liberation, to
bring about a reconciliation between his chancellor, William
Bishop of Ely, and the Archbishop of York, one of the conditions was that the chancellor should swear with a hundred
priestly compurgators that he had neither caused nor desired the arrest of the archbishop.[1] In the next century
Bracton alludes to the employment of conjurators in cases
of disputed feudal service between a lord and his vassal,
wherein the utmost exactness was rigidly required both as
to the number and fitness of the conjurators,[2] and we shall
see that no formal abrogation of it took place until the nineteenth century.

Soon after the time of Glanville, however, the system
received a severe shock from its most important patron, the
church. As stated above, in proceedings between ecclesiastics, it was everywhere received as the appropriate mode of
deciding doubtful cases. Innocent III. himself, who did so
much to abrogate the kindred absurdity of the ordeal, continued to prescribe its use in cases of the highest moment
involving dignitaries of lofty station ; though, sensible of
the abuses to which it led, he was careful in demanding
conjurators of good character, whose intimacy with the
accused would give weight to their oaths.[3] At the same
time, in endeavoring to remove one of the objections to its
use, he in reality destroyed one of its principal titles to
respect. He decreed that compurgators should only be
obliged to swear to their belief in the truth of their principal's oath,[4] and thus he attacked the very foundation of

---

[1] Roger de Hoveden, ann. 1194.

[2] Tunc vadiabit defendens legem se duodecima manu.—Bracton. Lib.
III. Tract. iii. cap. 37, § 1.—Et si ad diem legis faciendæ defuerit aliquis de
XII. vel si contra prædictos excipi possit quod non sunt idonei ad legem
faciendam, eo quod villani sunt vel alias idonei minus, tunc dominus incidet
in misericordiam.—Ibid. § 3. So also in Lib. v. Tract. v. cap. xiii. § 3.

[3] Can. vii. Extra, v. 34.

[4] Illi qui ad purgandam alicujus infamiam inducuntur, ad solum tenentur
juramento firmare quod veritatem credunt eum dicere qui purgatur.—Can.

the practice, and gave a powerful impulse to the tendency of
the times no longer to consider the compurgator as sharing
the guilt or innocence of the accused. Such an innovation could only be regarded as withdrawing the guarantee
which had immemorially existed. To recognize it as a legal
precept was to deprive the proceeding of its solemnity and
to render it no longer a security worthy the confidence of
the people or sufficient to occupy the attention of a court
of justice.

In the confusion arising from the long and varying contest as to the boundaries of civil and ecclesiastical jurisdiction, it is not easy to determine the exact authority
which this decretal may have exercised directly in secular
jurisprudence. We have seen above that the ancient form
of absolute oath was still employed without change, until
long after this period, but the moral effect of so decided a
declaration from the head of the Christian church could not
but be great. Another influence, not less potential, was also
at work. The revival of the study of the Roman jurisprudence, dating from about the middle of the twelfth
century, soon began to exhibit the results which were to
work so profound a change in the legal maxims and principles of half of Europe.[1] The criminal procedure of the

---

xiii. Extra, v. 34. Innocent also endeavored to put an end to the abuse
by which ecclesiastics, notoriously guilty, were able to escape the penalty
due their crimes, by this easy mode of purgation.—Can. xv. cod. loc.

[1] The rapidity with which the study of the civil law diffused itself throughout the schools and the eagerness with which it was welcomed were the sub
ject of indignant comment by the ecclesiastics of the day. As early as 1149
we find St. Bernard regretting that the laws of Justinian were already over-
shadowing those of God—"Et quidem quotidie perstrepent in palatio leges,
sed Justiniani, non Domini" (De Consideratione, Lib. i. cap. iv.) Even more
bitter were the complaints of Giraldus Cambrensis towards the end of the century. The highest of high churchmen, in deploring the decline of learning
among the prelates and clergy of his age, he attributes it to the exclusive attention bestowed on the jurisprudence of Justinian, which already offered the
surest prizes to cupidity and ambition, and he quotes in support of his opinion
the dictum of his teacher Mainier, a professor in the University of Paris ·

barbarians had rested to a great degree on the system of
negative proofs. In the absence of positive evidence of
guilt, and sometimes in despite of it, the accused was
bound to clear himself by compurgation or by the ordeal.
The cooler and less impassioned justice of the Roman law
saw clearly the futility of such attempts, and its system
was based on the indisputable maxim that it is morally
impossible to prove a negative—unless indeed that negative
should chance to be incompatible with some affirmative
susceptible of evidence—and thus the onus of proof was
thrown upon the accuser.[1] The enthusiastic worshippers
of the Pandects were not long in recognizing the truth of
this principle, and in proclaiming it far and wide. The
Spanish code of Alphonso the Wise, in the middle of the
thirteenth century, asserts it in almost the same words as

" Episcopus autem ille, de quo nunc ultimo locuti sumus, inter superficiales
numerari potuit, cujusmodi hodie multos novimus propter leges Justinianas,
quæ literaturam, urgente cupiditatis et ambitionis incommodo, adeo in multis
jam suffocarunt, quod magistrum Mainerium in auditorio scholæ suæ Parisius
dicentem et damna sui temporis plangentem, audivi, vaticinium illud Sibillæ
vere nostris diebus esse completum, hoc scilicet ' Venient dies, et væ illis,
quibus leges obliterabunt scientiam literarum.' " (Gemm. Ecclesiast. Dist.
II. cap. xxxvii.) This, like all other branches of learning, was as yet to a
great extent in the hands of the clergy, though already were arising the
precursors of those subtle and daring civil lawyers who were destined to do
such yeoman's service in abating the pretensions of the church.

It is somewhat singular to observe that at a period when the highest
offices of the law were frequently appropriated by ecclesiastics, they were
not allowed to perform the functions of advocates or counsel. See Horne's
Myrror of Justice, cap. II. sect. 5.

[1] Actor quod adseverat, probare se non posse profitendo, reum necessitate
monstrandi contrarium non adstringit : cum per rerum naturam factum
negantis probatio nulla sit. (Const. xxiii. C. de Probat. IV. 19.)—Cum inter
eum, qui factum adseverans, onus subiit probationis, et negantem numera-
tionem, cujus naturali ratione probatio nulla est . . . magna sit differentia.
(Const. x. C. de non numerat. IV. 30.) It is a little curious to see how completely this was opposed to the principle of the early Common Law of England,
by which in actions for debt "semper incumbit probatio neganti" (Fleta,
Lib. II. cap. lxiii. § 11).

the Roman jurisconsult.[1] Not long before, the Assises de Jerusalem had unequivocally declared that "nul ne peut faire preuve de non;" and Beaumanoir, in the "Coutumes du Beauvoisis," approvingly quotes the assertion of the civil doctors to the same effect, "Li clerc si dient et il dient voir, que negative ne doit pas quevir en proeve."

Abstract principles, however, though freely admitted, were not yet powerful enough to eradicate traditional customs rooted deeply in the feelings and prejudices of the age. The three bodies of law just cited contradict their own admissions, in retaining with more or less completeness the most monstrous of negative proofs—the ordeal of battle—and the introduction of torture soon after exposed the accused to the chances of the negative system in its most atrocious form. Still these codes show a marked progress as relates to the kindred procedure of compurgation. The Partidas, promulgated about 1262, is of comparative unimportance as an historical document, since it was of but uncertain authority, and rather records the convictions of an enlightened ruler as to what should be law than the existing institutions of a people. The absence of compurgation in Spain, moreover, was a direct legacy from the Wisigothic code, transmitted in regular descent through the Fuero Juzgo.[2] The Assises de Jerusalem is a more precious relic of mediæval jurisprudence. Constructed as a code for the government of the Latin kingdoms of the East, in 1099, by order of Godfrey of Bouillon, it has

---

[1] La cosa que non es non se puede probar nin mostrar segunt natura.—Las Siete Partidas, P. iii. Tit. xiv. l. 1.

[2] Though absent from the general laws of Spain, yet compurgation had been introduced as an occasional custom. Thus the Fuero of Madrid in 1202 provides that a man suspected of homicide and other crimes, in the absence of testimony, can clear himself with six or twelve conjurators, according to the grade of the offence—"iuret cum xii. uicinos bonos et ille de mays: et pergat in pace"—El Fuero de Madrid del año de 1202. (Mem. de la Real Acad. de Historia, 1852.) We shall see hereafter that it appears in the Fuero Viejo of Castile in 1356.

reached us only in the form assumed about the period under
consideration, and as it presents the combined experience
of the warriors of many Western races, its silence on the
subject of conjurators is not a little significant. The work
of Beaumanoir, written in 1283, is not only the most perfect embodiment of the jurisprudence of his time, but is
peculiarly interesting as a landmark in the struggle between the waning power of feudalism and the Roman theories which gave vigor and intensity of purpose to the
enlightened centralization aimed at by St. Louis; and
Beaumanoir likewise passes in silence over the practice of
compurgation, as though it were no longer an existing institution. All these legislators and lawyers had been preceded by the Emperor Frederic II., who, in 1231, promulgated his "Constitutiones Sicularum" for the government
of his Neapolitan provinces. Frederic was Latin, and not
Teutonic, both by education and predilection, and his system of jurisprudence is greatly in advance of all that had
preceded it. That conjurators should find no place in his
scheme of legal procedure is, therefore, only what might
be expected. The collection of laws known as the "Établissements" of St. Louis is by no means a complete code,
but it is sufficiently copious to render the absence of all
allusion to compurgation significant. In fact, the numerous
references to the Digest show how strong was the desire
to substitute the Roman for the customary law, and the
efforts of the king to do away with all negative proofs of
course included the one under consideration. The same
may be said of the "Livres de Justice et de Plet" and the
"Conseil" of Pierre de Fontaines, two unofficial books of
practice, which represent with tolerable fulness the procedures in vogue during the latter half of the thirteenth century; while the "Olim," or records of the Parlement of
Paris, the king's high court of justice, show that the same
principles were kept in view in the long struggle by which
that body succeeded in extending the royal jurisdiction at

the expense of the independence of the vainly resisting
feudatories.[1]

All these were the works of men deeply imbued with the
spirit of the resuscitated jurisconsults of Rome.   Their
labors bear testimony rather to the influences tending to
overthrow the institutions bequeathed by the barbarians to
the Middle Ages, than to a general acceptance of the innovations attempted.   Their authority was still circumscribed
by the innumerable jurisdictions which yet defied their
gradual encroachments, and which resolutely maintained
ancestral customs.   Thus, in 1250, we find in the settlement of a quarrel between Hugues Tirel Seigneur of Poix
in Picardy and the commune of that place, that one of the
articles was to the effect that the mayor with thirty-nine
of the bourgeois should kneel before the dame de Poix and
offer to swear that an insult inflicted on her had not been
done, or that if it had, it had been in honor of the Seigneur
de Poix.[2]   Even an occasional instance may be found
where the central power itself permitted the use of compurgation, showing how difficult it was to eradicate the

[1] In the " Olim," or records of the Parlement of Paris from 1254 to 1318,
I can find but two instances in which compurgation was required—one in
1279 at Noyon, and one in 1284 at Compiègne. As innumerable decisions are
given of cases in which its employment would have been equally appropriate,
these two can only be regarded as exceptional, and the inference is fair that
some local custom rendered it impossible to refuse the privilege on these
special occasions.   (Olim, II. 153, 237.)

A noteworthy instance of its employment occurred in 1234 at the Diet of
Frankfort, in the presence of Henry VII., son of that Frederic II. whom
we have seen discountenance its use in his Neapolitan laws.   When the fearful persecutions instigated by the grand inquisitor, Conrad of Marburg, drew
to a close, the last of his intended victims, the Counts of Seyne and Solms,
cleared themselves before the king of the charge of heresy with compurgatorial oaths in which each was supported by eight bishops, twelve Cistercian
abbots, twelve Franciscan and three Dominican friars, and a large number
of Benedictine abbots, clerks, and noble laymen. (Hartzheim Concil. German. III. 549.)   As we shall see, however, this was in accordance with the
rules of the Inquisition.

[2] Actes du Parlement de Paris, T. I. p. cccvii (Paris, 1863).

prejudices transmitted through ages from father to son, and that the policy adopted by St. Louis and Philippe-le-Bel, aided by the shrewd and energetic civil lawyers who assisted them so ably, was not in all cases adhered to. Thus, in 1283, when the bailli of Amiens was accused before the Parlement of Paris of having invaded the privileges of the church by trying three clerks accused of crime, it was decided that he should swear with six compurgators as to his ignorance that the criminals were ecclesiastics.[1] So, in 1303, a powerful noble of the court of Philippe-le-Bel was accused of a foul and treacherous murder, which a brother of the victim offered to prove by the wager of battle. Philippe was endeavoring to abolish the judicial duel, and the accused desired strongly to escape that ordeal. He was accordingly condemned to clear himself of the imputed crime, by a purgatorial oath with ninety-nine nobles, and at the same time to satisfy the fraternal claim of vengeance with an enormous fine[2]—a decision which offers the best practical commentary on the degree of faith reposed in this system of purgation. Even the Parlement of Paris in 1353 and a rescript of Charles-le-Sage in 1357 allude to compurgation as still in use and of binding force.[3]

It was in the provinces, however, that the system manifested its greatest vitality, protected both by the stubborn dislike to innovation, and by the spirit of independence which so long and so bitterly resisted the centralizing efforts of the crown. The Roman law concentrated all power in the person of the sovereign, and reduced his subjects to one common level of implicit obedience. The genius of the barbaric institutions and of feudalism localized power. The principles were essentially oppugnant,

[1] Actes du Parlement de Paris, T. I. p. 382.

[2] Statuunt . . . se manu centesima nobilium se purgare, et ad hæc benedicto juveni bis septem librarum milia pro sui rancoris satisfactione præsentare.—Wilelmi Egmond. Chron.

[3] Is qui reus putatur tertia manu se purgabit, inter quos sint duo qui dicentur denominati.—Du Cange s. v. *Juramentum*.

and the contest between them was prolonged and confused, for neither party could in all cases recognize the ultimate result of the minuter points involved, though each was fully alive to the broad issues of the struggle.

How obstinate was the attachment to bygone forms may be understood, when we see even the comparatively precocious civilization of a city like Lille preserve the compurgatorial oath as a regular procedure until the middle of the fourteenth century, even though the progress of enlightenment had long rendered it a mere formality, without serious meaning. Until the year 1351, the defendant in a civil suit was obliged to substantiate the oath of denial with two conjurators of the same sex, who swore to its truth, with some slight expression, indeed, of reserve.[1] The minutest regulations were enforced as to this ceremony, the position of every finger being determined by law, and though it was the veriest formality, serving merely as an introduction to the taking of testimony and the legal examination of the case,[2] yet the slightest error committed by either party lost him the suit irrecoverably.[3]

Normandy was even more faithful to the letter of the

[1] Et li deffendans, sour qui on a clamet se doit deffendre par lui tierche main, se chou est hom II. hommes et lui, se chou est fame II. femmes et li à tierche. . . . . "Tel sierment que Jehans chi jura boin sierment y jura au mien ensiant. Si m'ait Dius et chist Saint."—Roisin, Franchises, etc. de la Ville de Lille, pp. 30, 35.

[2] Ibid. p. 51. The system was abrogated by a municipal ordinance of September, 1351, in accordance with a special ordonnance to that effect issued by King John of France in March, 1350.

[3] The royal ordonnance declares that the oath was "en langage estraigne et de mos divers et non de legier a retenir ou prononchier," and yet that if either party "par quelconques maniere faloit en fourme ou en langage ou que par fragilite de langhe, huirans eu, se parolle faulsist ou oubvliast, ou eslevast se main plus que li dite maniere acoustumee en requeroit ou quelle ne tenist fermement sen poch en se paulme ou ne wardast et maintenist pluiseurs autres frivoles et vaines chozes et manieres appartenans au dit sierment, selonc le loy de la dite ville, tant em parole comme en fait, il avoit du tout sa cause perdue, ne depuis nestoit rechus sur che li demanderes a claim ou complainte, ne li deffenderes a deffensce."—Ibid. p. 390.

ancient traditions. The Coutumier in use until the revision of 1583 under Henry III. retains a remnant of the practice under the name of *desrene*, by which, in questions of little moment, a man could rebut an accusation with two or four compurgators, even when it was sustained by witnesses. The form of procedure was identical with that of old, and the oath, as we have already seen (page 51), was an unqualified assertion of the truth of that of the accused.[1] Practically, however, we may assume that the custom had long grown obsolete, for the letters patent of Henry III., ordering the revision in 1577, expressly state that the provisions of the existing laws "estoient la pluspart hors d'usage et peu ou point entendu des habitants du pays ;" and that compurgation was one of the forgotten formulas may fairly be inferred from the fact that Pasquier, writing previous to 1584, speaks of it as altogether a matter of the past.[2]

The fierce mountaineers of Béarn were comparatively inaccessible to the innovating spirit of the age, and preserved their feudal independence amid the progress and reform of the sixteenth century, long after it had become obsolete elsewhere throughout Southern Europe. Accordingly, we find the practice of compurgation maintained as a regular form of procedure in the latest revision of their code, made by Henry II. of Navarre in 1551, which continued in force until the eighteenth century.[3] The influence of the age is shown, however, even there, in a modification of the oath, which is no longer an unreserved confirmation of the principal, but a mere affirmation of belief.[4]

---

[1] Anc. Coutume de Normandie, chap. lxxxv. (Bourdot de Richebourg, IV. 53-4.)

[2] Recherches de la France, Liv. iv. chap. iii. Concerning the date of this, see La Croix du Maine, s. v. *Estienne Pasquier.*

[3] Fors et Cost. de Béarn, Rubr. de Juramentz (Bourdot de Richebourg, IV. 1082).

[4] Lo jurament deu seguido se fé, JURAN PER aquetz sanctz bertat ditz exi que io crey.

In Castile, a revival of the custom is to be found in the code compiled by Pedro the Cruel, in 1356, by which, in certain cases, the defendant was allowed to prove his innocence with the oath of eleven hidalgos.[1] This, however, is so much in opposition to the efforts made a century earlier, by Alfonso the Wise in the Partidas, to enforce the principles of the Roman jurisprudence, and is so contrary to the spirit of the Ordenamiento de Alcalà, which continued in force until the fifteenth century, that it can only be regarded as a tentative innovation, of mere temporary validity.

The Northern races resisted more obdurately the advances of the resuscitated influence of Rome. Though we have seen Frederic II. omitting all notice of compurgation in the code prepared for his Neapolitan dominions in 1231, he did not attempt to abrogate it among his German subjects, for it is alluded to in a charter granted to the city of Regensburg in 1230.[2] The "Speculum Suevicum," which during the thirteenth and fourteenth centuries was the municipal law of Southern Germany, directs the employment of conjurators in various classes of actions which do not admit of direct testimony.[3] In the early part of the sixteenth century, Maximilian I. did much to abrogate it,[4] but that he failed to eradicate it entirely is evident from a constitution issued by Charles V. in 1548, wherein its use is enjoined in doubtful cases in a manner to show that it was an existing resource of the law, and that it retained its hold upon public confidence, although the conjurators were only

[1] E si gelo negare e non gelo quisier probar, devel' facer salvo con once Fijosdalgo e èl doceno, que non lo fiço.—(Fuero Viejo de Castiella, Lib. I. Tit. v. l. 12.) It will be observed that this is an unqualified recognition of the system of negative proofs.

[2] Du Cange, s. v. *Juramentum.*

[3] Jur. Provin. Aleman. cap. xxiv. cccix. § 4; cccxxix. §§ 2, 3; cccxxxix. § 3. (Edit. Schilteri).

[4] Meyer, Institutions Judiciaires, V. 221.

required to swear as to their belief in the oath of their principal.[1]

In the Netherlands it likewise maintained its position. Damhouder, writing in 1554, after describing its employment in the Courts Christian, adds that by their example it was occasionally used also in secular tribunals.[2]

In Scotland, as late as the middle of the fourteenth century, its existence is proved by a statute which provides that if a thief escaped from confinement, the lord of the prison should clear himself of complicity with the evasion by the oaths of thirty conjurators, of whom three were required to be nobles.[3]

The Scandinavian nations adhered to the custom with even greater tenacity. In the code of Haco Haconsen, issued towards the close of the thirteenth century, it appears as the basis of defensive procedure in almost all criminal cases, and even in civil suits its employment is not unfrequently directed, the number of conjurators being proportioned to the nature of the crime or to the amount at stake, and regulations for administering the oath being given with much minuteness.[4] In Denmark, an allusion to it is found in 1537 in the laws of Christiern III.,[5] and its vitality among the people is shown by the fact that even in 1683, Christiern V., in promulgating a new code, found it necessary to formally prohibit accused persons from being

[1] Sique accusatus tanta ac tam gravi suspitione laboraret ut aliorum quoque purgatione necesse esset, in arbitratu stet judicis, sibi eam velit injungere, nec ne, qui nimirum compurgatores jurabunt, se credere quod ille illive qui se per juramentum excusarunt, recte vereque juraverint.—Constit. de Pace Publica cap. xv. § 1. (Goldast. Constit. Imp. I. 541.)

[2] Hac igitur forma utuntur curiæ spirituales, et earum imitatione subinde etiam tribunalia sæcularia, seu prophana in Flandria, nec non aliis in locis.— Damhouder. Rerum Criminalium Praxis cap. xliv. No. 6 (Antwerp. 1601).

[3] Statut. Davidi II. cap. i. § 6.

[4] Jarnsida, Mannhelge & Thiofa-Balkr *passim ;* Erfthatal cap. xxiv. ; Landabrigtha-Balkr cap. xxviii. ; Kaupa-Balkr cap. v., ix., etc.

[5] Quoted by Thorpe, Ancient Laws, &c., of England, I. 28.

forced to provide conjurators.[1]   In Sweden, its existence
was similarly prolonged.   Directions for its use are contained in the code which was in force until the seventeenth
century,[2] and it is even alluded to in an ordinance of Queen
Christina, issued in 1653.[3]

It is not a little singular that the latest active existence of
a custom which appears so purely Teutonic should be found
among a portion of the Sclavonic race.   In Poländ, it is
described as being in full force as late as the eighteenth
century, the defendant being obliged to support his purgatorial oath with conjurators, who swore as to its truth.[4]

The constitutional reverence of the Englishman for established forms and customs, however, nominally preserved
this relic of barbarism in the common law to a period later
by far than its disappearance from the codes of other
nations.   According to Bracton, in the thirteenth century,
in all actions arising from contracts, sales, donations, &c.,
when there was no absolute proof, the plaintiff came into
court with his "secta," and the defendant was bound to
produce two conjurators for each one advanced by the
plaintiff, the evidence apparently preponderating according
to quantity rather than quality.[5]   From the context, it
would appear that the "secta" of the plaintiff consisted of
his friends and followers willing to take the oath with him,
but not absolutely witnesses.   The Fleta, however, some
twenty-five years later, uses the term in the sense of wit-

---

[1] Nemini in causa ulla injungendum est ut duodecim virorum juramento
se purgare debeat.—Christiani V. Jur. Danic. Lib. i. c. xiv. § 8.

[2] Poteritque se tunc purgare cui crimen imponitur juramento XVIII. virorum.—Raguald. Ingermund. Leg. Suecorum Lib. i. c. xvi.

[3] Königswarter, op. cit. p. 168.

[4] Ludewig, Reliq. MSS. T. VII. p. 401.

[5] Et sic major praesumptio vincit minorem.   Si autem querens probationem habuerit, sicut instrumenta et chartas sigillatas, contra hujusmodi
probationes non erit defensio per legem.   Sed si in instrumento contradica-
tur, fides instrumenti probabiitur per patriam et per testes.—Bracton, Lib.
IV. Tract. vi. cap. 18, § 6.

7

nesses, and in actions of debt directs the defence to be
made with conjurators double in number the plaintiff's
witnesses,[1] thus offering an immense premium on dis-
honesty and perjury. In spite of this, it remained an integral part of the law. The "Termes de la Ley," compiled
in the early part of the sixteenth century, states as the
existing practice that "when one shall wage his law, he
shall bring with him 6, 8, or 12 of his neighbors, as the
court shall assign him, to swear with him." In the year
1596 the statute 38 Eliz. 3, 5, shows that it was still in common use in actions for debt.[2] Style's "Practical Register,"
published in 1657, also describes the process, but an absurd mistake as to the meaning of the traditional expression "jurare manu" shows that the matter was rather a
legal curiosity than a procedure in ordinary use; and, indeed, the author expressly states that the practice having
been "abused by the iniquity of the people, the law was
forced to find out another way to do justice to the nation."
Still the law remained unaltered, and a case is recorded
occurring in 1708, known as Gunner's case, where "the
plaintiff became nonsuit, when the defendant was ready to
perfect his law,"[3] and Jacob, in his "Review of the Statutes"
published not long after, treats of it as still part of the
existing judicial processes. As the wager of law came to
be limited to simple actions of debt, shrewd lawyers found
means of avoiding it by actions of "trespass upon the
case," and other indirect forms which required the intervention of a jury, but Burn in his Law Dictionary (Dublin,
1792) describes the whole process with all its forms as still
existing, and in 1799 a case occurred in which a defendant
successfully eluded the payment of a claim by producing
compurgators who "each held up his right hand, and then

[1] Ut si duos vel tres testes produxerit ad probandum, oportet quod defensio fiat per quatuor vel per sex ; ita quod pro quolibet teste duos producat
juratores usque ad duodecim.—Lib. II. c. lxiii. s. 10.
[2] Jacob's Review of the Statutes, 2d Ed., London, 1715, p. 532.
[3] Ibid.

laid their hands upon the book and swore that they believed what the defendant swore was true." The court endeavored to prevent this farce, but law was law, and reason was forced to submit. Even this did not provoke a change. In 1824, in the case of King v. Williams (2 Barnewall & Cresswell, 528), some black-letter lawyer revived the forgotten iniquity for the benefit of a client in want of testimony, and demanded that the court should prescribe the number of conjurators necessary for the defence, but the court refused assistance, desiring to give the plaintiff the benefit of any mistake that might be made. Williams then got together eleven conjurators, and appeared in court with them at his back, when the plaintiff, recognizing the futility of any further proceedings, abandoned his case in disgust.[1] Still, the fine reverential spirit postponed the inevitable innovation, and it was not until 1833 that the wager of law was formally abrogated by 3 and 4 William IV., c. 42, s. 13.[2]

It is quite possible that, strictly speaking, the wager of law may still preserve a legal existence in this country. In 1712 an act of the Colony of South Carolina, enumerating the English laws to be held as in force there, specifically includes those relating to this mode of defence, and I am not aware that they have ever been formally abrogated.[3] In 1811 Chancellor Kilty, of Maryland, speaks of the wager of law as being totally disused in consequence of the avoidance of the forms of suit which might admit of its employment, but he evidently regards it as not then specifically abolished.[4]

---

[1] I owe a portion of these references to a curious paper in the London "Jurist" for March, 1827, the writer of which instances the wager of law as an evidence of "that jealous affection and filial reverence which have converted our code into a species of museum of antiques and legal curiosities."

[2] Wharton's Law Lexicon, 2d ed., p. 758.

[3] Cooper's Statutes at Large of South Carolina, Columbia, 1837, II. 403.

[4] Kilty's Report on English Statutes, Annapolis, 1811, p. 140.

While the common sense of mankind was gradually elimi-
nating the practice from among the recognized procedures
of secular tribunals, the immutable nature of ecclesiastical
observances prolonged its vitality in the bosom of the
church. We have seen above that Innocent III., about the
commencement of the thirteenth century, altered the form
of oath from an unqualified confirmation to a mere assertion of belief in the innocence of the accused. That this
at once became the standard formula in ecclesiastical cases
is probable when we find it adopted for the oaths of the
compurgators who, during the Albigensian persecution,
were required by the nascent Inquisition in all cases to
assist in the purgation of such suspected heretics as were
allowed to escape so easily.[1] The practice thus commenced
at the foundation of the Inquisition was persevered in by
that terrible tribunal to the last.

"Our holy mother church," says Simancas, Bishop of
Badajos, a writer of the sixteenth century, "can in no
way endure the suspicion of heresy, but seeks by various
remedies to cure the suspect. Sometimes she forces them
to abjure or to purge themselves; sometimes she elicits
the truth by torture, and very often she coerces them with
extraordinary punishments." Therefore, any one whose
orthodoxy was doubtful, if he was unwilling to clear himself, at the command of the judge, was held to be convicted of heresy. By the secular law, he had a year's grace
before condemnation, but under the papal law he was in-
stantly punishable.[2]

Canonical purgation, according to the rules of the Inquisition, was indicated when public report rendered a
man suspected, and there was no tangible evidence against
him. The number of compurgators was left to the discre-

---

[1] Ego talis juro . . . me firmiter credere quod talis non fuit Insabbatus,
Valdensis, vel Pauperum de Lugduno . . . et credo firmiter eum in hoc
jurasse verum.—Doctrina de modo procedendi contra Hæreticos. (Martene,
Thesaur. T. V. p. 1801.)

[2] Jacob. Simancæ de Cathol. Instit. Tit. lvi. No. 3, 4 (Romæ, 1575).

tion of the judge, who at the same time decided whether
the deficiency of one, two, or more would amount to a
condemnation. They were to be peers of the accused;
and though he was allowed to select them, yet the qualifi-
cation that they were to be good men and orthodox practically left their nomination to the officials—even as the
customary accusation by the promotor-fiscal was held to
be in itself the requisite amount of suspicion required as a
condition precedent for the trial. The greater the suspicion, however, the larger was the number of compurgators
to be adduced.

When the accused had chosen his men, and they were
accepted by the judge, they were summoned, and each one
examined separately by the Inquisitors as to his acquaintance with the defendant—a process by which, it may
readily be conceived, the terrors of the Holy Office might
easily be so used as to render them extremely unwilling
to become his sponsors. They were then assembled together;
the accused was brought in, the charge against him was
read, and he took an oath denying it. Each conjurator
was then taken separately and sworn as to his belief in the
truth or falsity of the oath of denegation—and according
as they expressed their conviction of the veracity of the
accused the sentence was usually rendered, absolving or
condemning him.

No process of administering compurgation can well be
conceived more shrewdly adapted to reduce to a minimum
the chances of acquittal, or to leave the result subject to
the wishes of the officials. The testimony of the doctors
of law, both civil and canon, accordingly was that it was
blind, deceitful, and perilous.[1] In fact, it is easy to conceive of the impossibility of finding six or ten, or twelve
men willing to risk their lives and families by standing up

---

[1] Simancæ loc. cit. No. 31.—Villadiego, Fuero Juzgo, p. 318 b. (Madrid,
1600.)—Both of these authorities stigmatize it as "fragilis et periculosa,
cæca et fallax."

in support of any one who had fallen into the grasp of the
Holy Office.   The terrible apprehension which the Inquisition spread abroad among all classes, and the dread which
every man felt of being suspected and seized as an accomplice of heresy, are unconsciously intimated by Simancas
when, arguing against this mode of trial, he observes that
"the morals of mankind are so corrupt at the present day,
and Christian charity has grown so cold, that it is almost
impossible to find any one willing to join in clearing his
neighbor, or who does not easily believe the worst of him
and construe all doubtful things against him.   When it is
enough for the condemnation of the accused that the compurgators shall declare that they are ignorant or doubtful
as to his innocence, who is there that will not express
doubt when they know that he would not have been condemned to purge himself if he had not been violently suspected?"   For these reasons he says that those of Moorish
or Jewish stock should never be subjected to it, for it is
almost impossible not to think ill of them, and, therefore,
to send them to purgation is simply to send them to the
stake.[1]

For all this, there was a lively discussion in the time of
Simancas, whether if the accused succeeded in thus clearing himself, it was sufficient for acquittal. Many Inquisitors
indeed held to the older practice that the accused should
first be tortured, when if no confession could be forced from
him he was put on his purgation; if he passed safely through
this, he was then made to abjure the errors of which he
had not been convicted, and after all this he was punished
at the discretion of the judge.[2] Such an accumulation of
injustice seems incredible, and yet Simancas feels himself
obliged to enter into an elaborate discussion to prove its
impropriety.

In countries where the Inquisition had not infected society and destroyed all feeling of sympathy between man

[1] Simancæ, loc. cit. No. 12.   [2] Ibid. No. 17.

CORRECTED

---

and man this process of purgation was not impossible. Thus, in 1527, during one of the early persecutions of the reformers under Henry VIII., while numbers were convicted, two women, Margaret Cowbridge and Margery Bowgas, were allowed to clear themselves by compurgators, though there were several positive witnesses against them. It is also noteworthy that in these cases a portion of the compurgators were women.[1]

In the regular ecclesiastical courts, Lancelotti, at the end of the sixteenth century, speaks of compurgation as the only mode of defence then in use in doubtful cases, where the evidence was insufficient.[2] And amid certain orders of monks within the last century, questions arising between themselves were settled by this mode of trial.[3]

Even in England, after the Anglican Church had received its final shape under Cranmer, during the reign of Edward VI., the custom appears in a carefully compiled body of ecclesiastical law, of which the formal adoption was only prevented accidentally by the untimely death of the young king. By this, a man accused of a charge resting on presumptions and incompletely proved, was required to clear himself with four compurgators of his own rank, who swore, as provided in the decretals of Innocent III., to their belief in his innocence.[4]

Though not strictly a portion of our subject, the question is not without interest as to the power or obligation of the plaintiff or accuser to fortify his case with conjurators. There is little evidence of such a custom in primitive times, but one or two allusions to it in the "Leges Barbarorum" show that it was occasionally practised. Some of the

---

[1] Strype's Ecclesiastical Memorials, I. 87.
[2] Institut. Jur. Canon. Lib. iv. Tit. ii. § 2.
[3] Du Cange, loc. cit.
[4] Burnet, Reformation, Vol. II. p. 199 (Ed. 1681).

earlier texts of the Salique law contain a section providing
that in certain cases the complainant shall sustain his
action with a number of conjurators varying with the
amount at stake; a larger number is required of the defendant in reply; and it is presumable that the judges
weighed the probabilities on either side, and rendered a decision accordingly.[1] As this is omitted in the later revisions of the law, it probably was not widely practised, or
regarded as of much importance. Among the Baioarians,
a claimant of an estate produced six conjurators who took
the oath with him, and whose united efforts could be rebutted by the defendant with a single competent witness.[2]
These directions are so precise that there can be no doubt
that the custom prevailed to a limited extent among
certain tribes, as a natural expression of the individuality
of each house or family as distinguished from the rest of the
sept.   That it was, perhaps, more generally employed than
the scanty references to it in the codes would indicate may
be inferred from one of the ecclesiastical forgeries which
Charlemagne was induced to adopt and promulgate.
According to this, no accusation against a bishop could be
successful unless supported by seventy-two witnesses, all
of whom were to be men of good repute; forty-four were
required to substantiate a charge against a priest, thirty-
seven in the case of a deacon, and seven when a member of
the inferior grades was implicated.[3]   Though styled witnesses in the text, the number required is so large that
they evidently could have been only conjurators, with whom
the complainant supported his oath of accusation, and the
manufacture of such a law would seem to show that the
practice of employing such means of substantiating a
charge was familiar to the minds of men.

[1] Tit. LXXIV. of Herold's text. Cap. Extravagant. No. XVIII. of Pardessus.
[2] L. Baioar. Tit. XVI. cap. i. § 2.
[3] Capit. Car. Mag. VI. ann. 806, c. xxiii. (Concil. Roman. Silvestri PP. I.)

In England, the Anglo-Saxon laws required, except in trivial cases, a "fore-oath" from the accuser (*forath, ante-juramentum, præjuramentum*), and William the Conqueror, in his compilation of the laws of Edward the Confessor, shows that this was sometimes strengthened by requiring the addition of conjurators, who were in no sense witnesses, since their oath had reference, not to the facts of the case, but solely to the purity of intention on the part of the accuser.[1] Indications of the same procedure are to be found in the collection known as the laws of Henry I.[2]

In an age of comparative simplicity, it is natural that men should turn rather to the guarantees of individual character, or to the forms of venerable superstition, than to the subtleties of legal procedure. Even as the defendant was expected to produce vouchers of his truthfulness, so might the plaintiff be equally required to give evidence that his repute among his neighbors was such as to justify the belief that he would not bring a false charge or advance an unfounded claim. The two customs appear to arise from the same process of reasoning and to be identical in spirit, yet it is somewhat singular that, as the compurgatorial oath declined, the practice of sustaining the plaintiff's case with conjurators seems to have become more common. In Béarn the laws of the thirteenth century provide that in cases of debt under forty sous, where there was no testimony on either side, the claimant could substantiate his case by bringing forward one conjurator, while the defendant could rebut it with two.[3] A similar rule obtained in England in all actions arising from contracts and sales;[4]

---

[1] E li apelur jurra sur lui par VII. humes numez, sei siste main, que pur haur nel fait, ne pur auter chose, si pur sun dreit nun purchacer.—L. Guillel. I. cap. xiv.

[2] Omnis tihla tractetur ante-juramento plano vel observato.—L. Henrici I. Tit. lxiv. § 1. Ante-juramentum a compellante habeatur, et alter se sexto decime sue purgetur ; sicut accusator precesserit.—Ibid. Tit. lxvi. § 8.

[3] For de Morlaas, Rubr. xxxviii. art. 63.

[4] Bracton, Lib. iv. Tract. vi. cap. 18, § 6.

and in the laws of Soest in Westphalia, compiled at the
end of the eleventh or the commencement of the twelfth
century, an accusation of homicide could be proved by six
conjurators swearing with the prosecutor, while if this
failed the accused could then clear himself with eleven
compurgators.[1] Throughout Germany, in the thirteenth
century, we find the principle of accusing conjurators generally received, as is evident from the "juramentum supermortuum" already referred to, and other provisions of the
municipal law.[2] So thoroughly, indeed, was it established
that, in some places, in prosecutions for highway robbery,
arson, and other crimes, the accuser had a right to require
every individual in court, from the judge to the spectator,
to help him with an oath or to swear that he knew nothing
of the matter, and even the attorney for the defendant was
obliged to undergo the ceremony.[3] In Sweden it was likewise in use under the name of *jeffniteed*.[4] In Norway and
Iceland, in certain cases of imputed crime, the accuser
was bound to produce ten companions, of whom eight appeared simply as supporters, while two swore that they
had heard the offence spoken of, but that they knew nothing
about it of their own knowledge—the amount of weight attached to which asseveration is shown by the fact that the
accused only required two conjurators to clear himself.[5]

Perhaps the most careful valuation of the oath of a
plaintiff is to be found in the Coutumier of Bordeaux,
which provides that, in civil cases not exceeding four sols
in amount, the claimant should substantiate his case by an

---

[1] Statuta Susatensia, No. 10. (Hæberlin, Analecta Medii Ævi, p. 509.)—
The same provision is preserved in a later recension of the laws of Soest,
dating apparently from the middle of the thirteenth century (Op. cit. p. 520).

[2] Jur. Provin. Alaman. cap. cccix. § 4. (Ed. Schilter.)

[3] Ibid. cap. cccxcviii. §§ 19, 20.

[4] Du Cange *sub voce*.

[5] Ideo manus libro imponimus sacro, quod audivimus (crimen rumore
sparsum), at nobis ignotum est verum sit nec ne.—Jarnsida, Mannhelge
cap xxiv.

oath on the Gospels in the Mayor's Court; when from four
to twenty sols were at stake, he was sworn on the altar of
St. Projet or St. Antoine; from twenty sols to fifteen livres,
the oath was taken in the cemetery of St. Seurin, while for
amounts above that sum it was administered on the " Fort"
or altar of St. Seurin himself. Persons whose want of veracity was notorious were obliged in all cases, however unimportant, to swear on the Fort, and had moreover to
provide a conjurator who with an oath of equal solemnity
asserted his belief in the truth of his companion.[1]

The custom of supporting an accusatorial oath by conjurators was maintained in some portions of Europe to a
comparatively recent period. Wachter[2] prints a curious
account of a trial, occurring in a Swabian court in 1505,
which illustrates this, as well as the weight which was still
attached to the oath of a defendant. A woman accused
three men on suspicion of being concerned in the murder
of her husband. They denied the charge, but when the
oath of negation was tendered to them, with the assurance
that, if they were Swabians, it would acquit them, they
demanded time for consideration. Then the advocate of
the widow stepped forward to offer the oath of accusation,
and two conjurators being found willing to support him
the accused were condemned without further examination
on either side. A similar process was observed in the
Vehmgericht, or Court of the Free Judges of Westphalia,
whose jurisdiction in the fourteenth and fifteenth centuries
became extended over the whole of Germany. Accusations
were supported by conjurators, and when the defendant
was a Frei-graff, or presiding officer of a tribunal, the complainant was obliged to procure seven Frei-schöppen, or
free judges, to take the accusatorial oath with him.[3]

The latest indication that I have met with of established

[1] Rabanis, Revue Hist. de Droit, 1861, p. 511.
[2] Du Boys, Droit Criminel des Peuples Modernes, II. 595.
[3] Freher. de Secret. Judic. cap. xvii. § 26.

legal provisions of this nature occurs in the laws of Britanny, as revised in 1539.   By this, a man claiming compensation for property taken away is to be believed on oath as to his statement of its value, provided he can procure companions worthy of credence to depose "qu'ils croyent que le jureur ait fait bon et loyal serment."[1]   Even this last vestige disappears in the revision of the Coutumier made by order of Henry III. in 1580.

[1] Anc. Cout. de Bretagne, Tit. VIII. art. 168.

II.

THE WAGER OF BATTLE.

WHEN man is emerging from barbarism, the struggle
between the rising powers of reason and the waning forces
of credulity, prejudice, and custom, is full of instruction.
Wise in our generation, we laugh at the inconsistencies
of our forefathers, which, rightly considered as portions
of the great cycle of human progress, are rather to be
respected as trophies of the silent victory, winning its way
by almost imperceptible gradations. When, therefore, in
the dark ages, we find the elements of pure justice so
strangely intermingled with the arbitrament of force, and
with the no less misleading appeals to chance, dignified
under the forms of Christianized superstition, we should
remember that even this is an improvement on the all-per-
vading first law of brute strength. We should not wonder that barbarous tribes require to be enticed towards
conceptions of abstract right, through pathways which,
though devious, must reach the goal at last. When the
strong man is brought, by whatever means, to yield to the
weak, a great conquest is gained over human nature; and
if the aid of superstition is invoked to decide the struggle,
we have no right, while enjoying the result, to stigmatize
the means by which Providence has seen fit to bring it
about. With uneducated nations, as with uneducated men,
sentiment is stronger than reason, and sacrifices will be
made for the one which are refused to the other. If therefore, the fierce warrior, resolute to maintain an injustice

or a usurpation, can be brought to submit his claim to the chances of an equal combat or of an ordeal, he has already taken a vast step towards acknowledging the empire of right and abandoning the personal independence which is incompatible with the relations of human society. It is by such indirect means that mere aggregations of individuals, each relying on his sword and right hand, have been gradually led to endure regular forms of government, and, thus becoming organized nations, to cherish the abstract idea of justice as indispensable between man and man. Viewed in this light, the ancient forms of procedure lose their ludicrous aspect, and we contemplate their whimsical admixture of force, faith, and reason, as we might the first rude engine of Watt, or the "Clermont," which painfully labored in the waters of the Hudson—clumsy and rough it is true, yet venerable as the origin and prognostic of future triumphs.

There is a natural tendency in the human mind to cast the burden of its doubts upon a higher power, and to relieve itself from the effort of decision by seeking in mystery the solution of its difficulties. Between the fetish worshippers of Congo and the polished sceptics who frequented the *salon* of Mlle. le Normant, the distance, though great, is bridged over by this common weakness; and whether the information sought be of the past or of the future, the impulse is the same. When, therefore, in the primitive *mallum*, the wisdom of the *rachinborgs* was at fault, and the absence or equal balance of testimony rendered a verdict difficult, what was more natural than to seek a decision by appealing to the powers above, and to leave the matter to the judgment of God?[1] Nor, with the warlike instincts

---

[1] Thus, as late as the thirteenth century, the municipal law of Southern Germany, in prescribing the duel for cases destitute of testimony, says with a naïve impiety : "Hoc ideo statutum est, quod causa hæc nemini cognita est quam Deo, cujus est eandem juste decidere." Logical enough, if the

of the race, is it surprising that this appeal should be made to the God of battles, to whom, in the ardor of new and imperfect Christianity, they looked in every case for a special interposition in favor of innocence.   The curious mingling of procedure, in these untutored seekings after justice, is well illustrated in a form of process prescribed by the primitive Bavarian law.   A man comes into court with six conjurators to claim an estate; the possessor defends his right with a single witness, who must be a landholder of the vicinage.   The claimant then attacks the veracity of the witness—"Thou hast lied against me. Grant me the single combat, and let God make manifest whether thou hast sworn truth or falsehood;"[1] and, according to the event of the duel, is the decision as to the truthfulness of the witness and the ownership of the property.

In discussing the judicial combat, it is important to keep in view the wide distinction between the wager of battle as a judicial institution, and the custom of duelling which has obtained with more or less regularity among all races and at all ages.   When the Horatii met the Curiatii, or when Antony challenged Octavius to decide the empery of the world with their two swords, these were isolated pro-

---

premises be granted !   Even as late as 1617, August Viescher, in an elaborate treatise on the judicial duel, expressed the same reliance on the divine interposition : " Dei enim hoc judicium dicitur, soli Deo causa terminanda committitur, Deo igitur authore singulare hoc certamen suscipiendum, ut justo judicio adjutor sit, omnisque spes ad solam summæ providentiam Trinitatis referenda est."—(Vischer Tract. Juris Duellici Universi, p. 109.) This work is a most curious anachronism.   Viescher was a learned jurisconsult who endeavored to revive the judicial duel in the seventeenth century by writing a treatise of 700 pages on its principles and practice.   He exhibits the wide range of his studies by citations from no less than six hundred and seventy-one authors, and manages to convey an incredibly small amount of information on the subject.

[1] Mendacium jurasti contra me : sponde mihi pugnam duorum, et manifestet Deus si mendacium an veritatem jurasti.—L. Baioar. Tit. xiv. c. i. § 2.

posals to save the unnecessary effusion of blood, or to gratify individual hate. When the *raffiné* of the times of Henri Quatre, or the modern fire-eater, wiped out some imaginary stain in the blood of his antagonist, the duel thus fought, though bearing a somewhat closer analogy to the judicial combat, is not derived from it, but from the right of private vengeance which was common to all the Teutonic tribes, and from the cognate right of private warfare which was the exclusive privilege of the gentry during the feudal period.[1] The established euphuistic formula of demanding "the satisfaction of a gentleman," thus designates both the object of the custom and its origin. The abolition of private wars gave a stimulus to the duel at nearly the period when the judicial combat fell gradually into desuetude. The one thus succeeded to the other, and, being kindred in nature, it is not surprising that for a time there was some confusion in the minds of men respecting their distinctive characteristics. Yet it is not difficult to draw the line between them. The object of the one was vengeance and reparation; the theory of the other was the discovery of truth, and the impartial ministration of justice.

It is easy to multiply examples illustrating this. John Van Arckel, a knight of Holland, followed Godfrey of Bouillon to the first crusade. When some German forces joined the army, a Tyrolese noble, seeing Van Arckel's arms displayed before his tent, and recognizing them as identical with his own, ordered them torn down. The insult was flagrant, but the injured knight sought no satisfaction for his honor. He laid the case before the chiefs of the crusade as a judicial matter; an examination was made, and both

---

[1] The early edicts directed against the duel proper (Ordonn. Charles IX., an. 1566; Henri IV., an. 1602—in Fontanon I. 665) refer exclusively to the noblesse, and to those entitled to bear arms, as addicted to the practice, while the judicial combat, as we shall see, was open to all ranks, and was enforced indiscriminately upon all.

parties proved their ancestral right to the same bearings.
To decide the conflicting and incompatible claims, the
judges ordered the judicial combat, in which Van Arckel
deprived his antagonist of life and quarterings together,
and vindicated his right to the argent 2 bars gules, which
in gratitude to Heaven he bore for eight long years in
Palestine. This was not a quarrel on a punctilio, nor a
mode of obtaining redress for an insult, but an examination into a legal question which admitted of no other solution according to the manners of the age.[1] When, after the
Sicilian Vespers, the wily Charles of Anjou was sorely
pressed by his victorious rival Pedro I. of Arragon, and
desired to gain time in order to repress a threatened insur-
rection among his Neapolitan subjects, he sent a herald to
Don Pedro to accuse him of bad faith in having commenced the war without defiance. The fiery Catalan fell
into the snare, and in order to clear himself of the charge,
which was not ill-founded, he offered to meet his accuser in
the *champ-clos*. Both parties swore upon the Gospels to
decide the accusation by combat, a hundred on each side,
in the neutral territory of Bordeaux; and Charles, having
obtained the necessary suspension of arms, easily found
means to prevent the hostile meeting.[2] Though practically
this challenge may differ little from that of Antony—its
object in reality being the crown of the Two Sicilies—still
its form and purport were those of the judicial duel, the
accused offering to disprove the charge of *mala fides* on
the body of his accuser. So, when Francis I., in idle bra-
vado, flung down the gauntlet to Charles V., it was not to
save half of Europe from fire and sword, but simply to absolve himself from the well-grounded charge of perjury

---

[1] Chron. Domin. de Arkel. (Matthæi Analect. VIII. 296).

[2] Ramon Muntaner, cap. lxxi.—Nothing more picturesquely romantic is
to be found in the annals of chivalry than Muntaner's account of Don
Pedro's ride to Bordeaux and his appearance in the lists, where the seneschal was unable to guarantee him a fair field.

brought against him by the Emperor for his non-observance
of the treaty of Madrid.   This again, therefore, wore the
form of the judicial combat, whatever might be the motives
of personal hate and craving of notoriety which influenced
the last imitator of the follies of chivalry.[1] The celebrated
duel, fought in 1547, between Jarnac and La Chastaigneraye, so piteously deplored by honest old Brantôme, shows
the distinction maintained to the last.   It was conducted
with all judicial ceremonies, in presence of Henry II., not
to settle a point of honor, but to justify Jarnac from a disgusting accusation brought by his adversary.   Resulting
most unexpectedly in the death of La Chastaigneraye, who
was a favorite of the king, the monarch was induced to put
an end to all legalized combats, though the illegal practice
of the private duel not only continued to flourish, but increased beyond all precedent during the succeeding half-
century—Henry IV. having granted in twenty-two years
no less than seven thousand letters of pardon for duels
fought in contravention of the royal edicts.   Such a mode
of obtaining "satisfaction" is so repugnant to the spirit of
our age that it is perhaps not to be wondered at if its
advocates should endeavor to affiliate it upon the ancient
wager of battle.   Both relics of barbarism, it is true, drew
their origin from the same habits and customs, yet they
have coexisted as separate institutions; and, however
much intermingled at times by the passions of periods of
violence, they were practised for different ends, and were
conducted with different forms of procedure.

Our theme is limited to the combat as a judicial process.
Leaving, therefore, untouched the vast harvest of curious
anecdote afforded by the monomachial propensities of
modern times, we will proceed to consider briefly the
history of the legal duel from its origin to its abrogation.

[1] Du Bellay, Mémoires, Liv. III.

Its mediæval panegyrists sought to strengthen its title to respect by affirming that it was as old as the human race, and that Cain and Abel, unable to settle their conflicting claims in any other mode, agreed to leave the decision to the chances of single combat; but we will not enter into speculations so recondite. Though this origin will doubtless at the present day be considered apocryphal, it is not a little remarkable that a custom, unknown to the races of classical antiquity, or to the ancient civilizations of the East, should have prevailed with general unanimity from Sparti✓ento to the North Cape, and that, with but one or two exceptions, all the tribes which founded the European states should have adopted it with such common spontaneity that its introduction cannot be assigned with certainty to any one of them. It would seem to have been everywhere autochthonic, and the theories which would attribute its paternity especially to the Burgundians, to the Franks, or to the Lombards, are equally destitute of proof.

The earliest allusion to the practice occurs in Livy, who describes how some Spaniards seized the opportunity of a gladiatorial exhibition held by Scipio to settle various civil suits by combat, when no other convenient mode of solution had presented itself;[1] and he proceeds to particularize a case in which two rival cousins decided in this manner a disputed question in the law of descent, despite the earnest remonstrances of the Roman general.[2] This could hardly have been a prevailing custom, however, among the aborigines, for Cæsar makes no mention of it among the Gauls, nor does Tacitus among the Germans;[3] and their silence on

<hr/>

[1] Lib. xxvii. cap. xxi.

[2] Nec alium deorum hominumve quam Martem se judicem habituros esse. —*Ibid.*

[3] A passage in the "De Moribus Germaniæ," cap. x., is commonly, but erroneously, quoted as showing the existence of the duel as a means of evidence among the Germans. When about to undertake an important war, one of the enemy was captured and obliged to fight with a chosen champion,

the subject must be accepted as conclusive, since a system so opposed to the principles of the Roman law could not have failed to impress them, had it existed. Yet in the fourth century, an allusion which occurs in Claudian would seem to show that by that time the idea had become familiar to the Roman mind.[1]

If the fabulous antiquity attributed by the early historians to the Danish monarchy be accepted as credible, a statement may be quoted from Saxo Grammaticus to the effect that about the Christian era Frotho III., or the Great, ordered the employment of the duel to settle all controversies, preferring that his subjects should learn to rely on courage rather than on eloquence;[2] and however apocryphal the chronology may be, yet the tradition shows that even in those ancient times the origin of the custom was already lost in the night of ages. Among the Feini or ancient Irish, the battle ordeal undoubtedly existed in the earliest periods, for in the Senchus Mor, or code compiled under the supervision of St. Patrick, there is an allusion to a judicial combat long previous, when Conchobar and Sencha, father of Brigh, first decreed that a delay of five days should take place in such affairs.[3]   At the time of the con-

---

an augury being drawn from the result as to the event of the war.   There is a vast difference, however, between a special omen of the future, and a proof of the past in the daily affairs of life.

Du Cange quotes an expression from Paterculus to show that the judicial appeal to the sword was customary among the Germans, but, although I am diffident in dissenting from so absolute an authority, I cannot see such meaning in the passage.   Paterculus merely says (Lib. II. cap. cxviii.), in describing the stratagems which led to the defeat of Varus, " et solita armis decerni jure terminarentur."   Taken with the context, this would appear to refer merely to the law of the strongest which prevails among all savage tribes.

[1] Qui male suspectam nobis impensius arsit

  Vel leto purgare fidem : qui judice ferro

  Diluit immeritum laudato sanguine crimen.—De Bell. Getico v. 591.

[2] Saxon. Grammat. Hist. Dan. Lib. v.

[3] Senchus Mor, I. 251.—" Why is the distress of five days always more usual than any other distress ?   On account of the combat fought between two in Magh-inis.   When they had all things ready for plying their

version of Ireland, therefore, the duel was an ancestral
right firmly established, and subject to precise legal regulations. So general was it, indeed, that St. Patrick, in a
council held in 456, was obliged to forbid his clergy from
appealing to the sword, under a threat of expulsion from
the church.[1] Towards the end of the same century, King
Gundobald caused the laws of the Burgundians to be collected, and among them the wager of battle occupies so
conspicuous a place that it obtained in time the name of
Lex Gundebalda or Loy Gombette, giving rise to the be--
lief that it originated with that race.

In the ordinary texts of the Salique law, no mention is
made of it, but in one manuscript it is alluded to as a
regular form of procedure.[2] This silence, however, does
not justify the conclusion that the battle ordeal was not
practised among the Franks. Enough instances of it are
to be found in their early history to show that it was by
no means uncommon;[3] and, at a later period, the same
absence of reference to it is observable in the Lex Emendata of Charlemagne, though the capitularies of that

arms, except a witness alone, they met a woman at the place of combat, and
she requested of them a delay, saying, 'If it were my husband that was
there, I would compel you to delay.' 'I would delay,' said one of them,
'but it would be prejudicial to the man who sues me; it is his cause that
would be delayed.' 'I will delay,' said the other. The combat was then
put off, but they did not know till when it was put off, until Conchubhur
and Sencha passed judgment respecting it; and Sencha asked, 'What is
the name of this woman?' 'Cuicthi' (five), said she, 'is my name.' 'Let
the combat be delayed,' said Sencha, ' in the name of this woman, for five
days.' From which is derived 'The truth of the men of the Feini would
have perished, had it not been for Cuicthi.' It is Brigh that is here called
Cuicthi.''

[1] Rebus suis clericus ille solvat debitum ; nam si armis compugnaverit
cum illo, merito extra ecclesiam computetur.—Synod. S. Patricii, ann. 456,
can. VIII.

[2] Si tamen non potuerit adprobare . . . . et postea, si ausus fuerit, pugnet.
—Leyden MS.—Capit. Extravagant. No. xxviii. of Pardessus.

[3] Gregor. Turon. Hist. Franc. Lib. VII. c. xiv.; Lib. x. c. x.—Aimoini
Lib. IV. c. ii.

monarch frequently allude to it as a legal process in
general use. The off-shoots of the Salique law—the Ripuarian, Allemannic, and Bavarian codes—which were compiled by Thierry, the son of Clovis, revised successively
by Childebert and Clotair II., and put into final shape by
Dagobert I. about the year 630—in their frequent reference
to the "campus," show how thoroughly it pervaded the
entire system of Germanic jurisprudence. The Lombards
were, if possible, even more addicted to its use. Their
earliest laws, compiled by King Rotharis in 643, seventy-
six years after their occupation of Italy, make constant
reference to it, and the strong hold which it then had on
the veneration of the race, as an ancestral custom, is shown
by the fruitless efforts of that legislator and his successors
to restrict its employment and to abrogate it. Thus Rotharis forbids its use in some cases of importance, substituting
conjurators, with an expression of disbelief, which shows
how little confidence was felt in its results even then by
enlightened men.[1]   The next lawgiver, King Grimoald,
decreed that thirty years' possession of either land or
liberty relieved a defendant from maintaining his title by
battle, the privilege of employing conjurators being then
conceded to him.[2]   In the succeeding century, King Luitprand sought to abolish it entirely, but finding the prejudices of his people too strong to be overcome, he placed

[1] Quia absurdum et impossibile videtur esse ut tam grandis causa sub uno
scuto per pugnam dirimatur.—(L. Longobard. Lib. ii. Tit. lv. §§ 1, 2, 3.)
How completely this was at variance with the customs of the Lombards is
evident from a case which occurred under his immediate predecessor Ario-
valdus.   That monarch imprisoned his queen Gundeberga, a Merovingian
princess, on an accusation of conspiracy brought against her by Adalulf, a
disappointed suitor.   When Clotair the Great sent an embassay to rescue his
fair relative, the question was decided by a single combat between the accuser
and a champion named Pitto, and on the defeat of Adalulf, the queen was
pronounced innocent and restored to the throne after a confinement which
had lasted three years.—Aimoini Lib. iv. c. x

[2] L. Longobard. Lib. ii. Tit. xxxv. §§ 4, 5.

on record in the statute book a declaration of his contempt for it and a statement of his efforts to do away with it, while he was obliged to content himself with limiting the extent of its application, and diminishing the penalties incurred by the defeated party.[1] The laws of the Angles, the Saxons, and the Frisians, likewise bear testimony to the universality of the custom.[2]

The evidence adduced above of its existence among the Feini of Ireland previous to their conversion to Christianity gives probability to the assumption that it was likewise practised by the early inhabitants of Britain. If so, the long domination of the Romans was doubtless sufficient to extinguish all traces of it. The Welsh laws attributed to Hoel Dda in the early part of the tenth century, which are exceedingly minute and precise in their directions as to all forms of legal procedure, make no allusion to it whatever. It is true that an ancient collection of laws asserts that the code of Dyvnwal-moel-mud, a British king, prescribed the ordeals of battle, of hot iron and of boiling water, and that Hoel in his legislation considered them unjust, abrogated them, and substituted the proof by men, or *raith*.[3] This legend, however, is very apocryphal. There is no allusion to such customs in the Welsh codes up to the close of the twelfth century, and the few indications which occur in subsequent collections of laws would seem to indicate that they were rather innovations due to the

---

[1] Gravis causa nobis esse comparuit, ut sub uno scuto, per unam pugnam, omnem suam substantiam homo amittat. . . . . Quia incerti sumus de judicio Dei; et multos audivimus per pugnam sine justitia causam suam perdere. Sed propter consuetudinem gentis nostræ Longobardorum legem impiam vetare non possumus.—(L. Longobard, Lib I. Tit. ix. § 23.) Muratori, however, states that the older MSS. read "legem istam," in place of "impiam," as given in the printed texts, which would somewhat weaken the force of Luitprand's condemnation.

[2] L. Anglior. et Werinor. Tit. I. cap. iii. and Tit. xv.—L. Saxon. Tit. xv.—L. Frision. Tit. v. c. i. and Tit. xi. c. iii.

[3] Anomalous Laws, Book xiv. chap. xiii. § 4. (Owen, II. 623.)

influence of the English Conquest than revivals of ancient institutions.

It is not a little singular that the duel appears to have been unknown among the Anglo-Saxons. Employed so extensively as legal evidence throughout their ancestral regions, by the kindred tribes from which they sprang, and by the Danes and Norwegians who became incorporated with them; harmonizing moreover with their general habits and principles of action, it would seem impossible that they should not likewise have practised it. That such was the case is one of the anomalies which defy speculation; and the bare fact can only be stated that the judicial combat is not referred to in any of the Anglo-Saxon or Anglo-Danish codes.[1] There seems, indeed, to be no reason to doubt that its introduction into English jurisprudence dates only from the time of William the Conqueror.[2]

The only other barbarian race among whose laws the battle trial found no place was the Gothic, and here the exception is susceptible of easy explanation. The effect upon the invaders of the decaying but still majestic civilization of Rome, the Byzantine education of Theodoric, the leader

[1] In Horne's Myrror of Justice (cap. II. sect. 13), a work which is supposed to date from the reign of Edward II., there is a form of appeal of treachery " qui fuit trové en vielx rosles del temps du Roy Alfred,'' in which the appellant offers to prove the truth of his charge with his body ; but the whole proceeding bears so little resemblance to the Anglo-Saxon laws that one can have no hesitation in doubting either the antiquarian lore of the author or the fidelity of his paraphrase.

[2] A charter issued by William, which appears to date early in his reign, gives the widest latitude to the duel both for his French and Saxon subjects. —(L. Guillelmi Conquest. II. §§ 1, 2, 3. Thorpe, I. 488.) Another law, however, enabled a Norman defendant to decline the combat when a Saxon was appellant. "Si Francigena appellaverit Anglum. . . . Anglus se defendat per quod melius voluerit, aut judicio ferri, aut duello. . . . Si autem Anglus Francigenam appellaverit et probare voluerit, judicio aut duello, volo tunc Francigenam purgare se sacramento non fracto.''—(Ibid. III. § 12. Thorpe, I. 493.) Such immunity seems a singular privilege for the generous Norman blood.

of the Ostrogoths, and his settled policy of conciliating the Italians by maintaining as far as possible the existing state of society, preclude any surprise that no allusion to the practice should occur in the short but sensible code known as the "Edict of Theodoric," which shows how earnestly that enlightened conqueror endeavored to fuse the invaders and the vanquished into one body politic.[1] With regard to the Wisigoths, we must remember that early conversion to Christianity and long intercourse with civilization had already worn off much of the primitive ferocity of a race which could produce in the fourth century such a man as Ulphilas. They were the earliest of the invaders who succeeded in forming a permanent occupation of the conquered territories; and settling, as they did, in Narbonensian Gaul and Spain while the moral influence of Rome was yet all powerful, the imperial institutions exercised a much greater effect upon them than on the subsequent bands of Northern barbarians. Accordingly, we find their codes based almost entirely upon the Roman jurisprudence, with such modifications as were essential to adapt it to a ruder state of society. Their nicely balanced provisions and careful distinctions offer a striking contrast to the shapeless legislation of the races that followed, and neither the judicial combat nor canonical compurgation found a place in them. Even the vulgar ordeal would appear to have been unknown until a period long subsequent to the conquest of Aquitaine by Clovis, and but little anterior to the overthrow of the Gothic kingdom of Spain by the Saracens. That this ap-

[1] An epistle from Theodoric to the Gaulish provinces, which he had just added to his empire, congratulates them on their return to Roman laws and usages, which he orders them to adopt without delay. Its whole tenor shows his thorough appreciation of the superiority of the Imperial codes over the customs of the barbarians, and his anxiety for settled principles of jurisprudence. "Jura publica certissima sunt humanæ vitæ solatia, infirmorum auxilia, potentum frena."—(Cassiodor. Variar. Lib. iii. Epist. xvii.) Various other passages might be cited to the same effect "Jura veterum ad nostram cupimus reverentiam custodiri," "Delectamur jure Romano vivere," etc.

9

parent exception to the prevailing customs of the barbarians was due, however, to their acquiescence in the enlightened zeal of their legislators, Theodoric and Alaric
II., is rendered evident by passages in Cassiodorus, which
show that the Gothic races originally followed the same
practices as the other savage tribes.[1]　Even as in Italy the
Lombard domination destroyed the results of Theodoric's
labors, so in France the introduction of the Frankish element revived the barbarian instincts, and in the celebrated
combat before Louis-le-Débonnaire, between Counts Bera
and Sanila, who were both Goths, we find the "pugna
duorum" claimed as an ancient privilege of the race, with
the distinction of its being equestrian, in accordance with
Gothic usages.[2]

Nor was the wager of battle confined to races of Celtic
or Teutonic origin.　The Sclavonic tribes, as they successively emerge into the light of history, show the same tendency to refer doubtful points of civil and criminal law to
the arbitrament of the sword.　The earliest records of
Hungary, Bohemia, Poland, Servia, Silesia, Moravia, Pomerania, Lithuania, and Russia present evidences of the prevalence of the system.[3]

Arising thus spontaneously from the habits and character
of so many races, it is no wonder that the wager of battle,

---

[1] In sending Colosseus to govern the Pannonian Goths, Theodoric urges
strongly the abandonment of the duel, showing how firm a hold it still retained in those portions of the race which had not been exposed to the full
civilizing influence of Rome—"Cur ad monomachiam recurritis qui venalem
judicem non habetis? Deponite ferrum qui non habetis inimicum. Pessime
contra parentes erigitis brachium, pro quibus constat gloriose moriendum.
Quid opus est homini lingua, si causam manus agat armata? aut unde pax
esse creditur, si sub civilitate pugnatur?"—Cassiodor. Variar. Lib. III.
Epist. xxiii. xxiv.

[2] Ermold. Nigell. de Reb. Gest. Ludov. Pii Lib. III.—Astron. Vit. Ludov.
Pii cap. xxxiii.　So thoroughly was the guilt of Bera considered as proved
by his defeat in this combat, that his name became adopted in the Catalan
dialect as synonymous with traitor.—Marca Hispanica, Lib. III. c. 21.

[3] Königswarter, op. cit. p. 224.

adapting itself to their various usages, became a permanent institution. Its roots lay deep among the recesses of popular prejudice and superstition, and its growth was correspondingly strong and vigorous. In this it was greatly assisted by the ubiquitous evils of the facility for perjury afforded by the practice of sacramental purgation, and it seems to have been regarded by legislators as the only remedy for the crime of false swearing which was everywhere prevalent. Thus Gundobald assumes that its introduction into the Burgundian code arose from this cause;[1] Charlemagne urged its use as greatly preferable to the shameless oaths which were taken with so much facility;[2] while Otho II., in 983, ordered its employment in various forms of procedure for the same reason.[3] It can hardly be a source of surprise, in view of the manners of the times, and of the enormous evils for which a remedy was sought, that the effort was made in this mode to impress upon principals and witnesses the awful sanctity of the oath, thus subjecting them to a liability to support their asseverations by an appeal to arms under imposing religious ceremonies.

In the primitive codes of the barbarians, there is no distinction made between civil and criminal law. Bodily punishment being almost unknown, except for slaves, and

---

[1] L. Burgund. Tit. xlv.—The remedy, however, would seem to have proved insufficient, for a subsequent enactment provides an enormous fine (300 solidi) to be levied on the witnesses of a losing party, by way of making them share in the punishment. "Quo facilius in posterum ne quis audeat propria pravitate mentire."—L. Burgund. Tit. lxxx. § 2. The position of a witness in those unceremonious days was indeed an unenviable one.

[2] Ut palam apparet quod aut ille qui crimen ingerit, aut ille qui vult se defendere, perjurare se debeat. Melius visum est ut in campo cum fustibus pariter contendant, quam perjurium absconse perpetrent.—Capit. Car. Mag. ex Lege Longobard. c. xxxiv. (Baluze).

[3] L. Longobard. Lib. ii. Tit. lv. § 34.

nearly all infractions of the law being visited with fines, there was no necessity for such niceties, the matter at stake in all cases being simply money or money's worth. Accordingly, we find the wager of battle used indiscriminately, both as a defence against accusations of crime, and as a mode of settling cases of disputed property, real and personal. This gave it a wide sphere of action, which was speedily rendered almost illimitable by other causes.

In its origin, the judicial duel was doubtless merely an expedient resorted to in the absence of direct or sufficient testimony, and the judges or *rachinborgs* were probably the arbiters of its necessity. Some of the early codes refer to it but seldom, and allude to its employment in but few cases.[1] In others, however, it is appealed to on almost every occasion. Among the Burgundians, in fact, we may assume, from a remark of St. Agobard, that it superseded all evidence and rendered superfluous any attempt to bring forward witnesses.[2] If any limits, indeed, were originally imposed, they were not of long duration, for it was not difficult to find expedients to justify the extension of a custom which accorded so perfectly with the temper of the age. How little reason was requisite to satisfy the belligerent aspirations of justice is shown by a curious provision in the code of one of the Frisian tribes, by which a man unable to disprove an accusation of homicide was allowed to charge the crime on whomsoever he might select, and then the question between them was decided by combat.[3]

The elasticity with which the duel lent itself to the advantage of the turbulent and unscrupulous had no little

[1] Thus the Salique law, as has been said above, hardly recognizes the existence of the practice. The Ripuarian code refers to it but four times, that of the Alamanni but six times, while it fairly bristles throughout the cognate legislation of the Baioarians.

[2] Apud quorum legem non licet discussione aut veracium testimonio causas terminare; eo quod libuerit, armis comminari liceat, ne infirmior sua retinere aut reposcere audeat, tanquam veritas armis manifestari egeat. —Lib. Adversus Legem Gundobadi cap. x.

[3] L. Frision. Tit. xiv. § 4.

influence in extending its sphere of action. This feature in its history is well exemplified in a document containing the proceedings of an assembly of local magnates, held in the year 888 to decide a contention concerning the patronage of the church of Lessingon. After the testimony on one side had been given, the opposite party commenced in reply, when the leaders of the assembly, seizing their swords, vowed that they would affirm the truth of the first pleader's evidence with their blood before King Arnoul and his court—and the case was decided without more ado.[1] The strong and the bold are apt to be the ruling spirits in all ages, and were emphatically so in those periods of scarcely curbed violence when the jurisprudence of the European commonwealths was slowly developing itself. To such spirits the wager of battle gave increased preponderance to which may fairly be attributed a large share of the favor which it enjoyed.

It is no wonder therefore that means were readily found for extending its application as widely as possible. One of the most fruitful of these expedients was the custom of challenging witnesses. It was a favorite mode of determining questions of perjury, and there was nothing to prevent a suitor, who saw his case going adversely, from accusing an inconvenient witness of false swearing, and demanding the " campus" to prove it—a proceeding which adjourned the main case, and likewise decided its result. This summary process of course brought every action within the jurisdiction of force, and deprived the judges of all authority to control the abuse. That it obtained at a very early period is shown by a form of procedure occurring in the Bavarian law, already referred to, by which the claimant of an estate is directed to fight, not the defendant, but his witness;[2] and in 819 a capitulary of Louis-le-

---

[1] Goldast. Antiq. Alaman. chart. lxxxv.
[2] L. Baioar. Tit. XVI. cap. i. § 2.

Débonnaire gives a formal privilege to the accused on a criminal charge to select one of the witnesses against him with whom to decide the question in battle.[1]

Nor was this merely a temporary extravagance. Late in the thirteenth century, after enlightened legislators had been strenuously and not unsuccessfully endeavoring to limit the abuse of the judicial combat, the challenging of witnesses was still the favorite mode of escaping legal condemnation.[2] Even in the fourteenth century, the municipal law of Rheims, which allowed the duel between principals only in criminal cases, permitted witnesses to be indiscriminately challenged and forced to fight, affording them the privilege of employing champions only on the grounds of physical infirmity or advanced age.[3] A still more bizarre extension of the practice, and one which was most ingeniously adapted to defeat the ends of justice, is found in the English law of the thirteenth century. By this, a man was sometimes permitted to challenge his own witnesses. Thus in many classes of crimes, such as theft, forgery, coining, &c. the accused could summon a "warrantor." The warrantor could scarcely give evidence in favor of the accused without assuming the responsibility himself. If he refused, the accused was at liberty to challenge him; if he gave the required evidence, he was liable to a challenge from the accuser.[4] Another mode extensively used in France about the same time was to accuse the principal witness of some

[1] Capit. Ludov. Pii ann. 819, cap. xv. When such was the liability impending over witnesses, it is easy to understand why they were required to come into court armed, and to have their weapons blessed on the altar before giving testimony. If defeated, they were fined and obliged to make good any damage which their evidence would have caused the other side.— L. Baioar. Tit. xvi. c. v.

[2] Beaumanoir, Coutumes du Beauvoisis, chap. lxi. § 58.

[3] Lib. Pract. de Consuetud. Remens. §§ 14, 40 (Archives Législat. de Reims, Pt. i. pp. 37, 40).

[4] Bracton de Legibus Angl. Lib. iii. Tract. ii. cap. xxxvii. § 5.—Fleta, Lib. I. cap. xxii.

crime rendering him incapable of giving testimony, when he was obliged to dispose of the charge by fighting, either personally or by champion, in order to get his evidence admitted.[1]

It is not easy to imagine any cases which might not thus be brought to the decision of the duel; and the evidence of its universality is found in the restriction which prevented the appearance as witnesses of those who could not be compelled to accept the combat. Thus the testimony of women and ecclesiastics was not receivable in lay courts in suits where appeal of battle might arise;[2] and when in the twelfth century special privileges were granted by the kings of France empowering serfs to bear testimony in court, the disability which prevented a serf from fighting with a freeman was declared annulled in such cases, as the evidence was only admissible when the witness was capable of supporting it by arms.[3]

The result of this system was that, in causes subject to such appeals, no witness could be forced to testify, by the French law of the thirteenth century, unless his principal entered into bonds to see him harmless in case of challenge, to provide a champion, and to make good all damages in case of defeat;[4] though it is difficult to understand how this could be satisfactorily arranged, since the penalties inflicted on a vanquished witness were severe, being, in civil

---

[1] Beaumanoir, chap. vi. § 16.

[2] Ibid. chap. xxxix. §§ 30, 31, 66.—Assises de Jerusalem cap. 169.—A somewhat similar principle is in force in the modern jurisprudence of China. Women, persons over eighty or under ten years of age, and cripples who have lost an eye or a limb are entitled to buy themselves off from punishment, except in a few cases of aggravated crime. They are, therefore, not allowed to appear as accusers, because they are enabled by this privilege to escape the penalties of false witness.—Staunton, Penal Code of China, Sects. 20–22, and 339.

[3] The earliest of these charters is a grant from Louis-le-Gros in 1109 to the serfs of the church of Paris, confirmed by Pope Pascal II. in 1113. (Baluz. et Mansi III. 12, 62.)

[4] Beaumanoir, chap. lxi. § 59.

causes, the loss of a hand and a fine at the pleasure of the suzerain, while in criminal actions "il perderoit le cors avecques."[1] The only limit to this abuse was that witnesses were not liable to challenge in cases concerning matters of less value than five sous and one denier.[2]

If the position of a witness was thus rendered unenviable, that of the judge was little better. As though the duel had not received sufficient extension by the facilities for its employment just described, another mode of introducing it in all cases was invented by which it became competent for the defeated party in any suit to challenge the court itself, and thus obtain a reversal of judgment at the·sword's point. Towards the end of the twelfth century in England, we find Glanville acknowledging his uncertainty as to whether the court could depute such a quarrel to a champion, or whether the judge delivering the verdict was bound to defend it personally; and also as to what, in case of defeat, was the legal position of the court thus convicted of injustice.[3] These doubts would seem to indicate that the custom was still of recent introduction, and not as yet practised to an extent sufficient to afford a settled basis of precedents for its details. If so, it was not long in firmly establishing

---

[1] Beaumanoir, chap. lxi. § 57.   [2] Ibid. chap. xl. § 21.

[3] "Curia . . . tenetur tamen judicium suum tueri per duellum . . . Sed utrum curia ipsa teneatur per aliquem de curia se defendere, vel per alium extraneum hoc fieri possit, quero."—(De Leg. Angliæ Lib. VIII. cap. ix.) The result of a reversal of judgment must probably have been a heavy fine and deprivation of the judicial function, such being the penalty provided for injustice in the laws of Henry I.—" Qui injuste judicabit, cxx sol. reus sit et dignitatem judicandi perdat."—(L. Henrici I. Tit. xiii. § 4)—which accords nearly with the French practice in the time of Beaumanoir, as mentioned below.

It must be born in mind that, as the dispensing of justice was an attribute of the feudal nobility, the judges were generally warriors (except the royal judges in England, who were frequently ecclesiastics), and thus these proceedings were not as extraordinary as they may at first sight appear to us. In Germany, where the judges of the lower courts were elective, they were required to be active and vigorous of body—" nec manibus nec pedibus captus."—(Jur. Provin. Alaman. cap. lxviii. § 6.)

itself. In 1195, the customs of St. Quentin allow to the disappointed pleader unlimited recourse against his judge.[1] Towards the latter half of the thirteenth century, we find in the "Conseil" of Pierre de Fontaines the custom in its fullest vigor and just on the eve of its decline. No restrictions appear to be imposed as to the cases in which appeal by battle was permitted, except that it was not allowed to override the customary law.[2] The suitor selected any one of three judges agreeing in the verdict; he could appeal at any stage of the proceedings when a point was decided against him; if unsuccessful, he was only liable in a pecuniary penalty to the judges for the wrong done them, and the judge, if vanquished, was exposed to no bodily punishment.[3] The villein, however, was not entitled to the privilege, except by special charter.[4] The universality of the practice is shown by the fact that it was for a long time the only mode of reversing a judgment, and an appeal in any other form was an innovation introduced by the extension of the royal jurisdiction under St. Louis, who labored so strenuously and so effectually to modify the barbarism of

[1] Si ille contra quem fit judicium non concedit illud judicium, per campum et duellum poterit illud contradicere intra villam S. Quintini, contra illos qui judicium fecerint.—Cited by Marnier in his edition of Pierre de Fontaines.

[2] Car poi profiteroient les costumes el païs, s'il s'en covenoit combatre; ne dépecier ne les puet-om par bataille.—Edition Marnier, chap. XXII. Tit. xxxii.

[3] Chap. XXII. Tit. i. vi. viii. x. xxvii. xxxi.—"Et certes en fausement ne gist ne vie ne menbre de cels qui sont fausé, en quelconques point que li fausemenz soit faiz, et quele que la querele soit" (Ibid. Tit. xiv.). If the judge was accused of bribery, however, and was defeated, he was liable to confiscation and banishment (Tit. xxvi.). The increasing severity meted out to careless, ignorant, or corrupt judges manifests the powerful influence of the Roman law, which, aided by the active efforts of legists, was infiltrating the customary jurisprudence and altering its character everywhere. Thus de Fontaines quotes with approbation the Code, De pœna judicis (Lib. VII. Tit. xlix. l. 1) as a thing rather to be desired than expected, while in Beaumanoir we already find its provisions rather exceeded than otherwise.

[4] De Fontaines, chap. XXII. Tit. iii.

feudal institutions by subordinating them to the principles
of the Roman jurisprudence.   De Fontaines, indeed, states
that he himself conducted the first case ever known in
Vermandois of an appeal without battle.[1]   At the same
time, the progress of more rational ideas is manifested by
his admission that the combat was not necessary to reverse
a judgment manifestly repugnant to the law, and that, on
the other hand, the law was not to be set aside by the
duel.

Twenty years later, we find in Beaumanoir abundant evidence of the success of St. Louis in setting bounds to the
abuses which he was endeavoring to remove.   The restrictions which he enumerates are greatly more efficacious than
those alluded to by de Fontaines.   In capital cases, the
appeal did not lie; while in civil actions, the suzerain before
whom the appeal was made could refuse it when the justice
of the verdict was self-evident.   Some caution, moreover,
was requisite in conducting such cases, for the disappointed
pleader who did not manage matters rightly might find himself pledged to a combat, single-handed, with all his judges
at once; and as the bench consisted of a collection of the
neighboring gentry, the result might be the confirmation
of the sentence in a manner more emphatic than agreeable.
An important change is likewise observable in the severe
penalty imposed upon a judge vanquished in such an appeal, being a heavy fine and deprivation of his functions in
civil cases, while in criminal ones it was death and confiscation—"il pert le cors et quanques il a."[2]

The king's court, however, was an exception to the general rule.   No appeal could be taken from its judgments, for

[1] De Fontaines, chap. XXII. Tit. xxiii.—Et ce fu li premiers dont je oïsse
onques parler qui fust rapelez en Vermendois sanz bataille.

[2] Coutumes du Beauvoisis, chap. lxi. §§ 36, 45, 47, 50, 62.—It should be
borne in mind, however, that Beaumanoir was a royal bailli, and the difference between the "assise de bailli" and the "assises des chevaliers" is well
pointed out by Beugnot (Les Olim, T. II. pp. xxx. xxxi.).   Beaumanoir in
many cases evidently describes the law as he would wish it to be.

there was no tribunal before which they could be carried.[1]
The judges of the royal court were therefore safe from the
necessity of vindicating their decisions in the field, and
they even carried this immunity with them and communicated it to those with whom they might be acting. De
Fontaines accordingly advises the seigneur justicier who
anticipates the appeal of battle in his côurt to obtain a royal
judge to sit with him, and mentions an instance in which
Philip (probably Philip Augustus) sent his whole council
to sit in the court of the Abbey of Corbie, when an appeal
was to be entered.[2]

By the German law of the same period, the privilege of
reversing a sentence by the sword existed, but accompanied
with regulations which seem evidently designed to embarrass, by enormous trouble and expense, the gratification
of the impulse which disappointed suitors would have to
establish their claims in such manner. Thus, by the Swabian law, it could only be done in the presence of the
sovereign himself, and not in that of the immediate feudal
superior;[3] while the Saxon code requires the extraordinary
expedient of a pitched battle, with seven on each side.[4] It

---

[1] Et pour ce ne l'en puët fausser, car l'en ne trouveroit mie qui droit en
feist car li rois ne tient de nului fors de Dieu et de luy.—Établissements,
Liv. I. chap. lxxviii.

[2] Conseil, ch. XXII. tit. xxi.

[3] Si contingat ut de justitia sententiæ pugnandum sit, illa pugna debet
institui coram rege—(Jur. Provin. Alaman. cap. xcix. § 5—Ed. Schilt.). In
a French version of this code, made probably towards the close of the fourteenth century, the purport of this passage is entirely changed. " De chas-
cun iugemant ne puet lan trover leaul ne certain consoil si bien come per lo
consoil de sages de la cort lo roi."—Miroir de Souabe, P. I. c. cxiii. (Éd.
Matile, Neufchatel, 1843). We may hence conclude that by this period the
custom of armed appeal was disused, and the extension of the royal jurisdiction was established.

[4] Jur. Provin. Saxon. Lib. I. art. 18.—This has been questioned by modern
critics, but there seems to be no good reason for doubting its authority. The
whole formula for the proceeding is given in the Richstich Landrecht (cap.
41), a manual of procedure of the fourteenth century, adapted to the Saxon
code.

is not a little singular that the feudal law of the same period has no allusion to the custom, all appeals being regularly carried to and heard in the court of the suzerain.[1]

Apart from these side issues, the right of demanding the wager of battle as between the principals varied much with the age and race. When Beaumanoir composed his "Coutumes du Beauvoisis," in 1283, the practice may be considered to have entered upon its decadence; twenty years had elapsed since the determined efforts of St. Louis to abolish it; substitutes for it in legal processes had been provided; and the manner in which that enlightened jurist manifests his preference for peaceful forms of law shows that he fully appreciated the civilizing spirit in which the monarch had endeavored to soften the ferocity of his subjects. When, therefore, we see in Beaumanoir's treatise how few restrictions existed in his time, we may comprehend the previous universality of the custom. In criminal cases, if an accuser offered battle, the defendant was forced either to accept it or to confess his guilt, unless he could prove an alibi, or unless the accuser was himself notoriously guilty of the crime in question, and the accusation was evidently a mere device to shift the guilt to the shoulders of another; or unless, in case of murder, the victim had disculpated him, when dying, and had named the real criminals.[2] If, on the other hand, the accused demanded to wage his battle, the judge could only refuse it when his guilt was too notorious for question.[3] A serf could not challenge a freeman, nor a bastard a man of legitimate birth (though an appeal of battle might lie between two bastards), nor a leper a sound man.[4] In civil actions, the battle trial was not allowed in cases relating to dower, to

---

[1] Richstich Lehnrecht, cap. xxvii.
[2] Coutumes du Beauvoisis, chap. lxi. § 2; chap. xliii. § 6.
[3] Ibid. chap. lxi. § 2; chap. xxxix. § 12.
[4] Ibid. chap. lxiii. §§ 1, 2, 10.

orphans under age,[1] to guardianships, or to the equity of redemption afforded by the feudal laws to kinsmen in the sale of heritable property, or where the matter at stake was of less value than twelve deniers.[2] St. Louis also prohibited the duel between brothers in civil cases, while permitting it in criminal accusations.[3] The slenderness of these restrictions shows what ample opportunities were afforded to belligerent pleaders.

In Germany, as a general rule, either party had a right to demand the judicial combat,[4] subject, however, in practice, to several important limitations. Thus, difference of rank between the parties afforded the superior a right to decline a challenge, as we shall see more fully hereafter.[5] Relationship between the contestants was also an impediment,[6] and even the fact that the defendant was not a native of the territory in which the action was brought gave him the privilege of refusing the appeal.[7] Still, we find the principle laid down even in the fourteenth century that cases of homicide could not be determined in any other manner.[8] There were circumstances, indeed, in which the complainant, if he could bring the evidence of seven witnesses in his favor, could decline the duel; but if he chose to prove the

---

[1] Twenty-one years is the age mentioned by St. Louis as that at which a man was liable to be called upon to fight.—Établissements, Liv. I. chap. lxxiii., cxlii.

[2] Coutumes du Beauvoisis, chap. lxiii. §§ 11, 13, 18. The denier was the twelfth part of the solidus or sou.

[3] Établissements, Liv. I. chap. clxvii.

[4] Jur. Provin. Alaman. cap. clxvi. §§ 13, 27 ; cap. clxxvii. (Ed. Schilt.)

[5] As early as the time of Frederic Barbarossa this rule was strictly laid down. "Si miles adversus militem pro pace violata aut aliqua capitali causa duellum committere voluerit, facultas pugnandi ei non concedatur nisi probare possit quod antiquitus ipse cum parentibus suis natione legitimus miles existat."—Feudor. Lib. II. Tit. xxvii. § 3.

[6] Jur. Provin. Alaman. cap. ccclxxxvi. § 2. (Ed. Schilteri.)

[7] Ibid. cap. ccxcii. § 2.

[8] Sed scias si de perpetrato homicidio agitur, probationem sine duello non procedere.—Richstich Landrecht, cap. xlix.

10

charge by the combat, no examination or testimony was admitted.[1] Yet a general rule is found expressed to the effect that it was necessary only in cases where no other evidence was obtainable, when the result could be safely left to the judgment of Omniscience.[2]

By the English law of the thirteenth century, a man accused of crime had, in doubtful cases only, the right of election between trial by jury and the wager of battle. When a violent presumption existed against him, he was obliged to submit to the verdict of a jury; but in cases of suspected poisoning, as satisfactory evidence was deemed unattainable, the accused had only the choice between confession and the combat.[3] On the other hand, when the appellant demanded the duel, he was obliged to make out a probable case before it was granted.[4] When battle had been gaged, however, no withdrawal was permitted, and any composition between the parties to avoid it was punishable by fine and imprisonment[5]—a regulation, no doubt, intended to prevent pleaders from rashly undertaking it, and to obviate its abuse as a means of extortion. In accusations of treason, indeed, the royal consent alone could

---

[1] Jur. Provin. Aleman. cap. ccclxxxvi. §§ 28, 29. (Ed. Schilteri.)

[2] Hinc pervenit dispositio de duello. Quod enim homines non vident Deo nihilominus notum est optime, unde in Deo confidere possumus, eum duellum secundum jus diremturum.—Jur. Provin. Alaman. cap. clxviii. § 19. (Ed. Senckenberg.)

[3] Bracton. Lib. III. Tract. ii. cap. 18.—Fleta Lib. I. cap. xxxi. §§ 2, 3.

[4] Bracton. Lib. III. Tract. ii. cap. 23 § 1.

[5] Si autem uterque defaltam fecerit, et testatum sit quod concordati fuerunt, uterque capiatur, et ipsi et plegii sui in misericordia.—Ibid.

The custom with regard to this varied greatly according to local usage. Thus, a charter of the Count of Forez in 1270 concedes the right of avoiding battle, even at the last moment, by satisfying the adversary, and paying a fine of sixty sols.—Chart. Raynaldi Com. Forens. c. 4 (Bernard, Hist. du Forez, T. I. Preuves, p. 25). According to the customs of Lorris, in 1155, if a composition was effected after battle had been gaged and before security was given, each party paid a fine of two sous and a half. If after security was pledged, the fine was increased to seven sous and a half.—Chart. Ludov. Junior. ann. 1155, cap. xiv. (Isambert, Anciennes Lois Françaises, I. 155.)

prevent the matter from being fought out.[1] Any bodily injury on the part of the plaintiff, tending to render him less capable of defence or aggression, likewise deprived the defendant of the right to the wager of battle, and this led to such nice distinctions that the loss of molar teeth was adjudged not to amount to disqualification, while the absence of incisors was considered sufficient excuse, because they were held to be important weapons of offence.[2] Thus the knight who demanded that his antagonist should undergo the destruction of an eye to equalize the loss of his own, extinguished in the fight of Otterbourne, was strictly within the privileges accorded him by law. Notwithstanding these various restrictions, cases of treason were almost always determined by the judicial duel, according to both Glanville and Bracton.[3] This was in direct opposition to the custom of Lombardy, where such cases were especially exempted from decision by the sword.[4]

In Béarn, the duel was permitted at the option of the accuser in cases of murder and treason, but in civil suits only in default of testimony.[5] That in such cases it was in common use is shown by a treaty made, in the latter part of the eleventh century, between Centulla I. of Béarn and the Viscount of Soule, in which all doubtful questions arising between their respective subjects are directed to be settled by the combat, with the singular proviso that the combatants shall be men who have never taken part in war.[6]

---

[1] Nec erit locus concordiæ, nisi regis interveniat assensus.—Fleta Lib. II. cap. xxi. § 2.

[2] Bracton. Lib. III. Tract. ii. cap. 24 § 4.—Hujusmodi vero dentes multum adjuvant ad devincendum.

[3] Glanvil. Lib. XIV. cap. i.—Bracton. Lib. III. Tract. ii. cap. 3, § 1. Solet appellum istud per duellum terminari.

[4] Non est consuetudo Mediolani ut de felonia aut de infidelitate pugna fiat; licet contrarium sit, quod præcipit lex Longobardorum, ut de infidelitate pugna fiat.—Feudor. Lib. II. Tit. xxxix.

[5] For de Morlaas, Rubr. xxxviii. xxxix.

[6] Marca, Hist. de Béarn, p. 293. (Mazure et Hatoulet.)

In the thirteenth century, however, a provision occurs which must have greatly reduced the number of duels, as it imposed a fine of only sixteen sous on the party who made default, while, if vanquished, he was visited with a mulct of sixty sous and the forfeiture of his arms.[1] In the neighboring region of Bigorre an exemption was allowed in favor of the widow whose husband had been slain in war. Until she remarried or her sons were of age to bear arms, she was exempt from all legal process—a provision evidently intended to relieve her from the duel in which suits were liable to terminate.[2]

In some regions, greater restrictions were imposed on the facility for such appeals to the sword. In Catalonia, for instance, the judge alone had the power of deciding whether they should be permitted,[3] and a similar right was reserved in doubtful cases to the podestà in a code of laws enacted at Verona in 1228.[4] This must often have prevented the injustice inherent in the system, and an equally prudent reserve was exhibited in a statute of Montpellier, which required the assent of both parties.[5] On the other hand, in Normandy, at the commencement of the thirteenth century, many cases relating to real estate were examined in the first instance by a jury of twelve men, and if they failed of an unanimous verdict, the question was decided by the duel, whether the parties were willing or not.[6]

From a very early period, a minimum limit of value was established, below which a pugnacious pleader was not allowed to put the life or limb of his adversary in jeopardy. This varied of course with the race and the period. Thus,

---

[1] For de Morlaas, Rubr. iv.
[2] De Lagrèze, Hist. du Droit dans les Pyrénées, Paris, 1867, p. 68.
[3] Libell. Catalan. MS.   (Du Cange.)
[4] Meo arbitrio determinabo duellum, vel judicium judicabo. Lib. Juris Civil. Veronæ, cap. 78 (p. 63).
[5] Statut. Montispess. ann. 1204.   (Du Cange.)
[6] Établissements de Normandie, *passim* (Édition Marnier).

among the Angli and Werini, the lowest sum for which the combat was permitted was two solidi,[1] while the Baioarians established the limit at the value of a cow.[2] In the tenth century, Otho II. decided that six solidi should be the smallest sum worth fighting for.[3] The laws of Henry I. of England decreed that in civil cases the appeal of battle should not lie for an amount less than ten solidi.[4] In France, Louis-le-Jeune, by an edict of 1168, forbade the duel when the sum in debate was less than five sous,[5] and this remained in force for at least a century.[6] The custom of Normandy in the thirteenth century specifies ten sous as the line of demarcation between the "lex apparens" and the "lex simplex" in civil suits,[7] and the same provision retains its place in the Coutumier in use until the sixteenth century.[8] In the Frankish kingdom of Jerusalem,

---

[1] L. Anglior. et Werinor. Tit. xv. The variations in the coinage are so numerous and uncertain, that to express the values of the solidus or sou, at the different periods and among the different races enumerated, would occupy too much space. In general terms, it may be remarked that the Carlovingian solidus was the twentieth part of a pound of silver, and, according to the researches of Guérard, was equivalent in purchasing power to about thirty-six francs of modern money. The marc was half a pound of silver.

[2] L. Baioar. Tit. viii. cap. ii. § 5; cap. iii.

[3] L. Longobard. Lib. ii. cap. lv. § 37.

[4] L. Henrici I. cap. 59.

[5] Isambert, Anciennes Lois Françaises, I. 162. This occurs in an edict abolishing sundry vicious customs of the town of Orléans. It was probably merely a local regulation, though it has been frequently cited as a general law.

[6] Livres de Jostice et de Plet, Liv. xix. Tit. xvii. § 3, Tit. xxii. § 4, Tit. xxxviii. § 3. See also a coutumier of Anjou of the same period (Anciens Usages d'Anjou, § 32.—Marnier, Paris, 1853).

The "Livre de Jostice et de Plet" was the production of an Orléannais, which may account for his affixing the limit prescribed by the edict of Louis-le-Jeune. The matter was evidently regulated by local custom, since, as we have already seen, his contemporary, Beaumanoir (cap. lxiii. § 11), names twelve deniers, or one sou, as the minimum.

[7] Cost. Leg. Norman. P. ii. cap. xxi. § 7 (Ludewig, Reliq. MSS. VII. 307). The judgment of God was frequently styled "Lex apparens" or "paribilis."

[8] Anc. Coutum. de Normandie, cap. 87 (Bourdot de Richebourg, IV. 55).

10*

the minimum was a silver marc.[1]   A law of Arragon, in
1247, places the limit at ten sous.[2]   By the criminal procedure in England, at about the same period, the duel was
prescribed only for cases of felony or crimes of importance,
and it was forbidden in trifling misdemeanors.[3]   The contemporary law of Germany provides that in accusations
of personal violence, the duel was not to be allowed, unless
the injury inflicted on the complainant had been sufficiently
serious to cause permanent maiming,[4] thus showing how
thoroughly different in spirit was the judicial combat from
the modern code of honor which has been affiliated upon it.

No rank of life procured exemption from the duel between antagonists of equal station.   When in 1002, on the
death of Otho III., the German throne was filled by the
election of Henry the Lame, Duke of Bavaria, one of his
disappointed competitors, Hermann, Duke of Swabia, is said
to have demanded that their respective claims should be
determined by a judicial combat, and the new king, feeling
himself bound to accept the wager of battle, proceeded to
the appointed place, and waited in vain for the appearance
of his antagonist.[5]   Thus the champion of England, who
figures in the coronation pageant of Westminster Abbey,
is a relic of the times when it was not an idle ceremony
for the armed and mounted knight to fling the gauntlet
and proclaim aloud that he was ready to do battle with
any one who challenged the right of the new monarch to
his crown.[6]   A striking example of the liability attaching
to even the most exalted rank is afforded by a declaration

---

[1] Assises de Jerusalem, cap. 149.

[2] Laws of Huescar, by Don Jayme I. (Du Cange. s. v. *Torna.*)

[3] Bracton. Lib. III. Tract. ii. cap. 19 § 6, also cap. 23 § 2.

[4] Ob alia autem vulnera haud ita gravia, duellum non permittitur.—Jur.
Provin. Alaman. cap. clxxii. § 20. (Ed. Senckenberg.)

[5] Dithmari Chron. Lib. v.

[6] From the time of Henry I., the office of king's champion was one of
honor and dignity. See Spelman's Glossary.

of the privileges of the Duchy of Austria, granted by
Frederic Barbarossa in 1156, and confirmed by Frederic
II. in 1245. These privileges rendered the dukes virtually
independent sovereigns, and among them is enumerated
the right of employing a champion to represent the reign-
ing duke when summoned to the judicial duel.[1] Even
more instructive is the inference deducible from the For
de Morlaas, granted to his subjects by Gaston IV. of Béarn
about the year 1100. The privileges contained in it are
guaranteed by a clause providing that, should they be infringed by the prince, the injured subject shall substantiate
his complaint by his simple oath, and shall not be compelled to prove the illegality of the sovereign's acts by the
judicial combat,[2] thus indicating a pre-existing custom of
the duel between the prince and his vassals.

International litigation, even, was subject to the same
arbitrament. Allusion has already been made to the challenge which passed between Charles of Anjou and Pedro
of Arragon, and other instances might readily be given,
such as that of the Emperor Henry III. and Henry I. of
France during their interview at Ipsch in 1056 ;[3] or that of
the conflicting claims of the kings of Castile and Navarre
referred for adjudication to Henry II. of England, in 1177,
when both embassies to the English court were supplied
with champions as well as lawyers, so as to be ready in
case the matter should be submitted to the duel for decision.[4] These may perhaps be regarded rather as personal
than national quarrels, but that distinction does not apply
to a case which occurred in 1034, when the Emperor Conrad the Salique endeavored to pacify the Saxon Marches.

[1] Insuper potest idem Dux Austriæ, cum impugnatus fuerit ab aliquo de
duello, per unum idoneum non in enormitatis macula detentum vices suas
prorsus supplere.—Constit. Frid. II. ann. 1245, cap 9. (Goldast. Const.
Imp. I. 303.)

[2] For de Morlaas, Rubr. xxvi.

[3] Lambert. Hersfeld. ann. 1056.

[4] Benedicti Abbatis Gesta Henr. II. p. 139. (Rerum Britann. Script.)

On his inquiring into the origin of the mutual devastation of the neighboring races, the Saxons, who were really in fault, offered to prove by the duel that the Pagan Luitzes were the aggressors, trusting that their Christianity would counterbalance the injustice of their cause. The defeat of their champion by his heathen adversary was, however, a memorable example of the impartiality of God, and was received as a strong confirmation of the value of the battle trial.[1]

As regards the inferior classes of society, innumerable documents attest the right of peasants to decide their quarrels by the ordeal of battle. By the old Lombard law, slaves were allowed to defend themselves in this manner;[2] and they could even employ the duel to claim their liberty from their masters, as we may infer from a law of King Grimoald denying this privilege to those who could be proved to have served the same master for thirty continuous years.[3] Similarly, among the Frisians, a *litus* claiming his liberty was allowed to prove it against his master with arms.[4] The institutions of feudalism widened the distance between the different classes of society, and we have already seen that, in the thirteenth century, serfs were enfranchised in order to enable them to support their testimony by the combat; yet this was only the result of inequality of rank. In the time of Beaumanoir (1283), though an appeal would not lie from a serf to a freeman, it may be safely inferred from the context that a combat could be legally decreed between two serfs, if the consent of their masters were obtained,[5] and other contemporary authorities show that a

---

[1] Wippo. Vit. Chunradi Salici.

[2] L. Longobard. Lib. I. Tit. xxv. § 49.

[3] Ibid. Lib. I. Tit. ix. § 38.   [4] L. Frision. Tit. XI. cap. iii.

[5] Coutumes du Beauvoisis, cap. lxiii. § 1.—The consent of the master was necessary to authorize the risk of loss which he incurred by his serf venturing to engage in the duel. Thus, in a curious case which occurred in 1293, "idem Droetus corpus suum ad duellum in quo perire posset obligare non poterat sine nostri licentia speciali."—Actes du Parlement de Paris, I. 446.

man claimed as a serf could defend his freedom with the
sword against his would-be master.[1] Even Jews were held
liable to the appeal of battle, as we learn from a decision
of 1207, preserved in an ancient register of assizes in Normandy,[2] and they no doubt purchased the exemption, which
was granted to them, except in cases of flagrant murder,
by Philippe-le-Long, as a special favor, in 1317.[3]

Difference of condition thus became an impediment to the
duel, and formed the subject of many regulations, varying
with circumstance and locality. The free mountaineers of
Béarn, as has been seen, placed the prince and the subject
on an equality before the law, but this was a rare example
of independence, and the privileges of station were sometimes exhibited in their most odious form. In France, for
instance, while the battle trial could take place between the
gentilhomme and the *vilain*, the former was secured by the
distinction that if the villein presumed to challenge him,
he enjoyed the right of fighting on horseback with knightly
weapons, while the challenger was on foot and armed only
with shield and staff; but if the gentleman condescended
to challenge the villein, they met on equal terms.[4] In Ger-

---

[1] Livres de Jostice et de Plet, Liv. xix. Tit. 13.—Abnegavit se esse servum
S. Martini, et de hoc arramivit bellum contra nos.—Tabul. Vindocinens.
cap. 159. (Du Cange, s. v. *adramire*.)

[2] Assises de l'Echiquier de Normandie, p. 174. (Marnier.)

[3] Laurière, Table Chron. des Ordonnances, p. 105.

[4] Beaumanoir, op. cit. cap. lxi. §§ 9, 10.—Établissements de S. Louis,
Liv. I. chap. lxxxii.—Pierre de Fontaines, however, repudiates this barbarous custom in cases of appeal, and directs that the combat shall take
place on foot between champions. (Conseil, chap. xxi. Tit. xiv.) And in a
case recorded in 1280, when a *femme de corps* of Aimeri of Rouchechouart
accused the Sire of Montricher of burning her houses, when the duel was
adjudged, she placed in the lists an armed and mounted knight as her champion, who does not seem to have been objected to. (Actes du Parlement de
Paris, T. I. No. 2269 A. p. 217.) Even where the custom was observed,
Beaumanoir mentions a case which shows that practical justice was sometimes enforced without ceremony. A gentleman challenged a roturier, and
presented himself in the arena on horseback with his knightly arms. The
defendant reclaimed against the injustice, and the judges decided that the

many, where the minute distinctions of birth were guarded
with the most jealous care from a very early period, the
laws of the thirteenth century provide that a difference of
rank permitted the superior to decline the challenge of an
inferior, while the latter was obliged to accept the appeal of
the former.   So thoroughly was this principle carried into
practice, that, to compel the appearance of a *Semperfri*,
or noble of sixteen quarterings, the appellant was obliged
to prove himself of equally untarnished descent.[1]   In the
same spirit, a Jew could not decline the appeal of battle
offered by a Christian accuser, though we may safely infer
that the Jew could not challenge the Christian.[2]   So, in the
Latin kingdom of Jerusalem, the Greek, the Syrian, and the
Saracen could not challenge the Frank, but could not, in
criminal cases, decline the challenge of a Christian, though
they might in civil suits.[3]   In Arragon, no judicial duel was
permitted between a Christian and a Jew or a Saracen,[4]
while in Castile both combatants had to be gentlemen,
quarrels between parties of different ranks being settled by
the courts.[5]   On the other hand, in Wales, extreme difference of rank was held to render the duel necessary, as in

gentleman forfeited his horse and arms, and that if he desired to accomplish
the combat he must do so in the condition in which he was left by the dis-
armament—in his shirt, without weapon or shield, while his adversary retained his coat of mail, target, and club.   (Cout. de Beauvoi. cap. lxiv. § 3.)

[1] Jur. Provin. Alamann. cap. ccclxxxv. §§ 14, 15.   (Ed. Schilter.)   According to some MSS., however, this privilege of declining the challenge
of an inferior was not allowed in cases of homicide.—"Ibi enim corpus
corpori opponitur."—cap. liii. § 4.   (Ed. Senckenberg)   On the other
hand, a constitution of Frederic Barbarossa, issued in 1168 and quoted above,
forbids the duel in capital cases, unless the adversaries are of equal birth.

[2] Ibid. cap. cclviii. § 20.   (Ed. Schilter.)—We have already seen that
the converse of this rule was introduced in England, as regards questions
between Frenchmen and Englishmen, by William the Conqueror.

[3] Quia surien et greci in omnibus suis causis, præter quam in criminalibus
excusantur a duello.—Assises de Jerusalem, Baisse Court, cap. 269.

[4] Laws of Huescar, ann. 1247.   (Du Cange s. v. *Torna*.)

[5] Las Siete Partidas, P. VII. Tit. iii. 1. 3.

cases of treason against a lord, for there the lord was plaintiff against his vassal, and as no man could enter into law with his lord, the combat was considered the only mode of prosecution befitting his dignity.[1]

There were three classes—women, ecclesiastics, and those suffering under physical incapacity—with whom personal appearance in the lists would appear to be impossible. When interested in cases involving the judicial duel they were therefore allowed the privilege of substituting a champion, who took their place and did battle for the justice of their cause. So careful were legislators to prevent any failure in the procedure prescribed by law, that the Assises de Jerusalem ordered the suzerain to supply the expenses for forty days, when a suitor unable to fight was also too poor to pay for a champion to take his place; and when a murdered man left no relatives to prosecute the murderer, the suzerain was likewise obliged to furnish the champion in any trial that might arise.[2] Equally directed to the same purpose was the German law which provided that when a crippled defendant refused or neglected to procure a substitute, the judge was to seize one-half of his property with which to pay the services of a gladiator, who could claim nothing more.[3]

Women, however, did not always restrict themselves to fighting thus vicariously. The German laws refer to cases in which a woman might demand justice of a man personally in the lists, and not only are instances on record in which this was done, but it was of sufficiently frequent occurrence to have an established mode of procedure, which is preserved to us in all its details by illuminated MSS. of

---

[1] Anomalous Laws, Book XIV. chap. xiv. § 1. (Owen II. 625.)

[2] Assises de Jerusalem, cap. 266, 267.

[3] Si hoc facere non vult paralyticus ille, tunc judex mediante pecunia paralytici, campionem aliquem adsciscere debet, huic paralyticus semissem bonorum dare debet, et nihil amplius.—Jur. Provin. Alamann. cap. lx. § 5.

the period.[1] The chances between such unequal adversaries
were adjusted by burying the man to his waist, tying his
left hand behind his back, and arming him only with a
mace, while his fair opponent had the free use of her limbs
and was provided with a heavy stone securely fastened in
a piece of stuff.[2]

The liability of ecclesiastics to the duel varied with the
varying relations between the church and state. As early
as the year 819, Louis-le-Débonnaire, in his additions to the
Salique law, directs that, in doubtful cases arising between
laymen and ecclesiastics, the duel between chosen witnesses
shall be employed, but that when both parties are clerical
it shall be forbidden.[3] This restriction was not long observed. A decree of the Emperor Guy, in 892, gives to
churchmen the privilege of settling their quarrels either by
combat or by witnesses, as they might prefer;[4] and about
the year 945, Atto of Vercelli complains that the tribunals
allowed to ecclesiastics no exemption from the prevailing
custom.[5] Yet so far was this from being deemed a hardship by the turbulent spirits of the period, that clerks not
infrequently disdained to sustain their rights by the intervention of a champion, and, yielding to warlike aspirations,
boldly entered the lists themselves. In 1080 the Synod of
Lillebonne adopted a canon punishing by a fine such bel-

[1] Jur. Provin. Alamann. cap. ccxxix. § 2. This chapter is omitted in the
French version of the Speculum Suevicum.

[2] Königswarter, op. cit. p. 221.—In many places, however, crimes which
a man was forced to disprove by combat were subject to the ordeal of hot
iron or water when the accused was a woman. Thus, by the Spanish law of
the thirteenth century, "Muger . . salvese por fierro caliente; e si varon
fuere legador . . salvese por lid."—Fuero de Baeça. (Villadiego, Fuero
Juzgo fol. 317ª.)

[3] Capit. Ludov. Pii I. ann. 819, cap. x.

[4] Ughelli, T. II. p. 122 (Du Cange).

[5] Addunt insuper, quoniam si aliquis militum sacerdotes Dei in crimine
pulsaverit per pugnam sive singulari certamine esse decernendum.—De Pressuris Eccles.

ligerent churchmen as indulged in the luxury of duels
without having first obtained from their bishops a special
license authorizing it.[1] About the same period, Geoffry,
Abbot of Vendôme, in a letter to the Bishop of Saintes,
complains of one of his monks who had fought in a judicial
duel with a clerk of Saintes.[2] The practice continued, and
though forbidden by Pope Innocent II. in 1140,[3] Alexander
III. and Clement III. found it necessary to repeat the prohibition before the close of the century.[4] Yet Alexander,
when appealed to with respect to a priest of the Campagna
who had lost a finger in a duel, decided that neither the
offence nor the mutilation debarred him from the exercise
of his sacerdotal functions, and only directed him to undergo due penance.[5] The progress of the age, however,
was shown when, about thirty years afterwards, Celestin
III. pronounced sentence of deposition in a similar case
submitted to him;[6] and this was formally and peremp-
torily confirmed by Innocent III. at the great council of
Lateran in 1215.[7]

That the peaceful ministers of Christ should vindicate
their rights with the sword, either personally or by proxy,
was a sacrilege abhorrent to pious minds. As early as the
middle of the ninth century, Nicholas I., who did so much
to establish the supremacy of the church, endeavored to
emancipate it from this necessity, and declared that the
duel was not recognized by the ecclesiastical law.[8] The
utmost privilege which the secular law accorded the clergy,

---

[1] Clericus . . . si duellum sine episcopi licentia susceperit . . . aut assultum
fecerit, episcopis per pecuniam emendetur.—Orderic. Vital. P. II. Lib. v. c. 5.
[2] Goffrid. Vindocinens. Lib. III. Epist. 39.   [3] Du Cange.
[4] Ut clerici non pugnent in duello, nec pro se pugiles introducent.—Chron.
S. Ægid. in Brunswig.—Can. 1. Extra, Lib. v. Tit. xiv.
[5] Can. 1. Extra, Lib. I. Tit. xx.
[6] Can. 2 Extra, Lib. v. Tit. xiv.   [7] Concil. Lateran. IV. can. 18.
[8] Monomachiam in legem non assumimus, quam antecessores nostros
minime accepisse cognovimus.—Cap. Monomachiam caus. II. q. 5.—Nicolai
PP. I. Epist. 148.

11

however, was the right of presenting a champion in the
lists, which zealous churchmen naturally resented as an
arbitrary injustice.[1]   How thoroughly it was carried out
in practice, notwithstanding all remonstrances, is shown
by a charter granted in 1024 by St. Stephen of Hungary
to the monastery of St. Adrian of Zala, by which, among
other privileges, the pious king bound himself to supply a
champion in all suits against the abbey, in order that the
holy meditations of the monks might not be interrupted.[2]
It was long before the abuse was removed.   In 1112 we
find a certain Guillaume Maumarel, in a dispute with the
chapter of Paris concerning some feudal rights over the
domain of Sucy, appearing in the court of the Bishop of
Paris for the purpose of settling the question by the duel,
and though the matter was finally compromised without
combat, there does not seem to have been anything irregular in his proceeding.[3]   So, about the same period, in a case
of disputed property between the abbey of St. Aubin in
Anjou and a neighboring knight, the monks not only challenged their adversary, but the duel was held in the seignorial court of another monastery;[4] and in 1164, we find
a duel decreed at Monza, by the Archbishop of Cologne as
chancellor of Italy, between an abbey and a layman of the
vicinity.[5]   That such cases, indeed, were by no means uncommon is shown by their special prohibition in 1195 by
Celestin III.[6]   Yet, notwithstanding the repeated efforts
of the Holy See, it was almost impossible for the church
to exempt itself from the universal liability.   Though in

---

[1] Ad pugnam sacerdotes impingere quærunt, nullam amplius reverentiam
ipsis observantes, nisi quod non propriis manibus, sed per submissos illis in
tali discrimine judicant dimicare.—Atton. Vercell. De Pressuris Eccles.
Pt. I.

[2] Chart. S. Stephani. (Batthyani, Legg. Eccles. Hung. T. I. p. 384.)

[3] Cartulaire de l'Église de Paris, I. 378.

[4] The charter recording the suit and its results is given by Baluze and
Mansi, Miscell. III. 59.

[5] Ibid. p. 134.   [6] Can. 1 Extra, Lib. v. Tit. xxxv.

1174 Louis VII. granted a special privilege of exemption
to the church of Jusiers and its men, on the ground that
he was bound to abrogate all improper customs,[1] still no
general reform appears to have been practicable.   In 1239
a knight of Orléans, Gui de Santillac, testified before the
royal council that the chapter of Saint-Aignan had appealed him in wager of battle.[2]   As late as the year 1245,
some vassals of the chapter of Nôtre Dame at Paris denied
the service due by them, and demanded that the claim of
the chapter should be made good by the wager of battle.
That they had a legal right to do so is shown by the fact
that the churchmen were obliged to implore the intervention of the Pope; and Innocent IV. accordingly granted
to the chapter a special privilege, in which, on the ground
that single combats were forbidden by the canons, he declared that the church of Nôtre Dame should be entitled
to prove its rights by witnesses, deeds, and other legitimate proofs, notwithstanding the custom existing to the
contrary.[3]   It was probably his interference in this case
that led him a few years later, in 1252, to issue a decretal
in which he pointed out the manifest hardship of forcing
the clergy in France, when prosecuting such claims against
their serfs, to have recourse to the duel, and thus, under
the canon law, to forfeit their positions.   To remedy this
he proclaimed as a general rule that all verdicts should be
void when obtained against clerks either by means of the
duel or through reason of their refusing the combat.[4]   Even
a century later, when the judicial duel was going out of
fashion, a bishop of Liége so vexed the burghers of Louvain, by repeated citations to the combat to settle disputed

---

[1] Tenemur pravas consuetudines funditus extirpare.   (Du Boys, Droit
Criminel des Peuples Modernes, II. 187.)
[2] Actes du Parlement de Paris, T. I. p. cccvii.   (Paris, 1863.)
[3] Contraria consuetudine non obstante.—Cart. de l'Église de Paris, II.
393–4.
[4] Archives Administratives de Reims, T. I. p. 733.

questions, that John III. Duke of Brabant was obliged to appeal to the Emperor Charles IV., who accordingly wrote to the bishops of Trèves, Cambrai, and Verdun desiring them to find some means of putting an end to the bellicose tendencies of their episcopal brother.[1]

The customs and prejudices of the time were evidently too strong to be easily eradicated. It is therefore not surprising to find that the prelates, acting in their capacity of temporal seigneurs, should have been accustomed to award the duel as freely as any other form of legal procedure. To do this was not only one of the privileges which marked the feudal superior, but was also a source of revenue from the fees and penalties thence accruing, and these rights were as eagerly sought and as jealously guarded by the spiritual lords as by the warlike barons. It would scarce be necessary to multiply instances, but I may mention a charter granted by Fulk Nera, Count of Anjou, about the year 1010, bestowing these rights on the abbey of Beaulieu in Touraine,[2] and one by the Emperor Henry III., in 1052, to the bishop and church of Volaterra in Italy.[3] Some conscientous churchmen objected to a practice so antagonistic to all the teachings of the religion of which they were professors, and lifted up their voices to check the abuse. Thus, about the close of the eleventh century, we find the celebrated canonist, St. Ivo of Chartres, rebuking the Bishop of Orleans for ordering the combat to decide an important suit in his court.[4] Ivo even carried out his principles to the sacrifice of the jurisdiction usually so dear to the prelates of his day, for in

---

[1] Proost, Législation des Jugements de Dieu, p. 19.

[2] Du Cange, s. v. *Bellum.*

[3] Muratori, Antiq. Ital. Dissert. 39.—Among various other examples given by the same author is one of the year 1010, in which the court of the bishop of Aretino grants the combat to decide a case between a monastery and a layman.

[4] Ivon. Epist. cxlviii.

another case he refused to give judgment because it necessarily involved a trial by battle, and he eluded the responsibility by transferring the cause to the court of the Countess
of Chartres.[1] A century later the celebrated Peter Cantor
resolutely declared that as a priest he would in no case
furnish relics on which the preliminary oaths were to be
taken, for churchmen were prohibited from being concerned
in bloodshed.[2] These precepts and examples were equally
unavailing. Churchmen continued to award the wager of
battle, and resolutely resisted any invasion of their privileges. In 1150 the statutes of the chapter of Lausanne
direct that all duels shall be fought before the provost—
and the provost was Arducius, Bishop of Geneva.[3] Even
in the thirteenth century, in the archbishop's court or offi-
ciality of Rheims, the duel was a matter of course;[4] and a
case is recorded, occurring in 1224, in a dispute about the
ownership of a house, which was decided by a duel in the
court of the abbey of St. Remy, where the abbot presided
over the lists and they were guarded by the royal officials.[5]
In 1239 the Bishop of Orléans contested with the king as to
the right of the former to the jurisdiction of the duel in his
diocese;[6] and in a judgment rendered in 1269, concerning
a combat waged within the limits of the chapter of Nôtre
Dame of Paris, we find that the first blows of the fight,
usually known as "ictus regis" or "les cous lou roi," are
alluded to as "ictus capituli."[7] How eagerly these rights
were maintained is apparent from numerous decisions concerning contested cases. Thus, an agreement of 1193, be-

---

[1] Ivon. Epist. ccxlvii.
[2] Pet. Cantor. Verb. Abbreviat. cap. lxxviii.
[3] Migne's Patrologia, T. 188, p. 1287.
[4] Lib. Pract. de Consuetud. Remens. *passim.* (Archives Législ. de Reims.)
[5] Archives Administ. de Reims, T. I. p. 822.
[6] Actes du Parlement de Paris, T. I. p. cccvii. (Paris, 1863.)
[7] Cartulaire de l'Église de Paris, III. 432. After the first blows, the parties could be separated on payment of a fine to the court, from the recipient
of which the name is evidently derived.

tween the Countess of St. Quentin and the chapter of Nôtre
Dame, respecting the disputed jurisdiction of the town of
Viry, gives the official of the chapter the right to decree
duels, but places the lists under the supervision of both
parties, and divides the spoils equally between each.[1]   A
charter of 1199, concerning the village of Marne, shows
that the sergeant, or officer of the chapter, had the cognizance of causes up to the gaging of battle, after which
further proceedings were reserved for the court of the
bishop himself.[2]   In 1257, while St. Louis was exerting
himself with so much energy to restrict the custom, an
abbey is found engaged in a suit with the crown to prove
its rights to decree the duel, and to enjoy the fees and
mulcts thence arising;[3] and in 1277 a similar suit on the
part of the abbey of St. Vaast d'Arras was decided in favor
of the abbey.[4]   From a verdict given in 1293, the right of
the chapter of Soissons to decree the judicial combat
appears to be undoubted, as well as the earnestness of the
worthy ecclesiastics to exercise the privilege.[5]   Even more
significant is a declaration of the authorities of Metz, as
late as 1299, by which the granting of all wagers of battle
is expressly admitted by the civil magistrates of the city
to appertain to the court of the archbishop;[6] and even in
1311 a bishop of St. Brieuc ordered a duel between two
squires pleading in his court, in consequence of high words
between them.   From some cause the combat did not take
place, and the Christian prelate seized the arms and horses
of the parties as his mulct.   They appealed to the Parlement of Paris, which ordered the restoration of the confis-

---

[1] Cartulaire de l'Église de Paris, I. 234.   [2] Ibid. I. 79–80.

[3] Les Olim, I. 24.

[4] Actes du Parl. de Paris, T. I. No. 2122, C. p. 197.

[5] Ibid. p. 446.

[6] Faisons cognussant à tous que des arramies des champs et des batailles
nous avons recogneut et recognissons c'on ne les doit faire aillors, maiques
en la court de l'ostel nostre signour l'evesque de Metz.—Du Cange, s. v.
Arramiatio.

cated articles, and fined the bishop for his disregard of the royal edicts prohibiting the single combat.[1] By this time, probably, the dictum of Beaumanoir had become generally acknowledged, that the church could not be concerned in cases which involved the wager of battle, or of death or mutilation.[2]

There was one jurisdiction which held itself more carefully aloof from the prevailing influence of barbarism—that of the Admiralty Courts, which covered a large portion of practical mercantile law. This is a fact easily explicable, not only from the character of the parties and of the transactions for which those courts were erected, but from the direct descent of the maritime codes from the Roman law, less modified by transmission than any other portions of mediæval jurisprudence. These codes, though compiled at a period when the wager of battle flourished in full luxuriance, have no reference to it whatever, and the Assises de Jerusalem expressly allude to the Admiralty Courts as not admitting the judicial duel in proof,[3] while an English document of 12 Edward III. attests the same principle.[4] When, however, the case was one implying an accusation of theft or deception, as in denying the receipt of cargo, the matter entered into the province of criminal law, and the battle trial might be legitimately ordered.[5]

The forms and ceremonies employed in the judicial duel may furnish an interesting subject of investigation for the admirers of chivalry, but they teach in their details little concerning the habits and modes of thought of the

[1] Les Olim, III. 679.

[2] Voirs est que tuit li cas où il pot avoir gages de bataille ou peril de perdre vie ou membre, doivent estre justicié par le laie justice; ne ne s'en doit sainte Eglise meller.—Coutumes du Beauvoisis, cap. xi. art. 30.

[3] En la cort de la mer na point de bataille por prueve ne por demande de celuy veage.—Assises de Jerusalem, cap. xliii.

[4] Pardessus, Us et Coutumes de la Mer.

[5] Livres de Jostice et de Plet, Liv. VII. Tit. iv. § 2.

Middle Ages, and for the most part are therefore merely interesting to the pure archæologist. Although minute directions have come down to us in the manuals compiled for the guidance of judges of the lists, to enumerate them in their varying fashions would hardly be worth the space which would be required to accomplish the task with any fulness. Suffice it to say that the general principle on which the combat was conducted was the absolute assertion by each party of the justice of his cause, to which end a solémn oath on the Gospels, or on a relic of approved sanctity, was administered to each before the conflict commenced.[1] Defeat was thus not merely the loss of the suit, but was also a conviction of perjury, to be punished as such; and in criminal cases it was also a conviction of malicious prosecution on the part of a worsted appellant. Accordingly, we find the vanquished party, whether plaintiff or defendant, subjected to penalties more or less severe, varying with the time and place. Thus, in 819, Louis-le-Débonnaire decreed that, in cases where testimony was evenly balanced, one of the witnesses from each side should be chosen to fight it out, the defeated champion suffering the usual pen-

---

[1] According to Bracton, the appellant in criminal cases appears always obliged to swear to his own personal knowledge, *visu ac auditu*, of the crime alleged. This, however, was not the case elsewhere. Among the glossators on the Lombard law, there were warm disputes as to the propriety, in certain cases, of forcing one of the contestants to commit perjury. The matter will be found treated at some length in Savigny's Geschichte d. Rom. Recht, B. IV. pp. 159 sqq.

The formula of the oath as given in the Fleta is as follows : The parties take each other by the hand and first the appellee swears, " Hoc audis, homo quem per manum teneo, qui A. te facis appellari per nomen baptismi tui, quod ego C. fratrem tuum, vel alium parentem vel dominum non occidi, vel plagam ei feci ullo genere armorum per quod remotior esse debuit a vita et morti propinquior ; sic me Deus adjuvet et hæc Sancta etc." Then the appellant responds : " Hoc audis homo quem per manum teneo, qui te R. facis appellari per nomen baptismi tui, quod tu es perjurus et ideo perjurus quia tali anno, tali die, tali hora et tali loco nequiter et in felonia occidisti C. fratrem meum tali genere armorum, unde obiit infra triduum ; sic me Deus etc."—Lib. I. cap. xxxii. §§ 28, 29.

alty of perjury—the loss of a hand; while the remaining witnesses on the losing side were allowed the privilege of redeeming their forfeited members at the regular legal rate.[1] William the Conqueror imposed a fine of forty sous on the losing side impartially;[2] this was increased to sixty sous by the compilation known as the laws of Henry I.;[3] and the same regulation is stated by Glanville, with the addition that the defeated person was forever disqualified as a witness or champion;[4] while in the time of Edward II. the loser, except in cases of felony, paid to the victor forty sous besides a small gratification under the name of *ruaille*, in addition to the loss of the suit.[5] By the Lombard customs, early in the eleventh century, the appellant, if vanquished, had the privilege of redeeming his hand; the defendant, if defeated, lost his hand, and was of course subject in addition to the penalties of the crime of which he was proved guilty.[6] About the same time, the Bearnese

---

[1] Capit. Ludov. Pii ann. 819, cap. x. A somewhat similar provision occurs in the L. Burgund. Tit. xlv. and lxxx.

[2] L. Guillelmi Conquest. iii. xii. (Thorpe, I. 493.)—A previous law, however, had assessed a Norman appellant sixty sous when defeated. (Ibid. ii. ii.)

[3] L. Henrici I. cap. lix. § 15.

[4] Glanvil. de Leg. Angl. Lib. ii. cap. iii.

That defeat in the combat was regarded as much more damaging than the simple loss of a suit is shown by some provisions in the custom of Normandy, by which a vanquished combatant was classed with perjurers, false witnesses, and other infamous persons, as incapable thenceforth of giving testimony in court (Cod. Leg. Normann. P. I. cap. lxiv.—Ludewig Reliq. MSS. T. VII. p. 270), or of serving on a jury (Anc. Coutume de Normandie—Bourdot de Richebourg, T. IV. p. 29), "Ne doibvent estre receuz à la jurée, ne ceulx qui sont reprins de parjure, ou de porter faulx tesmoing, ou vaincu en champ de bataille, ou ceulx qui sont infames." This clause however, does not occur in the corresponding passage of the ancient Latin version above alluded to. (Ludewig, T. VII. p. 282.)

[5] Solement ceux vainqus sont quittes ou lour clients pur eux rendre aux combattants vanquishours 40 sous en nosme de recreantise et ruaille peur la bourse a mettre eins ses deniers oustre le judgement sur le principall.—Horne's Myrror of Justice, cap. iii. sect. 23

[6] Formul. Vetus in L. Longobard. (Georgisch, p. 1276.)

legislation embodies a similar principle in a milder form, a fine of sixty-six sous Morlaas being imposed impartially on the losing party.[1] In process of time, this system was abandoned in some countries. The English law of the thirteenth century admitted the justice of the *lex talionis* in principle, but did not put it in practice, a vanquished appellant in capital cases being merely imprisoned as a calumniator, while the defendant, if defeated, was executed, and his property confiscated.[2] The same distinction is to be found in the contemporary custom of Normandy.[3] So by the code in force in Verona in 1228 the Podestà in criminal cases had the power of ordering the duel, and of punishing at his pleasure the accuser if vanquished—the accused when convicted of course undergoing the penalty of his crime.[4]

Mediæval legislation, however, was not usually so lenient to a worsted appellant. The application of the *lex talionis* to the man who brought a false charge, thus adjudging to him the penalty which was incurred by the defendant if convicted, was widely current during the Middle Ages. This principle is to be found enunciated in the broadest and most decided manner in the ecclesiastical law,[5] and it was naturally brought into play in regulating the fate of those engaged in the wager of battle. Thus Guillaume-le-Breton

---

[1] For d'Oloron, Art. 21.

[2] Si autem appellans victus fuerit, gaolæ committatur tanquam calumniator puniendus, sed nec vitam amittat nec membrum, licet secundum leges ad taliones teneretur si in probatione deficeret (Bracton, Lib. III. Tract. ii. cap. 18 § 4). In another passage, Bracton gives a reason for this clemency— "Si autem victus sit in campo . . . quamvis ad gaolam mittendus sit, tamen sit ei aliquando gratia de misericordia, quia pugnat pro pace." (Ibid. cap. 21 § 7.) See also the Fleta, Lib. I. cap. xxxii. § 32.

[3] Étab. de Normandie, Tit. "De prandre fame à force" (Marnier).

[4] Lib. Juris Civilis Veronæ cap. 78 (p. 63).

[5] Qui calumniam illatam non probat, pœnam debet incurrere quam si probasset reus utique sustineret.—Can. Qui calumniam Caus. v. q. vi. (Decreti P. II.)

states that when Philip Augustus, in 1203, wrested Normandy from the feeble grasp of John Lackland, one of the few changes which he ventured to introduce in the local laws of the duchy was to substitute this rule of confiscation, mutilation, or death, according to the degree of criminality involved in the accusation, for the comparatively light pecuniary mulct and loss of legal status previously incurred by a worsted appellant.[1] The same system is followed throughout the legislation of St. Louis, whether the punishment be light or capital, of an equal responsibility on both parties.[2] In capital cases, when champions were employed, the principals were held in prison with the cord around them with which the defeated party was to be hanged; and if one were a woman, for the cord was substituted the spade wherewith she was to be buried alive.[3] The same principle of equal responsibility prevailed throughout the Frankish kingdoms of the East, where, in an appeal of murder, whichever party was defeated was hanged in his spurs;[4] and it finally established itself in England, where in the fourteenth century, we find it positively declared as an imperative regulation by Thomas, Duke of

[1]   .   .   .   ad poenas exigat æquas,
    Victus ut appellans sive appellatus, eadem
    Lege ligaretur mutilari aut perdere vitam.
    Moris enim extiterit apud illos hactenus, ut si
    Appellans victus in causa sanguinis esset,
    Sex solidos decies cum nummo solveret uno
    Et sic impunis, amissa lege, maneret :
    Quod si appellatum vinci contigeret, omni
    Re privaretur et turpi morte periret.
              Guillielmi Brito. Philippidos Lib. VIII.

It will be observed that the preëxisting Norman custom here described is precisely that indicated above by Glanville.

[2] *E. g.* Etablissements Lib. I. cap. 27 and 91.—" Cil qui seroit vaincus seroit pendus" (cap. 82).

[3] Beaumanoir, chap. lxiv. § 10.

[4] Assises de Jerusalem, cap. 317.

Gloucester, in an elaborate treatise on the rules of single combat printed by Spelman.[1]

In Germany, however, the custom was not uniform. In one text of the Swabian code, the principle is laid down that a defeated appellant escaped with a fine to the judge and to his adversary, while the defendant, if vanquished, was visited with the punishment due to his crime;[2] while another text directs that whichever party be defeated should lose a hand,[3] or be executed, according to the gravity of the crime alleged.[4] An exceptional case, moreover, was provided for, in which both antagonists might suffer the penalty; thus, when a convicted thief accused a receiver of stolen goods of having suggested the crime, the latter was bound to defend himself by the duel, and if defeated, both combatants were hanged with the strictest impartiality.[5]

The most hideous exaggeration of the system, however, was found in the Frankish kingdoms of the East, which reserved a special atrocity for women—one of the numerous instances to be observed in mediæval law of the injustice applied habitually to the weaker sex. When a woman appeared, either as appellant or defendant, in the lists by her champion, if he was defeated she was promptly burnt, no matter what was the crime for which the duel occurred—and as many accusations could only be determined by the wager of battle, she had no choice but to undergo the chance of the most dreadful of deaths.[6]

---

[1] Recta fides et æquitas et jus armorum volunt ut appellans eandem incurrat pœnam quam defendens, si is victus fuerit et subactus.—Formula Duelli, apud Spelman. Glossar. s. v. *Campus.*

[2] Jur. Provin. Alamann. cap. ccclxxxvi. §§ 19, 20. (Ed. Schilter.)

[3] Quique succumbit ei manus amputetur.—Ibid. cap. clxviii. § 20. (Ed. Senckenberg.)

[4] Ibid. cap. clxxii. § 18. (Ed. Senckenberg.)

[5] Ibid. cap. ccxix. § 6. (Ed. Schilter.)

[6] Assis. Hierosol. Alta Corte cap. cv. (Canciani, V. 208)

It was customary to require the parties to give security for their due appearance at the appointed time, various fines and punishments being inflicted on defaulters. By the old German law, when default was made by the defendant he was held guilty of the crime charged upon him : and either the defendant or appellant was declared infamous. According to some MSS., indeed, all the possessions of a defaulter were forfeited, either to his heirs, or to his feudal superior.[1] In a case occurring in the twelfth century in Hainault, between a seigneur and a man whom he claimed as a serf, the latter demanded the duel, which was allowed, but on the appointed day he failed to appear by nine o'clock. His adversary had waited for him since daybreak, and claimed the verdict which was awarded him by the council Hainault.   At this moment the missing man presented himself, but was adjudged to be too late, and was delivered to his claimant as a serf.   According to the custom of Flanders, indeed, the combatant who failed to appear suffered banishment, with confiscation of all his possessions.[2] This extreme rigor, however, did not obtain universally. Among the Béarnese, for instance, the forfeiture for a default was only sixteen sous Morlaas.[3] By the English law, the defaulter was declared infamous.[4] The Scandinavians punished him popularly by erecting a "nithstöng"—*pertica execrationis*—a post inscribed with defamatory runes, and so flagrant was this insult considered, that finally it was prohibited by law under pain of exile.[5]

The bail, of course, was liable for all legal penalties in-

[1] Jur. Provin. Alamann. cap. ccclxxxvi. § 31. (Ed. Schilter.)—Cap. clxxiii. §§ 7, 8. (Ed. Senckenb.)

[2] Proost. Législation des Jugements de Dieu, pp. 18, 21.

[3] For de Morlaas, Rubr. IV. art. 5.

[4] Horne's Myrror of Justice, cap. iv. sect. 13.

[5] Schlegel Comment. ad Grágás § 31.—Grágás sect. VIII. cap. 105.   A fanciful etymologist might trace to this custom the modern phrase of "posting a coward."

12

curred by a defaulter, and occasionally, indeed, would seem to be made to share the fate of his principal, when the latter appeared and was defeated. Thus, in a miracle play of the fourteenth century, a stranger knight at the court of Paris, compelled to fight in defence of the honor of the king's daughter, is unable to find security. The queen and princess offer themselves as hostages and are accepted, but the king warns them—

> Dame, par Dieu le roy celestre !
> Bien vous recevray pour hostage ;
> Mais de tant vous fas-je bien sage,
> Se le dessus en peut avoir
> Ardré, je vous feray ardoir
>   Et mettre en cendre.[1]

As regards the choice of weapons, much curious anecdote could be gathered from the pages of Brantôme and others learned in punctilio, without throwing additional light upon mediæval customs. It may be briefly observed, however, that when champions were employed on both sides, the law appears generally to have restricted them to the club and buckler, and to have prescribed perfect equality between the combatants.[2] An ordonnance of Philip Augustus, in 1215, directs that the club shall not exceed three feet in length.[3] When the principals appeared personally, it would seem that in early times the appellant had the choice of weapons, which not only gave him an enormous advantage,

[1] Un Miracle de Notre-Dame d'Amis et d'Amille. (Monmerqué et Michel, Théat. Français au Moyen-Age, p. 238.)

Another passage in the same play signalizes the equality of punishment for appellant and defendant in cases of defeat :—

> —Mais quant il seront
> En champ, jamais n'en ysteront
> Sanz combatre, soiez-en fis,
> Tant que l'un en soit desconfis ;
> Et celui qui vaincu sera,
> Je vous promet, pendu sera:
>   N'en doubte nulz.

[2] E. g. Constit. Sicular. Lib. II. Tit. xxxvii. § 1.

[3] Laurière, Table des Ordonn. p. 10.

but enabled him to indulge any whims which his taste or
fancy might suggest, as in the case of a Gascon knight in
the thirteenth century, who stipulated that each combatant
should be crowned with a wreath of roses. As every detail
of equipment was thus subject to the caprice of the challenger, those who were wealthy sometimes forced their
poorer adversaries to lavish immense sums on horses and
armor.[1] Where, however, the spirit of legislation became
hostile to the wager of battle, this advantage was taken from
the appellant.   Frederic II. appears to have been the first
to promulgate this rational idea, and, in decreeing that in
future the choice of arms shall rest with the defendant, he
stigmatizes the previous custom as utterly iniquitous and
unreasonable.[2] In this, as in so many other matters, he
was in advance of his age, and the general rule was that
neither antagonist should have any advantage over the
other—except the fearful inequality, to which allusion has
already been made, when a roturier dared to challenge a
gentleman.[3] According to Upton, in the fifteenth century,
the judges were bound to see that the arms were equal, but
he admits that on many points there were no settled or
definite rules.[4] In Wales, an extraordinary custom violated
all the principles of equality. Under the Welsh law, twins
were considered as one person, and as they were entitled
to but one share in the patrimony of the family, so they
were allowed to come into the field of combat as one man.[5]
In Russia, each combatant followed his own pleasure; and
a traveller in the sixteenth century relates that the Musco-
vites were in the habit of embarrassing themselves with
defensive armor to an extent which rendered them almost
helpless, so that in combats with Poles, Lithuanians, and

[1] Revue Historique de Droit, 1861, p. 514.
[2] Constit. Sicular. Lib. ii. Tit. xxxvii. § 4.
[3] This, however, was not permitted by Frederic.   (Ubi sup.)
[4] De Militari Officio Lib. ii. cap. viii.
[5] Book of Cynog, chap. xi. § 34.   (Owen, II. 211.)

Germans they were habitually worsted, until judicial duels between natives and foreigners were at length prohibited on this account.[1]

Allusions have occurred above to the employment of champions, a peculiarity of these combats which received an application sufficiently extended to deserve some special notice. It has been seen that those unable to wield the sword or club were not therefore exempted from the duel, and even the scantiest measure of justice would require that they should have the right to delegate their vindication to some more potential vehicle of the Divine decision. This would seem originally to have been the office of some member of the family, as in the cognate procedure of sacramental purgation. Among the Alamanni, for instance, a woman when accused could be defended by a kinsman " cum tracta spata;"[2] the same rule is prescribed by the Lombard law,[3] and by that of the Angli and Werini;[4] while the far-pervading principle of family unity renders the presumption fair that it prevailed throughout the other races in whose codes it is not specifically indicated. Restricted to cases of disability, the use of champions was a necessity to the battle ordeal, but at a very early period the practice received a remarkable extension, which was directly in conflict with the original principles of the judicial duel, in permitting able-bodied antagonists to put forward substitutes who fought the battle for their principals. With regard to this there appears to have been a considerable diversity of practice among the races of primitive barbarians. The laws of the Franks, of the Alamanni, and of the Saxons make no allusion to such a privilege, and apparently expect the principal to defend his rights himself,

---

[1] Du Boys, op. cit. I. 611.
[2] L. Alamann. Add. cap. xxi.
[3] L. Longobard. Lib. i. Tit. iii. § 6, and Lib. ii. Tit. lv. § 12.
[4] L. Anglior. et Werinor. Tit. xiv.

and yet an instance occurs in 590, where, in a duel fought by order of Gontran, the defendant was allowed to intrust his cause to his nephew, though, as he was accused of killing a stag in the king's forest, physical infirmity could hardly have been pleaded.[1] From some expressions made use of by St. Agobard, in his onslaught on the ordeal of battle, we may fairly presume that, under Louis-le-Débonnaire, the employment of champions, in the Burgundian law, was, if not forbidden, at least unusual as respects the defendant, even in cases where age or debility unfitted him for the combat, while it was allowed to the appellant.[2] On the other hand, the Baioarian law, which favored the duel more than any of the other cognate codes, alludes to the employment of champions in every reference to it, and with the Lombards the judicial combat and the champion seem to have been likewise convertible terms.[3] In a charter of the latter half of the tenth century in France, recording a judicial duel to decide a contest concerning property, the judge, in ordering the combat, calls upon the antagonists to produce skilled champions to defend their claims at the time and place indicated, which would show that the principals were not expected to appear personally.[4] There is in this something so repugnant to the fierce and self-relying spirit in which the wager of battle found its origin, and the use of a professional gladiator is so inconsistent with the pious reference to the judgment of God, which

---

[1] Greg. Turon. Hist. Lib. x. cap. x. In this case, both combatants perished, when the accused was promptly put to death, showing that such a result was regarded as proving the truth of the offence alleged.

[2] Horum enim causa accidit ut non solum valentes viribus, sed etiam infirmi et senes lacessantur ad certamen et pugnam etiam pro vilissimis rebus. (Lib. adv. Legem Gundobadi cap. vii.) Mitte unum de tuis, qui congrediatur mecum singulari certamine, ut probat me reum tibi esse, si occiderit. (Lib. contra Judicium Dei cap. i.)

[3] Liceat ei per campionem, id est per pugnam, crimen ipsum de super se si potuerit ejicere.—L. Longobard. Lib. i. Tit. i. § 8.

[4] Proost, Législation des Jugements de Dieu, p. 82.

formed the only excuse for the whole system, that some
external reason is required to account for its introduction.
This reason is doubtless to be found in the liberty allowed
of challenging witnesses, to which allusion has already
been made.   The prevalence of this throughout Western
Europe readily enabled parties, unwilling themselves to
encounter the risks of a mortal struggle, to put forward
some truculent bravo who swore unscrupulously, and whose
evidence would require him to be forced out of court at
the sword's point.   That this, indeed, was frequently done
is proved at a subsequent period by a remark of Bracton,
who states that a witness suspected of being a hired gladiator was not allowed to proceed to the combat, but was
tried for the attempt by a jury, and if convicted was
punished by the loss of a foot and hand.[1]

Although the custom of hiring champions existed from
a very early period, since the Frisian laws give the fullest
license for employing and paying them,[2] still, their identity
with witnesses cannot be readily proved from the simple
records of those primitive times.   It becomes very evident,
however, in the more detailed regulations of the twelfth
and thirteenth centuries.   In England, for instance, until
the first statute of Westminster, issued by Edward I., in
1275, the hired champion of the defendant, in a suit concerning real estate, was obliged to assume the position of
a witness, by swearing that he had been personally present
and had seen seizin given of the land, or that his father

[1] Intrat quandoque in defensionem et warantum aliquis malitiose et per
fraudem et per mercedem, sicut campio et conductitius, quod quidem si fuerit
coram justitiariis detectum, non procedatur ad duellum, sed per patriam inquiratur veritas si talis mercedem acceperit vel non; et si constiterit quod
sic, pedem amittat et pugnum.—Lib. III. Tract. ii. cap. 32 § 7.

This was not always the case, however.   In the primitive Icelandic laws
the procuring of champions was accomplished by the curious custom to which
I have already alluded, of buying and selling suits.

[2] Licet unicuique pro se campionem mercede conducere, si eum invenire
potuerit.—L. Frision. Tit. XIV. cap. iv.

when dying had enjoined him by his filial duty to maintain
the defendant's title as though he had been present.[1] This
curious legal fiction was common also to the Norman jurisprudence of the period, where in such cases the champion
of the plaintiff was obliged to swear that he had heard and
seen the matters alleged in support of the claim, while the
opposing champion swore that they were false.[2] In a similar spirit, an earlier code of Normandy prescribes that
champions shall be taken to see the lands and buildings in
dispute, before receiving the oath of battle, in the same
manner as a jury of view.[3] A more distant indication of the
same origin is observable in the regulation of the Assises de
Jerusalem and of the Sicilian constitutions, which directed
that the champion should swear on the field of battle as to
his belief in the justice of the quarrel which he was about
to defend.[4] An English legal treatise of the period, indeed,
assumes that the principals can only put forward witnesses
as substitutes, and gives as a reason why combats in civil
suits were always conducted by champions, that in such
cases the principals could not act as witnesses for themselves.[5] In a similar spirit, if on the field of battle one of
the parties presented a champion who was not receivable
as a witness and had not been accepted by the court, the
case could be decided against him by default.[6]

Looking on the profession of a champion in this light,
as that of a false witness, we can understand the heavy
penalties to which he was subjected in case of defeat, a
severity which would otherwise appear to be a purposeless
expression of the savage barbarity of the times. Thus, in

---

[1] Glanvil. de Leg. Angl. Lib. ii. cap. iii.

[2] Cod. Leg. Norman. P. ii. cap lxiv. (Ludewig Reliq. MSS. VII. 416.)

[3] Étab. de Normandie, p. 21.   (Marnier.)

[4] Assis. Hierosol. Bassa Corte, cap. ccxxxviii. (Canciani, II. 534.)—Constit. Sicular. Lib. ii. Tit. xxxvii. § 2.

[5] Horne's Myrror of Justice, cap. iii. sect. 23.

[6] Ibid. cap. iv. sect. 11.

the Norman coutumier above referred to, in civil suits as
to disputed landed possessions, the champion swearing to
the truth of his principal's claim was, if defeated, visited
with a heavy fine and was declared infamous, being thenceforth incapable of appearing in court either as plaintiff or
as witness, while the penalty of the principal was merely
the loss of the property in dispute;[1] and a similar principle was recognized in the English law of the period.[2]   In
criminal cases, from a very early period, while the principal
perhaps escaped with fine or imprisonment, the hired ruffian
was hanged, or at best lost a hand or foot, the immemorial
punishment for perjury;[3] while the laws of the Crusaders
prescribe that in combats between champions, the defeated
one shall be promptly hanged, whether dead or alive.[4]   In
later times, when the origin of the champion's office had
been lost sight of, and he was everywhere recognized as
simply a bravo who sold his skill and courage to the highest
bidder, a more practical reason was found for maintaining
this severity—the more necessary, because the principal
was bound by law to pay his champion, even when defeated,
the full sum agreed upon as the price of his services in
both swearing and fighting.[5]   Beaumanoir thus defends it
on the ground of the liability of champions to be bought
over by the adverse party, and he therefore commends the

---

[1] Cod. Leg. Norman. P. II. cap. lxiv. § 18.   (Ludewig, VII. 417.)

[2] Among the crimes entailing infamy is enumerated that of "ceux qui
combatent mortelment pur loyer qui sont vanquish en combate joyné per
judgement."—Horne's Myrror of Justice, cap. iv. sect. 13.

[3] Et campioni qui victus fuerit, propter perjuriam quod ante pugnam com-
misit, dextra manus amputetur.—(Capit. Ludov. Pii ann. 819, § x.)—Victus
vero in duello centum solidos et obolum reddere tenebitur.   Pugil vero conductitius, si victus fuerit, pugno vel pede privabitur.—(Charta ann. 1203
—Du Cange.)—Also Beaumanoir, Cout. du Beauv., cap. lxvii. § 10. (Du Cange
seems to me to have misinterpreted this passage.)—See also Monteil's admirable " Histoire des Français des Divers États," XVe Siècle, Hist. XIII.

[4] Assis. Hierosol. Bassa Corte, cap. ccxxxviii. Alta Corte, cap. cv. (Canciani II. 534 ; V. 208.)

[5] Cod. Leg. Norman. P. II. cap. lxiv. § 19.   (Ludewig, VII. 416).

gentle stimulus of prospective mutilation as necessary to prevent them from betraying their employers.[1]   In the same spirit, the Emperor Frederic II. prohibited champions from bargaining with each other not to use teeth and hands. He commanded them to inflict all the injury possible on their adversaries, and decreed that they should, in case of defeat, share the punishment incurred by the principal, if the judge of the combat should consider that through cowardice or treachery they had not conducted the duel with proper energy and perseverance.[2]

With such risks to be encountered, it is no wonder that the trade of the champion offered few attractions to honest men, who could keep body and soul together in any other way.   In primitive times, the solidarity of the family no doubt caused the champion in most cases to be drawn from among the kindred; at a later period he might generally be procured from among the freedmen or clients of the principal, and an expression in the Lombard law justifies the assumption that this was habitual, among that race at least.[3]   In the palmy days of chivalry, it was perhaps not uncommon for the generous knight to throw himself boldly into the lists in defence of persecuted and friendless innocence, as he was bound to do by the tenor of his oath of knighthood.[4]   Even as late as the fifteenth century, indeed, in a collection of Welsh laws, among the modes by which

[1] Et li campions vaincus a le poing copé; car se n'estoit por le mehaing qu'il emporte, aucuns, par barat, se porroit faindre par loier et se clameroit vaincus, par quoi ses mestres emporteroit le damace et le vilonie, et cil emporteroit l'argent; et por ce est bons li jugemens du mehaing.—(Cout. du Beauv. cap. lxi. § 14.)—A charter of 1372 shows that the mutilation of defeated champions was practised even at that late date.—(Isambert, V. 387.)

[2] Constit. Sicular. Lib. ii. Tit. xxxvii. § 3.

[3] Et post illam inquisitionem, tradat manum ipse camphio in manu parentis aut conliberti sui ante judicem.—L. Longobard. Lib. ii. Tit. lv. § 11.

[4] Thus the oath administered by the papal legate to William of Holland, on his receiving knighthood previous to his coronation as King of the Romans in 1247, contains the clause "pro liberatione cujuslibet innocentis duellum inire."—Goldast. Constit. Imp. T. III. p. 400.

a stranger acquired the rights of kindred is enumerated
the act of voluntarily undergoing the duel in the place of
a principal unable or unwilling to appear for himself.[1]   A
vast proportion of pleaders, however, would necessarily be
destitute of these chances to avoid the personal appearance in the arena for which they might be unfitted or dis-
inclined, and thus there gradually arose the regular profession of the paid gladiator. Reckless desperadoes, skilled
at quarter-staff, or those whose familiarity with sword and
dagger, gained by a life spent in ceaseless brawls, gave
them confidence in their own ability, might undertake it
as an occupation which exposed them to little risk beyond what they habitually incurred, and of such was the
profession generally composed.   This evil must have made
itself apparent early, for we find Charlemagne endeavoring
to oppose it by decreeing that no robber should be allowed
to appear in the lists as a champion;[2] and the order needed
to be frequently repeated.

When the Roman law commenced to exercise its powerful influence in moulding the feudal customs into a regular
body of procedure, and admiring jurists lost no opportunity of making use of the newly-discovered treasures of
legal lore, whether applicable or not, it is easy to understand that the contempt and the civil disabilities lavished
by the Imperial jurisprudence on the gladiator of antiquity came to be transferred to the mediæval champion;
although the latter, by the theory of the law, stood forth
to defend the innocent, while the former ignobly exposed his life for the gratification of an imbruted populace.
This curious legacy of shame is clearly traceable in Pierre
de Fontaines. To be a gladiator or an actor was, by the

---

[1] Anomalous Laws, Book x. chap. ii. § 9.   (Owen, II. 315.)   The position thus acquired was that of brother or nephew in sharing and paying *wehr-
gild*.

[2] Ut nemo furem camphium de mancipiis aut de qualibet causa recipere
præsumat, sicut sæpius dominus imperator commendavit.—Capit. Carol.
Mag. ex L. Longobard. cap. xxxv. (Baluze.)

Roman law, a competent cause for disinheritance.[1]   One of
the texts prescribing it is translated bodily by de Fontaines,
the "arenarius" of the Roman becoming the "champions"
of the Frenchman ;[2] and in another similar transcription
from the Digest, the "athleta" of the original is transformed
into a "champion."[3]   By the thirteenth century, the occupation of champion had thus become infamous.   Its professors were classed with the vilest criminals, and with the
unhappy females who exposed their charms for sale, as the
champion did his skill and courage.[4]   They were held incapable of appearing as witnesses, and the extraordinary
anomaly was exhibited of seeking to learn the truth in
affairs of the highest moment by a solemn appeal to God,
through the instrumentality of those who were already
considered as convicts of the worst kind, or who, by the
very act, were branded with infamy if successful in justifying innocence, and if defeated were mutilated or hanged.[5]
By the codes in force throughout Germany in the thirteenth and fourteenth centuries, they were not only deprived of all legal privileges, such as succeeding to property, bearing witness, &c., but even their children were
visited with the same disabilities.[6]   The utter contempt in

[1] Novel. cxv. cap. iii. § 10—more fully set forth in Lib. iii. Cod. Tit.
xxvii. 1. 11.

[2] Conseil. chap. xxxiii. tit. 32.

[3] Ibid. chap. xv. tit. 87, which is a translation of Lib. iv. Dig. Tit. ii. 1.
23, § 2.

[4] Percutiat si quis hominem infamem, hoc est lusorem vel pugilem, aut
mulierem publicam, &c.—Wichbild Magdeburg. Art. 129 (Du Cange).   "Plu-
sieurs larrons, ravisseurs de femmes, violleurs d'églises, batteurs à loyer,"
etc.—Ordonn. de Charles VII. ann. 1447, also Anciennes Coutumes de Bretagne.   (Monteil, ubi sup.)

[5] Johen de Beaumont dit que chanpions loiez, prové de tel chose, ne puet
home apelier à gage de bataille an nul quas, si n'est por chanpion loiez por sa
deffansse ; car la poine de sa mauvese vie le doit bien en ce punir.—Livres
de Jostice et de Plet, Liv. xix. Tit. ii. § 4.

[6] Campiones et eorum liberi (ita nati) et omnes qui illegitime nati sunt,
et omnes qui furti aut pleni latrocinii nomine satisfecere, aut fustigationem
sustinuere, hi omnes juris beneficiis carent.—Jur. Provin. Alamann. cap.
xxxvi. § 2.   (Ed. Schilter.)

which they were held was moreover quaintly symbolized in the same code by the provisions of a tariff of damages to be assessed for blows and other personal injuries. A graduated list of fines is given for such insults offered to nobles, merchants, peasants, &c., in compensation of their wounded honor; below the serf come the mountebank and juggler, who could only cuff the assailant's shadow projected on a wall; and last of all are rated the champion and his children, whose only redress was a glance of sunshine cast upon them by the offender from a polished shield. Deemed by law incapable of receiving an insult, the satisfaction awarded was as illusory as the honor to be repaired.[1] That this poetical justice was long in vogue is proved by the commentary upon it in the Richstich Landrecht, of which the date is shown to be not earlier than the close of the fourteenth century by an allusion in the same chapter to accidental deaths arising from the use of firearms.[2]

The Italians, however, took a more sensible and practical view of the matter. Accepting as a necessity the existence of champions as a class, they were disposed rather to elevate than to degrade the profession. In the Veronese code of 1228, they appear as an established institution, consisting of individuals selected and appointed by the magistrates, who did not allow them to receive more than one hundred sous for the performance of their office.[3]

It is evident that the evils attendant upon the employ-

[1] Campionibus et ipsorum liberis emendæ loco datur fulgur ex clypeo nitido, qui soli obvertitur, ortum; hoc is qui eis satisfactionem debet loco emendæ præstare tenetur.—(Ibid. cap. cccv. § 15.—Jur. Provin. Saxon. Lib. III. art. xlv.) In the French version of the Speculum Suevicum, these emblematic measures of damage are followed by the remark "cestes emandes furent estrablies an la vieillie loy per les roys," (P. II. c. lxxxvi.) which would appear to show that they were disused in the territories for which the translation was made.

[2] Richstich Landrecht, Lib. II. cap. xxv. This gives additional point to the insult by prescribing the use of a duelling shield for the reflection of the sunbeam.

[3] Lib. Juris civilis Veron. cap. 125, 126. (Veronæ, 1728, p. 95.)

ment of champions were generally recognized, and it is not singular that efforts were occasionally made to abrogate or limit the practice. Otho II., whose laws did so much to give respectability to the duel, decreed that champions should be permitted only to counts, ecclesiastics, women, boys, old men, and cripples.[1] That this rule was strictly enforced in some places we may infer from the pleadings of a case occurring in 1010 before the Bishop of Aretino, concerning a disputed property, wherein a crippled right hand is alleged as the reason for allowing a champion to one of the parties.[2] In other parts of Italy, however, the regulation must have been speedily disregarded, for about the same time Henry II. found it necessary to promulgate a law forbidding the employment of substitutes to able-bodied defendants in cases of parricide or of aggravated murder;[3] and when, two hundred years later, Frederic II. almost abolished the judicial combat in his Neapolitan dominions, we may fairly presume from one of his remarks that champions were almost universally employed.[4] Indeed, he made provision for supplying them at the public expense to widows, orphans, and paupers who might be unable to secure for themselves such assistance.[5] In Germany, early in the eleventh century, it would seem that champions were a matter of course, from the expressions made use of in describing the execution of a number of robbers convicted in this manner at Merseburg in 1017.[6] At a later period, it seems probable, from a comparison of two chapters of the Swabian laws, that efforts were made

---

[1] L. Longobard. Lib. ii. Tit. lv. §§ 38, 40.

[2] Muratori, Antiq. Ital. Dissert. 39.

[3] L. Longobard. Lib. i. Tit. ix. § 37 ; Tit. x. § 4.

[4] Vix enim aut nunquam duo pugiles inveniri poterunt sic æquales, etc.—Constit. Sicular. Lib. ii. Tit. xxxiii.

[5] Ibid. Lib. i. Tit. xxxiii.

[6] Ibi tunc multi latrones a gladiatoribus singulari certamine devicti, suspendio perierunt.—Dithmari. Chron. Lib. vii.

13

to prevent the hiring of professional gladiators,[1] but that
they were attended with little success may be inferred from
the disabilities which, as we have already seen, were so
copiously showered on the class by the same laws.

The English law manifests considerable variation at different periods with respect to this point.   In 1150, Henry
II. strictly prohibited the wager of battle with hired champions in his Norman territories,[2] and we learn from Glanville
that a champion suspected of serving for money might be
objected to by the opposite party, whence arose a secondary
combat to determine his fitness for the primary one.[3]   It is
evident from this that mercenary champions were not recognized as legal in England, a principle likewise deducible
from an expression of Bracton's in the succeeding century.[4]
This, however, was probably little regarded in practice.
There exists a charter of Bracton's date, by which John
"quondam porcarius de Coldingham" grants to the Priory
of Coldingham a tract of land which he had received from
Adam de Riston in payment for victoriously fighting a duel
for him.[5]   When John thus proclaimed himself to be a hired
champion there could have been little danger that legal disabilities would be visited either on him or his principal.   The
custom gradually became general, for eventually, in civil
cases, both parties were compelled by law to employ champions, which presupposes, as a matter of course, that in a great

---

[1] Jur. Provin. Alamann. cap. xxxvi. § 2; cap. lx. § 1.

[2] Nullus eorum duellum faciat contra aliquem qui testificatus sit pugil
conductitius per sacramentum decem legalium civium.—Concil. Eccles. Roto-
mag. p. 128.   (Du Cange.)

[3] De Leg. Angliæ Lib. ii. cap. iii.

[4] Ita posset quilibet in tali facto alium appellare per campionem conduc-
tivum, quod non est sustinendum.—Bracton. Lib. iii. Tract. ii. cap. 18 § 4.

[5] This charter, which has recently been found among the records of
Durham Cathedral, is printed in the London *Athenæum* of Nov. 10th, 1866.
It is not dated, but the names of the subscribing witnesses show that it must
have been executed about the year 1260.

majority of instances, the substitutes must have been hired.[1] In criminal cases, however, the rule was generally reversed; in felonies, the defendant was obliged to appear personally, while in cases of less moment he was at liberty to put forward a witness as champion;[2] and when the appellant, from sex or other disability, or the defendant from age, was unable to undergo the combat personally, it was forbidden, and the case was decided by a jury.[3] By the Scottish law of the twelfth century, it is evident that champions were not allowed in any case, since those disabled by age or wounds were forced to undergo the ordeal in order to escape the duel.[4] This strictness became relaxed in time, though the practice seems never to have received much encouragement. By a law of David II., about the year 1350, it appears that a noble had the privilege of putting forward a substitute; but if a peasant challenged a noble, he was obliged to appear personally, unless his lord undertook the quarrel for him and presented the champion as from himself.[5]

The tendency thus exhibited by the English law in distinguishing between civil and criminal cases is also manifested elsewhere. Thus, in France and the Frankish kingdoms of the East, there were limitations placed by

---

[1] Lord Eldon, in his speech advocating the abolition of trial by battle, in 1819, stated, "In these the parties were not suffered to fight *in propria persona*—they were compelled to confide their interests to champions, on the principle that if one of the parties were slain, the suit would abate."—Campbell's Lives of the Chancellors, VII. 279.

[2] Pur felony ne poit nul combattre pur autre ; en personal actions nequidant venials, list aux actors de faire les battailes per lour corps ou per loyal tesmoigne come en droit reals sont les combats.—Horne's Myrror of Justice, cap. iii. sect. 23.

[3] Bracton. Lib. III. Tract. ii. cap. 21, §§ 11, 12.—Ibid. cap. 24.

[4] Regiam Majestatem Lib. IV. cap. iii.

[5] Statut. David II. cap. xxviii. By the burgher laws of Scotland, a man who was incapacitated by reason of age from appearing in the field, was allowed to defend himself with twelve conjurators.—L. Burgor. cap. xxiv. §§ 1, 2.

law on the employment of champions in prosecutions for crime,[1] while in civil actions there appear to have been, at least in France, no restrictions whatever.[2] This distinction between civil and criminal practice is very clearly enunciated by Pierre de Fontaines, who states that in appeal of judgment the appellant in criminal cases is bound to show satisfactory cause for employing a champion, while in civil affairs the right to do so requires no argument.[3]   In practice, however, it is doubtful whether there was any effectual bar to their use in any case, for the Monk of St. Denis, in praising St. Louis for suppressing the battle-trial, gives as one of the benefits of its abrogation, the removal of the abuse by which a rich man could buy up all the champions of the vicinity, so that a poorer antagonist had no resource to avoid the loss of life or heritage.[4]   This hiring of champions, moreover, was legally recognized as a necessity attendant upon the privilege of employing them.[5]   High rank, or a marked difference between the station of parties to an action, was also admitted as justifying the superior in putting forward a champion in his place.[6]   Local variations, however, are observable in the customs regulating these matters.   Thus the municipal laws of Rheims, in the fourteenth century, not only restrict the admission of champions in criminal matters to cases in which age or physical disability may incapacitate the principals from

[1] Assises de Jerusalem, Baisse Court, cap. 145, 146.—Beaumanoir, cap. lxi. § 6 ; cap. lxiii. § 4.

[2] Beaumanoir cap. lxi. § 14.

[3] Conseil, chap. xxii. Tit. xiii.

[4] Grandes Chroniques T. IV. p. 427.

[5] Il est usage que se aucun demende la cort de bataille qui est juege par champions loées, il la tendra le jor maimes, et si ele est par le cors des quereléors il metra jor avenant à la tenir autre que celui.—Coutumes d'Anjou, XIII.ᵉ Siècle, § 74.

[6] Kar haute persone doit bien metre por lui, à deffendre soi, home, honeste persone, se l'an l'apele, ou s'il apele autre.—Livres de Jostice et de Plet, Liv. ii. Tit. xviii.

personally taking part in the combat, but also require the
accused to swear that the impediment has supervened since
the date of the alleged offence; and even this was of no
avail if the prosecutor had included in his appeal of battle
an assertion that such disability had existed at the time
specified.[1] Witnesses obliged to support their testimony by
the duel were not only subject to the same restrictions, but
in substituting a hired gladiator were obliged to swear that
they had vainly sought among their friends for some one
to voluntarily assume the office.[2] The whole tenor of these
provisions, indeed, manifests a decided intention to surround
the employment of champions with every practicable impediment.   In Béarn, again, the appellant in cases of treason
had a right to decide whether the defendant should be
allowed to put forward a substitute, and from the expressions in the text it may be inferred that in the selection of
champions there was an endeavor to secure equality of
age, size, and strength.[3]   This equalization of chances was
thoroughly carried out in the Veronese code of 1228, where,
as has been seen, the champions were a recognized body,
regulated and controlled by the state.   No one could engage a champion before a duel had been judicially decreed.
Then the magistrate was bound to choose gladiators of
equal prowess, and the choice between them was given
to the defendant: an arrangement which rendered the mutilation inflicted on the vanquished combatant only justifiable on the score of suspected treachery.[4]   In Bigorre,
the only restriction seems to have been that champions

[1] Lib. Pract. de Consuet. Remens. § 40. (Archives Législ. de Reims, Pt.
I. p. 40.)

[2] Etiam antequam campionem possit quis ponere, jurare debet quod bona
fide amicos suos requisivit quod pro ipso bellum facerent.—Ibid. § 14, p. 37.

[3] For de Morlaas, Rubr. liii. art. 188.

[4] Omnes camphiones . . . per me vel per judices communis Veronæ, sive
consules, bona fide coæquabo: facta coæquatione, defendenti electionem
dabo.—L. Jur. Civilis. Veronæ. cap. 125, 126 (p. 95).

13*

should be natives and not foreigners.[1] By the Spanish law
of the thirteenth century, the employment of champions
was so restricted as to show an evident desire on the part
of the legislator to discourage it as far as possible. The
defendant had the right to send a substitute into the field,
but the appellant could do so only by consent of his adversary. The champion was required to be of birth equal
to his principal, which rendered the hiring of champions
almost impossible, and not superior to him in force and
vigor. Women and minors appeared by their next of kin,
and ecclesiastics by their advocates.[2] In Russia, until the
sixteenth century, champions were never employed, contestants being always obliged to appear in person. In 1550,
the code known as the Soudebtnick at length permitted
the employment of champions in certain cases.[3]

There were two classes of pleaders, however, with whom
the hiring of champions was a necessity, and who could
not be bound by the limitations imposed on ordinary litigants. While the sexagenary, the infant, and the crippled
might possibly find a representative among their kindred,
and while the woman might appear by her husband or next
of kin, the ecclesiastical foundations and chartered towns
had no such resource. Thus, in a suit for taxes, in 1164,
before the court of Verona, Bonuszeno of Soavo proved
that the village of Soavo had exempted his father Petro-
batalla from all local imposts for having served as champion in a duel between it and a neighboring community, and
his claim to the reversion of the exemption was allowed.[4]
So a charter of 1104 relates how the monks of Noailles

---

[1] Pugiles in Bigorra non nisi indigenæ recipiantur. (Lagrèze, Hist. du
Droit dans les Pyrénées, p. 251.) By the same code, the tariff of payment to
the champion was 20 sous, with 12 for his shield and 6 for training—" pro
præparatione."

[2] Las Siete Partidas, Pt. vii. Tit. iv. l. 3.

[3] Du Boys, Droit Criminel des Peuples Modernes, I. 611–13.

[4] Campagnola, Lib. Juris Civ. Veronæ. (Veronæ, 1728, p. xviii.)

were harassed by the seizure of some mills belonging to
their abbey, claimed by an official of William Duke of
Aquitaine, until at length the duke agreed to allow the
matter to be decided by the duel, when the champion of
the church was victorious and the disputed property was
confirmed to the abbey.[1] At length their frequent occasion
for this species of service led to the employment of regularly appointed champions, who fought their battles for an
annual stipend, or for some other advantages bestowed in
payment. Du Cange, for instance, gives the text of an agreement by which one Geoffry Blondel, in 1256, bound himself
to the town of Beauvais as its champion for a yearly salary
of twenty sous Parisis, with extra gratifications of ten livres
Tournois every time that he appeared in arms to defend its
cause, fifty livres if blows were exchanged, and a hundred
livres if the combat were carried to a triumphant issue. It
is a little singular that Beaumanoir, in digesting the customs
of Beauvais but a few years later, speaks of this practice as
an ancient and obsolete one, of which he had only heard
through tradition.[2] That it continued to be in vogue until
long after, is shown by Monteil, who alludes to several
documents of the kind, bearing date as late as the fifteenth
century.[3]

The champions of the church occupied a higher position,
and were bound to defend the interests of their clients in
the field as well as in the court and in the lists; they also
led the armed retainers of the church when summoned by
the suzerain to national war. The office was honorable
and lucrative, and was eagerly sought by gentlemen of

---

[1] Polyptichum Irminonis, App. No. 33. (Paris, 1836, p. 372.)

[2] Une malvese coustume souloit courre anciemment, si comme nos avons
entendu des seigneurs de lois.—Cout. du Beauvoisis, cap. xxxviii. § 15.

[3] Hist. des Français, XVᵉ Siècle, Hist. xiii.—The tariff of rewards paid to
Blondel, and Beaumanoir's argument in favor of mutilating a defeated
champion, offer a strong practical commentary on the fundamental principle upon which the whole system of appeals to the judgment of God was based
—that success was an evidence of right.

station, who turned to account the opportunities of ag-
grandizement which it afforded; and many a noble family
traced its prosperity to the increase of ancestral property
thus obtained, directly or indirectly, by espousing the
cause of fat abbeys and wealthy bishoprics.[1] The influence
of feudalism early made itself felt, and the office of *Vidame*
or *Avoué* became generally hereditary. In many instances,
it was a consideration obtained for donations bestowed
upon churches, so that in some countries, and particularly
in England, the title of *advocatus* became gradually recognized as synonymous with patron. Thus, one of the worst
abuses of the Anglican Church is derived from this source,
and the forgotten wrongs of the Middle Ages are perpetuated, etymologically at least, in the advowson which renders the cure of souls too often a matter of bargain and
sale.

Thus arising spontaneously in the institutions of all the
European races, and carefully moulded to conform to the
popular prejudices or convictions of every age and country,
it may readily be imagined how large a part the judicial
combat played in the affairs of daily life. It was so skilfully interwoven throughout the whole system of jurisprudence that no one could feel secure that he might not, at
any moment, as plaintiff, defendant, or witness, be called
upon to protect his estate or his life either by his own right

---

[1] Thus, in the ninth century, the Abbot of Figeac, near Cahors, bestowed
on a neighboring lord sixty churches and five hundred mansi, on condition
of his fighting the battles of the abbey, "cum necessitas posceret, solo
jussu, absque lucro alio temporali, bella abbatis et suorum præliaretur."—
Hist. Monast. Figeacens.—(Baluz. et Mansi IV. p. 1.) When feudalism
fixed these chieftains firmly in possession, they rendered themselves independent of their benefactors. This process is graphically described by St.
Abbo of Fleury, about the year 996.—"Defensores ecclesiarum qui dicuntur
hodie, contra auctoritatem legum et canonum sibi defendunt quod fuerat
juris ecclesiarum, sicque violentiam clericis et monachis ingerendo, res ecclesiarum seu monasteriorum usufructuario diripiunt, colonos in paupertatem
redigunt, possessiones ecclesiarum non augent sed minuunt, et quorum
defensores esse debuerant, eos vastant."—Collect. Canonum, can. ii.

hand or by the club of some professional and probably treacherous bravo. This organized violence assumed for itself the sanction of a religion of love and peace, and human intelligence seemed too much blunted to recognize the shocking contradiction.

Having thus traced the origin and some of the leading features of the custom, a few illustrative examples may serve to show the estimation in which it was held, and the manner in which it was applied, not only to the trivial details of legal debate, but to the largest interests of states and governments. If Charlemagne, in dividing his vast empire, forbade the employment of the wager of battle in settling the territorial questions which might arise between his heirs,[1] the prohibition merely shows that it was habitually used in affairs of the highest moment, and the constant reference to it in his laws proves that it was in no way repugnant to his general sense of justice and propriety.

The next century affords ample evidence of the growing favor in which the judicial combat was held. About the year 930, Hugh, King of Provence and Italy, becoming jealous of his uterine brother, Lambert, Duke of Tuscany, asserted him to be a supposititious child, and ordered him in future to claim no relationship between them. Lambert, being "vir . . . bellicosus et ad quodlibet facinus audax," contemptuously denied the aspersion on his birth, and offered to clear all doubts on the subject by the wager of battle. Hugh accordingly selected a warrior named Teudinus as his champion; Lambert was victor in the ensuing combat, and was universally received as the undoubted son of his mother. His triumph, however, was illegally brought to a sudden close, for Hugh soon after succeeded in making him prisoner and deprived him of eye-

---

[1] Nec unquam pro tali caussa cujuslibet generis pugna vel campus ad examinationem judicetur.—Carol. Mag. Chart. Divisionis ann. 806 cap. xiv.

sight.[1] Still, the practice continued to be denounced by
some enlightened ecclesiastics, represented by Atto, Bishop
of Vercelli, who declared it to be totally inapplicable to
churchmen and not to be approved for laymen on account of
the uncertainty of its results;[2] but representations of this
kind were useless. About the middle of the century, Otho
the Great appears, throwing the enormous weight of his influence in its favor. As a magnanimous and warlike prince,
the wager of battle appears to have possessed peculiar attraction for his chivalrous instincts, and he extended its application as far as lay in his power. Not only did he force
his daughter Liutgarda, in defending herself from a villan-
ous accusation, to forego the safer modes of purgation, and
to submit herself to the perilous decision of a combat,[3] but
he also caused the abstract question of representation in the
succession of estates to be settled in the same manner; and
to this day in Germany the division of a patrimony among
children and grandchildren is regulated in accordance with
the law enacted by the doughty arms of the champions who
fought together nine hundred years ago at Steil.[4] There was
no question, indeed, which according to Otho could not be
satisfactorily settled in this manner. Thus when, in 963, he
was indulging in the bitter recriminations with Pope John
XII. which preceded the subjugation of the papacy under

[1] Liutprandi Antapodos. Lib. iii. cap. 46.

[2] Sed istud judicium quorundam laicorum solummodo est, quod nec ipsis
etiam omnino approbatur.   Nam saepe innocentes victi, nocentes vero
victores in tali judicio esse videntur.—(De Pressuris Eccles. Pt. ii.) This
was written about 945.

[3] Dithmari Chron. Lib. ii. ann. 950.

[4] Widukind. Rer. Saxon. Lib. ii. cap. x.—The honest chronicler considers that it would have been disgraceful to the nobility to treat questions
relating to them in a plebeian manner. "Rex autem meliori consilio usus,
noluit viros nobiles ac senes populi inhoneste tractari, sed magis rem inter
gladiatores discerni jussit."   In both these cases Otho may be said to have
had ancient custom in his favor. See L. Longobard. Lib. i. Tit. xii. § 2.—
L. Alamann. cap. LVI., LXXXIV.; Addit. cap. XXII.

the Saxon emperors, he had occasion to send Bishop Liutprand to Rome to repel certain accusations brought against
him, and he ordered the armed followers of his ambassador to sustain his assertions by the duel: a proposition
promptly declined by the pontiff, skilled though he was in
the use of weapons.[1] A duellist, in fact, seems to have
been reckoned a necessary adjunct to diplomacy, for when,
in 968, the same Liutprand was dispatched by Otho to
Constantinople on a matrimonial mission, and during the
negotiations for the hand of Theophania a discussion
arose as to the circumstances which had led to Otho's conquest of Italy, the warlike prelate offered to prove his
veracity by the sword of one of his attendants: a proposition which put a triumphant end to the argument.[2]

Nor was the readiness to commit the mightiest interests
to the decision of the judicial duel confined to Germany
and Lombardy. When, in 948, at the Synod of Ingelheim,
Louis d'Outremer invoked the aid of the church in his
death-struggle with the rising race of Capet, he closed the
recital of the wrongs endured at the hands of Hugh-le-
Grand by offering to prove the justice of his complaints in
single combat with the aggressor.[3] When the battle ordeal
was thus thoroughly incorporated in the manners of the
age, we need scarcely be surprised that, in a life of St.
Matilda, written by command of her son Otho the Great,
the author, after describing the desperate struggles of the
Saxons against Charlemagne, should gravely inform us
that the war was at last concluded by a duel between the
Christian hero and his great antagonist Witikind, religion
and empire being both staked on the issue as the prize of
the victor; nor does the pious chronicler shudder at the

---

[1] Liutprandi Hist. Otton. cap. vii.

[2] Liutprandi Legat. cap. vi.

[3] His si dux contraire audeat, nobis tantum singulariter congrediendum
sit.—Conquest. Ludov. in Synod. Ingilheim. ann. 948.

thought that the destiny of Christianity was intrusted to the sword of the Frank.[1]

The second Otho was fully imbued with his father's views, and so completely did he carry them out, that in a gloss on the Lombard law he is actually credited with the introduction of the duel.[2] In the preceding essay, allusion has been made to his substitution of the judicial combat for the sacramental oath in 983, and about the same period, he made an exception, in favor of the battle ordeal, to the immemorial policy of the barbarians which permitted to all subject races the enjoyment of their ancestral usages. At the council of Verona, where all the nobles of Italy, secular and ecclesiastical, were assembled, he caused the adoption of a law which forced the Italians in this respect to follow the customs of their conquerors.[3] Even the church was deprived of any exemption which she might previously have enjoyed, and was only allowed the privilege of appearing by her "advocati" or champions.[4] There were small chances of escape from the stringency of these regulations, for an edict of Otho I. in 971 had decreed the punishment of confiscation against any one who should refuse to undergo the chances of the combat.[5]

Under such auspices, and stimulated by the rising spirit of chivalry, it is no wonder that the judicial duel acquired fresh importance, and was more extensively practised than ever. From the wording of a constitution of the Emperor Henry II., it may even be assumed that in the early part

[1] Utrisque placuit principibus, ut ipsi singuli invicem dimicaturi consurgerent et cui sors victoriam contulisset, ipsi totus exercitus sine dubio pareret.—S. Mathild. Regin. Vit. c. 1.

[2] Nos belli dono ditat rex maximus Otto.

[3] Quacunque lege, sive etiam Romana, in omni regno Italico homo vixeret, hæc omnia ut in his capitulis per pugnam decernimus observare.—L. Longobard. Lib. ii. Tit. lv. § 38.

[4] De ecclesiarum rebus ut per advocatos fiat similiter jubemus.—Ibid. § 34.

[5] Si non audeat, res suæ infiscentur.—Convent. Papiens. ann. 971.

of the eleventh century it was no longer necessary that there should be a doubt as to the guilt of the accused to entitle him to the privileges of the combat, and that even the most notorious criminal could have a chance of escape by an appeal to the sword.[1]

Thus it came to pass that nearly every question that could possibly arise was finally deemed liable to the decision of the wager of battle. If Otho the Great employed champions to legislate respecting a disputed point of law, he was not more eccentric than the Spaniards, who settled in the same manner a controversy regarding the canonical observances of religion, when the fiery and indomitable Hildebrand endeavored to force the introduction of the Roman liturgy into Castile and Leon, in lieu of the national Gothic or Mozarabic rite. With considerable difficulty, some years before, Navarre and Arragon had been led to consent to the change, but the Castilians were doggedly attached to the observances of their ancestors, and stoutly refused compliance. In 1077, Alfonso I. procured the assent of a national council, but the people rebelled, and after repeated negotiations the matter was finally referred to the umpirage of the sword. The champion of the Gothic ritual was victorious, and tradition adds that a second trial was made by the ordeal of fire; a missal of each kind was thrown into the flames, and the national liturgy emerged triumphantly unscathed.[2]

Nearly contemporary with this was the celebrated case of Otho, Duke of Bavaria, perhaps the most noteworthy example of a judicial appeal to the sword. A worthless adventurer, named Egeno, accused the proud and powerful Otho of conspiring against the life of Henry IV. In a diet held at Mainz, the duke was commanded to disprove the

---

[1] Qui vero infra treugam, post datum osculum pacis, alium hominem interfecerit, et negare voluerit, pugnam pro se faciat.—L. Longobard. Lib. I. Tit. ix. § 38.

[2] Ferreras, Hist. Gén. d'Espagne, Trad. d'Hermilly, III. 245.

14

charge by doing battle with his accuser within six weeks. According to some authorities, his pride revolted at meeting an adversary so far his inferior; according to others, he was prevented from appearing in the lists only by the refusal of the Emperor to grant him a safe conduct. Be this as it may, the appointed term elapsed, his default of appearance caused judgment to be taken against him, and his duchy was confiscated accordingly. It was bestowed on Welf, son of Azo d'Este and of Cunigunda, descendant and heiress of the ancient Guelfic Agilolfings; and thus, on -the basis of a judicial duel, was founded the second Bavarian house of Guelf, from which have sprung so many royal and noble lines, including their Guelfic Majesties of Britain. Some years later, the Emperor himself offered to disprove by the same means a similar accusation brought against him by a certain Reginger, of endeavoring to assassinate his rival, Rodolph of Swabia. Ulric of Cosheim, however, who was involved in the accusation, insisted on taking his place; and a day was appointed for the combat, which was prevented only by the opportune death of Reginger.[1]

Scarcely less impressive in its results, and even more remarkable in itself, as exhibiting the duel invested with legislative as well as judicial functions, is the case wherein the wager of battle was employed in 1180 to break the overgrown power of Henry the Lion. That puissant Duke of Saxony and Bavaria had long divided the power of the empire, and defied the repeated efforts of Frederic Barbarossa to punish his constantly recurring rebellions. Cited to appear and answer for his treasons in successive diets, he constantly refused, on the plea that the law required him to have a trial within his own dominions. At length, in the diet of Wurzburg, a noble arose and declared himself ready to prove by the single combat that

[1] Lambert. Hersfeld. ann. 1070, 1073, 1074.—Conrad. Ursperg. ann. 1071. —Bruno de Bello Saxonico.

the Emperor could legally cite his princes before him at any place that he might select within the limits of the empire. Of course there was none to take up the challenge, and Frederic was enabled to erect the principle thus asserted into a binding law. Henry was condemned by default, and his confiscated possessions were shared between those who had arranged and enacted the comedy.[1]

To such an extent was carried the respect entertained for the judicial duel, that, by the English law of the thirteenth century, a pleader was sometimes allowed to alter the record of his preliminary plea, by producing a man who would offer to prove with his body that the record was incorrect, the sole excuse for the absurdity being that it was only allowed in matters which could not injure the other side;[2] and a malefactor turning king's evidence was obliged, before receiving his pardon, to pledge himself to convict all his accomplices, if required, by the duel.[3]

A case which occurred about the year 1100 shows the robustness of the faith with which the duel was regarded. A sacrilegious thief named Anselm stole the sacred vessels from the church of Laon and sold them to a merchant, from whom he exacted an oath of secrecy. Frightened at the excommunications fulminated by the authorities of the plundered church, the unhappy traitor revealed the name of the robber. Anselm denied the accusation, offered the wager of battle, defeated the unfortunate receiver of stolen goods, and was proclaimed innocent. Encouraged by impunity, he repeated the offence, and after his conviction by the ordeal of cold water, he confessed the previous crime. The doubts cast by this event on the efficacy of the judicial combat were, however, happily removed by the suggestion

---

[1] Conrad. Ursperg. ann. 1175.—Cumque nullus isti se offerret ad pugnam, edicto Imperatoris præfata sententia pro jure perpetuo statuta est, quam non dubium est autoritate et ratione firmari.

[2] Bracton. Lib. iii. Tract. ii. cap. 37 § 5.

[3] Ibid. cap. 33, § 2, and 34, § 2.

that the merchant had suffered for the violation of the oath which he had sworn to Anselm; and the reputation of the duel remained intact.[1]

It may readily be imagined that cases of this nature frequently arose, and as they often did not admit of so ingenious an explanation of the criminal's escape, legal casuists assumed a condition of being, guilty in the sight of God, but not in that of man—a refinement of speculation which even finds place in the German codes of the thirteenth century;[2] and men contented themselves then, as they do still, with predicting future misfortunes and an eternity of punishment. The more direct solution, in cases of unjust condemnation, was very much like that which justified the defeat of Anselm's merchant—that the unfortunate victim, though innocent of the special offence charged, suffered in consequence of other sins. This doctrine was even supported by the infallible authority of the papacy, as enunciated in 1212 by Innocent III. in a case wherein the priory of St. Sergius was unjustly convicted of theft by the judicial duel, and its possessions were consequently seized by the authorities of Spoleto.[3] That the combatants themselves did not always feel implicit confidence in the justice of the event, or rely solely upon the righteousness of their cause, is shown by the custom of occasionally bribing

[1] Guibert. Noviogent. de Vita sua Lib. III. cap. xvi.—Hermann. de Mirac. S. Mariæ Laudun. Lib. III. cap. 28.—Forsitan ut multi putarunt, pro fidei violatæ reatu, qua promiserat fidem Anselmo, quod eum non detegeret.

[2] Und diser vor Got schuldig, und vor den luten nit.—(Jur. Provin. Alamann. cap. ccxix. § 8.) This is a provision for cases in which a thief accuses a receiver of having suggested and assisted in the crime. The parties are made to fight, when, if the receiver is worsted, both are hanged; if the thief, he alone, and the receiver escapes though criminal. The French version enlarges somewhat on the principle involved: "Se il puet vancre lautre il est quites et li autre sera panduz. et sera an colpe anver lo munde et anver dex andui. ce avient a assez de genz, que aucons sunt an colpe anver dex et ne mie anver le seigle."—(Miroir. de Souabe, P. II. c. vi.)

[3] Can. Significantibus, Extra, De Purgatione Vulgari.—"Duellum in quo aliis peccatis suis præpedientibus, ceciderunt."

Heaven either to assist the right or to defend the wrong. Thus, in the eleventh century, we find the monastery of St. Peter at Bèze in the enjoyment of certain lands bestowed on the Saint by Sir Miles the Stammerer, who thus endeavored to purchase his assistance in a combat about to take place—a bargain no doubt highly appreciated by the worthy monks.[1]

Notwithstanding the wrong and injustice perpetually arising from the indiscriminate and universal application of the duel, it was so thoroughly engrafted in the convictions and prejudices of Europe that centuries were requisite for its extirpation. Curiously enough, the earliest decisive action against it took place in Iceland, where it was formally interdicted as a judicial proceeding in 1011;[2] and though the assumption that this was owing to the introduction of Christiani'y has been disproved, still, the fact that both events were contemporaneous allows us to conclude that some influence may have been exercised by even so imperfect a religion as that taught to the new converts.[3] The Danes were the first to follow the example. Indeed, Saxo Grammaticus in one passage attributes to them the priority, asserting that when Poppo, in 965, converted Harold Blaatand by the ordeal of red-hot iron, it produced so powerful an effect as to induce the substitution of that

[1] Isdem quoque Milo . . . monomachi certaturus pugna, attribuit sancto Petro terram quam habebat in Luco, prope atrium ecclesiæ, quo sibi adjutor in disposito bello existerit.—Chron. Besuense, Chart. de Luco.

[2] Schlegel, Comment. ad Grágás, p. xxii.—Dasent, in his Icelandic Chronology (Burnt Njal I. cciii.) places this in 1006.

[3] The kind of Christianity introduced may be estimated by the character of the Apostle of Iceland. Deacon Thangbrand was the son of Willibald Count of Saxony, and even after he had taken orders continued to ply his old vocation of viking or sea-robbing. To get rid of him and to punish him, King Olaf of Denmark imposed upon him the task of converting Iceland, which he accomplished with the sword in one hand and the Bible in the other. —See Dasent, Burnt Njal, II. 361.

mode of trial for the previously existing wager of battle.[1]
Yet it evidently was not abrogated for a century later, for
when Harold the Simple, son of Sven Estrith, ascended
the throne in 1074, among the legal innovations which he
introduced was the substitution of the purgatorial oath for
all other forms of defence, which, Saxo specifically states,
put an end to the wager of battle, and opened the door to
great abuses.[2]

Fiercer tribes than these in Europe there were none, and
their abrogation of the battle trial at this early age is an
inexplicable anomaly. It was an exceptional movement,
however, without results beyond their own narrow boundaries. Other causes had to work slowly and painfully for
ages before man could throw off the bonds of ancestral
prejudice. One of the most powerful of these causes was
the gradual rise of the Tiers-État to consideration and
importance. The sturdy bourgeois, though ready enough
with morion and pike to defend their privileges, were usually
addicted to a more peaceful mode of settling private quarrels. Devoted to the arts of peace, seeing their interest
in the pursuits of industry and commerce, enjoying the
advantage of settled and permanent tribunals, and exposed to all the humanizing and civilizing influences of
close association in communities, they speedily acquired
ideas of progress very different from those of the savage
feudal nobles living isolated in their fastnesses, or of the
wretched serfs who crouched for protection around the
castles of their masters and oppressors. Accordingly, the
desire to escape from the necessity of purgation by battle
is almost coeval with the founding of the first communes.
The earliest instance of this tendency that I have met
with is contained in the charter granted to Pisa by the
Emperor Henry IV. in 1081, by which he agrees that any
accusations which he may bring against citizens can be

---

[1] Saxon. Grammat. Hist. Dan. Lib. x.   [2] Ibid. Lib. xi.

tried without battle by the oaths of twelve compurgators, except when the penalties of death or mutilation are involved; and in questions concerning land, the duel is forbidden when competent testimony can be procured.[1] Limited as these concessions may seem, they were an immense innovation on the prejudices of the age, and are important as affording the earliest indication of the direction which the new civilization was assuming. Not long after, about the year 1105, the citizens of Amiens received a charter from their bishop, St. Godfrey, in which the duel is subjected to some restriction—not enough in itself, perhaps, to effect much reform, yet clearly showing the tendency which existed.[2] Perhaps the earliest instance of absolute freedom from the judicial combat occurs in a charter granted to the town of Ypres, in 1116 by Baldwin VII. of Flanders, when he substituted the oath with four conjurators in all cases where the duel or the ordeal was previously in use.[3] This was followed by a similar grant to the inhabitants of Bari by Roger, King of Naples, in 1132.[4] Curiously enough, almost contemporary with this is a similar exemption bestowed on the rude mountaineers of the Pyrenees. Centulla I. of Bigorre, who died in 1138, in the Privileges of Lourdes, specifies that the inhabitants can prosecute their claims without the duel;[5] and his de-

---

[1] Lünig Cod. Diplom. Ital. I. 2455.—The liberal terms of this charter show the enlightenment of the Emperor, and explain the fidelity manifested for him by the imperial cities in his desperate struggles with his rebellious nobles and an implacable papacy.

[2] Si conventio aliqua facta fuerit ante duos vel plures scabinos, de conventione illa amplius non surget campus vel duellum, si scabini qui conventioni interfuerint hoc testificati fuerint.—Chart. Commun. Ambianens. c. 44. (Migne's Patrolog. T. 162, p. 750.)

[2] The charter is given by Proost, op. cit. p. 96.

[4] Ferrum, cacavum, pugnam, aquam, vobis non judicabit vel judicari faciet. (Muratori, Antiq. Ital. Dissert. 38.)

[5] Item damus et concedimus omnibus habitatoribus Lorde, quod ipsi omnia eis debita sine imbargio possint probare sine duello etc.—Priviléges de Lourdes, cap. ii. (Lagrèze, op. cit. p. 482.)

sire to discourage the custom is further shown by a clause
permitting the pleader who has gaged his battle to withdraw on payment of a fine of only five sous to the seigneur,
in addition to what the authorities of the town may levy.[1]
Still more decided was a provision of the laws of Soest in
Westphalia, somewhat earlier than this, by which the citizens were absolutely prohibited from appealing each other
in battle;[2] and this is also to be found in a charter granted
to the town of Tournay by Philip Augustus in 1187.[3]   In
the charter of Nieuport, bestowed in 1163, by Philip of
Alsace, while the ordeal of red-hot iron and compurgatorial oaths are freely alluded to as means of rebutting
accusations, there is no reference whatever to the battle
trial, showing that it was by that time no longer in use.[4]
In the customs of Maubourguet, granted in 1309, by
Bernard VI. of Armagnac, privileges similar to those of
Lourdes, alluded to above, were included, rendering the
duel a purely voluntary matter.[5]   Even in Scotland, partial exemptions of the same kind in favor of towns are
found as early as the twelfth century.   A stranger could
not force a burgher to fight, except on an accusation of
treachery or theft, while, if a burgher desired to compel a
stranger to the duel, he was obliged to go beyond the con-

---

[1] Priviléges de Lourdes, cap. xiii. (Lagrèze p. 484.)   These privileges
were confirmed at various epochs, until 1407.

[2] Statuta Susatensia, No. 41 (Hæberlin, Analect. Med. Ævi. p. 513).   This
is retained in the subsequent recension of the law, in the thirteenth century.
(Op. cit. p. 526.)

[3] Proost, op. cit. p. 51.

[4] Oudegherst, Annales de Flandre ed. Lesbroussart. T. II. note ad fin —
The laws bestowed by Philip on the city of Ghent in 1178 have no allusion
to any species of ordeal, and appear to rest altogether on ordinary legal processes.—Ibid. T. I. pp. 426 sqq.

[5] E sobre ayso que dam e autreyam als borges de la vielle de Maubourguet que totz los embars pusquen provar sens batalhe etc.—Coutumes de
Maubourguet, cap. v.   That this, however, was not expected to do away entirely with the battle trial is shown by the regulation prescribed in cap.
xxxvii.   (Lagrèze, op. cit. pp. 470, 474.)

fines of the town. A special privilege was granted to the royal burghs, for their citizens could not be challenged by the burghers of nobles or prelates, while they had the right to offer battle to the latter.[1]   Much more efficient was the clause of the third *Keure* of Bruges, granted in 1304 by Philip son of Count Guy of Flanders, which strictly prohibited the duel. Any one who gave or received a wager of battle was fined sixty sols, one-half for the benefit of the town, and the other for the count.[2]

The special influence exercised by the practical spirit of trade in rendering the duel obsolete is well illustrated by the privilege granted, in 1127, by William Clito to the merchants of St. Omer, declaring that they should be free from all appeals to single combat in all the markets of Flanders.[3] In a similar spirit, when Frederic Barbarossa, in 1173, was desirous of attracting to the markets of Aix-la-Chapelle and Duisbourg the traders of Flanders, in the code which he established for the protection of such as might come, he specially enacted that they should enjoy immunity from the duel.[4] Even Russia found it advantageous to extend the same exemption to foreign merchants, and in the treaty which Mstislas Davidovitch made in 1228 with the Hansetown of Riga, he granted to the Germans who might seek his dominions immunity from liability to the red-hot iron ordeal and wager of battle.[5]

Germany seems to have been somewhat later than France or Italy in the movement, yet her burghers evidently regarded it with favor. In 1219, the charter granted to Nürnberg by Frederic II. expressly exempts the citizens from

---

[1] L. Burgorum, c. 14, 15.   (Skene.)

[2] Warnkœnig, Hist. de la Flandre, IV. 129.

[3] In omni mercato Flandriæ si quis clamorem adversus eos suscitaverit, judicium scabinorum de omni clamore sine duello subeant ; ab duello vero ulterius liberi sint.—(Warnkönig, Hist. de la Flandre, II. 411.)

[4] Nemo mercatorem de Flandria duello provocabit. (Ibid. II. 426.)

[5] Traité de 1228, art. 3.   Esneaux, Hist. de Russie, II. 272.

the appeal of battle throughout the empire.[1] The statutes
of Eisenach, in 1283, provide that no duel shall be adjudged in the town, except in cases of homicide, and then
only when the hand of the murdered man shall be produced in court at the trial.[2] In 1291, Rodolph of Hapsburg issued a constitution declaring that the burghers of
the free imperial cities should not be liable to the duel outside of the limits of their individual towns,[3] and in the
Kayser-Recht this privilege is extended by declaring the
burghers exempt from all challenge to combat, except in a
suit brought by a fellow-citizen.[4]

All these, however, were special privileges for a limited
class of men, and their local regulations had no direct
bearing on general legislation, except in so far as they
might assist in softening the manners of their generation
and aiding in the general spread of civilization. A more
efficient cause was to be found in the opposition of the
church. From Liutprand the Lombard to Frederic II., a
period of five centuries, no secular lawgiver seems to have
thought of abolishing the judicial combat, and those
whose influence was largest were the most conspicuous in
fostering it. During the whole of this period the church
was consistently engaged in discrediting it, notwithstanding that the local interests or pride of individual prelates

[1] Item, nemo aliquem civem loci illius duello impetere debet in toto Romano imperio.—Constit. Frid. II. de Jur. Norimb. § 4 (Goldast. Constit.
Imp. I. 291).

[2] Henke, Gesch. des Deut. Peinlichen Rechts I. 192 (Du Boys, op. cit.
II. 590).

[3] Nullus vos vel vestrum aliquem modo duellico vel per viam duelli extra
civitatem citare possit vel debeat evocare. (Goldast. op. cit. I. 314.)

[4] Imperator eos immunes declaravit a duello, . . . ut non possint con-
veniri nisi civibus in eadem civitate habitantibus, ubi vir ille moratur cui
lis movetur.—Jur. Cæsar. P. iv. cap. i. (Senckenberg, Corp. Jur. German.
I. 118.) This portion of the Kayser-Recht is probably therefore posterior to
the rise of the Hapsburg dynasty.

might lead them to defend their vested privileges arising under it.

When King Gundobald gave form and shape to the battle ordeal in digesting the Burgundian laws, Avitus, Bishop of Vienne, remonstrated loudly against the practice as unjust and unchristian. A new controversy arose on the occasion of the duel between the Counts Bera and Sanila, to which allusion has already been made as one of the important events in the reign of Louis-le-Débonnaire. St. Agobard, Archbishop of Lyons, took advantage of the opportunity to address to the Emperor a treatise in which he strongly deprecated the settlement of judicial questions by the sword; and he subsequently wrote another tract against ordeals in general, consisting principally of scriptural texts with a running commentary, proving their incompatibility with these unchristian practices.[1] Some thirty-five years later, the Council of Valence in 855 denounced the wager of battle in the most decided terms, praying the Emperor Lothair to abolish it throughout his dominions, and adopting a canon which not only excommunicated the victor in such contests, but refused the rites of Christian sepulture to the victim.[2] By this time the forces of the church were becoming consolidated in the Papacy, and the Vicegerent of God was beginning to make his voice heard authoritatively throughout Europe. The popes accordingly were not long in protesting energetically against the custom. Nicholas I. denounced it vigorously,[3] and his successors constantly endeavored, as we have already seen, to

---

[1] "Liber adversus Legem Gundobadi" and "Liber contra Judicium Dei." (Agobardi Opp. Ed. Baluz. I. 107, 301.) Both of these works display marked ability, and a spirit of enlightened piety, mingled with frequent absurdities which show that Agobard could not in all things rise superior to his age. One of his favorite arguments is that the battle ordeal was approved by the Arian heretic Gundobald, whom he stigmatizes as "quidam superbus ac stultus hæreticus Gundobadus Burgundionum rex."

[2] Concil. Valentin. ann. 855 can. 12.

[3] Can. Monomachiam cans. II. q. v.

discredit it.   In the latter half of the twelfth century, Peter Cantor argues that a champion undertaking the combat relies either on his superior strength and skill, which is manifest injustice; or on the justice of his cause, which is presumption; or on a special miracle, which is a devilish tempting of God.[1] Near the close of the same century, Celestin III. prohibited it in general terms,[2] and he further pronounced that champions in such contests, together with principals, were guilty of homicide, and liable to all the ecclesiastical penalties of that crime.[3]   Innocent III., moreover, took care that the great council of Lateran in 1215 should confirm all the previous prohibitions of the practice.[4] It was probably this papal influence that led Simon de Montfort, the special champion of the church, to limit the use of the duel in the terriories which he won in his crusade against the Counts of Toulouse.   In a charter given December 1, 1212, he forbids its use in all the seignorial courts in his dominions, except in cases of treason, theft, robbery and murder.[5] De Montfort's dependence on Rome, however, was exceptional, and Christendom at large was not as yet prepared to appreciate the reformatory efforts of the popes.   How difficult it was to enforce respect for these precepts, even among churchmen, has been shown above, and the persistence of ecclesiastical belief in the divine interposition is fairly illustrated by a case, re-

---

[1] Pet. Cantor. Verb. Abbrev. cap. LXXVIII.

[2] "In eo casu, vel aliis etiam, hoc non debes aliquatenus tolerare" (Can. 1, Extra, Lib. v. Tit. xxxv.).   The rubric of this canon is even more decided.—"Duella et aliæ purgationes vulgares prohibitæ sunt, quia per eas multoties condemnatur absolvendus, et Deus tentari videtur."

[3] Quod tales pugiles homicidæ veri existunt. . . . Homicidium autem, tam facto quam præcepto, sive consilio, aut defensione, non est dubium perpetrari.—Can. 2, Extra, Lib. v. Tit. xv.

[4] Concil. Lateranens. IV. can. 18.

[5] Item, nullus Baro, sive Miles, vel quilibet alius Dominus in terra nostra recipiat in curia sua duellum pro aliqua causa, nisi pro proditione, vel pro latrocinio, vel pro rapina, vel pro murtro.—Consuetud. S. Montisfortis. —Contre le Franc-Alleu sans Tiltre, p. 229. Paris, 1629.

lated with great triumph by monkish chroniclers, as late as the fourteenth century, when a duel was undertaken by direction of the Virgin Mary herself. In 1325, a French Jew feigned conversion to Christianity in order to gratify his spleen by mutilating the images in the churches, and at length he committed the sacrilege of carrying off the holy wafer to aid in the unknown and hideous rites of his fellows. The patience of the Virgin being at last exhausted, she appeared in a vision to a certain smith, commanding him to summon the impious Israelite to the field. A second and a third time was the vision repeated without effect, till at last the smith, on entering a church, was confronted by the Virgin in person, scolded for his remissness, promised an easy victory, and forbidden to pass the church door until his duty should be accomplished. He obeyed and sought the authorities. The duel was decreed, and the unhappy Hebrew, on being brought into the lists, yielded without a blow, falling on his knees, confessing his unpardonable sins, and crying that he could not resist the thousands of armed men who appeared around his adversary with threatening weapons. He was accordingly promptly burned, to the great satisfaction of all believers.[1] Yet for all this, the opposition of the church, as authoritatively expressed by successive pontiffs, could not but have great influence in opening the minds of men to a sense of the cruelty and injustice of the custom.[2]

But perhaps the most potential cause at work was the revival of the Roman jurisprudence, which in the thirteenth century commenced to undermine all the institutions of

[1] Willelmi Egmond. Chron. (Matthæi Analect. IV. 231.) Proost (Législation des Jugements de Dieu, p. 16) gives this story, with some variations, as occurring at Mons, and states that the duel was authorized by no less a personage than the pope John XXII.

[2] As late as 1492, the Synod of Schwerin promulgated a canon prohibiting Christian burial to those who fell in the duel or in tournaments.—Synod. Swerin. ann. 1492, Can. xxiv. (Hartzheim Concil. German. V. 647.)

15

feudalism. Its theory of royal supremacy was most agreeable to sovereigns whose authority over powerful vassals
was scarcely more than nominal; its perfection of equity
between man and man could not fail to render it enticing
to clear-minded jurists, wearied with the complicated and
fantastic privileges of ecclesiastical, feudal, and customary
law. Thus recommended, its progress was rapid. Monarchs
lost no opportunity of inculcating respect for that which
served their purpose so well, and the civil lawyers, who
were their most useful instruments, speedily rose to be a
power in the state. Of course the struggle was long, for
feudalism had arisen from the necessities of the age, and a
system on which were based all the existing institutions of
Europe could only be attacked in detail, and could only be
destroyed when the advance of civilization and the general
diffusion of enlightenment had finally rendered it obsolete.
The French Revolution was the final battle-field, and that
terrible upheaval was requisite to obliterate a form of
society whose existence had numbered nine hundred years.

The wager of battle was not long in experiencing the
first assaults of the new power. The earliest efficient steps
towards its abolition were taken in 1231 by the Emperor
Frederic II. in his Neapolitan code. He pronounces it to
be in no sense a legal proof, but only a species of divination,
incompatible with every notion of equity and justice, and
he prohibits it for the future, except in cases of murder and
treason where other proof is unattainable; and even in
these it is placed at the option of the accuser alone, as if
to render it a punishment and not a trial.[1] The German
Imperial code, known as the Kayser-Recht, which was probably compiled about the same time, contains a similar
denunciation of the uncertainty of the duel, but does not
venture on a prohibition, merely renouncing all responsi-

---

[1] Constit. Sicular. Lib. ii. Tit. xxxii. xxxiii.—"Non tam vera probatio
quam quædam divinatio . . . quæ naturæ non consonans, a jure communi
deviat, æquitatis rationibus non consentit." Cf. Lib. I. Tit. xxi. cap. 2.

bility for it, while recognizing it as a settled custom.[1] In
the portion, however, devoted to municipal law, which is
probably somewhat later in date, the prohibition is much
more stringently expressed, manifesting the influences at
work;[2] but even this is contradicted by a passage almost
immediately preceding it. How little influence these wise
counsels had, in a state so intensely feudal and aristocratic,
is exemplified in the Swabian and Saxon codes, where the
duel plays so important a part. Yet the desire to escape
it was not altogether confined to the honest burghers of the
cities, for in 1277, Rodolph of Hapsburg, even before he
granted immunity to the imperial towns, gave a charter
to the duchy of Styria, securing to the Styrians their privileges and rights, and in this he forbade the duel in all cases
where sufficient testimony could be otherwise obtained;
while the general tenor of the document shows that this
was regarded as a favor.[3]

In 1248, Don Jayme I. of Arragon, in revising the franchises of Majorca, prohibited the judicial combat in both
civil and criminal cases.[4] Within fifteen years from this,
Alfonso the Wise of Castile issued the code generally known
as Las Siete Partidas. In this he evidently desired to curb
the practice as far as possible, stigmatizing it as a custom
peculiar to the military class (por lid de caballeros ò de
peones), and as reprehensible both as a tempting of God
and as a source of perpetual injustice.[5] Accordingly, he

[1] Cum viderit innocentes in duello succubuisse, et sontes contra in suâ
iniustitia nihilominus victoriam obtinuisse. Et ideo in jura imperii scrip-
tum est, ubi duo ex more in duellum procedunt, hoc non pertinet ad imperium.
—Jur. Cæsar. P. II. c. 70. (Senckenberg I. 54.)

[2] Quilibet sciat imperatorem jussisse ut nemo alterum ad duellum provocet.
. . . Nemo enim unquam fortiores provocari vidit, sed semper debiliores,
et fortiores semper triumpharunt.—Ibid. P. IV. cap. 19.

[3] Rudolphi I. Privileg. (Ludewig Reliq. MSS. T. IV. p. 260.)

[4] Du Cange, s. v. Batalia.

[5] Los sabios antiguos que ficieron las leyes non lo tovieron por derecha
prueba : ed esto por dos razones ; la una porque muchas vegadas acaesce

subjected it to very important limitations. The wager of
battle could only be granted by the king himself;[1] it could
only take place between gentlemen,[2] and in personal actions
alone which savored of treachery, such as murder, blows,
or other dishonor, inflicted without warning or by surprise.   Offences committed against property, burning,
forcible seizure, and other wrongs, even without defiance,
were specifically declared not subject to its decision, the
body of the plaintiff being its only recognized justification.[3] Even in this limited sphere, the consent of both
parties was requisite, for the appellant could prosecute in
the ordinary legal manner, and the defendant, if challenged
to battle, could elect to have the case tried by witnesses or
inquest, nor could the king himself refuse him the right to
do so.[4] When to this is added that a preliminary trial was
requisite to decide whether the alleged offence was treacherous in its character or not, it will be seen that the combat
was hedged around with such difficulties as rendered its
presence on the statute book scarcely more than an unmean-
ing concession to popular prejudice; and if anything were
wanting to prove the utter contempt of the legislator for
the decisions of the battle-trial, it is to be found in the regulation that if the accused was killed on the field, without
confessing the imputed crime, he was to be pronounced
innocent, as one who had fallen in vindicating the truth.[5]
The same desire to restrict the duel within the narrowest

que en tales lides pierde la verdat e vence la mentira : la otra porque aquel
que ha voluntad de se adventurar á esta prueba semeja que quiere tentar á
Dios nuestro señor.—Partidas, P. I:I. Tit. xiv. 1. 8.

[1] Ibid. P. VII. Tit. iii. 1. 2.

[2] Ibid. P. VII. Tit. iii. 1. 3.

[3] Ibid. P. VII. Tit. iii. 1. 3.

[4] Tres dias débese acordar el reptado para escoger una de las tres maneras
que desuso dixiemos, qual mas quisiere porque se libre el pleyto. . . . ca el
re nin su corte non han de mandar lidiar por riepto.—Ibid. P. VII. Tit. iii.
1. 4.

[5] Muera quito del riepto ; ca razon es que sea quito quien defendiendo la
verdad recibió muerte.—Ibid. P. VII. Tit. iv. 1. 4.

possible limits is shown in the rules concerning the employment of champions, which have been already alluded to.
Although the Partidas as a scheme of legislation was not
as successful as it deserved to be, and although it was most
unwillingly received, still, these provisions were lasting, and
produced the effect designed. The Ordenamiento de Alcalá,
issued by Alfonso XI. in 1348, which remained in force
for nearly two centuries, repeats the restrictions of the
Partidas, but in a very cursory manner, and rather incidentally than directly, showing that the judicial combat
was then a matter of little importance, and that the ordinances of Alfonso the Wise had become part of the national
law, to be received as a matter of course.[1] In fact, the jurisprudence of Spain was derived so directly from the Roman
law through the Wisigothic code and its Romance recension, the Fuero Juzgo, that the wager of battle could never
have become so deeply rooted in the national faith as among
the more purely barbarian races.   It was therefore more
readily eradicated, and yet, as late as the sixteenth century,
a case occurred in which the judicial duel was prescribed
by Charles V., in whose presence the combat took place.[2]

The varying phases of the struggle between progress and
centralization on the one side, and chivalry and feudalism
on the other, were exceedingly well marked in France, and
as the materials for tracing them are abundant, a more
detailed account of the gradual reform may perhaps have
interest, as illustrating the long and painful strife which
has been necessary to evoke order and civilization out of
the incongruous elements from which modern European
society has sprung.   The sagacity of St. Louis, so rarely
at fault in the details of civil administration, saw in the
duel not only an unchristian and unrighteous practice, but

[1] Ordenamiento de Alcalá, Tit. xxxii. ll.vii.—xi.
[2] Meyer, Institutions Judiciaires, I. 337.

a symbol of the disorganizing feudalism which he so energetically labored to suppress.   His temper led him rather
to adopt pacific measures, in sapping by the forms of law
the foundations of the feudal power, than to break it down
by force of arms as his predecessors had attempted.   The
centralization of the Roman polity might well appear to
him and his advisers the ideal of a well ordered state, and
the royal supremacy had by his time advanced to a point
where the gradual extension of the judicial prerogatives of
the crown might prove the surest mode of humbling eventually the haughty vassals who had so often bearded the
sovereign.   No legal procedure was more closely connected
with feudalism, or embodied its spirit more thoroughly
than the wager of battle, and Louis accordingly did all
that lay in his power to abrogate the custom.   The royal
authority was strictly circumscribed, however, and though,
in his celebrated Ordonnance of 1260, he formally prohibited the battle trial in the territory subject to his jurisdiction,[1] he was obliged to admit that he had no power to
control the courts of his barons beyond the domains of the
crown.[2]   Even within this comparatively limited sphere,
we may fairly assume from some passages in the Établissements, compiled about the year 1270, that he was unable
to do away entirely with the practice.   It is to be found

[1] Nous deffendons à tous les batailles par tout nostre demengne, més nous
n'ostons mie les clains, les respons, les convenans, etc. . . . fors que nous
ostons les batailles, et en lieu des batailles nous meton prueves de tesmoins,
et si n'oston pas les autres bones preuves et loyaux, qui ont esté en court
laye siques à ore.—Isambert, I. 284.

Laurière (Tabl. des Ordonn. p. 17) alludes to an edict to the same purport
under date of 1240, of which I can nowhere else find a trace.   There is no
reference to it in the Table des Ordonnances of Pardessus (Paris, 1847).

[2] Se ce est hors l'obeissance le Roy, gage de bataille. (Étab. de St. Louis,
Liv. II. chap. xi , xxix., xxxviii.)   Beaumanoir repeats it, a quarter of a
century later, in the most precise terms, "Car tout cil qui ont justice en le
conté poent maintenir lor cort, s'il lor plest, selonc l'ancienne coustume ; et
s'il lor plest il le poent tenir selonc l'establissement le Roy." (Cout. du
Beauv. cap. xxxix. § 21.)   And again, "Car quant li rois Loïs les osta de sa
cort il ne les osta pas des cours à ses barons." (Cap. LXI. § 15.)

permitted in some cases both civil and criminal, of peculiarly knotty character, admitting of no other apparent solution.[1] It seems, indeed, remarkable that he should even have authorized personal combat between brothers, in criminal accusations, only restricting them in civil suits to fighting by champions,[2] when the German law of nearly the same period forbids the duel, like marriage, between relations in the fifth degree, and states that previously it had been prohibited to those connected in the seventh degree.[3]

Even this qualified reform provoked determined opposition. Every motive of pride and interest prompted resistance. The prejudices of birth, the strength of the feudal principle, the force of chivalric superstition, the pride of self-reliance gave keener edge to the apprehension of losing an assured source of revenue. The right of granting the wager of battle was one of those appertaining to the *hauts-justiciers*, and so highly was it esteemed that paintings of champions fighting frequently adorned their halls as emblems of their prerogatives; Loysel, indeed, deduces from it a maxim, "The pillory, the gibbet, the iron collar, and paintings of champions engaged, are marks of high jurisdiction."[4] This right had a considerable money value, for

[1] Liv. I. chap. xxvii., xci., cxiii. etc. This is so entirely at variance with the general belief, and militates so strongly with the opening assertion of the Établissements (Ordonn. of 1260) that I should observe that in the chapters referred to the direction for the combat is absolute ; no alternative is provided, and there is no allusion to any difference of practice prevailing in the royal courts and in those of the barons, such as may be seen in other passages. (Liv. I. chap. xxxviii., lxxxi., cxi., etc.) Yet in a charter of 1263, Louis alludes to his having interdicted the duel in the domains of the crown, in the most absolute manner.—"Sed quia duellum perpetuo de nostris domaniis duximus amovendum."—(Actes du Parlement de Paris No. 818 A. T. I. p. 75, Paris 1863.)

[2] Ibid. Liv. I. chap. clxvii.

[3] Jur. Provin. Alamann. cap. CLXXI. §§ 10, 11, 12.

[4] Pilori, échelle, carquant, et peintures de champions combattans sont marques de haute justice.—Instit. Coutum. Liv. II. Tit. ii. Règle 47.

the seigneur at whose court an appeal of battle was tried
received from the defeated party a fine of sixty livres if he
was a gentleman, and sixty sous if a roturier, besides a
perquisite of the horses and arms employed, and heavy
mulcts for any delays which might be asked.[1] Nor was this
all, for during the centuries of its existence there had
grown and clustered around the custom an immeasurable
mass of rights and privileges which struggled lustily against
destruction.   Thus, hardly had the ordonnance of prohibition been issued when, in 1260, a knight named Mathieu-le-
Voyer actually brought suit against the king for the loss
it inflicted upon him.   He dolefully set forth that he enjoyed the privilege of guarding the lists in all duels adjudged
in the royal court at Corbón, for which he was entitled to
receive a fee of five sous in each case; and, as his occupation
thus was gone, he claimed compensation, modestly suggest-
ing that he be allowed the same tax on all inquests held
under the new law.[2]

How closely all such sources of revenue were watched is
illustrated by a case occurring in 1286, when Philippe-le-Bel
remitted the fines accruing to him from a duel between two

[1] Beaumanoir, op. cit. chap. LXI. §§ 11, 12, 13.

In Normandy, these advantages were enjoyed by all seigneurs justiciers.
"Tuit chevalier et tuit sergent ont en leurs terres leur justice de bataille en
cause citeaine; et quant li champions sera vaincuz, il auront LX. sols et I
denier de la récréandise."—Etab. de Normandie (Ed. Marnier, p. 30).
These minutely subdivided and parcelled out jurisdictions were one of the
most prolific causes of debate during the middle ages, not only on account
of the power and influence, but also from the profits derived from them.
That the privilege of decreeing duels was not the least remunerative of these
rights is well manifested by the decision of an inquest held during the reign
of Philip Augustus to determine the conflicting jurisdictions of the ducal
court of Normandy and of the seigneurs of Vernon. It will be found quoted
in full by Beugnot in his notes to the Olim, T. I. p. 969.

[2] Les Olim, I. 491. It is perhaps needless to add that Mathieu's suit was
fruitless. There are many cases recorded in the Olim showing the questions
which arose and perplexed the lawyers, and the strenuous efforts made by
the petty seigneurs to preserve their privileges.

squires adjudged in the royal court of Tours. The sene-
chal of Anjou and Touraine brought suit before the Parlement of Paris to recover one-third of the amount, as he
was entitled to that proportion of all dues arising from
combats held within his jurisdiction, and he argued that the
liberality of the king was not to be exercised to his disad-
vantage. His claim was pronounced just, and a verdict
was rendered in his favor.[1]

But the loss of money was less important than the cur-
tailment of privilege and the threatened absorption of
power of which this reform was the precursor. Every step
in advancing the influence of peaceful justice, as expounded
by the jurists of the royal courts, was a heavy blow to the
independence of the feudatories. They felt their ancestral
rights assailed at the weakest point, and they instinctively
recognized that, as the jurisdiction of the royal bailiffs
became extended, and as appeals to the court of the Parlement of Paris became more frequent, their importance was
diminished, and their means of exercising a petty tyranny
over those around them were abridged. Entangled in the
mazes of a code in which the unwonted maxims of Roman
law were daily quoted with increasing veneration, the impetuous seigneur found himself the prey of those whom he
despised, and he saw that subtle lawyers were busily undo-
ing the work at which his ancestors had labored for centuries. These feelings are well portrayed in a song of the
period, exhumed not long since by Le Roux de Lincy.
Written apparently by one of the sufferers, it gives so
truthful a view of the conservative ideas of the thirteenth
century that a translation of the first stanza may not be
amiss :—

[1] Actes du Parlement de Paris, I. 407.

Gent de France, mult estes esbahis !
Je di à touz ceus qui sont nez des fiez, etc.[1]

> Ye men of France, dismayed and sore
>   Ye well may be.   In sooth, I swear,
> Gentles, so help me God, no more
>   Are ye the freemen that ye were !
> Where is your freedom ? Ye are brought
>   To trust your rights to inquest-law,
> Where tricks and quibbles set at naught
>   The sword your fathers wont to draw.
> Land of the Franks !—no more that name
>   Is thine—a land of slaves art thou,
> Of bondsmen, wittols, who to shame
>   And wrong must bend submissive now !

Even legists—de Fontaines, whose admiration of the Digest led him on all occasions to seek an incongruous alliance between the customary and imperial law, and Beaumanoir, who in most things was far in advance of his age, and who assisted so energetically in the work of centralization—even these enlightened lawyers hesitate to object to the principles involved in the battle trial, and while disapproving of the custom, express their views in language which contrasts strongly with the vigorous denunciations of Frederic II. half a century earlier.[2]

---

[1] Recueil de Chants Historiques Français, I. 218.—It is not unreasonable to conjecture that these lines may have been occasioned by the celebrated trial of Enguerrand de Coucy in 1256. On the plea of baronage, he demanded trial by the Court of Peers, and claimed to defend himself by the wager of battle. St. Louis proved that the lands held by Enguerrand were not baronial, and resisted with the utmost firmness the pressure of the nobles who made common cause with the culprit. On the condemnation of de Coucy, the Count of Britanny bitterly reproached the king with the degradation inflicted on his order by subjecting its members to inquests.—Beugnot, Olim I. 954.—Grandes Chroniques ann. 1256.

[2] Et se li uns et li autres est si enreués, qu'il n'en demandent nul amesurement entrer pueent par folie en périll de gages.—(Conseil, chap. xv. Tit. xxvii.)   Car bataille n'a mie leu ou justise a mesure.— (Ibid. Tit. xxviii.) Mult a de perix en plet qui est de gages de bataille, et mult est grans mestiers c'on voist sagement avant en tel cas.—Cout. du Beauv. chap. lxiv. § 1.)

How powerful were the influences thus brought to bear
against the innovation is shown by the fact that when the
mild but firm hand of St. Louis no longer grasped the
sceptre, his son and successor could not maintain his
father's laws.   In 1280 there is a record of a duel adjudged
in the king's court between Jeanne de la Valete and the
Sire of Montricher on an accusation of arson,[1] and about
1283 Philippe even allowed himself to preside at a judicial
duel, scarcely more than twenty years after the promulga-
tion of the ordonnance of prohibition.[2]   The next monarch, Philippe-le-Bel, was at first guilty of the same weakness, for when in 1293 the Count of Armagnac accused
Raymond Bernard of Foix of treason, a duel between
them was decreed, and they were compelled to fight before
the King at Gisors; though Robert d'Artois interfered
after the combat had commenced, and induced Philippe to
separate the antagonists.[3]   Philippe, however, was too astute
not to see that his interests lay in humbling feudalism in
all its forms; while the rapid extension of the jurisdiction
of the crown, and the limitations on the seignorial courts,
so successfully invented and asserted by the lawyers, acting by means of the Parlement through the royal bailiffs,
gave him power to carry his views into effect such as had
been enjoyed by none of his predecessors. Able and unscrupulous, he took full advantage of his opportunities in
every way, and the wager of battle was not long in experiencing the effect of his encroachments. Still, he proceeded step by step, and the vacillation of his legislation
shows how obstinate was the spirit with which he had to
deal.   In 1296 he prohibited the judicial duel in time of

Car ce n'est pas coze selonc Diu de soufrir gages en petite querele de meubles
ou d'eritages ; mais coustume les suefre ès vilains cas de crieme.—Ibid.
chap. vi. § 31.

[1] Actes du Parlement de Paris, T. I. No. 2269 A. p. 217.
[2] Beaumanoir, op. cit. chap. lxi. § 63.
[3] Grandes Chroniques, T. IV. p. 104.

war,[1] and in 1303 he was obliged to repeat the prohibition.[2]
It was probably not long after this that he interdicted the
duel wholly[3]—possibly impelled thereto by a case occurring
in 1303, in which he is described as forced to grant the
combat between two nobles, on an accusation of murder,
very greatly against his wishes, and in spite of all his
efforts to dissuade the appellant.[4]

In thus abrogating the wager of battle, Philippe-le-Bel
was in advance of his age. Before three years were over
he was forced to abandon the position he had assumed;
and though he gave as a reason for the restoration of the
duel that its absence had proved a fruitful source of encouragement for crime and villany,[5] yet at the same time
he took care to place on record the assertion of his own
conviction that it was worthless as a means of seeking
justice.[6] In thus legalizing it by the Ordonnance of 1306,

[1] Quod durante guerra regis, inter aliquos gagia duelli nullatenus admittantur, sed quilibet in curiis regis et subditorum suorum jus suum via ordinaria prosequatur.—Isambert, II. 702.

[2] Ibid. II. 806.

[3] I have not been able to find this Ordonnance. Laurière alludes to it
(Tabl. des Ordonn. p. 59), but the passage of Du Cange which he cites refers
only to prohibition of tournaments. The catalogue of Pardessus and the
collection of Isambert contain nothing of the kind, but that some legislation
of this nature actually occurred is evident from the preamble to the Ordonnance of 1306—"Savoir faisons que comme ça en arrière, pour le commun
prouffit de nostre royaume, nous eussions deffendu généraument à tous noz
subgez toutes manières de guerres et tous gaiges de batailles, etc." It is
worthy of note that these ordonnances of Philippe were no longer confined to
the domain of the crown, but purported to regulate the customs of the whole
kingdom.

[4] Willelmi Egmond. Chron. (Matthæi Analect. IV. 135-7.)

[5] Dont pluseurs malfaicteurs se sont avancez par la force de leurs corps et
faulx engins à faire homicides, traysons et tous autres maléfices, griefz et
excez, pource que quant ilz les avoient fais couvertement et en repost, ilz ne
povoient estre convaincuz par aucuns tesmoings dont par ainsi le maléfice se
tenoit.—Ordonnance de 1306 (Éd. Crapelet, p. 2).

[6] Car entre tous les périlz qui sont, est celui que on doit plus craindre et
doubter, dont maint noble s'est trouvé déceu ayant bon droit au non, par
trop confier en leurs engins et en leurs forces ou par leurs ires oultrecuidées.
—Ibid. p. 34. A few lines further on, however, the Ordonnance makes a con-

however, he by no means replaced it on its former footing. It was restricted to criminal cases involving the death penalty, excepting theft, and it was only permitted when the crime was notorious, the guilt of the accused probable, and no other evidence attainable.[1] The ceremonies prescribed, moreover, were fearfully expensive, and put it out of the reach of all except the wealthiest pleaders. As the Ordonnance, which is very carefully drawn, only refers to appeals made by the prosecutor, it may fairly be assumed that the defendant could merely accept the challenge and had no right to offer it.

Even with these limitations, Philippe was not disposed to sanction the practice within the domains of the crown, for, the next year (1307), we find him commanding the seneschal of Toulouse to allow no duel to be adjudged in his court, but to send all cases in which the combat might arise to the Parlement of Paris for decision.[2] This was equivalent to a formal prohibition. During the whole of the period under consideration, numerous causes came before the Parlement concerning challenges to battle, on appeals from various jurisdictions throughout the country, and it is interesting to observe how uniformly some valid reason was found for its refusal. In the public register of decisions, extending from 1254 to 1318, scarcely a single instance of its permission is to be found.[3] The only doubtful

cession to the popular superstition of the time in expressing a conviction that those who address themselves to the combat simply to obtain justice may expect a special interposition of Providence in their favor.   " Et se l'intéressé, sans orgueil ne maltalent, pour son bon droit seulement, requiert bataille, ne doit doubter engin ne force, car le vray juge sera pour lui."

[1] Ordonnance de 1306, cap. i.

[2] Isambert, II. 850.

[3] See Les Olim, *passim*. Two judgments of the Parlement in 1309 show the observance of the Ordonnance of 1306, for, while admitting that the duel could take place, the cases are settled by inquest, as capable of proof by investigation.   In another instance, however, the appellant is fined at the pleasure of the king, for challenging his opponent without due grounds. (Olim, III. 381-7.)   Considerable ingenuity was manifested by the Parle-

16

instance which I have observed is a curious case occurring
in 1292, wherein a man accused a woman of homicide in
the court of the Chapter of Soissons, and the royal officers interfered on the ground that the plaintiff was a
bastard.   As by the local custom he thus was in some
sort a serf of the crown, they assumed that he could not
risk his body without the express permission of the king.
The Chapter contended for the appellant's legitimacy, and
the case became so much obscured by the loss of the record
of examinations made, that the Parlement finally shuffled
it out of court without any definite decision.[1] In general,
however, the civil lawyers composing that powerful body
knew too well the work for which they were destined to
hesitate as to their conclusions.

In spite of these efforts, the progress of reform was
slow.   On the breaking out afresh of the perennial contest
with Flanders, Philippe found himself, in 1314, obliged to
repeat his order of 1296, forbidding all judicial combats
during the war, and holding suspended such as were in progress.[2] As these duels could have little real importance
in crippling his military resources, it is evident that he
seized such occasions to accomplish under the war power
what his peaceful prerogative was unable to effect, and it
is a striking manifestation of his zeal in the cause, that he
could turn aside to give attention to it amid the preoccu-
pations of the exhausting struggle with the Flemings.
Yet how little impression he made, and how instinctively
the popular mind still turned to the battle ordeal, as the
surest resource in all cases of doubt, is well illustrated by

ment in thus finding some sufficient excuse for refusing the duel in the vast
variety of cases brought before it.   This is sometimes effected by denying
the jurisdiction of the court which had granted it, and sometimes for other
reasons more or less frivolous, the evident intention discernible in all the
arrêts being to restrict the custom within limits so narrow as to render it
practically a nullity.

[1] Actes du Parlement de Paris, I. 116.

[2] Isambert, III. 40.

a passage in a rhyming chronicle of the day. When the
close of Philippe's long and prosperous reign was dark-
ened by the terrible scandal of his three daughters-in-law,
and two of them were convicted of adultery, Godefroy de
Paris makes the third, Jeanne, wife of Philippe-le-Long,
offer at once to prove her innocence by the combat:—

> Gentil roy, je vous requier, sire,
> Que vous m'oiez en deffendant.
> Se nul ou nule demandant
> Me vait chose de mauvestie,
> Mon cuer sens si pur, si haitie,
> Que bonement me deffendrai,
> Ou tel champion baillerai,
> Qui bien saura mon droit deffendre,
> S'il vous plest à mon gage prendre.[1]

The iron hand of Philippe was no sooner withdrawn
than the nobles made desperate efforts to throw off the
yoke which he had so skilfully and relentlessly imposed
on them.   His son, Louis-le-Hutin, not yet firmly seated
on the throne, was constrained to yield a portion of the
newly-acquired prerogative.   The nobles of Burgundy, for
instance, in their formal list of grievances, demanded the
restoration of the wager of battle as a right of the accused
in criminal cases, and Louis was obliged to promise that
they should enjoy it according to ancient custom.[2]   Those
of Amiens and Vermandois were equally clamorous, and
for their benefit he re-enacted the ordonnance of 1306, permitting the duel in criminal prosecutions, where other
evidence was deficient, with an important extension autho-
rizing its application to cases of theft, in opposition to
previous usage.[3]   A legal record, compiled about 1325 to

---

[1] Chronique Métrique, I. 6375.

[2] Et quant au gage de bataille, nous voullons que il en usent, si comme
l'en fesoit anciennement.—Ordonn. Avril 1315, cap. 1. (Isambert, III. 62.)

[3] Nous voullons et octroions que en cas de murtre, de larrecin, de rapt, de
trahison et de roberie, gage de bataille soit ouvert, se les cas ne pouvoient
estre prouvez par tesmoings—Ordonn. 15 Mai 1315. (Isambert, III. 74.)

illustrate the customs of Picardy, shows by a group of cases that it was still quite common, and that indeed it was the ordinary defence in accusations of homicide.[1] The nobles of Champagne demanded similar privileges, but Louis, by right of his mother, Jeanne de Champagne, was Count of Champagne, and his authority was less open to dispute. He did not venture on a decided refusal, but an evasive answer, which was tantamount to a denial of the request,[2] showed that his previous concessions were extorted, and not willingly granted. Not content with this, the Champenois repeated their demand, and received the dry response, that the existing edicts on the subject must be observed.[3]

The threatened disturbances were avoided, and during the succeeding years the centralization of jurisdiction in the royal courts made rapid progress. It is a striking evidence of the successful working of the plans of St. Louis and Philippe-le-Bel that several ordonnances and charters granted by Philippe-le-Long in 1318 and 1319, while promising reforms in the procedures of the bailiffs and seneschals, and in the manner of holding inquests, are wholly silent on the subject of the duel, affording a fair inference that complaints on that score were no longer made.[4] Philip of Valois was especially energetic in maintaining the royal jurisdiction, and when in 1330 he was obliged to restrict the abusive use of appeals from the local courts to the Parlement,[5] it is evident that the question of granting or withholding the wager of battle had become practically a prerogative of the crown. That the challenging of witnesses must ere long have fallen into desuetude is shown by an edict of Charles VI., issued in 1396, by which he ordered

[1] Ancien Coutumier inédit de Picardie, p. 48 (Marnier, Paris, 1840).

[2] Ordonn. Mai 1315, P. i. chap. 13. (Isambert, III. 90.)

[3] Ibid. P. ii. chap. 8. (Isambert, III. 95.)

[4] Isambert, III. 196–221.

[5] Ordonn. 9 Mai 1330 (Isambert, IV. 369).

that the testimony of women should be received in evidence in all the courts throughout his kingdom.[1]

Though the duel was thus deprived, in France, of its importance as an ordinary legal procedure, yet it was by no means extinguished, nor had it lost its hold upon the confidence of the people. An instructive illustration of this is afforded by the well-known story of the Dog of Montargis. Though the learned Bullet[2] has demonstrated the fabulous nature of this legend, and has traced its paternity up to the Carlovingian romances, still, the fact is indubitable that it was long believed to have occurred in 1371, under the reign of Charles-le-Sage, and that authors nearly contemporary with that period recount the combat of the dog and the knight as an unquestionable fact, admiring greatly the sagacity of the animal, and regarding as a matter of course both the extraordinary judicial proceedings and the righteous judgment of God which gave the victory to the greyhound.

In 1386, the Parlement of Paris was occupied with a subtle discussion as to whether the accused was obliged, in cases where battle was gaged, to give the lie to the appellant, under pain of being considered to confess the crime charged, and it was decided that the lie was not essential.[3] The same year occurred the celebrated duel between the Chevalier de Carrouges and Jacques le Gris, to witness which the King shortened a campaign, and in which the appellant was seconded by Waleran, Count of St. Pol, son-in-law of the Black Prince. Nothing can well be more impressive than the scene so picturesquely described by Froissart. The cruelly wronged Dame de Carrouges, clothed in black, is mounted on a sable scaffold, watching the varying chances of the unequal combat between her husband, weakened by disease, and his vig-

---

[1] Neron, Récueil d'Édits, I. 16.

[2] Dissertations sur la Mythologie Française.

[3] De Laurière, note on Loysel, Instit. Coutum. Lib. vi. Tit. i. Règle 22.

16*

orous antagonist; with the fearful certainty that, if might
alone prevail, he must die a shameful death and she be
consigned to the stake.   Hope grows faint and fainter; a
grievous wound seems to place Carrouges at the mercy of
his adversary, until at the last moment, when all appeared
lost, she sees the avenger drive his sword through the body
of his prostrate enemy, vindicating at once his wife's honor
and his own good cause.[1]   Froissart, however, was rather
an artist than an historian; he would not risk the effect
of his picture by too rigid an adherence to facts, and he
omits to mention, what is told by the cooler Juvenal des
Ursins, that Le Gris was subsequently proved innocent by
the death-bed confession of the real offender.[2]   To make
the tragedy complete, the Anonyme de S. Denis adds that
the miserable Dame de Carrouges, overwhelmed with re-
morse at having unwittingly caused the disgrace and death
of an innocent man, ended her days in a convent.[3]   So
striking a proof of the injustice of the battle ordeal is said
by some writers to have caused the abandonment of the
practice; but this, as will be seen, is an error, though no
further trace of the combat as a judicial procedure is to be
found on the registers of the Parlement of Paris.[4]

Still, it was popularly regarded as an unfailing resource.
Thus, in 1390, two women were accused at the Châtelet of
Paris of sorcery.   After repeated torture, a confession im-
plicating both was extracted from one of them, but the
other persisted in her denial, and challenged her companion
to the duel by way of disproving her evidence.   In the
record of the proceedings the challenge is duly entered,
but no notice whatever seems to have been taken of it by
the court, showing that it was no longer a legal mode of
trial in such cases.[5]

[1] Froissart, Liv. III. chap. xlix. (Éd. Buchon, 1846.)
[2] Hist. de Charles VI. ann. 1386.
[3] Hist. de Charles VI. Liv. VI. chap. ix.
[4] Buchon, notes to Froissart, II. 537.
[5] Registre du Châtelet de Paris, I. 350 (Paris, 1861).

In 1409, the battle trial was materially limited by an ordonnance of Charles VI. prohibiting its employment except
when specially granted by the King or the Parlement;[1]
and though the latter body may never have exercised the
privilege thus conferred upon it, the King occasionally did,
as we find him during the same year presiding at a judicial
duel between Guillaume Bariller, a Breton knight, and John
Carrington, an Englishman.[2] The English occupation of
France, under Henry V. and the Regent Bedford, revived
the practice, and removed for a time the obstacles to its
employment. Nicholas Upton, writing in the middle of
the fifteenth century, repeatedly alludes to the numerous
cases in which he assisted as officer of the Earl of Salis-
bury, Lieutenant of the King of England; and in his
chapters devoted to defining the different species of duel
he betrays a singular confusion between the modern ideas
of reparation of honor and the original object of judicial
investigation, thus fairly illustrating the transitional character of the period.[3]

It was about this time that Philippe-le-Bon, Duke of
Burgundy, formally abolished the wager of battle, as far
as lay in his power, throughout the extensive dominions of
which he was sovereign, and in the Coutumier of Burgundy, as revised by him in 1459, there is no trace of it to
be found. The code in force in Britanny until 1539 permitted it in cases of contested estates, and of treason,
theft, and perjury—the latter, as usual, extending it over
a considerable range of civil actions, while the careful par-
ticularization of details by the code shows that it was not
merely a judicial antiquity.[4] In Normandy, the legal ex-

---

[1] Que jamais nuls ne fussent receus au royaume de France à faire gages
de bataille ou faict d'armes, sinon qu'il y eust gage jugé par le roy, ou la
cour de parlement.—Juvenal des Ursins, ann. 1409.

[2] Monstrelet, Liv. i. chap. lv.

[3] Nic. Uptoni de Militari Officio Lib. ii. cap. iii. iv. (pp. 72-73).

[4] Très Ancienne Cout. de Bretagne, chap. 99, 129-135 (Bourdot de
Richebourg).

istence of the judicial duel was even more prolonged, for it was not until the revision of the coutumier in 1583, under Henry III., that the privilege of deciding in this way numerous cases, both civil and criminal, was formally abolished.[1] Still, it may be assumed that, practically, the custom had long been obsolete, though the tardy process of revising the local customs allowed it to remain upon the statute book to so late a date. The fierce mountaineers of remote Béarn clung to it more obstinately, and in the last revision of their code, in 1552, which remained unaltered until 1789, it retains its place as a legitimate means of proof, in default of other testimony, with a heavy penalty on the party who did not appear upon the field at the appointed time.[2]

During this long period, examples are to be found which show that although the combat was falling into disuse, it was still a legal procedure, which in certain cases could be claimed as a right, or which could be decreed and enforced by competent judicial authority. Among the privileges of the town of Valenciennes was that any homicide taking refuge there could swear that the act had been committed in self-defence, when he could be appealed only in battle. This gave occasion to a combat in 1455 between a certain Mahuot and Jacotin Plouvier, the former of whom had killed a kinsman of the latter. Neither party desired the battle, but the municipal government insisted upon it, and furnished them with instructors to teach the use of the staff and buckler, allowed as arms. The Count de Charolois, Charles-le-Téméraire, endeavored to prevent the useless cruelty, but the city held any interference as an infringement of its chartered rights ; and, after long negotiations, Philippe-le-Bon, the suzerain, authorized the combat, and was present at it. The combatants, according to cus-

[1] Ancienne Cout. de Normandie, chap. 53, 68, 70, 71, 73, etc. (Bourdot de Richebourg).
[2] Fors et Cost. de Béarn, Rubr. de Batalha (Bourdot de Richebourg, IV. 1093).

tom, had the head shaved and the nails pared on both hands and feet; they were dressed from head to foot in a tight fitting suit of hardened leather, and each was anointed with grease to prevent his antagonist from clutching him. The combat was long and desperate, but at length the appellant literally tore out the heart of his antagonist.[1] Such incidents among roturiers, however, were rare. More frequently some fiery gentleman claimed the right of vindicating his quarrel at the risk of his life.   Thus, in 1482, shortly after the battle of Nancy had reinstated René, Duke of Lorraine, on the ruins of the second house of Burgundy, two gentlemen of the victor's court, quarrelling over the spoils of the battle-field, demanded the *champclos;* it was duly granted, and on the appointed day the appellant was missing, to the great discomfiture and no little loss of his bail.[2] When Charles d'Armagnac, in 1484, complained to the States General of the inhuman destruction of his family, committed by order of Louis XI., the Sieur de Castelnau, whom he accused of having poisoned his mother, the Countess d'Armagnac, appeared before the assembly, and his advocate denying the charge, presented his offer to prove his innocence by single combat.[3]   In 1518, Henry II. of Navarre ordered a judicial duel at Pau between two contestants, of whom the appellant made default; the defendant was accordingly pronounced innocent, and was empowered to drag through all cities, villages, and other places through which he might pass, the escutcheon and effigy of his adversary, who was further punished by the prohibition thenceforth to wear arms or

[1] Mathieu de Coussy, chap. cxii.—Ol. de la Marche ch. xxii.
[2] D. Calmet, Hist. de Lorraine. By the old German law, the bail of a defaulting combatant was condemned to lose a hand, which, however, he had the privilege of redeeming at its legal value (Jur. Provin. Alamann. cap. ccclxxxvi. § 32—Ed. Schilter.), or, according to another text, he was liable to the punishment incurred by his principal if convicted. (Ibid. cap. clxxiii. § 13—Ed. Senckenberg.)
[3] Jehan Masselin, Journal des États de Tours, p. 320.

knightly bearings.[1]   In 1538, Francis I. granted the combat
between Jean du Plessis and Gautier de Dinteville, which
would appear to have been essentially a judicial proceeding, since the defendant not appearing at the appointed
time was condemned to death by sentence of the high
council, Feb. 20, 1538.[2]   The duel thus was evidently still
a matter of law, which vindicated its majesty by punishing
the unlucky contestant who shrank from the arbitrament
of the sword.

Allusion has already been made to the celebrated combat between Chastaigneraye and Jarnac, in 1547, wherein
the death of the former, a favorite of Henry II., led the
monarch to take a solemn oath never to authorize another
judicial duel.   Two years later, two young nobles of his
court, Jacques de Fontaine, Sieur de Fendilles, and Claude
des Guerres, Baron de Vienne-le-Châtel, desired to settle
in this manner a disgusting accusation brought against the
latter by the former.   The king, having debarred himself
from granting the appeal, arranged the matter by allowing
Robert de la Marck, Marshal of France and sovereign
Prince of Sedan, to permit it in the territory of which he
was suzerain.   Fendilles was so sure of success that he
refused to enter the lists until a gallows was erected and
a stake lighted, where his adversary after defeat was to be
gibbeted and burned.   Their only weapons were broad-
swords, and at the first pass Fendilles inflicted on his opponent a fearful gash in the thigh.   Des Guerres, seeing that
loss of blood would soon reduce him to extremity, closed
with his antagonist, and being a skilful wrestler, speedily
threw him.   Reduced to his natural weapons, he could only
inflict blows with the fist, which failing strength rendered

---

[1] Archives de Pau, *apud* Mazure et Hatoulet, Fors de Béarn, p. 130.
There may have been something exceptional in this case, since the punishment was so much more severe than the legal fine of 16 sous quoted above.
(Fors de Morlaas, Rubr. IV)
[2] D. Calmet, Hist. de Lorraine.

less and less effective, when a scaffold crowded with ladies and gentlemen gave way, throwing down the spectators in a shrieking mass. Taking advantage of the confusion, the friends of des Guerres violated the law which imposed absolute silence and neutrality on all, and called to him to blind and suffocate his adversary with sand. Des Guerres promptly took the hint, and Fendilles succumbed to this unknightly weapon. Whether he formally yielded or not was disputed. Des Guerres claimed that he should undergo the punishment of the gallows and stake prepared for himself, but de la Marck interfered, and the combatants were both suffered to retire in peace.[1] This is the last recorded instance of the wager of battle in France. The custom appears never to have been formally abolished, and so little did it represent the thoughts and feelings of the age which witnessed the Reformation, that when, in 1566, Charles IX. issued an edict prohibiting duels, no allusion was made to the judicial combat. The encounters which he sought to prevent were solely those which arose from points of honor between gentlemen, and the offended party was ordered not to appeal to the courts, but to lay his case before the Marshals of France, or the governor of his province.[2] The custom had died a natural death. No ordonnance was necessary to abrogate it; and, seemingly from forgetfulness, the crown appears never to have been divested of the right to adjudge the wager of battle.

In Hungary, it was not until 1492 that any attempt was made to restrict the judicial duel. In that year Vladislas II. prohibited it in cases where direct testimony was pro-

---

[1] Brantôme, Discours sur les Duels. An account of this duel, published at Sedan, in 1620, represents it as resulting even less honorably to Fendilles. He is there asserted to have formally submitted, and to have been contemptuously tossed out of the lists like a sack of corn, des Guerres marching off triumphantly, escorted with trumpets.

[2] Fontanon, 1. 665.

curable ; where such evidence was unattainable, he still
permitted it, both in civil and criminal matters, and he
alleged as his reason for the restriction, the almost universal employment of champions who treacherously sold out
their principals.   The terms of the decree show that previously its use was general, though he declared it to be a
custom unknown elsewhere.[1]   Even the precocious civilization of Italy, which usually preferred astuteness to force,
could not altogether shake off the traditions of the Lombard law until the sixteenth century.   In 1505, Julius II.
forbade the duel under the severest penalties, both civil
and ecclesiastical, in a decretal of which the expressions
allow the fair conclusion that until then the wager of battle was still in some cases employed as a legal process
within the confines of the pontifical states.[2]

In Flanders, it is somewhat remarkable that the duel
should have lingered until late in the sixteenth century,
when, as we have seen above, the commercial spirit of that
region had sought its abrogation at a very early period,
and had been seconded by the efforts of Philippe-le-Bon
in the fifteenth century.   Damhouder, writing about the
middle of the sixteenth century, states that it was still
legal in matters of public concern, and even his severe
training as a civil lawyer cannot prevent his declaring it
to be laudable in such affairs.[3]   Indeed, when the Council
of Trent, in 1563, stigmatized the duel as a work of the

---

[1] Quia in duellorum dimicatione plurimæ hinc inde fraudes committi possunt ; raro enim illi inter quos illud fit judicium per se decertant, sed pugiles conducunt, qui nonnunquam dono, favore, et promissis corrumpuntur.—
L. Uladis. II. c. ix.   (Batthyani, I. 531).

[2] Duellorum et gladiatorum hujusmodi usum damnamus et improbamus,
et in terris Rom. Ecclesiæ mediate vel immediate subjectis . . . . e quacunque
causa, etiam a legibus permissa, fieri omnino prohibemus.—Can. Regis
Pacifici, De Duello, in Septimo.

[3] Reperio tamen indubie vulgarem purgationem sive duellum in casu sine
scrupulo admittendum quum publicæ salutis caussa fiat : et istud est admodum laudabile.—Damhouder. Rer. Crimin. Praxis cap. xlii. No. 12. (Antwerp. 1601.)

devil and prohibited all potentates from granting it under pain of excommunication and forfeiture of all feudal possessions,[1] the state Council of Flanders, in their report to the Duchess of Parma on the reception of the Council, took exception to this canon, and decided that the ruler ought not to be deprived of the power of ordering the combat.[2] In this view, the Council of Namur agreed.[3]

In Russia, under the code known as the Oulogenié Zakonof, promulgated in 1498, any culprit, after his accuser's testimony was in, could claim the duel; and as both parties went to the field accompanied by all the friends they could muster, the result was not infrequently a bloody skirmish. These abuses were put an end to by the Soudebtnick, issued in 1550, and the duel was regulated after a more decent fashion, but it continued to flourish legally, until it was finally abrogated in 1649 by the Czar Alexis Mikhailowitch, in the code known as the Sobornoié Oulogenié. The more enlightened branch of the Sclavonic race, however, the Poles, abolished it in the fourteenth century; but Macieiowski states that in Servia and Bulgaria the custom has been preserved to the present day.[4]

In other countries, the custom likewise lingered to a comparatively late period. Scotland, indeed, was somewhat more forward than her neighbors; for in the year 1400, the Parliament showed the influence of advancing civilization by limiting the practice in several important particulars, which, if strictly observed, must have almost rendered it obsolete. Four conditions were pronounced essential prerequisites: the accusation must be for a capital crime;

---

[1] Concil. Trident. Sess. xxv. De Reform. cap. xix. Detestabilis duellorum usus fabricante diabolo introductus.

[2] Anne is usus reliquendus sit arbitrio principis? Videtur quod sic, et respiciendum esse principi quid discernat.—*Ap.* le Plat, Monument. Concil. Trident. VII. 19.

[3] Le Plat, VII. 75.

[4] For these details I am indebted to Du Boys, Droit Criminel des Peuples Modernes, I. 611-17, 650.

17

the offence must have been committed secretly and by treachery; reasonable cause of suspicion must be shown against the accused, and direct testimony both of witnesses and documents must be wanting.[1]

Still the "perfervidum ingenium Scotorum" clung to the arbitrament of the sword with great tenacity. Knox relates that in 1562, when the Earl of Arran was consulting with him and others respecting a proposed accusation against Bothwell for high treason, arising out of a plan for seizing Queen Mary which Bothwell had suggested, the Earl remarked, "I know that he will offer the combate unto me, but that would not be suffered in France, but I will do that which I have proposed." In 1567, also, when Bothwell underwent a mock trial for the murder of Darnley, he offered to justify himself by the duel; and when the Lords of the Congregation took up arms against him, alleging as a reason the murder and his presumed designs against the infant James II., Queen Mary's proclamation against the rebels recites his challenge as a full disproval of the charges. When the armies were drawn up at Carberry Hill, Bothwell again came forward and renewed his challenge. James Murray, who had already offered to accept it, took it up at once, but Bothwell refused to meet him on account of the inequality in their rank. Murray's brother, William of Tullibardin, then offered himself, and Bothwell again declined, as the Laird of Tullibardin was not a peer of the realm. Many nobles then eagerly proposed to take his place, and Lord Lindsay especially insisted on being allowed the privilege of proving the charge on Bothwell's body, but the latter delayed on various pretexts, until Queen Mary was able to prohibit the combat.[2]

In England, the resolute conservatism, which resists innovation to the last, prolonged the existence of the wager of battle until a period unknown in other civilized nations.

[1] Statut. Roberti III. cap. iii.
[2] Knox's Hist. of Reform. in Scotland, pp. 322, 116–7.

At the close of the fourteenth century, when France was engaged in rendering it rapidly obsolete, Thomas, Duke of Gloucester, dedicated to his nephew Richard II., a treatise detailing elaborately the practice followed in the Marshal's court with respect to judicial duels.[1] Even a century later, legislation was obtained to prevent its avoidance in certain cases. The "Statute of Gloucester" (6 Ed. III. cap. 9), in 1333, had given to the appellant a year and a day in which to bring his appeal of death—a privilege allowed the widow or next of kin to put the accused on a second trial after an acquittal on a public indictment—which, as a private suit, was usually determined by the combat. In practice, this privilege was generally rendered unavailing by postponing the public prosecution until the expiration of the delay, so as to prevent the appeal. In 1486, however, a law was passed to diminish the frequency of murder which required the trial to be finished before the expiration of the year and day, and ordered the justices, in case of acquittal, to hold the defendant in prison or on bail until the time had passed, so as to insure to the widow or next of kin the opportunity of prosecuting the appeal of death.[2] Another evidence of the prevalence of the custom is to be found in the rule which permitted a priest in the fifteenth century to shrive a man who was about to wage his battle, without regard to the fact as to whose parishioner he might legally be—

> And of mon that schal go fyghte
> In a bateyl for hys ryghte,
> Hys schryft also thou myghte here,
> Thagh he thy pareschen neuer were.[3]

With the advance of civilization and refinement, the custom gradually declined, but it was not abolished. In 1571

---

[1] Spelman (Gloss. s. v. *Campus*) gives a Latin translation of this interesting document, from a MS. of the period.

[2] 3 Henr. VII. cap. 1.

[3] John Myrc's Instructions for Parish Priests, p. 26. (Early English Text Society, 1868.)

a case occurred, as Spelman says, "non sine magna juris-consultorum perturbatione," when to determine the title to an estate in Kent, Westminster Hall was forced to adjourn to Tothill Fields, and all the forms of a combat were literally enacted, though an accommodation between the parties saved the skulls of their champions.[1]

A curious custom, peculiar to the English jurisprudence, allowed a man indicted for a capital offence to turn "approver," by confessing the crime and charging or appealing any one he chose as an accomplice, and this appeal was usually settled by the single combat. This was sufficiently frequent to require legislation as late as the year 1599, when the Act 41 Eliz. chap. 3 was passed to regulate the nice questions which attended appeals of several persons against one, or of one person against several. In the former case, the appellee, if victorious in the first duel, was acquitted; in the latter, the appellor was obliged to fight successively with all the appellees.[2] Even in the seventeenth century, instances occurred of the battle ordeal between persons of high station. In civil suits the last case on record, I believe, is that of Claxton v. Lilburn, which shows curiously enough the indisposition to put an end to what was regarded by common consent as a solecism. A valuable estate in Durham, said to be worth more than £200 a year, was the subject in dispute. Claxton had been unsuccessful in a suit for its recovery, and had brought a new action, to which Lilburn responded, Aug. 6th, 1638, by producing in court his champion, George Cheney, in array, armed with a sandbag and battoon, who cast into the court his gauntlet with five small pence in it and demanded battle. Claxton rejoined by producing a champion similarly armed, and gaged his battle. The court was nonplussed, putting off the proceedings from day to day and seeking some excuse for refusing the combat. The champions

[1] Spelman. Gloss. p. 103.
[2] Hale, Pleas of the Crown, II. chap. xxix.

were interrogated, and both admitted that they were hired for money. King Charles demanded the opinion of the Chief Justice and all his barons whether this was sufficient to invalidate the proceedings, but they unanimously replied that after battle was gaged and sureties given, such confession was no bar to its being carried out. The King then ordered his judges if possible to find some just way for its prevention, but they apparently could do nothing but procrastinate the matter for years, for in 1641 Lilburn petitioned the Long Parliament, setting forth that he had repeatedly claimed his right of battle and had produced his champion, but was ever put off by the judges finding some error in the record. Parliament thereupon ordered a bill to be brought in taking away the judicial combat.[1] It was not acted on, however, and Sir Matthew Hale, writing towards the close of the century, feels obliged to describe with considerable minuteness the various niceties of the law, though he is able to speak of the combat as "an unusual trial at this day."[2]

In 1774, the subject incidentally attracted attention in a manner not very creditable to the enlightenment of English legislation. When, to punish the rebellious Bostonians for destroying the obnoxious tea, a "Bill for the improved administration of justice in the province of Massachusetts Bay" was passed, it originally contained a clause depriving the New Englanders of the appeal of death, by which, it will be remembered, a man acquitted of a charge of murder could be again prosecuted by the next of kin, and the question could be determined by the wager of battle. The denial of this ancestral right aroused the indignation of the liberal party in the House of Commons, and the point was warmly contested. The learned and eloquent Dunning, afterwards Lord Ashburton, one of the leaders of opposition, defended the ancient custom in the strongest terms.

[1] Rushworth's Collections, Vol. I. P. i. pp. 788–90, P. iii. p. 356.
[2] Hale, loc. cit.

"I rise," said he, "to support that great pillar of the constitution, the appeal for murder; I fear there is a wish to establish a precedent for taking it away in England as well as in the colonies. It is called a remnant of barbarism and gothicism. The whole of our constitution, for aught I know, is gothic. . . . . I wish, sir, that gentlemen would be a little more cautious, and consider that the yoke we are framing for the despised colonists may be tied round our own necks!" Even Burke was heard to lift a warning voice against the proposed innovation, and the obnoxious clause had to be struck out before the ministerial majority could pass the bill.[1] Something was said about reforming the law throughout the empire, but it was not done, and the beauty of the "great pillar of the constitution," the appeal of death, was shown when the nineteenth century was disgraced by the resurrection of all the barbaric elements of criminal jurisprudence. In 1818, the case of Ashford vs. Thornton created much excitement. Ashford was the brother of a murdered girl, whose death, under circumstances of peculiar atrocity, was charged upon Thornton, with every appearance of probability. Acquitted on a jury trial, Thornton was appealed by Ashford, when he pleaded "Not guilty, and I am ready to defend the same by my body." After elaborate argument, Lord Ellenborough, with the unanimous assent of his brother justices, sustained the appellee's right to this as "the usual and constitutional mode of trial," expounding the law in almost the same terms as those which we read in Bracton and Beaumanoir.[2] The curious crowd was sorely disappointed when the appellant withdrew, and the chief justice was relieved from the necessity of presiding over a gladiatorial exhibition. A similar case occurred

---

[1] Campbell's Lives of the Chancellors of England, VI. 112.

[2] I. Barnewall & Alderson, 457.—In April 1867 the journals record the death at Birmingham of William Ashford the appellant in this suit. Thornton emigrated to America and disappeared from sight.

almost simultaneously in Ireland, and the next year the
act 59 Geo. III. chap. 46, at length put an end to this last
remnant of the age of chivalry.[1]

America, inheriting the blessings of English law, inherited also its defects. The colonies enjoyed the privilege
of the appeal of death, against the abrogation of which, in
the province of Massachusetts Bay, Dunning protested so
vehemently. At least one instance of its employment is
to be found here, when in 1765, in Maryland, Sarah Soa-
per appealed a negro slave named Tom for the murder of
her husband. The negro, however, was probably not aware
of his privilege to demand the wager of battle, so he submitted to be tried by a jury and was duly condemned and
executed.[2] John C. Gray, Jr., Esq., of Boston, to whom
I am indebted for calling my attention to this and some
other sources of information on the subject, informs me
of a tradition that a disputed question of boundary between two townships in New Hampshire was once settled
by combat between champions; but the most conservative
State in this respect appears to be South Carolina. An
act of that colony, in 1712, enumerating the English laws
to be held in force, specifically includes those concerning
appeal of death, and Dr. Cooper, in his " Statutes at Large
of South Carolina," writing in 1837, seems to think that
both the wager of battle and appeal of death were still
legally in force there at that time.[3] So Chancellor Kilty,
in his Report on English Statutes applicable to Maryland,
made in 1811, apparently considers that the appeal of death
was still legally existent, but regards it as unimportant in
view of the pardoning power and other considerations.[4]

[1] Campbell, Chief Justices, III. 169.
[2] I. Harris and McHenry's Md. Reps. 227.
[3] Cooper's Statutes at Large of S. C. II. 403, 715.
[4] Kilty's Report on English Statutes, Annapolis, 1811, p. 141.

III.

THE ORDEAL.

It is only in an age of high and refined mental culture that man can entertain an adequate conception of the Supreme Being. An Omnipotence that can work out its destined ends, and yet allow its mortal creatures free scope to mould their own fragmentary portions of the great whole; a Power so infinitely great that its goodness, mercy, and justice are compatible with the existence of evil in the world which it has formed, so that man has full liberty to obey the dictates of his baser passions, without being released from responsibility, and, at the same time, without disturbing the preordained results of Divine wisdom and beneficence—these are not the conceptions which prevail in the formative periods of society. Accordingly, in the earlier epochs of almost all races, a belief in a Divine Being is accompanied with the expectation that special manifestations of power will be made on all occasions, and that the interposition of Providence may be had for the asking, whenever man, in the pride of his littleness, condescends to waive his own judgment, and undertakes to test the inscrutable ways of his Creator by the touchstone of his own limited reason. Thus miracles come to be expected as matters of every-day occurrence, and the laws of nature are to be suspended whenever man chooses to tempt his God with the promise of right and the threat of injustice to be committed in His name.

To these elements of the human mind is attributable the

almost universal adoption of the so-called Judgment of God, by which men, oppressed with doubt, have essayed in all ages to relieve themselves from responsibility by calling in the assistance of Heaven. Nor, in so doing, have they seemed to appreciate the self-exaltation implied in the act itself, but in all humility have cast themselves and their sorrows at the feet of the Great Judge, making a merit of abnegating the reason which, however limited, has been bestowed to be used and not rejected. In the Carlovingian Capitularies there occurs a passage, dictated doubtless by the spirit of genuine trust in God, which well expresses the pious sentiments presiding over acts of the grossest practical impiety. "Let doubtful cases be determined by the judgment of God. The judges may decide that which they clearly know, but that which they cannot know shall be reserved for Divine judgment. Whom God hath kept for his own judgment may not be condemned by human means. 'Therefore judge nothing before the time, until the Lord come, who both will bring to light the hidden things of darkness, and will make manifest the counsels of the hearts.'"[1]   (1 *Cor.* iv. 5.)

With but one exception, the earliest records of the human race bear witness to the existence of the superstition thus dignified with the forms of Christian faith, and this exception, as might be anticipated, is furnished by China. Her strange civilization presents itself, in the Sacred Books collected by Confucius five hundred years before the Christian era, in nearly the same form as it exists to this day, guided by a religion destitute of life, and consisting of a system of cold morality, which avoids the virtues as well

---

[1] "In ambiguis, Dei judicio reservetur sententia Quod certe agnoscunt suo, quod nesciunt divino reservent judicio. Quoniam non potest humano condemnari examine quem Deus suo judicio reservavit Incerta namque non debemus judicare quoadusque veniat Dominus, qui latentia producet in lucem, et inluminabit abscondita tenebrarum, et manifestabit consilia cordium."—Capit. Lib VII. cap 259.

as the errors of a more imaginative and generous faith. In
the most revered and authoritative of the Chinese scriptures, the Chou-King, or Holy Book, of which the origin
is lost in fabulous antiquity, we find a theo-philosophy
recognizing a Supreme Power (Tai-Ki), or Heaven, which
is pure reason, or the embodiment of the laws and forces
of Nature, acting under the pressure of blind destiny.
Trace back the Chinese belief as far as we may, we cannot
get behind this refined and philosophical scepticism. The
flowery kingdom starts from the night of Chaos intellec-
tually full-grown, like Minerva, and from first to last there
is no semblance of a creed which would admit of the direct
practical intervention of a higher power. The fullest admission which this prudent reserve will allow is expressed
by the legislator Mou-Vang (about 1000 B. C.) in his instructions to his judges in criminal cases: "Say not that
Heaven is unjust—it is that man brings these evils on himself. If it were not that Heaven inflicts these severe punishments, the world would be ungoverned."[1] In the modern
penal code of China there is accordingly no allusion to
evidence other than that of witnesses, and even oaths are
neither required nor admitted in judicial proceedings.[2]

When we turn, however, to the other great source of
Asiatic jurisprudence, whose fantastic intricacy forms so
strange a contrast to the coeval sober realism of China, we
find in the laws of Manu abundant proof of our general
proposition. There is no work of the human intellect
which offers so curious a field of speculation to the student of human nature; none in which the transitions are
so abrupt, or the contradictions so startling, between the
most sublime doctrines of spiritual morality, and the
grossest forms of puerile superstition—between elevated

---

[1] Chou-King, Part iv. chap. 27 § 21 (after Goubil's translation).

[2] Staunton, Penal Code of China, p. 364.—A curious exception to this
general principle will be found noted hereafter.

precepts of universal justice, and the foulest partiality in specific cases. Its very complexity reveals a highly civilized state of society, and the customs and observances which it embodies are evidently not innovations on an existing order of things, but merely a compilation of regulations and procedures established through previous ages, whose origin is lost in the trackless depths of remote antiquity. When, therefore, we see in the Hindoo code the same strange and unnatural modes of purgation which two thousand years later[1] greet us on the threshold of European civilization, adorned but not concealed by a thin veil of Christianized superstition, the coincidence seems more than accidental. That the same principle should be at work in each, we can account for by the general tendencies of the human mind; but that this principle should manifest itself under identical forms in races so far removed by time and space, offers a remarkable confirmation of the community of origin of the great Aryan family of mankind. In the following texts, the principal forms of Ordeal prescribed are precisely similar to the most popular of the mediæval judgments of God :—

" Or, according to the nature of the case, let the judge cause him who is under trial to take fire in his hand, or to plunge in water, or to touch separately the heads of his children and of his wife.

" Whom the flame burneth not, whom the water rejects not from its depths, whom misfortune overtakes not speedily, his oath shall be received as undoubted.

" When the Richi Vatsa was accused by his young half-brother, who stigmatized him as the son of a Soûdra, he sware that it was false, and passing through fire proved the truth of his oath ; the fire, which attests the guilt and the innocence of all men, harmed not a hair of his head, for he spake the truth."[2]

---

[1] Sir William Jones places the composition of the Laws of Manu about 880 B. C. More recent investigators, however, have arrived at the conclusion that they are anterior to the Christian era by at least thirteen centuries.

[2] Laws of Manu, Book VIII. v. 114-116 (after Delongchamp's translation).

That this was not merely a theoretical injunction is shown by a subsequent provision (Book VIII. v. 190), enjoining the ordeal on both plaintiff and defendant, even in certain civil cases. From the immutable character of Eastern institutions, we need not be surprised to see the custom flourishing in India to the present day, and to find that, in the popular estimation, the right of plaintiff or defendant, or the guilt or innocence of the accused, is to be tested by his ability to carry red-hot iron, to plunge his hand unhurt in boiling oil, to pass through fire, to remain under water, to swallow consecrated rice, to drink water in which an idol has been immersed, and by various other forms which still preserve their hold on public veneration,[1] as many of them did within five or six centuries among our own forefathers.

The numerous points of resemblance existing between the Indian and Egyptian civilizations, which render it probable that the one was derived from the other, lead us also to presume that these superstitions were common to both races. Detailed evidence, such as we possess in the case of Hindostan, is, however, not to be expected with regard to Egypt, of which the literature has so utterly perished ; but an incident related by Herodotus shows us that the same belief existed in the land of the Pharaohs, in at least one form, and that in judicial proceedings an appeal was occasionally made to some deity, whose response had all the weight of a legal judgment, a direct interposition of the

---

[1] The *purrikeh* or ordeal is prescribed in the modern Hindoo law in all cases, civil and criminal, which cannot be settled by written or oral evidence or by oath. It is sometimes indicated for the plaintiff and sometimes for the defendant.—Gentoo Code, Halhed's Translation, chap. iii. §§ 5, 6, 9, 10 ; chap. xviii. (E. I. Company, London, 1776.) The different forms of ordeal will be found described in Gladwin's Translation of the *Ayeen Akbery*, or Institutes of the Sultan Akbar, Vol. II. pp. 496 sqq. (London, 1800.) Under English rule, however, their practical observance has been interdicted within the present generation.

18

divinity being expected as a matter of course by all parties.
King Amasis, whose reign immediately preceded the invasion of Cambyses, "is said to have been, even when a
private person, fond of drinking and jesting, and by no
means inclined to serious business; and when the means
failed him for the indulgence of his appetites, he used to go
about pilfering. Such persons as accused him of having
their property, on his denying it, used to take him to the
oracle of the place, and he was oftentimes convicted by the
oracles, and oftentimes acquitted. When, therefore, he had
come to the throne, he acted as follows: Whatever gods
had absolved him from the charge of theft, of their temples
he neither took any heed, nor contributed anything toward
their repair; neither did he frequent them nor offer sacrifices, considering them of no consequence at all, and as
having only lying responses to give. But as many as had
convicted him of the charge of theft, to them he paid the
highest respect, considering them as truly gods, and delivering authentic responses."[1]

A passing allusion only is necessary to the instances,
which will readily occur to the Biblical student, in the
Hebrew legislation and history. The bitter water by which
conjugal infidelity was revealed (*Numbers* v. 11–31), was
an ordeal pure and simple, as were likewise the special
cases of determining criminals by lot, such as that of Achan
(*Joshua* vii. 16–18) and of Jonathan (I *Samuel* xiv. 41, 42),
—precedents which were duly put forward by the monkish
defenders of the practice, when battling against the efforts
of the Papacy to abolish it.

Looking to the farthest East, we find the belief in full
force in Japan. Fire is there considered, as in India, to be
the touchstone of innocence,[2] and other superstitions, less

1 Euterpe, 174 (Cary's translation).

2 Königswarter, Études Historiques sur le Développement de la Société
Humaine, p. 203

dignified, have equal currency. The *goo*, a paper inscribed
with certain cabalistic characters, and rolled up into a
bolus, when swallowed by an accused person, is believed
to afford him no internal rest, if guilty, until he is relieved
by confession; and a beverage of water in which the *goo*
has been soaked is attended with like happy effects.[1] The
immobility of Japanese customs authorizes us to conclude that these practices have been observed from time
immemorial.

In Pegu, the same ordeals are employed as in India, and
Java and Malacca are equally well supplied.[2] Thibetan
justice has a custom of its own, which is literally even-
handed, and which, if generally used, must exert a powerful
influence in repressing litigation. Both plaintiff and defendant thrust their arms into a caldron of boiling water
containing a black and a white stone, victory being assigned
to the one who succeeds in obtaining the white.[3]

Among the crowd of fantastic legends concerning Zoro-
aster is one which, from its resemblance to the ordeal of
fire, may be regarded as indicating a tendency to the same
form of superstition among the Guebres. They relate that,
when an infant, he was seized by the magicians, who pre-
dicted his future supremacy over them, and was thrown
upon a blazing fire. The pure element refused to perform
its office, and was changed into a bath of rose-water for
the wonderful child.[4]

To some extent, the Moslems are an exception to the
general rule; and this may be attributed to the doctrine of
predestination which forms the basis of their creed, as well
as to the elevated ideas of the Supreme Being which Mahomet drew from the Bible, and which are so greatly in

[1] Collin de Plancy, Dictionnaire Infernal, pp. 255 and 305.
[2] Königswarter, op. cit. p. 202.
[3] Duclos, Mém. sur les Épreuves.
[4] Collin de Plancy, op. cit. p. 555.

advance of all the Pagan forms of belief. There is accordingly no authority in the Korán for any description of ordeal; but yet it is occasionally found among the true believers. Among some tribes of Arabs, for instance, the ordeal of red-hot iron appears in the shape of a gigantic spoon, to which, when duly heated, the accused applies his tongue, his guilt or innocence being apparent from his undergoing or escaping injury.[1] The tendency of the mind towards superstitions of this nature, in spite of the opposite teaching of religious dogmas, is likewise shown by a species of divination employed among the Turks, through which thieves are discovered by observing the marks on wax slowly melted while certain cabalistic sentences are repeated over it.[2] A more direct instance of divine interposition to guide the course of justice may be found in the ancient Turkish legend, which relates that a youth, accused of murder before Mahomet, asserted that the act was committed in self-defence. The prophet ordered the corpse to be buried, and postponed his decision to the following day. The brethren of the murdered man, still insisting on their right of vengeance, were then told that they could inflict upon the accused precisely the same wounds as those which they should find upon the body. On opening the tomb for the purpose of inspection, they returned affrighted to the tribunal and reported that they had found in it nothing but Stygian smoke and stench; whereupon Mahomet pronounced that Satan had carried off the body of the guilty man and that the accused was innocent.[3]

A similar tendency is visible in a custom prevalent in Tahiti, where in cases of theft, when the priest is applied to for the discovery of the criminal, he digs a hole in the clay floor of the house, fills it with water, and, invoking his god, stands over it with a young plantain in his hand.

[1] Königswarter, op. cit. p. 203.
[2] Collin de Plancy, s. v. *Céromancie.*
[3] Loniceri Chron. Turcic. Lib. II. cap. xvii.

The god to whom he prays is supposed to conduct the spirit of the thief over the water, and the priest recognizes the image by looking in the pool.[1]

The gross and clumsy superstitions of Africa have this element in common with the more refined religions of other races, modified only in its externals. Thus, among the Kalabarese, various ordeals are in use, of a character which reveals the rude nature of the savage. The "afia-edet-ibom" is administered with the curved fang of a snake, which is cunningly inserted under the lid and round the ball of the defendant's eye; if innocent, he is expected to eject it by rolling the eye, while, if unable to perform this feat, it is removed with a leopard's tooth, and he is condemned. The ceremony of the "afia-ibnot-idiok" is even more childish. A white and a black line are drawn on the skull of a chimpanzee, which is then held up before the accused, when an apparent attraction of the white line towards him indicates his innocence, or an inclination of the black towards him pronounces his guilt. The use of the ordeal-nut is more formidable, as it contains an active principle which is a deadly poison, manifesting its effects by frothing at the mouth, convulsions, paralysis, and speedy death. In capital cases, or even when sickness is attributed to unfriendly machinations, the "abiadiong," or sorcerer, decides who shall undergo the trial, and as the poisonous properties of the nut can be eliminated by preliminary boiling, liberality on the part of the accused is supposed to be an unfailing mode of rendering the ordeal harmless.[2]

The ordeal of red water, or infusion of "sassy bark," also prevails throughout a wide region in Western Africa. As described by Dr. Winterbottom, it is administered in the neighborhood of Sierra Leone, by requiring the accused to

[1] Ellis, Polynesian Researches, Vol. I. chap. 14.
[2] Hutchinson's Impressions of Western Africa. London, 1858.

18*

fast for the previous twelve hours, and to swallow a small quantity of rice previous to the trial. The infusion is then taken in large quantities, as much as a gallon being sometimes employed; if it produces emesia, so as to eject all of the rice, the proof of innocence is complete, but if it fails in this, or if it acts as a purgative, the accused is condemned. It has narcotic properties also, a manifestation of which is likewise fatal to the sufferer. Among some of the tribes this is determined, as described by the Rev. Mr. Wilson, by placing small sticks on the ground at distances of about eighteen inches apart, among which the patient is required to walk, a task rendered difficult by the vertiginous effects of the poison. Although death not infrequently results from the ordeal itself, without the subsequent punishment, yet the faith reposed in these trials is well expressed by Dr. Livingstone, who describes the eagerness with which they are demanded by those accused of witchcraft, confiding in their innocence, and believing that the guilty alone can suffer. When the emetic effects are depended on, the popular explanation is that the fetish enters with the draught, examines the heart of the accused, and, in cases of innocence, returns with the rice as evidence.[1]

In Madagascar, the ordeal is administered with the nut of the Tangena, the decoction of which is a deadly poison. In the persecution of the Malagasy Christians, in 1836, many of the converts were tried in this manner, and numbers of them died. It was repeated with the same effect in the persecution of 1849.[2]

Although the classical nations of antiquity were not in the habit of employing ordeals as a judicial process, during

---

[1] See an elaborate "Examination of the Toxicological Effects of Sassy-Bark," by Drs. Mitchell and Hammond, in the Proceedings of the Biological Dep. of the Acad. of Nat. Sciences, Philadelphia, 1859.

[2] Ellis's Three Visits to Madagascar, chap. I. VI.

the periods in which their laws have become known to us, still there is sufficient evidence that a belief in the efficacy of such trials existed before philosophical skepticism had reduced religion to a system of hollow observances. The various modes of divination by oracles and omens, which occupy so prominent a position in history, manifest a kindred tendency of mind, in demanding of the gods a continual interference in human affairs, at the call of any suppliant, and we are therefore prepared to recognize among the Greeks the relics of pre-existing judicial ordeals in various forms of solemn oaths, by which, under impressive ceremonies, actions were occasionally terminated, the party swearing being obliged to take the oath on the heads of his children (κατὰ τῶν παίδων), with curses on himself and his family (κατ' ἐξωλείας), or passing through fire (διὰ τοῦ πυρός).[1] The secret meaning of these rites becomes fully elucidated on comparing them with a passage from the Antigone of Sophocles, in which, the body of Polynices having been secretly carried off for burial against the commands of Creon, the guard endeavor to repel the accusation of complicity by offering to vindicate their innocence in various forms of ordeal, which bear a striking similarity to those in use throughout India, and long afterwards in medieval Europe.

> "Ready with hands to bear the red-hot iron,
>   To pass through fire, and by the gods to swear,
>   That we nor did the deed, nor do we know
>   Who counselled it, or who performed it."[2]

The water ordeal, which is not alluded to here, may, nevertheless, be considered as having its prototype in several fountains, which were held to possess special power in cases of suspected female virtue. One at Artecomium, mentioned by Eustathius, became turbid as soon as en-

---

[1] Smith, Dict. Greek and Roman Antiq. s. v. *Martyria*.
[2] Antigone, ver. 264—267.

tered by a guilty woman. Another, near Ephesus, alluded to by Achilles Tatius, was even more miraculous. The accused swore to her innocence, and entered the water, bearing suspended to her neck a tablet inscribed with the oath. If she were innocent, the water remained stationary, at the depth of the midleg; while, if she were guilty, it rose until the tablet floated. Somewhat similar to this was the Lake of Palicr in Sicily, commemorated by Stephanus Byzantinus, where the party inscribed his oath on a tablet, and committed it to the water, when if the oath were true it floated, and if false it sank.[1]

The Roman nature, sterner and less impressible than the Greek, offers less evidence of weakness in this respect, but traces of it are nevertheless to be found. The medieval *corsnæd*, or ordeal of bread, finds a prototype in a species of alphitomancy practised near Lavinium, where a sacred serpent was kept in a cave under priestly care. Women whose virtue was impeached offered to the animal cakes made by themselves, of barley and honey, and were condemned or acquitted according as the cakes were eaten or rejected.[2] The fabled powers of the *ætites*, or eagle-stone, mentioned by Dioscorides,[3] likewise remind us of the *corsnæd*, as bread in which it was placed, or food with which it was cooked, became a sure test for thieves, from their being unable to swallow it. Special instances of miraculous interposition to save the innocent from unjust condemnation may also be quoted as manifesting the same general tendency of belief. Such was the case of the vestal

[1] Eustathii de Amor. Ismenii, Lib. vii., xi.; Achill. Tatii de Amor. Clitoph. Lib. viii.; Steph. Byzant. s. v. Παλικη (apud Spelman, Gloss. p. 324). Superstitions of this nature have obtained in all ages, and these particular instances find their special modern counterpart in the fountain of Bodilis, near Landivisiau in Britanny, in which a girl when accused places the pin of her collar, her innocence or guilt being demonstrated by its floating or sinking.

[2] Collin de Plancy, op. cit. p. 31.

[3] Lib. v. cap. 161 (ap. Lindenbrog.).

Tucca, accused of incest, who demonstrated her purity by carrying water in a sieve,[1] and that of Claudia Quinta, who, under a similar charge, made good her defence by dragging a ship against the current of the Tiber, after it had run aground, and had resisted all other efforts to move it.[2] As somewhat connected with the same ideas, we may allude to the imprecations accompanying the most solemn form of oath among the Romans, known as "Jovem lapidem jurare,"[3] whether we take the ceremony, mentioned by Festus, of casting a stone from the hand, and invoking Jupiter to reject in like manner the swearer if guilty of perjury, or that described by Livy as preceding the combat between the Horatii and Curiatii, in which an animal was knocked on the head with a stone, under a somewhat similar adjuration.[4] As Christianity inculcated a closer reliance upon the divine nature than the Pagan superstitions, it is no wonder that the true religion revived occasionally the feeling which led to such experiments as those of Tucca and Claudia. St. Augustine re-

---

[1] Valer. Maxim. Lib. VIII. cap. 1.

[2] " Supplicis, alma, tuæ, genetrix fœcunda Deorum,
      Accipe sub certa conditione preces.
    Casta negor ; si tu damnas, meruisse fatebor.
      Morte luam pœnas, judice victa Dea.
    Sed si crimen abest, tu nostræ pignora vitæ
      Re dabis ; et castas casta sequere manus.
    Dixit, et exiguo funem conamine traxit," etc.
                                    Ovid. Fastorum Lib. IV. 1. 305 sqq.

This invocation to the goddess to absolve or condemn, and the manner in which the entire responsibility is thrown upon the supernal judge, give the whole transaction a striking resemblance to an established judicial form of ordeal.

[3] Quod sanctissimum jusjurandum est habitum.—Aulus Gellius, I. 21.

[4] "Si sciens fallo, tum me Diespiter salva urbe arceque bonis ejiciat, ut ego hunc lapidem." (Festus, Lib. X.; Livy, I. 24.) If we can receive as undoubted Livy's account of a similar ceremony performed by Hannibal to encourage his soldiers before the battle of Ticinus (Lib. XXI. cap. 45), we must conclude that the custom had obtained a very extended influence.

lates that at Milan a thief who swore upon some holy relics with the intention of bearing false witness was suddenly forced to confess himself the author of the crime which he had designed fastening on another; and Augustine himself, when unable to decide between two of his ecclesiastics, who mutually accused each other of revolting crime, sent them both to the shrine of St. Felix of Nola in the full expectation of a miraculous interference that should bring the truth to light.[1] There is no trace of the system, however, in the Roman jurisprudence, which, with the exception of the use of torture at the later periods, is totally in opposition to its theory. Nothing can be more contrary to the spirit in which the ordeal is conceived than the maxim of the civil law—" Accusatore non probante, reus absolvitur."

In turning to the Barbarian races from which the nations of modern Europe are descended, we are met by the question, which has been variously mooted, whether the ordeals that form so prominent a part of their jurisprudence were customs derived from remote Pagan antiquity, or whether they were inventions of the priests in the early periods of rude Christianity, to enhance their own authority, and to lead their reluctant flocks to peace and order under the influence of superstition. There would seem to be no doubt that the former is the correct opinion, and that the religious ceremonies surrounding the ordeal, as we find it judicially employed, were introduced by the Church to Christianize the pagan observances, which in this instance, as in so many others, it was judged impolitic, if not impossible to eradicate. Various traces of such institutions are faintly discernible in the darkness from which the wild tribes emerge into the twilight of history; and as they had no

---

[1] Augustin. Epist. 78 §§ 2, 3. (Ed. Benedict.)—"Ut quod homines invenire non possunt, de quolibet eorum divino judicio propaletur."

written language, it is impossible to ask more.[1] Thus an
anonymous epigram preserved in the Greek Anthology

---

[1] There has been much discussion among the learned as to whether the
barbarian dialects were written, and especially whether the Salique Law was
reduced to writing before its translation into Latin. In the dearth of testimony, it is not easy to arrive at a positive conclusion, but the weight of
evidence decidedly inclines to the negative of the question. We have the
authority of Tacitus for the assertion that letters were utterly unknown to
the Germans of his period—" Literarum secreta viri pariter ac fœminæ ignorant"—and though four or five centuries of contact with the Roman civilization may be thought to have familiarized them with the necessity of written speech, yet had it been adopted at the time of the compiling of the
Salique law it would not have been left for Charlemagne, three hundred
years later, to put into writing the heroic poems of his race, which form so
important a portion of the literature of a barbaric and warlike people.
" Barbara et antiquissima carmina, quibus veterum regum acta et bella
canebantur, et scripsisse et memoriæ mandasse. Inchoavit et grammaticam
patriæ sermonis." (Eginh. Vit. Carol. Mag. cap. xxix.) Even Charlemagne, with all his culture, could not write, and when, in advanced life, he
sought to learn the art, it was too late (Ibid. cap. xxv.)—which shows how
little the wild Saliens and Ripuarians could have thought of converting their
language into written characters. Charlemagne's efforts accomplished
nothing, for though in 842 the contemporary Count Nithard gives us the
earliest specimen of written Tudesque in the celebrated oath of Charles-le-
Chauve at Strasburg, yet, not long afterwards, Otfrid, in the preface to his
version of the Gospels, details the difficulties of his task in a manner which
shows that it was without precedent, and that he was himself obliged to
adapt the language to the exigencies of writing. Indeed, he asserts positively
that writing was not used and that no written documents existed, and he
expresses surprise that the annals of the race should have been intrusted
exclusively to foreign tongues. " Hujus enim linguæ barbaries ut est inculta
et indisciplinabilis, atque insueta capi regulari frœno grammaticæ artis, sic
etiam in multis dictis scriptu est propter literarum aut congeriem aut incog-
nitam sonoritatem difficilis. Nam, interdum tria uuu, ut puto, quærit in
sono, priores duo consonantes, ut mihi videtur, tertium vocali sono manente.
Interdum vero nec a nec e nec i neo u vocalium sonos præcanere potui, ibi
y Græcum mihi videbatur adscribi etc. . . . Lingua enim hæc velut agrestis
habetur; dum a propriis nec scriptura, nec arte aliqua ullis est temporibus ex-
polita, quippe qui nec historias suorum antecessorum, ut multæ gentes cæteræ,
commendant memoriæ, nec eorum gesta vel vitam ornant dignitatis amore.
Quodsi raro contigit, aliarum gentium lingua, id est, Latinorum vel Græco-
rum potius explanant. . . . Res mira . . . cuncta hæc in alienæ linguæ gloriam
transferre, et usam scripturæ in propria lingua non habere." (Otfrid. Liut-

informs us of a singular custom existing in the Rhine-land,
anterior to the conversion of the inhabitants, by which the
legitimacy of children was established by exposure to an
ordeal of the purest chance.

Θαρσαλέοι Κελτοὶ ποταμῷ ζηλήμονι ʹΡήνῳ, κ. τ. λ.[1]

Upon the waters of the jealous Rhine
    The savage Celts their children cast, nor own
Themselves as fathers, till the power divine
    Of the chaste river shall the truth make known.
Scarce breathed its first faint cry, the husband tears
    Away the new-born babe, and to the wave
Commits it on his shield, nor for it cares
    Till the wife-judging stream the infant save,
And prove himself the sire.   All trembling lies
    The mother, racked with anguish, knowing well
The truth, but forced to risk her cherished prize
    On the inconstant water's reckless swell.

We learn from Cassiodorus that Theodoric, towards the
close of the fifth century, sought to abolish the battle ordeal
among the Ostrogoths, whence we may conclude that the

berto Mogunt. in Schilt. Thesaur. Antiq. Teuton. I. 11–12.)   Otfrid's partiality for his native tongue is sufficiently proved by his labors as a translator,
and the scope of his general learning is shown by his references to Greek and
Hebrew, and his quotations from the Latin poets, such as Virgil, Ovid, and
Lucan.   His testimony is therefore irreproachable.

It is true that the Gothic language was employed in writing by Ulphilas in
the fourth century, and that the Malbergian glosses in Herold's text of the
Salique law preserve some fragmentary words of the ancient Frankish
speech.   It is also true that there has been high antiquity claimed for the
Scandinavian runic letters, but the balance of testimony is decidedly in
favor of the opinion that the Germanic tribes were innocent of any rudi-
ments of a written language.

[1] Anthol. Lib. IX. Ep. 125.   This charming trait of Celtic domestic manners has been called in question by some writers, but it rests on fair
authority.   Claudian evidently alludes to it as a well-known fact in the lines—

        . . . . . "Galli
Quos Rhodanus velox, Araris quos tardior ambit,
Et quos nascentes explorat gurgite Rhenus."—In Rufinum, Lib. II. l. 110.

appeal to the judgment of God was an ancestral custom of the race.[1] At an even earlier period, the Senchus Mor, or Irish law, compiled for the Brehons at the request of St. Patrick, contains unequivocal evidence of the existence of the ordeal, in a provision which grants a delay of ten days to a man condemned to undergo the test of hot water.[2] Equally convincing proof is found in the Salique Law, of which the earliest known text may safely be assumed to be coeval with the conversion of Clovis, as it contains no allusion to Christian rules such as appear in recensions made somewhat later. In this text, the ordeal of boiling water finds its place as a judicial process in regular use, as fully as in the subsequent revisions of the code.[3] In the decree of Tassilo, Duke of the Baioarians, issued in 772, there is a reference to a pre-existing custom, named *stapfsaken*, used in cases of disputed debt, which is

[1] Variarum. Lib. iii. Epist. 23, 24.

[2] Senchus Mor. I. 195. Compare Gloss, p. 199.—In an ancient Gloss on the Senchus, there is preserved a curious tradition which illustrates the belief in divine interposition, though manifested upon the judge rather than on the culprit.

"However, before the coming of Patrick there had been remarkable revelations. When the Brehons deviated from the truth of nature, there appeared blotches upon their cheeks; as first of all on the right cheek of Sen Mac Aige, whenever he pronounced a false judgment, but they disappeared again whenever he had pronounced a true judgment, &c.

"Sencha Mac Col Cluin was not wont to pass judgment until he had pondered upon it in his breast the night before. When Fachtna, his son, had passed a false judgment, if in the time of fruit, all the fruit in the territory in which it happened fell off in one night, &c.; if in time of milk, the cows refused their calves; but if he passed a true judgment, the fruit was perfect on the trees; hence he received the name of Fachtna Tulbrethach.

"Sencha Mac Aillila never pronounced a false judgment without getting three permanent blotches on his face for each judgment. Fithel had the truth of nature, so that he pronounced no false judgment. Morann never pronounced a judgment without having a chain around his neck. When he pronounced a false judgment, the chain tightened around his neck. If he pronounced a true one, it expanded down upon him."—Ibid. p. 25.

[3] Tit. liii. lvi. (First Text of Pardessus.)

19

denounced as a relic of Pagan rites,—" in verbis quibus ex
vetusta consuetudine paganorum, idolatriam reperimus,"—
and which is there altered to suit the new order of ideas,
affording an instructive example of the process to which
I have alluded.   It is evidently a kind of ordeal, as is
manifested by the expression, " Let us stretch forth our
right hands to the just judgment of God.'"   These proofs
would seem amply sufficient to demonstrate the existence
of the practice as a primitive custom of some of the Barbarian races, prior to their occupation of the Roman empire.
If more be required, it must be remembered that the records
of those wild tribes do not extend beyond the period of
their permanent settlement, when baptism and civilization
were received together, so that we cannot reasonably ask
for codes and annals at a time when each sept was rather
a tumultuous horde of freebooters than a people living
under a settled form of organized society.   Tacitus, it is
true, makes no mention of anything approaching nearer
to the Judgment of God than the various forms of rude
divination common to all superstitious savages.   It is
highly probable that to many tribes the ordeal was unknown, and that it had nowhere assumed the authority
which it afterwards acquired, when the Church found in
it a powerful instrument to enforce her authority, and to
acquire influence over the rugged nature of her indocile
converts.[2]   Indeed, we have evidence that in some cases it
was introduced, and its employment enforced, for the purpose of eradicating earlier Pagan observances; as, for
instance, when Bishop Geroldus, about the middle of the

---

[1] " Extendamus dextera nostra ad justum judicium Dei."—Decret. Tassi-
lonis Tit ii. § 7.

[2] Thus, in the laws of St. Stephen, King of Hungary, promulgated soon
after his conversion, in 1016, there is no allusion to the ordeal, while in
those of King Coloman, issued about a century later, it is freely directed as
a means of legal proof.

twelfth century, converted the Sclavonians of Mecklen-burg.[1]

Be this as it may, the custom was not long in extending itself throughout Europe. The laws of the Salien Franks we have already alluded to, and the annals of Gregory of Tours and of Fredegarius, the Merovingian Capitularies, and the various collections of Formularies, show that it was not merely a theoretical prescription, but an every day practice among them. The Ripuarian Franks were some-what more cautious, and the few references to its employ-ment which occur in their code would seem to confine its application to slaves and strangers.[2] The code of the Ala-manni makes no allusion to any form except that of the "tracta spata," or judicial duel. The code of the Baioa-rians, in its original shape, while referring constantly to the combat, seems ignorant of any other mode. The supple-mentary Decree of Tassilo, however, affords an instance, quoted above, and another which seems to show that force was sometimes necessary to carry out the decision to em-ploy it.[3] The Wisigoths, who, like their kinsmen the Ostro-goths, immediately on their settlement adapted themselves in a great degree to Roman laws and customs, for nearly two centuries had no allusion in their body of laws to any form of ordeal. It was not until 693, long after the destruc-tion of their independence in the South of France, and but little prior to their overthrow in Spain by the Saracens, that their king, Egiza, with the sanction of the Council of Toledo, issued an edict commanding the employment of the *æneum*, or ordeal of boiling water. The expressions of the

---

[1] "Et vetavit Comes ne Sclavi de cetero jurarent in arboribus, fontibus, et lapidibus ; sed offerrent criminibus pulsatos sacerdoti, ferro ac vomeribus examinandos."—Anon. Chron. Sclavic. cap. xxv. (Script. Rer. German. Septent. Lindenbrog. p. 215.)

[2] L. Ripuar. Tit. xxx. §§ 1, 2 ; Tit. xxxi. § 5.

[3] "Ut . . . . . liberi . . . . . ad eadem cogantur judicia quæ Baioarii *Urtella* dicunt."—Decret. Tassilon. Tit. ii. § 9.

law, however, warrant the conclusion that this was only
the extension of a custom previously existing, by removing
the restrictions which had prevented its application to all
questions, irrespective of their importance.[1] The Burgundian code refers more particularly to the duel, which was
the favorite form of ordeal with that race, but from the
writings of. St. Agobard we may safely assume that the
trials by hot water and by iron were in frequent use. The
primitive Saxon jurisprudence also prefers the battle ordeal;
but the other kinds are met with in the codes of the Frisians[2]
and of the Thuringians.[3] The earliest Lombard law as
compiled by Rotharis, refers only to the wager of battle;
but the additions of Liutprand, made in the eighth century,
allude to the employment of the hot-water ordeal as a
recognized procedure.[4] In England, the Britons appear to
have regarded the ordeal with much favor, as a treaty
between the Welsh and the Saxons, about the year 1000,
provides that all questions between individuals of the two
races should be settled in this manner, in the absence of a
special agreement between the parties.[5] The Anglo-Saxons
seem to have been somewhat late in adopting it; for the
dooms of the earlier princes refer exclusively to the refutation of accusations by oath with compurgators, and we
find no allusion made to the ordeal until the time of Edward the Elder, at the commencement of the tenth century,
that allusion, however, being of a nature to show that it

---

[1] " Multas cognovimus querelas, et ab ingenuis multa mala pati, credentes
in ccc. solidis quæstionem agitari. Quod nos modo per salubrem ordina-
tionem censemus, ut quamvis parva sit actio rei facta ab aliquo criminis, eum
per examinationem aquæ ferventis a judice distringendum ordinamus."—L.
Wisigoth. Lib. vi. Tit. i. § 3.

[2] L. Frision. Tit. iii. §§ 4, 5, 6.

[3] L. Anglior. et Werinor. Tit. xiv.

[4] L. Longobard. Lib. i. Tit. xxxiii. § 1.

[5] "Non stat alia lada (i. e. purgatio) de tyhla (i. e. compellatione) nisi
ordalium, inter Walos et Anglos."—Senatus-Consult. de Monticolis Waliæ
cap. ii.

was then a settled custom, and not an innovation.[1] Among
the northern races it was probably indigenous, the earliest
records of Iceland, Denmark, and Sweden exhibiting its
vigorous existence at a period anterior to their conversion
to Christianity;[2] and the same may be said of the Sclavonic tribes in Eastern Europe. In Bohemia, the laws of
Brzetislas, promulgated in 1039, make no allusion to any
other form of evidence in contested cases,[3] while in Russia
it was the final resort in all cases of murder, theft and
false accusation.[4] The Majjars placed equal reliance on
this mode of proof, as is shown by the statutes of Kings
Ladislas and Coloman, towards the end of the eleventh
century, which allude to various forms of ordeal as in
common use.[5] Scotland likewise employed it in her jurisprudence, as developed in the code known as " Regiam Majestatem Scotiæ," attributed to David I., in the first half of
the twelfth century.[6] Even the Byzantine civilization became contaminated with the prevailing custom, and various
instances of its use are related by the historians of the
Lower Empire, to a period as late as the middle of the
fourteenth century.

One cause of the general prevalence of the ordeal among
the barbarian tribes settled in the Roman provinces may
perhaps be traced to the custom, which prevailed universally, of allowing all races to retain their own jurisprudence, however socially intermingled the individuals might
be. The confusion thus produced is well set forth by St.
Agobard, when he remarks that frequently five men shall
be in close companionship, each owning obedience to a

[1] Dooms of King Edward, cap. iii. ; Laws of Edward and Guthrum, cap. ix.
[2] Saxo. Grammat. Hist. Danic. Lib. v.; Widukindi Lib. iii. c. 65.—
Grágás, Sect. vi. c. 55.
[3] Similiter de his qui homicidiis infamantur . . . . si negant, ignito ferro
sive adjurata aqua examinentur.—Annalista Saxo, ann. 1039.
[4] Rouskaïa Prawda, art. 28. (Esneaux, Hist. de Russie I. 181.)
[5] Batthyani Legg. Eccles. Hung T. I. p. 439, 454.
[6] For instance, Lib. iv. cap. iii. § 4.

different law.[1] He further states, that, under the Burgundian rules of procedure, no one was admitted to bear witness against a man of different race;[2] so that in a large
proportion of cases there could be no legal evidence attainable, and recourse was had of necessity to the judgment of
God. No doubt a similar tendency existed generally, and
the man who appealed to Heaven against the positive testimony of witnesses of different origin would be very apt to
find the court disposed to grant his request.

During the full fervor of the belief that the Divine interposition could at all times be had for the asking, almost
any form of procedure conducted under priestly observances could assume the position and influence of an ordeal. As early as 592, we find Gregory the Great alluding to a simple purgatorial oath, taken by a bishop on
the relics of St. Peter, in terms which convey evidently
the idea that the accused, if guilty, had exposed himself to
imminent danger, and that by performing the ceremony
unharmed he had sufficiently proved his innocence.[3] But
such unsubstantial refinements were not sufficient for the
vulgar, who craved the evidence of their senses, and
desired material proof to rebut material accusations. In
ordinary practice, therefore, the principal modes by which
the will of Heaven was ascertained were the ordeal of fire,
whether administered directly, or through the agency of
boiling water or red-hot iron; that of cold water; of bread
or cheese; of the Eucharist; of the cross; the lot; and the
touching of the body of the victim in cases of murder.

---

[1] Lib. adv. Legem Gundobadi, cap. iv.

[2] "Ex qua re oritur res valde absurda, ut si aliquis eorum in cœtu populi,
aut etiam in mercato publico commiserat aliquam pravitatem, non coar-
guatur testibus."—Ibid. cap. vi.

[3] "Quibus (sacramentis) præstitis, magna sumus exultatione gavisi, quod
hujuscemodi experimento innocentia ejus evidenter enituit."—Can. Habet
hoc proprium, caus. ii. quæst. 5.

Some of these, it will be seen, required a miraculous interposition to save the accused, others to condemn; some depended altogether on volition, others on the purest chance; while others, again, derived their power from the influence exerted on the mind of the patient. They were all accompanied with solemn religious observances, and the most impressive ceremonies of the Church were lavishly employed to give authority to the resultant decisions, and to impress on the minds of all the directness of the interference which was expected of the Creator.

The ordeal of boiling water (*æneum, judicium aquæ ferventis, cacabus, caldaria*) is probably the oldest form in which the application of fire was judicially administered in Europe as a mode of proof. It is the one usually referred to in the most ancient texts of laws, and its universal adoption denotes a very high antiquity. It is particularly recommended by Hincmar as combining the elements of water and of fire: the one representing the deluge—the judgment inflicted on the wicked of old; the other authorized by the fiery doom of the future—the day of judgment.[1] A caldron of water was brought to the boiling-point, and the accused was obliged with his naked hand to find a small stone or ring thrown into it; sometimes the latter portion was omitted, and the hand was simply inserted, in trivial cases to the wrist, in crimes of magnitude to the elbow; the former being termed the single, the latter the triple ordeal;[2] or, again, the stone was employed, suspended by a string, and the severity of the trial was regulated by the length of the line, a palm's breadth being counted as single, and the distance to the elbow as triple.[3] A good

---

[1] Quapropter fieri aquam ignitam ad hæc duo copulata in unum indaganda judicia, illud videlicet quod jam per aquam factum est, et illud quod per ignem fiendum est . . . . in quibus sancti liberantur illæsi, et reprobi punientur addicti.—Hincmar de Divort. Lothar. Interrog. VI.

[2] Dooms of King Æthelstan, iv. cap. 7.

[3] Adjuratio ferri vel aquæ ferventis (Baluz. II. 655.)

example of the process, in all its details, is furnished us by
Gregory of Tours, who relates that an Arian priest and
a Catholic deacon, disputing about their respective tenets,
and being unable to convince each other, the latter proposed to refer the subject to the decision of the *æneum*,
and the offer was accepted. Next morning the deacon's
enthusiasm cooled, and he mingled his matins with precautions of a less spiritual nature, by bathing his arm in oil,
and anointing it with protective unguents. The populace
assembled to witness the exhibition, the fire was lighted,
the caldron boiled furiously, and a little ring thrown into
it was whirled around like a straw in a tornado, when the
deacon politely invited his adversary to make the trial first.
This was declined, on the ground that precedence belonged
to the challenger, and with no little misgiving the deacon
proceeded to roll up his sleeve, when the Arian, observing
the precautions that had been taken, exclaimed that he had
been using magic arts, and that the trial would amount to
nothing. At this critical juncture, when the honor of the
orthodox faith was trembling in the balance, a stranger
stepped forward—a Catholic priest named Jacintus, from
Ravenna—and offered to undergo the experiment. Plung-
ing his arm into the bubbling caldron, he was two hours
in capturing the ring, which eluded his grasp in its
fantastic gyrations; but finally, holding it up in triumph
to the admiring spectators, he declared that the water felt
cold at the bottom, with an agreeable warmth at the top.
Fired by the example, the unhappy Arian boldly thrust
in his arm; but the falseness of his cause belied the confidence of its rash supporter, and in a moment the flesh was
boiled off the bones up to the elbow.[1]

This was a volunteer experiment. As a means of judicial
investigation, the process was surrounded with all the solem-

[1] De Gloria Martyrum Lib. i. cap. 81.—Injecta manu, protinus usque ad
ipsa ossium internodia caro liquefacta defluxit.

nity which the most venerated rites of the Church could impart. Fasting and prayer were enjoined for three days previous, and the ceremony commenced with special prayers and adjurations, introduced for the purpose into the litany, and recited by the officiating priests; mass was celebrated, and the accused was required to partake of the sacrament under the fearful adjuration, "This body and blood of our Lord Jesus Christ be to thee this day a manifestation!" This was followed by an exorcism of the water, of which numerous formulas are on record, varying in detail, but all presenting a vivid picture of robust faith and self-confident ignorance. A single specimen will suffice.

"O creature of water, I adjure thee by the living God, by the holy God who in the beginning separated thee from the dry land; I adjure thee by the living God wno led thee from the fountain of Paradise, and in four rivers commanded thee to encompass the world; I adjure thee by Him who in Cana of Galilee by His will changed thee to wine, who trod on thee with His holy feet, who gave thee the name Siloa; I adjure thee by the God who in thee cleansed Naaman, the Syrian, of his leprosy;—saying, O holy water, O blessed water, water which washest the dust and sins of the world, I adjure thee by the living God that thou shalt show thyself pure, nor retain any false image, but shalt be exorcised water, to make manifest and reveal and bring to naught all falsehood, and to make manifest and bring to light all truth; so that he who shall place his hand in thee, if his cause be just and true, shall receive no hurt; but if he be perjured, let his hand be burned with fire, that all men may know the power of our Lord Jesus Christ, who will come, with the Holy Ghost, to judge with fire the quick and the dead, and the world! Amen!"[1]

After the experiment had taken place, the hand was carefully enveloped in a cloth, sealed with the signet of the judge, and three days afterwards it was unwrapped, when

[1] Formulæ Exorcismorum, Baluz. II. 639 sqq. Various other formulas are given by Baluze, Spelman, Muratori, Goldast, and other collectors, all manifesting the same unconscious irreverence.

the guilt or innocence of the party was announced by the condition of the member.[1]

The justification of this mode of procedure by its most able defender, Hincmar, Archbishop of Rheims, is similar in spirit to this form of adjuration. King Lothair, great-grandson of Charlemagne, desiring to get rid of his wife, Teutberga, accused her of the foulest incest, and forced her to a confession, which she afterwards recanted, proving her innocence by undergoing the ordeal of hot water by proxy. Lothair, nevertheless, married his concubine, Waldrada, and for ten years the whole of Europe was occupied with the disgusting details of the quarrel, council after council assembling to consider the subject, and the thunders of Rome being freely employed. Hincmar, the most conspicuous ecclesiastic of his day, stood boldly forth in defence of the unhappy queen, and in his treatise " De Divortio Lotharii et Teutbergæ," he was led to justify the use of ordeals of all kinds. The species of reasoning which was deemed conclusive in the ninth century may be appreciated from his arguments in favor of the *æneum*, " Because in boiling water the guilty are scalded and the innocent are unhurt, because Lot escaped unharmed from the fire of Sodom, and the future fire which will precede the terrible Judge will be harmless to the Saints, and will burn the wicked as in the Babylonian furnace of old."[2]

In the Life of St. Athewold is recorded a miracle, which, though not judicial, yet, from its description by a contemporary, affords an insight into the credulous faith which intrusted the most important interests to decisions of this nature. The holy saint, while Abbot of Abingdon, to test

---

[1] Doom concerning hot iron and water (Laws of Æthelstan, Thorpe, I. 226) ; Baluze, II. 644.

[2] " Quia in aqua ignita coquuntur culpabiles et innoxii liberantur incocti, quia de igne Sodomitico Lot justus evasit inustus, et futurus ignis qui præibit terribilem judicem, Sanctis erit innocuus et scelestos aduret, ut olim Babylonica fornax, quæ pueros omnino non contigit."—Interrog. vi.

the obedience of Elfstan the cook of the Monastery, ordered him to extract with his hand a piece of meat from the bottom of a caldron in which the conventual dinner was boiling. Without hesitation the monk plunged his hand into the seething mass and unhurt presented the desired morsel to his wondering superior. Faith such as this could not go unrewarded, and Elfstan, from his humble station, rose to the episcopal seat of Winchester.[1]

This form of trial was in use among all the races in whose legislation the *purgatio vulgaris* found place. It is the only mode alluded to in the Salique Law, from the primitive text to the amended code of Charlemagne.[2] The same may be said of the Wisigoths, as we have already seen; while the codes of the Frisians, the Anglo-Saxons, and the Lombards, all refer cases to its decision.[3] In Iceland, it was employed from the earliest times;[4] in the primitive jurisprudence of Russia its use was enjoined in cases of minor importance,[5] and it continued in vogue throughout Europe until the general discredit attached to this mode of judgment led to the gradual abandonment of the ordeal as a legal process. It is among the forms enumerated in the sweeping condemnation of the whole system, in 1215, by Innocent III. in the Fourth Council of Lateran; but even subsequently we find it prescribed in certain cases by the municipal laws in force throughout the whole of Northern and Southern Germany,[6] and as late as 1282 it is specified in a charter of Gaston of Béarn, conferring on a

---

[1] Vit. S. Athewoldi c. x. (Chron. Abingd. II. 259.)

[2] First text of Pardessus, Tit. liii., lvi. ; MS. Guelferbyt. Tit. xiv., xvi.; L. Emend. Tit. lv., lix.

[3] L. Frision. Tit. iii. ; L. Æthelredi iv. § 6 ; L. Lombard. Lib. i. Tit. xxxiii. § 1.

[4] Grágás, Sect. vi. cap. 55.

[5] Rouskaïa Prawda, Art. 28.

[6] Jur. Prov. Saxon. Lib. i. Art. 39 ; Jur. Provin. Alaman. cap. xxxvii. §§ 15, 16.

church the privilege of holding ordeals.[1] At a later date,
indeed, it was sometimes administered in a different and
more serious form, the accused being expected to swallow
the boiling water. I have met with no instances recorded
of this, but repeated allusions to it by Rickius show that
it could not have been unusual.[2]

The modern Hindoo variety of this ordeal consists in
casting a piece of gold into a vessel of boiling *ghee* or
sesame oil, of a specified size and depth. If the person to
be tried can extract it between his finger and thumb, without scalding himself, he is pronounced victorious.[3] Of
course, under the influence of English rule, this and all
other ordeals are legally obsolete, but the popular belief in
them is not easily eradicated. As late as 1867 the Bom-
bay *Gazette* records a case occurring at Jamnuggur, when a
camel-driver named Chakee Soomar, under whose charge a
considerable sum of money was lost, was exposed by a
local official to the ordeal of boiling oil. The authorities,
however, took prompt measures to punish this act of
cruelty. The "karbharee" who ordered it escaped chastisement by opportunely dying, but the owner of the trea-
sure, who had urged the trial, was condemned to pay to the
camel-driver a pension of 100 rupees during life. In 1868,
the Madras *Times* chronicled an attempt to revive the
practice among the Brahmins of Travancore. About thirty
years ago it was abolished by the British authorities, but
previous to that time it was performed by placing a small
silver ball in a brazen vessel eight inches deep, filled with
boiling ghee. After various religious ceremonies, the accused plunged in his hand, and sometimes was obliged to
repeat the attempt several times before he could bring out
the ball. The hand was then wrapped up in tender palm

---

[1] Du Cange.   [2] Defens. Probæ Aquæ Frigid. §§ 167, 169, &c.
[3] Ayeen Akbery, II. 498. This work was written about the year 1600 by
Abulfazel, vizier of the Emperor Akbar. Gladwin's Translation was published under the auspices of the East India Company in 1800.

leaves and examined after an interval of three days. In 1866 some Brahmins in danger of losing caste endeavored to regain their position by obtaining permission to undergo a modification of this trial, substituting cold oil for boiling ghee. The authorities made no objection to this, but the holy society refused to consider it a valid purgation.

Occasionally heaven interposed to reverse the ordinary form of the hot water ordeal. D'Achery quotes from a contemporary MS. life of the holy Ponce, Abbot of Andaone near Avignon, a miracle which relates that one morning after mass, as he was about to cross the Rhone he met two men quarrelling over a ploughshare, which, after being lost for several days, had been found buried in the ground, and which each accused the other of having purloined and hidden. As the question was impenetrable to human wisdom, Ponce intervened and told them to place the ploughshare in the water of the river, within easy reach. Then, making over it the sign of the cross, he ordered the disputant who was most suspected to lift it out of the river. The man accordingly plunged his arm into the stream only to withdraw it, exclaiming that the water was boiling, and showed his hand fearfully scalded, thus affording the most satisfactory evidence of his guilt.[1] Similar to this was the incident which drove the holy St. Gengulphus from the world. While yet a warrior and favorite of King Pepin, during his travels in Italy he was attracted by a way-side fountain, and bought it from the owner, who imagined that it could not be removed from his possessions. On his return to France, Gengulphus drove his staff into the ground near his house, in a convenient place, and on its being withdrawn next day, the obedient stream, which had followed him from Italy, burst forth. He soon learned that during his absence his wife had proved unfaithful to him with a priest, and desiring to test her innocence, he

---

[1] D'Achery, Not. 119 ad Opp. Guibert. Noviogent.

20

took her to the fountain and told her that she could disprove the reports against her by picking up a hair which
lay at the bottom of the pool. She boldly did this, but on
withdrawing her hand it was fearfully scalded, the skin
and flesh hanging in strips from her finger ends. He pardoned her and retired from the world, but it is melancholy
to add that she took her revenge by inciting her paramour
to murder him.[1]

The trial by red-hot iron (*judicium ferri, juise*) was in
use from a very early period, and became one of the favorite
modes of determining disputed questions. It was administered in two essentially different forms. The one (*vomeres
igniti, examen pedale*) consisted in laying on the ground at
certain distances six, nine, or in some cases twelve, red-hot
ploughshares, among which the accused walked barefooted,
sometimes blindfolded, when it became an ordeal of pure
chance, and sometimes compelled to press each iron with
his naked feet.[2] The other and more usual form obliged
the patient to carry in his hand for a certain distance,
usually nine feet, a piece of red-hot iron, the weight of
which was determined by law and varied with the importance of the question at issue or the magnitude of the
alleged crime.[3] The hand was then wrapped up and sealed,

[1] Pet. Cantor. Verb. Abbrev. Not. in cap. lxxviii. (Migne's Patrol. T.
205, p. 471.)

[2] " Si titubaverit, si singulos vomeres pleno pede non presserit, si quantu-
lumcunque læsa fuerit, sententia proferatur."—Annal. Winton. Eccles.
(Du Cange, s. v. *Vomeres.*) Six is the number of ploughshares specified in
the celebrated trial of St. Cunigunda, wife of the emperor St. Henry II.—
Mag. Chron. Belgic.

[3] Thus, among the Anglo-Saxons, in the "simple ordeal" the iron weighed
one pound, in the "triple ordeal" three pounds. The latter is prescribed
for incendiaries and "morth-slayers" (secret murderers), Æthelstan, iv. § 6 ;
—for false coining, Ethelred, iii. § 7 ;—for plotting against the king's life,
Ethelred, v. § 30, and Cnut, Secular. § 58—while at a later period, in the
collection known as the Laws of Henry I., we find it extended to cases of
theft, robbery, arson, and felonies in general, Cap. lxvi. § 9. In Spain, the
iron had no definite weight, but was a palm and two fingers in length, with

and three days afterwards the decision was rendered in accordance with its condition.[1] These proceedings were accompanied by the same solemn observances which have been already described, the iron itself was duly exorcised, and the intervention of God was invoked in the name of all the manifestations of Divine clemency or wrath by the agency of fire—Shadrach, Meshach, and Abednego, the burning bush of Horeb, the destruction of Sodom, and the day of judgment.[2] Occasionally, when several criminals were examined together, the same piece of heated iron was borne by them successively, giving a manifest advantage to the last one, who had to endure a temperature considerably less than his companions.[3]

So, in the form ordinarily in use throughout modern India, the patient bathes and performs certain religious ceremonies. After rubbing his hands with rice bran, seven green Peepul leaves are placed on the extended palms and bound round seven times with raw silk. A red-hot iron of a certain weight is then placed on his hands, and with this he has to walk across seven concentric circles, each with a radius sixteen fingers' breadth larger than the preceding. If this be accomplished without burning the hands, he gains his cause.[4]

In the earlier periods, the burning iron was reserved for

four feet, high enough to enable the criminal to lift it conveniently (Fuero de Baeça, *ap.* Villadiego, Fuero Juzgo, fol. 317*a*). The episcopal benediction was necessary to consecrate the iron to its judicial use. A charter of 1082 shows that the Abbey of Fontanelle in Normandy had one of approved sanctity, which, through the ignorance of a monk, was applied to other purposes. The Abbot thereupon asked the Archbishop of Rouen to consecrate another, and before the latter would consent, the institution had to prove its right to administer the ordeal.—Du Cange, s. v., *Ferrum candens.*

[1] Laws of Æthelstan, iv. § 7.—Adjuratio ferri vel aquæ ferventis, Baluz. II. 656.—Fuero de Baeça (ubi sup.)

[2] For instance, see various forms of exorcism given by Baluze, II. 651–654. Also Dom Gerbert (Patrologiæ, T. 138, p. 1127) ; Goldast. Alamann. Antiquitat. T. II. p. 150 (Ed. Senckenberg.)

[3] Petri Cantor. Verb. Abbreviat. cap. lxxviii. (Patrol. ccv. 233.)

[4] Ayeen Akbery, II. 497.

cases of peculiar atrocity. Thus we find it prescribed by
Charlemagne in accusations of parricide;[1] the Council of
Risbach in 799 directed its use in cases of sorcery and
witchcraft;[2] and among the Thuringians it was ordered for
women suspected of poisoning or otherwise murdering
their husbands[3]—a crime visited with peculiar severity in
almost all codes. Subsequently, however, it became rather
an aristocratic procedure, as contradistinguished from
the water ordeals, as stated by Horne, a legal writer of the
reign of Edward II.[4] This nevertheless was not universal,
for both kinds were employed indiscriminately by the
Anglo-Saxons,[5] and at a later period throughout Germany;[6]
while in the Assises de Jerusalem the hot iron is the only
form alluded to as employed in the *roturier* courts;[7] in the
laws of Nieuport, granted by Philip of Alsace in 1163, it is
prescribed as a plebeian ordeal;[8] about the same period, in
the military laws enacted by Frederic Barbarossa during his
second Italian expedition, it appears as a servile ordeal;[9]
and as early as 848 the Council of Mainz indicates it especially for slaves.[10] In the Russian law of the eleventh cen-

---

[1] Capit. Carol. Mag. ii. Ann. 803, cap. 5.

[2] Concil. Risbach. can. ix. (Hartzheim Concil. German. II. 692.)

[3] L. Anglior. et Werinor. Tit. xiv.

[4] Après les serements des parties soloit lon garder la partie, et luy porter
a la maine une piece de fer flambant sil fuit frank home, ou de mettre le
main ou la pié en eaw boillant s'il ne fuit frank.—Myrror of Justice, cap.
iii. sect. 23.

[5] Laws of Æthelred. iv. § 6—where the accuser had the right to select the
mode in which the ordeal should be administered.

[6] The Jus Provin. Alaman. (Cap. xxxvii. §§ 15, 16; Cap. clxxxvi. §§ 4,
6, 7; Cap. ccclxxiv.) allows thieves and other malefactors to select the ordeal
they prefer. The Jus Provin. Saxon. (Lib. i. Art. 39) affords them in addition the privilege of the duel.

[7] Baisse Court, Cap. 132, 261, 279, 280, etc.

[8] Lesbroussart's Oudegherst, II. 707.

[9] Radevic. de Reb. Frid. Lib. i. cap. xxvi.

[10] "Si Presbyterum occidit . . . si liber est, cum xii. juret; si autem
servus, per xii. vomeres ferventes se expurget." Concil. Mogunt. ann. 848,
can. xxiv. That of Tribur, however, in 895, prescribes it for men of rank,
"fidelis libertate notabilis."—Concil. Tribur. c. xxii.

tury, it is ordered in all cases where the matter at stake
amounts to more than half a *grivna* of gold, while the
water ordeal is reserved for matters of less importance.[1]
Notwithstanding this, we find it to have been the mode
usually selected by persons of rank when compelled to
throw themselves upon the judgment of God. The Empress Richarda, wife of Charles-le-Gros, accused in 887 of
adultery with Bishop Liutward, offered to prove her innocence either by the judicial combat or the red-hot iron.[2]
So when the Emperor St. Henry II. indulged in unworthy
doubts of the purity of his virgin-wife St. Cunigunda, she
eagerly appealed to the judgment of God and established
her innocence by treading unharmed the burning ploughshares.[3] The tragical tradition of Mary, wife of the Third
Otho, contains a similar example, with the somewhat unusual variation of an accuser undergoing an ordeal to prove
a charge. The empress, hurried away by a sudden and un-
conquerable passion for Amula, Count of Modena, in 996,
repeated in all its details the story of Potiphar's wife. The
unhappy count, unceremoniously condemned to lose his
head, asserted his innocence to his wife, and entreated her
to clear his reputation. He was executed, and the countess,
seeking an audience of the emperor, disproved the calumny
by carrying unharmed the red-hot iron, when Otho, convinced of his rashness by this triumphant vindication,
immediately repaired his injustice by consigning his empress
to the stake.[4] When Edward the Confessor, who entertained

---

[1] Rouskaïa Prawda, Art. 28.

[2] Regino. ann. 887.—Annales Metenses.

[3] Vit. S. Kunegundæ cap. 2. (Ludewig Script. Rer. German. I. 346–7.)

[4] Gotfridi Viterbiensis Pars xvii., " De Tertio Othone Imperatore." Siff-
ridi Epit. Lib. i. ann. 998. Ricobaldi Hist. Impp. sub Ottone III.—The
story is not mentioned by any contemporary authorities, and Muratori has
well exposed its improbability (Annali d'Italia, ann. 996); although he
had on a previous occasion argued in favor of its authenticity (Antiq. Ital.
Dissert. 38). In convicting the empress of calumny, the Countess of Modena
appeared as an accuser, making good the charge by the ordeal : but if we

a not unreasonable dislike for his mother Emma, listened
eagerly to the accusation of her criminal intimacy with
Alwyn, Bishop of Winchester, she was condemned to
undergo the ordeal of the burning shares, and walking over
them barefooted and unharmed, she established beyond per-
adventure the falsehood of the charge.[1] Robert Curthose,
son of William the Conqueror, while in exile during his
youthful rebellion against his father, formed an intimacy
with a pretty girl. Years afterwards, when he was Duke of
Normandy, she presented herself before him with two likely
youths, whom she asserted to be pledges of his former affection. Robert was incredulous; but the mother, carrying
unhurt the red-hot iron, forced him to forego his doubts,
and to acknowledge the paternity of the boys, whom he
thenceforth adopted.[2] Indeed this was the legal form of
proof in cases of disputed paternity established by the
legislation of Iceland at this period,[3] and in that of Spain
a century later.[4] Remy, Bishop of Dorchester, when ac-

---

look upon her as simply vindicating her husband's character, the case enters
into the ordinary course of such affairs. Indeed, among the Anglo-Saxons,
there was a special provision by which the friends of an executed criminal
might clear his reputation by undergoing the triple ordeal, after depositing
pledges, to be forfeited in case of defeat.—Ethelred, iii. § 6.

[1] Rapin, Hist. d'Angleterre, I. 123—Giles states (note to William of Malmesbury, ann. 1043) that Richard of Devizes is the earliest authority for this
story.

[2] Order. Vitalis Lib. x. cap. 13.   [3] Grágás, Sect. vi. cap. 45.

[4] "E si alguna dixiere que preñada es dalguno, y el varon no la creyere,
prendo fierro caliente ; e si quemada fuere, non sea creyda, mas si sana esca-
pare del fierro, de el fijo al padre, e criel assi como fuero es."—Fuero de
Baeça (Villadiego, Fuero Juzgo, fol. 317 a).

An important question of the same kind was settled in the tenth century
by a direct appeal to Heaven, through which the rights of Ugo, Marquis
of Tuscany, were determined. His father Uberto, incurring the enmity of
Otho the Great, fled to Pannonia, whence returning after a long exile,
he found his wife Willa with a boy, whom he refused to acknowledge.
After much parleying, the delicate question was thus settled : A large
assembly, principally of ecclesiastics, was convened ; Uberto sat undistin-
guished among the crowd ; the boy, who had never seen him, was placed in

cused of treason against William the Conqueror, was cleared
by the devotion of a follower, who underwent the ordeal
of hot iron.[1] In 1143, Henry I., Archbishop of Mainz, ordered
its employment, and administered it himself, in a controversy between the Abbey of Gerode and the Counts of
Hirschberg. In the special charter issued to the abbey
attesting the decision of the trial, it is recorded that the
hand of the ecclesiastical champion was not only uninjured
by the fiery metal, but was positively benefited by it.[2]
About the same period, Centulla IV. of Béarn caused it to
be employed in a dispute with the Bishop of Lescar concerning the fine paid for the murder of a priest, the ecclesiastic,
as usual, being victorious.[3] But perhaps the instance of
this ordeal most notable in its results was that by which
Bishop Poppo, in 962, succeeded in convincing and converting the Pagan Danes. The worthy missionary, dining with
King Harold Blaatand, denounced, with more zeal than
discretion, the indigenous deities as lying devils. The king
dared him to prove his faith in his God, and on his assent-
ing, caused next morning an immense piece of iron to be
duly heated, which the undaunted Poppo grasped and carried round to the satisfaction of the royal circle, displaying
his hand unscathed by the glowing mass. The miracle was
sufficient, and Denmark thenceforth becomes an integral
portion of Christendom.[4] The most miraculous example of

the centre, and prayers were offered by all present that he should be led by
Divine instinct to his father. Either the prayers were answered, or his
training had been good, for he singled out Uberto without hesitation, and
rushed to his arms; the cautious parent could indulge no longer in unworthy
doubts, and Ugo became the most powerful prince of Italy (Pet. Damian.
Opusc. LVII. Diss. ii. c. 3, 4).

[1] Roger of Wendover, Ann. 1085.

[2] Quod ferrum manum portantis non solum non combussit, sed, ut videbatur, postmodum saniorem reddidit.—Gudeni Cod. Diplom. Mogunt. T. I.
No. liii.

[3] Mazure et Hatoulet, Fors de Béarn, p. xxxviii.

[4] Widukindi Lib. III. cap. 65.—Sigebert. Gemblac. Ann 966.—Dithmari
Chron. Lib. II. cap. viii.—Saxo. Grammat. Hist. Danic. Lib. x.

this form of ordeal, however, was one by which the holy Suidger, Bishop of Munster, reversed the usual process. Suspecting his chamberlain of the theft of a cap, which was stoutly denied, he ordered the man to pick up a knife lying on the table, having mentally exorcised it. The cold metal burned the culprit's hands, as though it were red hot, and he forthwith confessed his guilt.[1]

No form of ordeal was more thoroughly introduced throughout the whole extent of Europe. From Spain to Constantinople, and from Scandinavia to Naples, it was appealed to with confidence as an unfailing mode of ascertaining the will of Heaven. The term "judicium," indeed, was at length understood to mean an ordeal, and generally that of hot iron, and in its barbarized form, "juise," may almost always be considered to indicate this particular kind. In the code of the Frankish kingdoms of the East, it is the only mode alluded to, except the duel, and it there retained its legal authority long after it had become obsolete elsewhere. The Assises de Jerusalem were in force in the Venetian colonies until the sixteenth century, and the manuscript preserved officially in the archives of Venice, described by Morelli as written in 1436, retains the primitive directions for the employment of the *juise*.[2] Even the Venetian translation, commenced in 1531, and finished in 1536, is equally scrupulous, although an act of the Council of Ten, April 10, 1535, shows that these customs had fallen into desuetude and had been formally abolished.[3]

This ordeal even became partially naturalized among the Greeks, probably as a result of the Latin domination at Constantinople. In the middle of the thirteenth century, the Emperor Theodore Lascaris demanded that Michael Paleologus, who afterwards wore the imperial crown,

---

[1] Annalista Saxo, ann. 993.

[2] This text is given by Kausler, Stuttgard, 1839, together with an older one compiled for the lower court of Nicosia.

[3] Pardessus, Us et Coutumes de la Mer, I. 268 sqq.

should clear himself of an accusation in this manner; but the Archbishop of Philadelphia, on being appealed to, pronounced that it was a custom of the barbarians, condemned by the canons, and not to be employed except by the special order of the emperor.[1] Yet George Pachymere speaks of the custom as one not uncommon in his youth, and he describes at some length the ceremonies with which it was performed.[2]

In Europe, even as late as 1310, in the proceedings against the Order of the Templars, at Mainz, Count Frederic, the master preceptor of the Rhenish provinces, offered to substantiate his denial of the accusations by carrying the red-hot iron.[3] Perhaps one of the latest instances of its actual employment was that which occurred in Modena in 1329, in a dispute between the German soldiers of Louis of Bavaria and the citizens. The Germans offered to settle the question by carrying a red-hot bar; but when the townsfolks themselves accomplished the feat, and triumphantly showed that no burn had been inflicted, the Germans denied the proof, and asserted that magic had been employed.[4]

The ordeal of fire was sometimes administered directly, without the intervention of water or of iron; and in this, its simplest form, it may be considered the origin of the proverbial expression, "J'en mettrois la main au feu," as an affirmation of positive belief,[5] showing how thoroughly

---

[1] Du Cange, s. v. *Ferrum candens.*

[2] Pachymeri Hist. Mich. Palæol. Lib. I. cap. xii.

[3] Et super hoc paratus esset experientiam subire et ferrum ardens portare. —Raynouard, Monuments relatifs à la Condamn. des Chev. du Temple, p. 269.

[4] Bonif. de Morano Chron. Mutinense.—*ap.* Muratori Antiq. Ital. Diss. 38.

[5] Thus Rabelais, "en mon aduiz elle est pucelle, toutesfoys ie nen vouldroys mettre mon doigt on feu" (Pantagruel, Lib. II. chap. xv.) : and the Epist. Obscur. Virorum (P. II. Epist. 1) "Quamvis M. Bernhardus diceret, quod vellet disputare ad ignem quod hæc est opinio vestra."

the whole system engrained itself in the popular mind. The earliest legal allusion to it occurs in the code of the Ripuarian Franks, where it is prescribed as applicable to slaves and strangers, in some cases of doubt.[1] From the phraseology of these passages, we may conclude that it was then administered by placing the hand of the accused in a fire. Subsequently, however, it was conducted on a larger and more impressive scale; huge pyres were built, and the individual undergoing the trial literally walked through the flames. The celebrated Petrus Igneus gained his surname and reputation by an exploit of this kind, which attracted great attention in its day. Pietro di Pavia, Bishop of Florence, unpopular with the citizens, but protected by Godfrey, Duke of Tuscany, was accused of simony and heresy. Being acquitted by the Council of Rome, in 1063, and the offer of his accusers to prove his guilt by the ordeal of fire being refused, he endeavored to put down his adversaries by tyranny and oppression. Great disturbances resulted, and at length, in 1067, the monks of Vallombrosa, who had borne a leading part in denouncing the Bishop, and who had suffered severely in consequence (the episcopal troops having burned the monastery of S. Salvio and slaughtered the cenobites), resolved to decide the question by the ordeal, incited thereto by no less than three thousand enthusiastic Florentines, who assembled there for the purpose. Pietro Aldobrandini, a monk of Vallombrosa, urged by his superior, the holy S. Giovanni Gualberto, offered himself to undergo the trial.

---

[1] Quodsi servus in ignem manum miserit, et læsam tulerit, etc.—·Tit. xxx. Cap. i.; also Tit. xxxi. If we may credit. Cedrenus (Compend. Histor. Ann. 16 Anastasii), as early as the year 507, under the Emperor Anastasius, a Catholic bishop, who had been worsted in a theological dispute with an Arian, vindicated his tenets by standing in the midst of a blazing bonfire, and thence addressing an admiring crowd; but Cedrenus being a compiler of the eleventh century, and zealous in his orthodoxy, the incident can hardly be thought to possess much importance except as illustrating the age of the writer, not that attributed to the occurrence.

After imposing religious ceremonies, he walked slowly between two piles of blazing wood, ten feet long, five feet wide, and four and a half feet high, the passage between them being six feet wide and covered with an inch or two of glowing coals. The violence of the flames agitated his dress and hair, but he emerged without hurt, even the hair on his legs being unsinged, barelegged and barefooted though he was. Desiring to return through the pyre, he was prevented by the admiring crowd, who rushed around him in triumph, kissing his feet and garments, and endangering his life in their transports, until he was rescued by his fellow monks. A formal statement of the facts was sent to Rome by the Florentines, the Papal court gave way, and the bishop was deposed; while the monk who had given so striking a proof of his steadfast faith was marked for promotion, and eventually died Cardinal of Albano.[1] An example of a similar nature occurred in Milan, in 1103, when the Archbishop Grossolano was accused of simony by a priest named Liutprand, who, having no proof to sustain his charge, offered the ordeal of fire. All the money he could raise, he expended in procuring fuel, and when all was ready the partisans of the archbishop attacked the preparations and carried off the wood. The populace, deprived of the promised exhibition, grew turbulent, and Grossolano was obliged not only to assent to the trial, but to join the authorities in providing the necessary materials. In the Piazza di S. Ambrogio two piles were accordingly built, each ten cubits long, by four cubits in height and width, with a gangway between them of a cubit and a half. As the undaunted priest entered the blazing mass, the flames divided before him, and closed as he passed, allowing him to emerge in safety, although with two slight injuries, one a burn on the hand, received while sprinkling the fire before entering, the other on the foot, which he attributed to a kick from a

---

[1] Vit. S. Johannis Gualberti c. lx.-lxiv.

horse in the crowd that awaited his exit. The evidence
was accepted as conclusive by the people, and Grossolano
was obliged to retire to Rome. Pascal II., however, received him graciously, and the Milanese suffragans disap-
proved of the summary conviction of their metropolitan,
to which they were probably all equally liable. The injuries received by Liutprand were exaggerated, a tumult was
excited in Milan, the priest was forced to seek safety in
flight, and Grossolano was restored.[1]

But the experiment was not always so successful for the
rash enthusiast. In 1098, during the first crusade, after
the capture of Antioch, when the Christians were in turn
besieged in that city, and, sorely pressed and famine-struck,
were well-nigh reduced to despair, an ignorant peasant named
Peter Bartholomew, a follower of Raymond of Toulouse,
announced a series of visions in which St. Andrew and the
Saviour had revealed to him that the lance which pierced
the side of Christ lay hidden in the church of St. Peter.
After several men had dug in the spot indicated, from
morning until night, without success, Peter leaped into the
trench, and by a few well-directed strokes of his mattock
exhumed the priceless relic, which he presented to Count
Raymond. Cheered by this, and by various other manifestations of Divine assistance, the Christians gained heart,
and defeated the Infidels with immense slaughter. Peter
became a man of mark, and had fresh visions on all important conjunctures. Amid the jealousies and dissensions
which raged among the Frankish chiefs, the possession of
the holy lance vastly increased Raymond's importance, and
rival princes were found to assert that it was merely a rusty
Arab weapon, hidden for the occasion, and wholly unde-
serving the veneration of which it was the object. At
length, after some months, during the leisure of the siege

---

[1] Landulph. Jun. Hist. Mediol. cap. ix., x., xi. (Rer Ital. Script. T. V.)
—Muratori, Annal. Ann. 1103.

of Archas, the principal ecclesiastics in the camp investigated the matter, and Peter, to silence the doubts expressed as to his veracity, offered to vindicate the identity of the relic by the fiery ordeal. He was taken at his word, and after three days allowed for fasting and prayer, a pile of dry olive-branches was made, fourteen feet long and four feet high, with a passage-way one foot wide. In the presence of forty thousand men all eagerly awaiting the result, Peter, bearing the object in dispute, and clothed only in a tunic, boldly rushed through the flames, amid the anxious prayers and adjurations of the multitude. As the chroniclers lean to the side of the Neapolitan Princes or of the Count of Toulouse, so do their accounts of the event differ; the former asserting that Peter sustained mortal injury in the fire; the latter assuring us that he emerged safely, with but one or two slight burns, and that, the crowd enthusiastically pressing around him in triumph, he was thrown down, trampled on, and injured so severely that he died in a few days, asseverating with his latest breath the truth of his revelations. Raymond persisted in upholding the sanctity of his relic, but it was subsequently lost.[1]

Even after the efforts of Innocent III. to abolish the ordeal, and while the canons of the Council of Lateran were still fresh, St. Francis of Assisi, in 1219, offered himself to the

---

[1] Fulcher. Carnot. cap. x.; Radulf. Cadomensis cap. c., ci., cii., cviii.; Raimond. de Agiles (Bongars, I. 150–168). The latter was chaplain of the Count of Toulouse, and a firm asserter of the authenticity of the lance. He relates with pride, that on its discovery he threw himself into the trench and kissed it while the point only had as yet been uncovered. He officiated likewise in the ordeal, and delivered the adjuration as Peter entered the flames: "Si Deus omnipotens huic homini loquutus est facie ad faciem, et beatus Andreas Lanceam Dominicam ostendit ei, cum ipse vigilaret, transeat iste illæsus per ignem. Sin autem aliter est, et mendacium est, comburatur iste cum lancea quam portabit in manibus suis." Raoul de Caen, on the other hand, in 1107 became secretary to the chivalrous Tancred, and thus obtained his information from the opposite party. He is very decided in his animadversions on the discoverers. Fulcher de Chartres was chaplain to Baldwin I. of Jerusalem, and seems impartial, though sceptical.

21

flames for the propagation of the faith. In his missionary trip to the East, finding the Sultan deaf to his proselyting eloquence, he proposed to test the truth of their respective religions by entering a blazing pile in company with some imams, who naturally declined the perilous experiment. Nothing daunted, the enthusiastic Saint then said that he would traverse the flames alone if the Sultan would bind himself, in the event of a triumphant result, to embrace the Christian religion and to force his subjects to follow the example. The Turk, more wary than the Dane whom Poppo converted, declined the proposition, and St. Francis returned from his useless voyage unharmed.[1] The honors which the unbelievers rendered to their self-sacrificing guest may perhaps be explained by the reverence with which they are accustomed to regard madmen.

In this St. Francis endeavored unsuccessfully to emulate the glorious achievement of Boniface, the Apostle of Russia, who, according to the current martyrologies, converted the King of Russia to the true faith by means of such a bargain and ordeal.[2] It is a little curious that Peter Cantor, in his diatribe against the judgment of God, presents the supposition of a trial of this kind as an unanswerable argument against the system—the church, he says, could not assent to such an experiment, and therefore it ought not to be trusted in affairs of less magnitude.[3]

A still more remarkable attempt at this kind of ordeal occurred at a much later period, when the whole system had long become obsolete, and though not carried into execution, it is worthy of passing notice, as it may be said to have produced results affecting permanently the destinies of civilization. When at the close of the fifteenth century, Savonarola, the precursor of the Reformation, was commencing at Florence the career which Luther afterwards

[1] Raynaldi Annal. Eccles. ann. 1219, c. 56.
[2] Martyrol. Roman. 19 Jun.—Petri Damian. Vit. S. Romualdi. c. 27.
[3] Petri Cantor. Verb. Abbreviat. cap. lxxviii. (Patrol. ccv. 229.)

accomplished, and was gradually throwing off all reverence
for the infamous Borgia, who then occupied the chair of St.
Peter, he challenged any of his adversaries to undergo with
him the ordeal of fire, to test the truth of his propositions
that the Church needed a thorough reformation, and that
the excommunication pronounced against him by the Pope
was null and void. In 1497, the Franciscan Francesco di
Puglia, an ardent opponent, accepted the challenge, but left
Florence before the preliminaries were arranged. On his
return, in the following year, the affair was again taken up,
but the principals readily found excuses to devolve the dangerous office on enthusiastic followers. Giuliano Rondi-
nelli, another Franciscan, agreed to replace his companion,
declaring that he expected to be burned alive; while on the
other side the ardor was so great that two hundred and
thirty-eight Dominicans and numberless laymen subscribed
a request to be permitted to vindicate their cause by triumphantly undergoing the trial unhurt, in place of Do-
menico da Peschia, who had been selected as Savonarola's
champion. At length, after many preliminaries, the Signiory
of Florence assigned the 7th of April, 1498, for the experiment. An immense platform was erected, on which a huge
pile of wood was built, charged with gunpowder and other
combustibles, and traversed by a narrow passage, through
which the champions were to walk. All Florence assembled
to see the show; but, when everything was ready, quibbles
arose about permitting the champions to carry crucifixes,
and to have the sacrament with them, about the nature of
their garments, and other like details, in disputing over
which the day wore away, and at vespers the assemblage
broke up without result. Each party, of course, accused
the other of having raised the difficulties in order to escape
the ordeal ; and the people, enraged at being cheated of the
promised exhibition, and determined to have compensation
for it, easily gave credit to the assertions of the Franciscans,
who stimulated their ardor by affirming that Savonarola

had endeavored to commit the sacrilege of burning the sacrament. In two days a tumult was thus raised, during which Savonarola's convent of San Marco was attacked. Notwithstanding a gallant resistance by the friars, he was taken prisoner, and after undergoing frightful tortures, was hanged and burned. Thus was repressed a movement which at one time promised to regenerate Italy, and to restore purity to a corrupted Church.[1]

It will be observed that the ordeal of fire was principally affected by ecclesiastics in church affairs, perhaps because it was of a nature to produce a powerful impression on the spectators, while at the same time it could no doubt in many instances be so managed as to secure the desired results by those who controlled the details. In like manner, it was occasionally employed on inanimate matter to decide points of faith or polity. Thus, in the question which excited great commotions in Spain in 1077, as to the substitution of the Roman for the Gothic or Mozarabic rite, after a judicial combat had been fought and determined in favor of the national ritual, the partisans of the Roman offices continued to urge their cause, and the ordeal of fire was appealed to. A missal of each kind was committed to the flames, and, to the great joy of all patriotic Castilians, the Gothic offices were unconsumed.[2]   More satisfactory to the orthodox

---

[1] I have principally followed a very curious and characteristic account of the "Sperimento del Fuoco," contained in a Life of Savonarola by the P. Pacifico Burlamacchi. given by Mansi in his edition of the Miscellanea of Baluze, I. 530 sqq. Burlamacchi, as a disciple and ardent follower of the reformer, of course throws all the blame of defeating the ordeal on the quibbles raised by the Franciscans, while the Diary of Burchard, master of ceremonies of the Papal Chapel to Borgia (Diarium Curiæ Romanæ, ann. 1498), roundly asserts the contrary. Guicciardini (Lib. III. cap. vi.) briefly states the facts, without venturing an opinion, except that the result utterly destroyed the credit of Savonarola, and enabled his enemies to make short work with him.

[2] Ferreras, Hist. Gén. d'Espagne, trad. d'Hermilly, III. 245. The authenticity of this miracle has somewhat exercised orthodox writers, and Mabillon states that the earliest authority for it is Roderic, Archbishop of Toledo, who flourished in the middle of the thirteenth century (Proœm. ad

was the result of a similar ordeal which marked the opening of St. Dominic's career against the Albigenses. In a dispute with some heretics he wrote out his argument on the points of faith, and gave it to them for examination and reply. That night, as they were seated around the hearth, the paper was produced and read, when one of them proposed that it should be cast into the flames, when, if it remained unconsumed, they would see that its contents were true. This was promptly done, when the saintly document was unharmed. One, more obstinate than the rest, asked for a second and then for a third trial, with the same result. The perverse heretics, however, closed their hearts against the truth, and bound themselves by oath to keep the affair secret; and so glorious a victory for the true faith would have remained unknown but for the indiscretion of one of them, a knight, who had a covert inclination towards orthodoxy.[1] A somewhat similar instance occurred in Constantinople, as late as the close of the thirteenth century, when Andronicus II., on his accession, found the city torn into factions relative to the patriarchate, arising from the expulsion of Arsenius, a former patriarch. All attempts to soothe the dissensions proving vain, at length both parties agreed to write out their respective statements and arguments, and, committing both books to the flames, to abide by the result, each side hoping that its manuscript would be preserved by the special interposition of Heaven. The ceremony was conducted with imposing state, and, to the general surprise, both books were reduced to ashes. Singularly enough, all parties united in the sensible conclusion that God had thereby commanded them to forget their differences, and to live in peace.[2]

Vit. Greg. VII. No. 10). If this be so, it only shows to how late a period the superstition extended.
[1] Pet. Val Cernaii Hist. Albigens. cap. III.
[2] Niceph. Gregor. Lib. VI.

21*

The genuineness of relics was often tested in this manner by exposing them to the action of fire. When, in 1065, the pious Ægelwin, Bishop of Durham, miraculously discovered the relics of the holy martyr King Oswyn, he gave the hair to Judith, wife of Tosti, Earl of Northumberland, and she with all reverence placed it on a raging fire, whence it was withdrawn, not only uninjured, but marvellously increased in lustre, to the great edification of all beholders.[1] Guibert de Nogent likewise relates that, when his native town became honored with the possession of an arm of St. Arnoul, the inhabitants, at first doubting the genuineness of the precious relic, cast it into the flames; when it vindicated its sanctity, not only by being fire-proof, but also by leaping briskly away from the coals, testimony which was held to be incontrovertible.[2]

The cold-water ordeal (*judicium aquæ frigidæ*) differed from most of its congeners in requiring a miracle to convict the accused, as in the natural order of things he escaped. The preliminary solemnities, fasting, prayer, and religious rites, were similar to those already described; holy water sometimes was given to the accused to drink; the reservoir of water, or pond, was then exorcised with formulas exhibiting the same combination of faith and impiety, and the accused, bound with cords, was lowered into it with a rope, to prevent fraud if guilty, and to save him from drowning if innocent.[3] According to Anglo-Saxon rule the length of rope allowed under water was an ell and a half;[4] but in process of time nice questions arose as to the precise

---

[1] Matthew of Westminster, Ann. 1065.

[2] Guibert. Noviogent. de Vita sua Lib. III. cap. xxi.

[3] Ne aut aliquem possit fraudem in judicio facere, aut si aqua illum velut innoxium reciperit, ne in aqua pericletetur, ad tempus valeat retrahi.— Hincmar. de Divort. Lothar. Interrog. vi. It may readily be supposed that a skilful management of the rope might easily produce the appearance of floating, when a conviction was desired by the priestly operators.

[4] L. Æthelstani, I. cap. xxiii.

amount of submergence requisite for acquittal. Towards
the close of the twelfth century we find that some learned
doctors insisted that sinking to the very bottom of the water
was indispensable; others decided that if the whole person
were submerged it was sufficient; while others again reasoned that as the hair was an accident or excrement of the
body, it had the privilege of floating without convicting its
owner, if the rest of his body was satisfactorily covered.[1]

The basis of this ordeal was the superstitious belief that
the pure element would not receive into its bosom any one
stained with the crime of a false oath, a belief which, as we
have seen, was entertained in primeval India, and which
bears considerable resemblance to the kindred superstition
of old, that the earth would eject the corpse of a criminal,
and not allow it to remain quietly interred.   The ecclesiastical doctrines on the subject are clearly enunciated by
Hincmar: " He who seeks to conceal the truth by a lie will
not sink in the waters over which the voice of the Lord
hath thundered; for the pure nature of water recognizes as
impure, and rejects as incompatible, human nature which,
released from falsehood by the waters of baptism, becomes
again infected with untruth."[2] The baptism in the Jordan,
the passage of the Red Sea, and the crowning judgment of
the Deluge, were freely adduced in support of this theory,
though these latter were in direct contradiction to it; and
the most figurative language was boldly employed to give
some show of probability to the results expected. Thus, in
St. Dunstan's elaborate formula, the prayer offered over the
water metaphorically adjures the Supreme Being—" Let not
the water receive the body of him who, released from the

[1] Petri Cantor. Verb. Abbreviat. cap. lxxviii. (Patrol. ccv. 233.)

[2] Qui veritatem mendacio cupit obtegere, in aquis, super quas vox Domini
Dei majestatis intonuit, non potest mergi, quia pura natura aquæ naturam
humanam per aquam baptismatis ab omni mendacii figmento purgatam,
iterum mendacio infectam, non recognoscit puram, et ideo eam non recipit,
sed rejicit ut alienam.—De Divort. Lothar. Interrog vi.

weight of goodness, is upborne by the wind of iniquity!"[1]
As practised in modern India, however, the trial is rather
one of endurance.   The patient stands in water up to his
middle, facing the East.   He dives under, while simultaneously an arrow of reed without a head is shot from a bow,
106 fingers' breadth in length, and if he can remain under
water until the arrow is picked up and brought back, he
gains his cause.[2]

Although the use of this form of ordeal prevailed wher-
ever the judgment of God was appealed to, and although it
enjoyed a later existence than any of its kindred practices,
it was the last to make its appearance in Europe.   There
seems to be good reason for attributing its introduction as
a Christian mode of trial to Pope Eugenius II., who occupied the pontifical throne from 824 to 827, although some
critics have denied to it this paternity, on what would seem
to be insufficient grounds.   Baluze gives a formula for conducting it which is thought to be of the ninth century, and
which expressly states that Eugenius invented it at the
request of Louis-le-Débonnaire, as a means of repressing
the prevalent vice of perjury; and another manuscript to
which Mabillon attributes the same date makes a similar
assertion.[3]   All this derives additional probability from

---

[1] Nec patiantur recipere corpus, quod ab onere bonitatis evacuatum, ven-
tus iniquitatis allevavit et inane constituit.—Ordo S. Dunstani Dorobern.
(Baluze, II. 650.)

[2] Ayeen Akbery, II. 497.   The use of this ordeal was confined to the
Vaisya or caste of husbandmen and merchants.

[3] Hoc judicium autem, petente Domno Hludovico Imperatore, constituit
beatus Eugenius, ... ne perjuri super reliquias sanctorum perdant suas
animas in malum consentientes (Baluze, II. 646).—Hoc autem judicium
creavit omnipotens Deus, et verum est; et per Domnum Eugenium Apostoli-
cum inventum est (Mabillon, Analecta, pp. 161, 162, ap. Cangium.).—The
same assertion is made in several other rituals which are given at length by
Muratori (Antiq. Ital. Dissert. 38); and by Juretus (Observat. ad Ivon.
Epist. 74).   Two ancient formulæ, however, given by Canciani (Barbaror.
Ll. Antiq. T. I. pp. 282-3), attribute it to Leo III., a quarter of a century
earlier, stating that when in 799 the Romans revolted against him, he fled

the fact that the cold-water ordeal is not alluded to in any
of the codes or laws anterior to the ninth century, while it
is continually referred to in subsequent ones; and another
evidence of weight is afforded by St. Agobard, Archbishop
of Lyons, who, in his celebrated treatise against the judgment of God, written a few years before the accession of
Eugenius, while enumerating and describing the various
modes in use, says nothing about that of cold water.[1] The
only arguments alleged in favor of an earlier date are certain passages in Gregory of Tours, relating legends in
which innocent persons unjustly condemned to be drowned
were miraculously preserved—cases which have evidently
nothing ·to do with the question, as they were interposi-
tions of Providence to save, not to condemn, and were
inflictions of punishment, not legal investigations.[2]

The new process had a hard struggle for existence. But
a few years after its introduction, it was condemned by
Louis-le-Débonnaire at the Council at Worms, in 829; its
use was strictly prohibited, and the "missi dominici" were
instructed to see that the order was carried into effect,
regulations which were repeated by the Emperor Lothair,
son of Louis.[3] These interdictions were of little avail.
The ordeal found favor with popular superstition, and

to Charlemagne, and that, on the Emperor's bringing him back to Rome,
this form of ordeal was introduced to try the authors of the disturbance.

[1] Non oportet . . . suspicari quod omnipotens Deus occulta hominum in
præsenti vita per aquam calidam aut ferrum revelari velit; quanto minus per
crudelia certamina?—(Lib. adv. L. Gundobadi cap. ix.)   And again, in the
Liber contra Judicium Dei, cap. i. : "Mitte unum de tuis, qui congrediatur
mecum singulari certamine, ut probet me reum tibi esse, si occiderit; aut
certe, jube ferrum vel aquas calefieri, quas manibus illæsus attrectem; aut
constitue cruces, ad quas stans immobilis perseverem."

[2] Gregor. Turon Miracul. Lib. i. c. 69, 70.   The Epistle given in Gratian
(C. Mennam caus. 2, q. 5) as written by St. Gregory to Queen Brunhilda,
scarcely needs a reference, its allusions to the ordeal having long since been
restored to their true author, Alexander II. (Epist. 122).

[3] Capit. Wormat. Ann. 829, Tit. ii. cap. 12;—L. Longobard. Lib. ii. Tit.
lv. § 31.

Hincmar contents himself with remarking that the imperial prohibition was not confirmed by the canons of authoritative councils.[1] The trial by cold water spread throughout Europe, and by all the continental races it was
placed on an equal footing with the other forms of ordeal.
Among the Anglo-Saxons, indeed, its employment has
been called in question by some modern writers; but the
Dooms of Æthelstan, and the formula of St. Dunstan of
Canterbury, already quoted, sufficiently manifest its existence in England before the Conquest, while as late as the
close of the twelfth century its employment would seem
to have been almost universal. The assizes of Clarendon
in 1166, confirmed at Northampton in 1176, direct an inquest to be held in each shire, and all who are indicted for
murder, robbery, harboring of malefactors, and other felonies are to be at once, without further trial, passed through
the water ordeal to determine their guilt or innocence.[2]

The ordeals of both hot and cold water were stigmatized
as plebeian from an early period, as the red-hot iron and the
duel were patrician. Thus Hincmar, in the ninth century,
alludes to the former as applicable to persons of servile
condition;[3] a constitution of the Emperor St. Henry II.,
about A.D. 1000, in the Lombard law, has a similar bearing;[4] an Alsatian document in the eleventh,[5] and the laws

---

[1] De Divort. Lothar. Interrog. vi.

[2] Assisa facta apud Clarendune §§ 1, 2.—Assisa apud Northamtoniam.—
(Gesta Henrici II. T. II. p. cxlix.—T. I. p. 108.—Ed. Rer. Britann. Script.)

[3] Ut si præfati sui homines quia non liberæ conditionis sunt, aut cum
aqua frigida, aut cum aqua calida, inde ad judicium Dei exirent, quid inde
Deus ostenderet mihi sufficeret.—Opusc. adv. Hincmar. Laudun. cap. xliii.

[4] Si quis . . . accusatus negare voluerit, aut per duellum si liber est; si
vero servus, per judicium ferventis aquæ defendat se.—L. Longobard. Lib.
I. Tit. ix. § 39.

[5] Et si . . . ipse innocentiæ suæ expurgationem appellaverit, liber vel
personatus serviens, si infra patriam est, post septem dierum inducias cum
totidem suæ comparitatis testibus; plebejus autem et minoris testimonii
rusticus, aquæ frigidæ se expurget judicio.—Recess. Convent. Alsat. anno
1051, § 6. (Goldast. Constit. Imp. II. 48.)

of Scotland in the twelfth century, assume the same position;[1] and Glanville at the end of the twelfth century
expressly asserts it.[2] This, however, was an innovation;
for in the earliest codes there was no such distinction, a
provision in the Salique law prescribing the *æneum*, or hot-
water ordeal, even for the Antrustions, who constituted the
most favored class in the state.[3] Nor even in later times
was the rule by any means absolute. In the tenth century,
Sanche, Duke of Gascony, desirous of founding the monastery of Saint Sever, claimed some land which was necessary
for the purpose, and being resisted by the possessor, the
title was decided by reference to the cold-water ordeal.[4]
In 1027, Guelf II., Count of Altorf, ancestor of the great
houses of Guelf in Italy and England, having taken part
in the revolt of Conrad the Younger and Ernest of Suabia,
was forced by the Emperor Conrad the Salique to prove his
innocence in this manner.[5] This may have been, perhaps,
intended rather as an humiliation than as a judicial proceeding, for Guelf had been guilty of great excesses in the conduct of the rebellion; but about the same period Othlonus
relates an incident in which a man of noble birth accused
of theft submitted himself to the cold water ordeal as a
matter of course;[6] and we find, nearly two centuries later,
when all the vulgar ordeals were falling into disuse, the

---

[1] Regiam Majestatem Lib. IV. cap. iii. § 4.

[2] In tali autem causa tenetur se purgare is qui accusatur per dei judicium
. . . . scilicet per ferrum calidum si fuerit homo liber, per aquam si fuerit
rusticus.—De Legg. Angliæ Lib. XIV. cap. i.

There may be, however, some question as to this. In 1177 a citizen of London who is qualified as "nobilissimus et ditissimus," accused of robbery,
was tried by the water ordeal and on being found guilty offered Henry II.
five hundred marks for a pardon. The dazzling bribe was refused and he
was duly hanged.—Gesta Henrici II. T. I. p. 156.

[3] Text. Herold. Tit. LXXVI.

[4] Mazure et Hatoulet, Fors de Béarn, p. xxxi.

[5] Conrad. Ursperg. sub Lothar. Saxon.

[6] Quidam illustris vir.—Othlon. de Mirac. quod nuper accidit etc. (Migne's
Patrol. T. 140, p. 242.)

water ordeal established among the nobles of Southern Germany, as the mode of deciding doubtful claims on fiefs.[1]

In 1083, during the deadly struggle between the Empire and the Papacy, as personified in Henry IV. and Hildebrand, the imperialists related with great delight that some of the leading prelates of the Papal court submitted the cause of their chief to this ordeal. After a three days' fast, and proper benediction of the water, they placed in it a boy to represent the Emperor, when to their horror he sank like a stone. On referring the result to Hildebrand, he ordered a repetition of the experiment, which was attended with the same result. Then, throwing him in as a representative of the Pope, he obstinately floated during two trials, in spite of all efforts to force him under the surface, and an oath was exacted from them to maintain inviolable secrecy as to the unexpected result.[2]

Perhaps the most extensive instance of the application of this form of ordeal was that proposed when the sacred vessels were stolen from the cathedral church of Laon, as related by a contemporary. At a council convened on the subject, Master Anselm, the most learned doctor of the diocese, suggested that, in imitation of the plan adopted by Joshua at Jericho, a young child should be taken from each parish of the town and tried by immersion in conse-crated water. From each house of the parish which should be found guilty, another child should be chosen to undergo the same process. When the house of the criminal should thus be discovered, all its inmates should be submitted to the ordeal, and the author of the sacrilege would thus be revealed. This plan would have been adopted had not the frightened inhabitants rushed to the Bishop and insisted that the experiment should commence with those whose access to the church gave them the best opportunity to

[1] Juris Feud. Alaman. cap. lxxvii. § 2.
[2] MS. Brit. Mus. inserted by Pertz in Hugo. Flaviniac. Lib. II.

perpetrate the theft. Six of these latter were accordingly selected, among whom was Anselm himself. While in prison awaiting his trial, he caused himself to be bound hand and foot and placed in a tub full of water, in which he sank satisfactorily to the bottom, and assured himself that he should escape. On the day of trial, in the presence of an immense crowd, in the cathedral which was chosen as the place of judgment, the first prisoner sank, the second floated, the third sank, the fourth floated, the fifth sank, and Anselm, who was the sixth, notwithstanding his previous experiment, obstinately floated, and was condemned with his accomplices, in spite of his earnest protestations of innocence.[1]

Although the cold-water ordeal disappears from the statute-book in civil and in ordinary criminal actions at the same time that the other similar modes of purgation were abandoned, there was one class of cases in which it maintained its hold upon the popular faith to a much later period. These were the accusations of sorcery and witchcraft which form so strange and prominent a feature of mediæval society, and its use for this purpose may apparently be traced to various causes. For such crimes, drowning was the punishment inflicted by the customs of the Franks, as soon as they had lost the respect for individual liberty of action which excluded personal punishments from their original code;[2] and in addition to the general belief that

---

[1] Hermann. de Mirac. S. Mariæ Laudun. Lib. III. cap. 28.

[2] Lodharius . . . Gerbergam, *more maleficorum*, in Arari mergi præcepit.—Nithardi Hist. Lib. I. Ann. 834.

The Salique law merely inflicts fines in cases of witchcraft, even when the offender had, according to a widely spread superstition of the times, eaten the victim bodily (L. Emendat. cap. xxi. § 3; cap. lxvii. § 3). So also the L. Ripuarior. (Tit. lxxxiii.) Charlemagne allowed suspected persons to be tortured for confession, provided the process was not carried to the point of death, and after conviction they were to be imprisoned until amendment. (Capit. II. Ann. 805, § xxv.) The legislation of other races was very various in this respect. The Ostrogoths visited all such practices with death (Edict.

22

the pure element refused to receive those who were tainted
with crime, there was in this special class of cases a

Theoderici, cap. CVIII.), relaxing somewhat on the laws of Constantius, who
sought to extirpate them with fire and torments (Const. 3, 6, 7, C. De Male-
ficis IX. 18). The Wisigoths more humanely contented themselves with
stripes, shaving the head, and exposure (L. Wisigoth. Lib. VI. Tit. ii. cap. 3).
Gregory the Great directed that slaves guil'y of such practices should be
punished with stripes and torments, while freemen were to be closely imprisoned and subjected to penance (Gregor. PP. I. Lib. IX. Epist. 65). The
Lombard law (Lib. II. Tit. xxxviii. § 2) ordered them to be sold as slaves
beyond the boundaries of the province, and the earliest legislator, King
Rotharis, denounced severe penalties against those who put women to death
under the absurd belief that they could eat living men.—" Quod Christianis
mentibus nullatenus est credendum, nec possibile est, ut hominem mulier
vivum intrinsecus possit comedere" (L. Longobard. Lib. I. Tit. xi. § 9).
The Pagan Saxons entertained a similar superstition, for which they were in
the habit of burning witches and sorcerers, and even of eating them in turn,
as we learn from the civilizing and Christianizing capitulary of Charlemagne:
" Si quis, a diabolo deceptus, crediderit, secundum morem paganorum, virum
aliquem aut feminam strigam esse et homines comedere, et propter hoc ipsam
incenderit, vel carnem ejus ad comedendum dederit, vel ipsam comederit,
capitis sententia punietur etc." (Capit. de Partibus Saxoniæ, Ann. 789,
§ vi.). The Anglo-Saxons merely banished the witch who would not reform,
with the penalty of death for disobedience (Laws of Edward and Guthrum,
Tit. XI.; Ethelred, VI. § 7; Cnut. Secular. cap. IV.); unless the death of a
victim had been compassed, when the offender was executed (Æthelstan, I.
§ 6), or delivered to the kindred to be punished at their pleasure (Henrici I.
Tit. LXXI. § 1). The primitive law of Scotland, if Boethius may be believed,
was more severe, condemning to the stake all engaged in such practices
(Kenethi Leg. Civil. cap. 18—Spelman. Concil. I. 341); while in Hungary,
for ordinary witchcraft, on a first offence the criminal was only handed to
the bishop to be reformed by fasting and the catechism; a second offence
was visited with branding on the forehead, head, and back, in the form of a
cross with a church key; but when life was attempted in such practices, the
sorcerer was delivered to the kindred to be punished at their pleasure (Henrici I.
discretion (Legg. S. Stephani, c. xxxi xxxii.). The progress of enlightenment in Hungary was rapid, for, by the end of the century, we find King
Coloman contenting himself with the brief remark, " De strigis vero quæ
non sunt, nulla quæstio fiat" (Decret. Coloman. c. 20—Batthyani, Legg.
Eccles. Hung. T. I. p. 455).

The cause of humanity gained but little when, all such accusations being
included in the convenient general charge of heresy, for five hundred years,
luckless sharpers and dupes were committed pitilessly to the flames. King

widely spread superstition that adepts in sorcery and magic lost their specific gravity. Pliny mentions a race of enchanters on the Euxine who were lighter than water— "eosdem non posse mergi . . . ne veste quidam degravatos;" and Stephanus Byzantinus describes the inhabitants of Thebe as magicians who could kill with their breath, and floated when thrown into the sea.[1] This whimsical opinion was perpetuated to a comparatively late period, and gave rise to a species of ordeal known as the *trial by balance*, in which the suspected sorcerer was weighed to ascertain his guilt, enabling him, we may presume, to escape, except when the judges, determined to procure a conviction, managed to elude the vigilance of the inspectors.[2] To the

James I. coldly dismisses the question of their punishment with the appropriate observation, "Passim obtinuit ut crementur. Quanquam in hac re sua cuique genti permittenda est consuetudo." (Demonologiæ, Lib. III. c. vi.) Even in the enlightenment of the seventeenth century, who can read without grim disgust and wonder the terrible farce of the trial of Urbain Grandier, hurrying, amid details ludicrously revolting, its unfortunate victim through torture to the stake, to gratify the quenchless malice of Cardinal Richelieu? Nor did the tragedy cease for yet a hundred years. In the middle of the eighteenth century, Muratori could still write—" Novimus etiam innocentes præsertim mulieres interdum in veneficii suspicionem adductas fuisse in quibusdam Christiani orbis partibus, et aut igni datas, aut mortis periculum vix evasisse: neque alia de caussa reas vulgo creditas quam quod sub fasce annorum illarum humeri jam curvarentur."—(Antiq. Ital. Dissert. 59.) Even as late as the year 1850, in the department of the Hautes-Pyrénées, a husband and wife named Subervie were convicted of having burned alive an old woman whom they regarded as a witch. (Lagrèze, Hist. du Droit dans les Pyrénées, Paris, 1867, p. 293.)

Perhaps the superstition of the devouring of living men by witches may find its last lingering remnants in the vampirism of Eastern Europe.

[1] Ameilhon, de l'Épreuve de l'Eau Froide.

[2] Rickius (Defens. Probæ Aq. Frigid. § 41), writing in 1594, speaks of this as a common practice in many places, and gravely assures us that very large and fat women had been found to weigh only thirteen or fifteen pounds. Königswarter (op. cit. p. 186) states that as late as 1728, at Szegedin in Hungary, thirteen persons suspected of sorcery were, by order of court, subjected to the ordeal of cold water, and then to that of the balance. At Oudewater in Holland, according to the same authority, the scales used on

concurrence of these notions we may attribute the fact
that when the cold-water ordeal was abandoned, in the
thirteenth century, as a judicial practice in ordinary cases,
it still maintained its place as a special mode of trying
those unfortunate persons whom their own folly, or the
malice and fears of their neighbors, pointed out as witches
and sorcerers.[1] No less than a hundred years after the
efforts of Innocent III. had virtually put an end to all the
other forms of vulgar ordeals, we find Louis Hutin ordering
its employment in these cases.[2] At length, however, it fell
into desuetude, until the superstitious panic of witchcraft
which took possession of the popular mind in the second
half of the sixteenth century caused its revival.[3] The
crime was one so difficult to prove judicially, and the
ordeal offered so ready and so satisfactory a solution to
the doubts of timid and conscientious judges, that its
extensive use is not to be wondered at. The professed
Dæmonographers, Bodin, Binsfeld, Godelmann, and others,
either openly rejected it, or omitted all reference to it, but

these occasions are still to be seen. A modification of the trial by balance
consisted in putting the accused into one scale and a Bible into the other.
(Collin de Plancy, s. v. *Bibliomancie*.)

As the simplest, least painful, and perhaps most easily manipulated form
of ordeal, this was monopolized in India by the Brahmins. As practised by
them, the suitor was weighed, and then, after certain religious ceremonies,
he was weighed again. If he had lost weight meanwhile, he was pronounced
victorious, but if his density remained stationary, he was condemned
(Ayeen Akbery, II. 496.)

[1] In earlier times, various other modes of proof were habitually practised.
Among the Lombards, King Rotharis prescribed the judicial combat (L.
Longobard. Lib. I. Tit. xvi. § 2). The Anglo-Saxons (Æthelstan, cap. VI.)
direct the triple ordeal, which was either red-hot iron or boiling water.

[2] Ille adversus quem maleficium factum fuerit vel proditio, si alium accusaverit, de quo aliqua suspicio sit curiæ, accusatus recipiet judicium aquæ
frigidæ.—Regest. Ludovici Hutini (*op.* Cangium).

[3] Scribonius, writing in 1583, speaks of it as a novelty "utpote quæ in
aliis Germaniæ partibus vix audita esset;" but Neuwald assures us that it
had been universally employed for eighteen years previous—"sed in Westphalia ferme ante annos octodecim est passim observata."

still it did not want defenders. In 1583, a certain Scribonius, on a visit to Lemgow, saw three unfortunates burnt as witches, and three other women, the same day, exposed to the ordeal on the accusation of those executed. He describes them as stripped naked, hands and feet bound together, right to left, and then cast upon the river, where they floated like logs of wood. Profoundly impressed with the miracle, in a letter to the magistrates of Lemgow he expresses his warm approbation of the proceeding, and endeavors to explain its rationale, and to defend it against unbelievers. Sorcerers, from their intercourse with Satan, partake of his nature; he resides within them, and their human attributes become altered to his; he is an imponderable spirit of air, and therefore they likewise become lighter than water. Two years later, Hermann Neuwald published a tract in answer to this, gravely confuting the arguments advanced by Scribonius, who, in 1588, returned to the attack with a larger and more elaborate treatise in favor of the ordeal. In 1594, a more authoritative combatant entered the arena—Jacob Rickius, a learned jurisconsult of Cologne, who, as judge in the court of Bonn, had ample opportunity of considering the question, and of putting his convictions into practice.[1] He describes vividly the perplexities of the judges hesitating between the enormity of the crime and the worthlessness of the evidence, and his elaborate discussions of all the arguments in its favor may be condensed into this: that the offence is so difficult of proof that there is no other certain evidence than the ordeal; that without it we should be destitute of absolute

[1] These various tracts were collected together and reprinted in 1686 at Leipsic, in 1 vol. 4to. It contains Rickius's "Compendiosa certisque modis astricta defensio Probæ Aquæ Frigidæ, quæ in examinatione maleficarum plerique judices hodie utuntur;" the "Epistola de Purgatione Sagarum super Aquam frigidam projectarum" of Scribonius; and Neuwald's "Exegesis Purgationis sive Examinis Sagarum, &c." There are few more curious pictures of the age to be found by the student of the mysteries of human intelligence.

22*

proof, which would be an admission of the superiority of
the Devil over God, and that anything would be preferable
to such a conclusion.   He states that he never administered
it when the evidence without it was sufficient for conviction,
nor when there was not enough other proof to justify the
use of torture; and that in all cases it was employed as a
prelude to torture—"præparandum•et muniendum torturæ
viam"—the latter being frequently powerless in consequence
of diabolical influences.   The sickening instances which he
details with much complacency as irrefragable proofs of
his positions show how frequent and how murderous were
the cases of its employment, but would occupy too much
space for recapitulation here; while the learning displayed
in his constant citations from the Scriptures, the Fathers,
the Roman and the Canon Law, is in curious contrast with
the superstitious cruelty of his acts and doctrines.

In France, the central power had to be invoked to put
an end to the atrocity of such proceedings.   In 1588, an
appeal was taken to the supreme tribunal from a sentence
pronounced by a Champenois court, ordering a prisoner to
undergo the experiment, and the Parlement, in December,
1601, registered a formal decree against the practice; an
order which it found necessary to repeat, August 10th, 1641.[1]
That this latter was not uncalled for, we may assume from
the testimony of the celebrated Jerôme Bignon, who, writing
nearly at the same time, says that, to his own knowledge,
within a few years, judges were in the habit of elucidating
doubtful cases in this manner.[2]   In England, James I. gratified at once his conceit and his superstition by eulogizing
the ordeal as an infallible proof in such cases.   His argument was the old one, which pronounced that the pure
element would not receive those who had renounced the

---

[1] Königswarter, op. cit. p. 176.
[2] "Porro, nostra memoria, paucis abhinc annis, solebant judices reos
maleficii accusatos mergere, pro certo habentes incertum crimen hac ratione
patefieri."—Notæ ad Legem Salicam.

privileges of their baptism,[1] and his authority no doubt
gave encouragement to innumerable instances of cruelty
and oppression. In Scotland, indeed, the indecency of
stripping women naked for the immersion was avoided by
wrapping them up in a sheet before binding the thumbs
and toes together—and a portion of the Bay of St. An-
drews is still called the "Witch Pool," from its use in the
trial of these unfortunates.[2] How slowly the belief was
eradicated from the minds of even the educated and enlightened may be seen in a learned inaugural thesis presented by J. P. Lang, in 1661, for the Licentiate of Laws in
the University of Bâle, in which, discussing incidentally
the question of the cold-water ordeal for witches, he concludes that perhaps it is better to abstain from it, though
he cannot question its efficaciousness as a means of investigation.[3] Even in the middle of the eighteenth century, the
learned and pious Muratori affirms his reverent belief in
the miraculous convictions recorded by the mediæval writers as wrought in this manner by the judgment of God,[4]
and he further informs us that it was common throughout
Transylvania in his time;[5] while in West Prussia, as late
as 1745, the Synod of Culm describes it as a popular abuse
in common use, and stringently forbids it for the future.[6]

[1] Tanquam aqua suum in sinum eos non admitteret, qui excussa baptismi
aqua, se omni illius sacramenti beneficio ultro orbarunt.—Demonologiæ, Lib.
III. cap. vi.

[2] Rogers' Scotland, Social and Domestic, p. 266. (Grampian Club, 1869.)

[3] Tutius erit ab eo abstinere, neque refragatur quod sæpe per hoc tentamen
veritas explorata fuit.—Dissert. Inaug. de Torturis Th. XVIII. § xi. Basil.
1661.

[4] Quibus in exemplis vides, sese Deum accommodasse interdum ad hominum piam fidem et preces.—Antiq. Ital. Dissert. 38.

[5] Si vera sunt etiam quæ interdum audivi, in Transylvania, perdurat adhuc
experimentum aquæ ad dignoscendas sagas, sive incantatrices maleficas,
quarum ingens copia ibi traditur esse.—Ibid.

[6] Qui ex levi suspicione, in tali crimine delatas, nec confessas, nec con-
victas, ad torturas, supernatationem aquarum, et alia eruendæ veritatis
media, tandem ad ipsam mortem condemnare . . . non verentur, exempla

We have already alluded to the employment of the water ordeal by an Hungarian tribunal as late as the eighteenth century. Although, within the last hundred years, it has disappeared from the authorized legal procedures of Europe, still the popular mind has not as yet altogether overcome the superstitions and prejudices of so many ages, and occasionally in some benighted spot an outrage occurs to show us that mediæval ignorance and brutality still linger amid the triumphs of modern civilization. In 1815 and 1816, Belgium was disgraced by trials of the kind performed on unfortunates suspected of witchcraft;[1] and in 1836, the populace of Hela, near Dantzic, twice plunged into the sea an old woman reputed to be a sorceress, and as the miserable creature persisted in rising to the surface, she was pronounced guilty, and beaten to death.[2] Even in England it is not many years since a party of credulous people were prosecuted for employing the water ordeal in the trial of a woman whom they believed to be a witch.[3]

Perhaps we may class as a remnant of this superstition a custom described by a modern traveller as universal in Southern Russia. When a theft is committed in a household, the servants are assembled, and a sorceress, or *vorogeia*, is sent for. Dread of what is to follow generally extorts a confession from the guilty party without further proceedings, but if not, the *vorogeia* places on the table a vase of water and rolls up as many little balls of bread as there are suspected persons present. Then, taking one of the balls, she addresses the nearest servant—"If you have committed the theft, this ball will sink to the bottom of the vase, as will your soul in Hell; but if you are innocent, it will float on the water." The truth or falsehood of this assertion is

proh dolor! plurima testantur.—Synod. Culmens. et Pomesan. ann. 1745, c. v. (Hartzheim. Concil. German. X. 510.)

[1] Meyer, Institutions Judiciaires, I. 321.

[2] Königswarter, op. cit. p. 177.

[3] Spottiswoode Miscellany, Edinburgh, 1845, II. 41.

never tested, for the criminal invariably confesses before his turn arrives to undergo the ordeal.[1]

The ordeal of the cross (*judicium crucis, stare ad crucem*) was one of simple endurance.   The plaintiff and defendant, after appropriate religious ceremonies and preparation, stood with uplifted arms before a cross, while divine service was performed, victory being adjudged to the one who was able longest to maintain his position.[2]   The earliest allusion to it which I have observed occurs in a Capitulary of Pepin-le-Bref, in 752, where it is prescribed in cases of application by a wife for dissolution of marriage.[3]   Charlemagne appears to have regarded it with much favor; for he not only frequently refers to it in his edicts, but, when dividing his mighty empire, in 806, he directs that all territorial disputes which may arise in the future between his sons shall be settled in this manner.[4]   An example occurring during his reign shows the details of the process.   A controversy between the bishop and citizens of Verona, relative to the building of certain walls, was referred to the decision of the cross.   Two young ecclesiastics, selected as champions, stood before the sacred emblem from the commencement of mass ; at the middle of the Passion, Aregaus, who represented the citizens, fell lifeless to the ground, while his antagonist, Pacificus, held out triumphantly to the end, and the bishop gained his cause, as ecclesiastics were wont to do.[5]

---

[1] Hartausen, Études sur la Russie.   (Du Boys, Droit Criminel des Peuples Modernes, I. 256.)

[2] A formula for judgments obtained in this manner by order of court, in cases of disputed title to land, occurs in the Formulæ Bignonianæ, No. xii.

[3] Capit. Pippini ann. 752, § xvii.

[4] Chart. Division. cap. xiv. The allusion to it throughout the Capitularies of this monarch are very frequent ; for instance, Capit. ann. 779, § x. ; Capit. iv. ann. 803, §§ iii. vi. ; in L. Longobard. Lib. ii. Tit. xxviii. § 3 ; Tit. lv. § 25, etc.

[5] Ughelli, Italia Sacra, T. V. p. 610 (*ap.* Baluz. Not. ad Libb. Capit.).

When a person desired to discredit the compurgators of an adversary, he had the right to accuse them of perjury, and the main question was then adjourned until this secondary point was decided by this process.[1] In a similar spirit, witnesses too infirm to undergo the battle-trial, by which in the regular process of law they were bound to substantiate their testimony, were allowed, by a Capitulary of 816, to select the ordeal of the cross, with the further privilege, in cases of extreme debility, of substituting a relative or other champion, whose robustness promised an easier task for the Divine interference.[2]

A slight variation of this form of ordeal consisted in standing with the arms extended in the form of a cross, while certain portions of the service were recited. In this manner St. Lioba, Abbess of Bischoffsheim, triumphantly vindicated the purity of her flock, and traced out the offender, when the reputation of her convent was imperilled by the discovery of a new-born child drowned in a neighboring pond.[3]

The sensitive piety of Louis-le-Débonnaire was shocked at this use of the cross, as tending to bring the Christian symbol into contempt, and in 816, soon after the death of Charlemagne, he prohibited its continuance, at the Council of Aix-la-Chapelle;[4] an order which was repeated by his son, the Emperor Lothair.[5] Baluze, however, considers, with

---

[1] Si ille homo cujus causa jurata fuerit, dicere voluerit quod ille qui juravit se sciens perjurâsset, stent ad crucem.—Capit. Car. Mag. incerti anni c. x. (Hartzheim. Concil. German. I. 426.)

[2] Namque si debiliores ipsi testes fuerint, tunc ad crucem examinentur. Nam si majoris ætatis, et non possint ad crucem stare, tunc mittant aut filios aut parentes, aut qualescunque homines possint, qui pro eis hoc tendunt.— Capit. Lud. Pii ann. 816, § i. (Eccardi L. Francorum, pp. 183, 184.)

[3] Rudolph. Fuldens. Vitæ S. Liobæ, cap. xv. (Du Cange, s. v. *Crucis Judicium.*)

[4] Sancitum est ut nullus deinceps quamlibet examinationem crucis facere præsumat, ne quæ Christi passione glorificata est, cujuslibet temeritate contemptui habeatur.—Concil. Aquisgran. cap. xvii.

[5] L. Longobard. Lib. ii. Tit. lv. § 32.

apparent reason, that this command was respected only in the Rhenish provinces and in Italy, from the fact that the manuscripts of the Capitularies belonging to those regions omit the references to the ordeal of the cross, which are retained in the copies used in the other territories of the Frankish empire.[1] Louis himself would seem at length to have changed his opinion ; for, in the final division of his succession between his sons, he repeats the direction of Charlemagne as regards the settlement of disputed bound-aries.[2] The procedure, however, appears to have soon lost its popularity, and indeed never to have obtained the wide and deeply-seated hold on the veneration of the people enjoyed by the other forms of ordeal. We see little of it at later periods, except the trace it has left in the proverbial allusion to an *experimentum crucis*.

The ordeal of consecrated bread or cheese (*judicium offæ, panis conjuratio*, the *corsnæd* of the Anglo-Saxons)

[1] Not. ad Libb. Capit. Lib. i. cap. 103. This derives additional proba-bility from the text cited immediately above, relative to the substitution of this ordeal for the duel, which is given by Eckhardt from an apparently contemporary manuscript, and which, as we have seen, is attributed to Louis-le-Débonnaire in the very year of the Council of Aix-la-Chapelle. It is not a simple Capitulary, but an addition to the Salique Law, which invests it with much greater importance. Lindenbruck (Cod. Legum Antiq. p. 355) gives a different text, purporting likewise to be a supplement to the Law, made in 816, which prescribes the duel in doubtful cases between laymen, and orders the ordeal of the cross for ecclesiastical causes—" in Ecclesi-asticis autem negotiis, crucis judicio rei veritas inquiratur"—and allows the same privilege to the " imbecillibus aut infirmis qui pugnare non valent." Baluze's collection contains nothing of the kind as enacted in 816, but under date of 819 there is a much longer supplement to the Salique law, in which cap. x. presents the same general regulations, almost verbatim, except that in ecclesiastical affairs the testimony of witnesses only is alluded to, and the *judicium crucis* is altogether omitted. The whole manifestly shows great confusion of legislation.

[2] Chart. Divisionis ann. 837, cap. x. The words used are identical with those of Charlemagne, with the substitution of "vexillo crucis" for "judicio crucis." The word *vexillum* is frequently employed in the sense of *signum* or *testimonium* in signatures to diplomas.

was administered by presenting to the accused a piece of bread (generally of barley) or of cheese, about an ounce in weight,[1] over which prayers and adjurations had been pronounced. After appropriate religious ceremonies, including the communion, the morsel was eaten, the event being determined by the ability of the accused to swallow it. This depended of course on the imagination, and we can readily understand how, in those times of faith, the impressive observances which accompanied the ordeal would affect the criminal, who, conscious of guilt, stood up at the altar, took the sacrament, and pledged his salvation on the truth of his oath. The mode by which a conviction was expected may be gathered from the forms of the exorcism employed, of which a number have been preserved.

"O Lord Jesus Christ, . . . grant, we pray thee, by thy holy name, that he who is guilty of this crime in thought or in deed, when this creature of sanctified bread is presented to him for the proving of the truth, let his throat be narrowed, and in thy name let it be rejected rather than devoured. And let not the spirit of the Devil prevail in this to subvert the judgment by false appearances. But he who is guilty of this crime, let him, chiefly by virtue of the body and blood of our Lord which he has received in communion, when he takes the consecrated bread or cheese tremble, and grow pale in trembling, and shake in all his limbs; and let the innocent quietly and healthfully, with all ease, chew and swallow this morsel of bread or cheese, crossed in thy holy name, that all may know that thou art the just Judge," &c.[2]

And even more whimsical in its devout impiety is the following :—

"O God Most High, who dwellest in Heaven, who through thy Trinity and Majesty hast thy just angels, send, O Lord, thy Angel Gabriel to stick in the throat of those who have committed this theft, that they may neither chew nor swallow this bread and cheese created by Thee. I invoke the patriarchs, Abraham, Isaac, and Jacob, with twelve thousand Angels and Archangels. I invoke the four Evan-

---

[1] Half an ounce, according to a formula in a MS. of the ninth century, printed by Dom Gerbert (Migne's Patrolog. 138, 1142).

[2] Baluze, II. 655.

gelists, Matthew, Mark, Luke, and John. I invoke Moses and Aaron, who divided the sea. That they may bind to their throats the tongues of the men who have committed this theft, or consented thereto. If they taste this bread and cheese created by Thee, may they tremble like a trembling tree, and have no rest, nor keep the bread and cheese in their mouths, that all may know Thou art the Lord and there is none other but Thee !"[1]

A striking illustration of the superstitions connected with this usage is found in the story related by most of the English chroniclers concerning the death of the powerful Godwin, Duke of Kent, father of King Harold, and in his day the king-maker of England. As he was dining with his royal son-in-law, Edward the Confessor, some trivial circumstance caused the king to repeat an old accusation that his brother Alfred had met his death at Godwin's hands. The old but fiery duke, seizing a piece of bread, exclaimed: "May God cause this morsel to choke me if I am guilty in thought or in deed of this crime." Then the king took the bread and blessed it, and Godwin, putting it in his mouth, was suffocated by it, and fell dead.[2] A poetical life of Edward the Confessor, written in the thirteenth century, gives a graphic picture of the death of the duke and the vengeful triumph of the king:—

[1] Muratori, Antiq. Ital. Dissert. 38.

[2] This account, with unimportant variations, is given by Roger of Wendover, ann. 1054, Matthew of Westminster, ann. 1054, the Chronicles of Croyland, ann. 1053, Henry of Huntingdon, ann. 1053, and William of Malmesbury, Lib. II. cap. 13; which shows that the legend was widely spread and generally believed, although the Anglo-Saxon Chronicle, ann. 1052, and Roger de Hoveden, ann. 1053, in mentioning Godwin's death, make no allusion to its being caused in this manner. A similar reticence is observable in an anonymous Life of Edward (Harleian MSS. 526), p. 408 of the collection in Rer. Britann. Script., and although this is perhaps the best authority we have for the events of his reign, still the author's partiality for the family of Godwin renders his evidence in this respect liable to suspicion.

No great effort of scepticism is requisite to suggest that Edward, tired of the tutelage in which he was held, may have made way with Godwin by poison, and then circulated the story related by the annalist to a credulous generation.

23

> " L'aleine e parole pert
>   Par le morsel ki ferm s'ahert.
>   Morz est li senglant felun ;
>   Mut out force la benaicun,
>   Ke duna a mors vertu,
>   Par une la mort provée fu.
>   ' Atant' se escrie li rois,
>   ' Treiez hors ceu chen punois.' "[1]

This form of ordeal never obtained the extended influence which characterized some of the other modes, and it seems to have been chiefly confined to the populations allied to the Saxon race. In England, before the Conquest, it was enjoined on the lower orders of the clergy,[2] and it may be considered as a plebeian mode of trial, rarely rising into historical importance. Its vitality, however, is demonstrated by the fact that Lindenbruck, writing in 1613, states that it was then still in frequent use.[3]

Aimoin relates a story which, though in no sense judicial, presents us with an instance of the same superstition. A certain renowned knight named Arnustus unjustly occupied a property belonging to the Benedictine Abbey of Fleury. Dining there one day, and boasting of his contempt for the complaints of the holy monks, he took a pear and exclaimed—" I call this pear to witness that before the year is out I will give them ample cause for grumbling." Choking with the first morsel, he was carried speechless to bed, and miserably perished unhouselled, a warning to evil-doers not to tempt too far the patience of St. Benedict.[4] These stories are by no means uncommon, and are interesting as a picture of the times, when they were reverently received, and formed a portion of the armory by which the weak defended themselves against the strong. Somewhat

---

[1] Lives of Edward the Confessor, p. 119 (Rer. Britann. Script.).

[2] Dooms of Ethelred, IX. § 22 : Cnut. Eccles. Tit. v.

[3] Aliam examinis modum, nostro etiamnunc sæculo, sæpe malo modo usitatum.—Cod. Legum Antiq. p. 1418.

[4] De Mirac. S. Benedicti. Lib. I. c. v.

similar is an occurrence related about the year 1090, when
Duke Henry of Limburg was involved in a quarrel with
Engilbert, Archbishop of Trèves, and treated the excommunication and anathema inflicted upon him with contempt.
Joking upon the subject with his followers one day at dinner, he tossed a fragment of food to his dog, remarking
that if the animal ate it, they need not feel apprehensive of
the episcopal curse. The dog refused the tempting morsel,
though he manifested his hunger by eagerly devouring food
given him by another hand, and the duke, by the advice of
his counsellors, lost no time in reconciling himself with his
ghostly adversary. This is the more remarkable, as Engilbert himself was under excommunication by Gregory VII.,
being a stanch imperialist, who had received his see from
Henry IV. and his pallium from the antipope Guiberto.[1]

In India, this ordeal is performed with a kind of rice
called *sathee*, prepared with various incantations. The
person on trial eats it, with his face to the East, and then
spits upon a Peepul leaf. " If the saliva is mixed with
blood, or the corners of his mouth swell, or he trembles,
he is declared to be a liar."[2]

A simplification of the ordeal of consecrated bread was
the trial by the Eucharist, which indeed may be regarded
as bearing a similar relation to all the forms of ordeal, as
its administration was invariably a portion of the preparatory ceremony, with the awful adjuration, " May this body
and blood of our Lord Jesus Christ be a judgment to
thee this day!" The apostle had said that " he that eateth
and drinketh unworthily eateth and drinketh damnation
to himself" (I. *Corinth.* XI. 28, 29) and the pious veneration
of the age accepted the admonition literally. Perhaps the
most instructive illustration of the mysteries of human su-

[1] Gesta Treverorum, continuat. I.   (Migne's Patrol. 154, 1205-6.)
[2] Ayeen Akbery, II. 498.

perstition in this respect that I have met with is the case
of a dissolute priest of Turgau, in the fourteenth century.
An habitual drunkard, gambler, and fornicator, he yet celebrated mass daily with exemplary regularity. On being
warned of the dangers to which he was thus exposing himself in partaking of the Eucharist, he at length confessed
that he never consecrated the host, but that he carried
about him a small round piece of wood, resembling the
holy wafer, which he exhibited to the people and passed it
off for the body of Christ. The honest chronicler fairly
explodes with indignation in relating this trick, and assures
us that while the priest succeeded in escaping one danger
he fell into a much greater, as he was the cause of leading
his flock into the unpardonable sin of idolatry. Apparently
his parishioners thought so too, for though they had pa-
tiently endured the scandals of his daily life, as soon as
this trick became known they drove him away unceremoniously.[1] What the priest might properly have dreaded is
to be learned from the story of a volunteer miracle vouchsafed to an unchaste priest at Lindisfarne, who being suddenly summoned to celebrate mass without having had
time to purify himself, when he came to partake of the
sacramental cup, saw the wine change to an exceeding
blackness. After some hesitation he took it, and found it
bitter to the last degree. Hurrying to his bishop, he
confessed his sin, underwent penance, and reformed his life.[2]

The general use of the sacrament to lend authority and
solemnity to transactions, and the binding force it was
thought to give to treaties, agreements, and the testimony
of witnesses, might seem to remove it, in its simplicity,
from among the list of ordeals proper, were it not for the
superstition of the age which believed that, when the consecrated wafer was offered under appropriate invocations,

---

[1] Vitodurani Chron. ann. 1336, p. 45. (Thes. Hist. Helvet.)
[2] Roger of Wendover, ann. 1051.

the guilty could not receive it, or that, if it were taken, immediate convulsions and speedy death, or some other miraculous manifestation, ensued. This is well illustrated by a form of exorcism preserved by Mansi: " We humbly pray thy Infinite Majesty that this priest, if guilty of the accusation, shall not be able to receive this venerated body of thy Son, crucified for the salvation of all, and that what should be the remedy of all evil shall prove to him hurtful, full of grief and suffering, bearing with it all sorrow and bitterness."[1] What might be expected under such circumstances is elucidated by a case which occurred in the early part of the eleventh century, as reported by Rodolphus Glaber, a contemporary, in which a monk, condemned to undergo the trial, boldly received the sacrament, when the Host, indignant at its lodgment in the body of so perjured a criminal, immediately slipped out at the navel, white and pure as before, to the immense consternation of the accused, who forthwith confessed his crime.[2]

The antiquity of this mode of trial is shown in its employment by Cautinus, Bishop of Auvergne, towards the close of the sixth century. A certain Count Eulalius was popularly accused of parricide, whereupon he was suspended from communion. On his complaining of thus being punished without a trial, the bishop administered the sacrament under the customary adjuration, and Eulalius, taking it without harm, was relieved from the imputation.[3] It was usually, however, a sacerdotal form of purgation, as is shown by the Anglo-Saxon laws,[4] and by the canons of the Councils of Tribur and Worms directing its employment, in all cases of ecclesiastics charged with crimes, to relieve them from the necessity of taking oaths.[5] Thus, in 941,

---

[1] Baluz. et Mansi Miscell. II. 575.   [2] Lib. v. cap. i.

[3] Greg. Turon. Hist. Lib. x. cap. 8.

[4] Dooms of Ethelred, x. § 20 ; Cnut. Eccles. Tit. v.

[5] Can. Statuit quoque. Caus. ii. quæst. v.—Concil. Vormat. ann. 868, can. 15.

Frederic, Archbishop of Mainz, publicly submitted to an ordeal of this kind, to clear himself of the suspicion of having taken part in an unsuccessful rebellion of Henry, Duke of Bavaria, against his brother, Otho the Great.[1] After the death of Henry, slander assailed the fame of his widow, Juthita, on account of an alleged intimacy between her and Abraham, Bishop of Frisingen. When she, too, died, the bishop performed her funeral rites, and, pausing in the mass, he addressed the congregation: "If she was guilty of that whereof she was accused, may the Omnipotent Father cause the body and blood of the Son to be my condemnation to just perdition, and perpetual salvation to her soul!"—after which he took the sacrament unharmed, and the people acknowledged the falsity of their belief.[2] So in 1050, Subico, Bishop of Speyer, cleared himself of a similar accusation at the Council of Mainz, in the same manner.[3]

Perhaps the most striking instance recorded of its administration was, however, in a secular matter, when in 869 it closed the unhappy controversy between King Lothair and his wives, to which reference has been already made. To reconcile himself to the Church, Lothair took a solemn oath before Adrian II. that he had obeyed the ecclesiastical mandates in maintaining a complete separation from his pseudo-wife Waldrada, after which the pontiff admitted him to communion, under an adjuration that it should prove the test of his truthfulness. Lothair did not shrink from the ordeal, nor did his nobles, to whom it was given on their declaring that they had not abetted the designs of the concubine; but, leaving Rome immediately afterwards,

---

[1] Reginonis Continuat. ann. 941.   [2] Dithmari Chron. Lib. II.
[3] Hist. Archiep. Bremens. ann. 1051. (Lindenbrog. Script. Septentrion. p. 90.) Lambert. Hersfeld. ann. 1050. Another account of the transaction, however, states that the bishop's jaw became paralyzed in the act, "terrifico sacramento Dominici corporis," and remained in that condition until his death (Hartzheim. Concil. German. III. 112).

the royal *cortége* was stopped at Piacenza by a sudden epidemic which broke out among the courtiers, and there Lothair died, August 8th, with nearly all of his followers— an awful example held out by the worthy chroniclers as a warning to future generations.[1]

In this degradation of the Host to the level of daily life there was a profanity which could hardly fail to disgust a reverential mind, and we are therefore not surprised to find King Robert the Pious, in the early part of the eleventh century, raising his voice against its judicial use, and threatening to degrade the Archbishop of Sens for employing it in this manner, especially as his biographer informs us that the custom was daily growing in favor.[2] Robert's example was soon afterwards imitated by Alexander II., who occupied the pontifical chair from 1061 to 1073.[3] The next pope, however, the impetuous Hildebrand, made use of it on a memorable occasion. When, in 1077, the unhappy Emperor Henry IV. had endured the depths of humiliation before the arrogant pontiff's castle gate at Canosa, and had at length purchased peace by submitting to all the exactions demanded of him, the excommunication under which he had lain was removed in the chapel. Then Gregory, referring to the crimes imputed to himself by the emperor's partisans, said that he could easily refute them by abundant witnesses; "but lest I should seem to rely rather on human than divine testimony, and that I may remove from the minds of all, by immediate satisfaction, every scruple, behold this body of our Lord which I am about to take. Let it be to me this day a test of my innocence, and may the Omnipotent God this day by his judgment absolve me of the accusations if I am innocent, or let me perish by sudden death, if guilty!" Swallowing

---

[1] Regino, ann. 869 ; Annal. Bertiniani.
[2] Helgaldi Epitome Vitæ Roberti Regis.
[3] Duclos, Mémoire sur les Épreuves.

the wafer, he turned to the emperor, and demanded of him the same refutation of the charges urged against him by the German princes. Appalled by this unexpected trial, Henry in an agony of fear evaded it, and, trembling, consulted hurriedly with his councillors how to escape the awful test, which he finally declined on the ground of the absence of both his friends and his enemies, without whose presence the result would establish nothing.[1] In estimating the mingled power of imagination and conscience which rendered the proposal insupportable to the emperor, we must allow for the influence which a man like Hildebrand with voice and eye can exert over those whom he wishes to impress. At an earlier stage of his career, in 1055, he improvised a very effective species of ordeal, when presiding as papal legate at the Council of Lyons, assembled for the repression of simony. A guilty bishop had bribed the opposing witnesses, and no testimony was obtainable for his conviction. Hildebrand addressed him: "The episcopal grace is a gift of the Holy Ghost. If, therefore, you are innocent, repeat, ' Glory to the Father, and to the Son, and to the Holy Ghost!'" The bishop boldly commenced, "Glory to the Father, and to the Son, and to—" here his voice failed him, he was unable to finish the sentence; and, confessing the sin, he was deposed.[2]

The necessity of Henry's prudence in declining the Eucharistic ordeal was proved by the fate of the unfortunate Imbrico, Bishop of Augsburg, who, in the same year, 1077, after swearing fealty to Rodolph of Suabia, abandoned him and joined the emperor. Soon after, while saying mass before Henry, to prove the force of his loyal convictions, he declared that the sacrament he was about to take should attest the righteousness of his master's cause; and

---

[1] Lambert. Hersfeld. ann. 1077.

[2] This anecdote rests on good authority. Peter Damiani states that he had it from Hildebrand himself (Opusc. xix. cap. vi.), and Calixus II. was in the habit of relating it (Pauli Bernried. Vit. Greg. VII. No. 11).

the anti-imperialist chronicler duly records that a sudden
disease overtook him, to be followed by speedy death.[1]
In the case of William, Bishop of Utrecht, as related by
Hugh of Flavigny, the Eucharist was less an ordeal than
a punishment. He dared, at the Assembly of Utrecht, in
1076, to excommunicate Gregory, at the command of
Henry IV.; but when, at the conclusion of the impious
ceremony, he audaciously took the Host, it turned to fire
within him, and, shrieking "I burn! I burn!" he fell down
and miserably died.[2]

The ordeal of the lot left the decision to pure chance,
in the hope that Heaven would interpose to save the
innocent and punish the guilty. We may assume that
this was extensively practised in Pagan times, but that,
on the introduction of Christianity, it gradually became
obsolete, as the various modes of appealing to the Deity,
which are described above, acquired importance and threw
the less impressive reference to the lot into insignificance.
The only allusions to it occur in the earlier laws, and no

[1] Bernald. Constant. Chron. ann. 1077.
[2] Hugon. Flaviniac. Chron. Lib. II. ann. 1080; Lambert. Hersfeld. ann.
1076.—Among the manifestations of belief in the miraculous powers of the
Host may be mentioned the practice of throwing on a conflagration the cloth
used to cover the sacred cup, in the expectation that it would extinguish the
flames. This superstition was sufficiently important to attract the reprehen-
sion and prohibition of the Council of Selingenstadt in 1022. "Conques-
tum est . . . de quibusdam stultissimis presbyteris ut quando incendium
videant, corporale dominico corpore consecratum, ad extinguendum incendium temeraria præsumptione in ignem projiciant. Ideoque decretum est
sub anathematis interdictione, ne ulterius fiat."—(Concil. Selingens. cap.
vi.) A less harmless belief in the virtues of the body of our Lord was
shown during the terrible persecution which repressed the religious movement of Germany in the second quarter of the thirteenth century. It is
gravely related that among the thousands of unfortunate heretics who ex-
piated their perverseness at the stake, one poor wretch would not burn, and
obstinately resisted the efforts of his torturers, until some one brought to the
pile a holy wafer, when the unbeliever was promptly reduced to a cinder.
(Alberic. Trium Fontium Chron. ann. 1233.)

trace of it is to be met with in the subsequent legislation of any race. Mention of it is made in the Ripuarian code,[1] and in some of the earlier Merovingian documents its use is prescribed in the same brief manner.[2] Indeed, as late as the middle of the eighth century, Ecgberht, Archbishop of York, quotes from the canons of an Irish Council a direction for its employment in cases of sacrilegious theft, as a means of determining the punishment to be inflicted.[3] On the other hand, shortly after, the Council of Calchuth condemned the practice between litigants as a remnant of paganism.[4]

No explanation is given of the details of the process by which this appeal to fortune was made, and I know of no contemporary applications by which its formula can be investigated; but in the primitive Frisian laws there is described a singular ordeal of the lot, which may reasonably be assumed to bear some relation to it. When a man was killed in a chance-medley and the murderer remained unknown, the friends had a right to accuse seven of the participants in the brawl. Each of these defendants had then to take the oath of denial with twelve conjurators, after which they were admitted to the ordeal. Two pieces of twig, precisely similar, were taken, one of which was marked with a cross; they were then wrapped up separately in white wool and

---

[1] Ad ignem seu ad sortem se excusare studeat.—Tit. xxxi. § 5.

[2] Pact. Childeberti et Chlotarii, ann. 593, § 5. "Et si dubietas est, ad sortem ponatur." Also § 8 : "Si litus de quo inculpatur ad sortem ambulaverit." As in § 4 of the same document the *æneum* or hot-water ordeal is provided for freemen, it is possible that the lot was reserved for slaves. This, however, is not observed in the Decret. Chlotarii, ann. 595, § 6, where the expression, "Si de suspicione inculpatur, ad sortem veniat," is general in its application, without reservation as to station.

[3] Si quis furatus fuerit pecuniam ab æcclesia, mittatur sors, ut aut illius manus abscindatur, aut in carcerem mittatur, diu jejunans ac gemens.— Ecgberti Excerpt. cap. lxxxiv. (Thorpe, II. 108).

[4] Audivimus etiam quod dum inter vos litigium versatur, sortes more gentilium mittatis, quod omnino sacrilegium istis temporibus reputatur.—Conc. Calchuth. can. 19 (Spelman, Concil. Brit. I. 300).

laid on the altar; prayers were recited, invoking God to
reveal the innocence or guilt of the party, and the priest,
or a sinless youth, took up one of the bundles. If it contained the marked fragment, the defendants were absolved;
if the unmarked one, the guilty man was among them.
Each one then took a similar piece of stick and made a
private mark upon it; these were rolled up as before,
placed on the altar, taken up one by one, and unwrapped,
each man claiming his own. The one whose piece was left
to the last was pronounced guilty, and was obliged to pay
the wehr-gild of the murder.[1] The various modes of ecclesiastical divination, so frequently used in the Middle Ages
to obtain an insight into the future, sometimes assumed
the shape of an appeal to Heaven to decide questions of
the present or of the past.[2] Thus, when three bishops,
of Poitiers, Arras, and Autun, each claimed the holy
relics of St. Liguaire, and human means were unavailing
to reconcile their pretensions, the decision of the Supreme
Power was resorted to, by placing under the altar-cloth
three slips with their respective names inscribed, and after
a becoming amount of prayer, on withdrawing one of them,
the See of Poitiers was enriched with the precious remains
by Divine favor.[3]

[1] L. Frision. Tit. xiv. §§ 1, 2. This may not improbably be derived from
the mode of divination practised among the ancient Germans, as described
by Tacitus, De Moribus German. cap. x.

[2] When used for purposes of divining into the future, these practices were
forbidden. Thus, as early as 465, the Council of Vannes denounced those
who "sub nomine fictæ religionis quas sanctorum sortes vocant divinationis
scientiam profitentur, aut quarumcumque scripturarum inspectione futura
promittant," and all ecclesiastics privy to such proceedings were to be ex-
pelled from the church. (Concil. Venet. can. xvi.) This canon is repeated
in the Council of Agde in 506, where the practice is denounced as one "quod
maxime fidem catholicæ religionis infestat." (Conc. Agathens. can. xlii.)

[3] Baldric. Lib. i. Chron. Camerac. cap. 21. (Du Cange, s. v. Sors.)—In
this the bishops were guilty of no contravention of ecclesiastical rules. That
such trials were allowed by the canon law, when properly conducted for appropriate purposes, is shown by Gratian, Decret. Caus. 26, q. 2, can. 3, 4.

Somewhat similar in character was an appeal to heaven made by the pious monks of Abingdon, about the middle of the tenth century, to determine their right to the meadows of Beri against the claims of some inhabitants of Oxfordshire. For three days, with fasting and prayer, they implored the Divine Omnipotence to make manifest their right; and then, by mutual assent, they floated on the Thames a round buckler, bearing a handful of wheat, in which was stuck a lighted taper. The sturdy Oxonians gaped at the spectacle from the distant bank, while a deputation of the more prudent monks followed close upon the floating beacon. Down the river it sailed, veering from bank to bank, and pointing out, as with a finger, the various possessions of the Abbey, till at last, on reaching the disputed lands, it miraculously left the current of the stream, and forced itself into a narrow and shallow channel, which in high water made an arm of the river around the meadows in question. At this unanswerable decision, the people with one accord shouted "Jus Abbendoniæ, jus Abbendoniæ!" and so powerful was the impression produced, that the worthy chronicler assures us that thenceforth neither king, nor duke, nor prince dared to lay claim to the lands of Beri; showing conclusively the wisdom of the abbot who preferred thus to rely upon his right rather than on mouldy charters or dilatory pleadings.[1]

As administered in India, the ordeal of chance consists in writing the words *dherem* and *adherem* on plates of

The most extraordinary application, however, is that by which, under the Spanish Wisigoths, episcopal elections were sometimes decided. The second Council of Barcelona, in 599, directs that two or three candidates shall be chosen by the clergy and people, and from among these the metropolitan and suffragan bishops shall select by lot, "quem sors, praeunte episcoporum jejunio, Christo domino terminante, monstraverit, benedictio consecrationis accumulet."—(Concil. Barcinon. II. can. iii.) This is evidently suggested by the election of Matthias (Acts I. 26).

[1] Hist. Monast. de Abingdon, Lib. I. (Rer. Brit. Med. Ævi Script. Vol. I. p. 89.)

silver and lead respectively, or on pieces of white and black linen, which are placed in a vessel that has never held water. The party on trial draws out one of the pieces, and if it proves to be "*dherem*" he gains his cause.[1]

The powerful temptation felt by human nature to seek by such means the solution of its doubts is shown in the adoption of a singular form of chance ordeal by even the strict materialism of China. If an injured husband finds his wife *flagrante delicto* he is at liberty to kill both the woman and her seducer on the spot, but he is then obliged to cut off their heads and carry them to the nearest magistrate, when it is incumbent on him to prove the truth of his story. . As external evidence is scarcely to be expected in such cases, the mode usually adopted is to place the two heads in a large tub of water, which is then stirred violently around. The heads in revolving naturally come together in the centre, when, if they meet back to back, the victims are pronounced innocent, and the husband is punished as a murderer; if face to face, it is regarded as full proof of their guilt, the husband is gently bastinadoed in retribution for not having kept better watch over his wife, and is presented with a small sum of money wherewith to purchase another spouse.[2] Even amid our boasted civilization we may occasionally see evidences of the same spirit at work around us. In 1867 the London *Times* recorded a case occurring at Southampton, where a sailor boy on board a collier was brought before court on a charge of theft, the only evidence against him being that afforded by securing a key in a Bible opposite the first chapter of Ruth. The Bible was then swung round while the names of several suspected persons were repeated, and on the mention of the prisoner's name the book fell on the floor.

[1] Ayeen Akbery, II. 498. This ordeal is allowed for all the four castes, Brahmins, Kchatryas, Vaisyas, and Soûdras.

[2] See a note by W. T. Stronach in the "Journal of the North China Branch of the Royal Asiatic Society," New Series No. 2, Dec. 1865, p. 176.

24

The credulity of mediæval belief could surely go no farther than this.

The superstition that, at the approach of a murderer, the body of his victim would bleed, or give some other manifestation of recognition, is one of ancient origin, and, under the name of "bier-right," it has been made a means of investigation and detection. Shakspeare introduces it, in King Richard III., where Gloster interrupts the funeral of Henry VI., and Lady Anne exclaims:

> "O gentlemen, see, see ! dead Henry's wounds
> Open their congealed mouths, and bleed afresh."

The story is well known which relates that, when Richard Cœur-de-Lion hastened to the funeral of his father, Henry II., and met the procession at Fontevraud, the blood poured from the nostrils of the dead king, whose end he had hastened by his disobedience and rebellion.[1] A notable instance of its practical application occurred in 1331 at Ueberlingen in Swabia. The body of a child of one of the burghers was found in a pond, and from certain wounds the populace recognized that Jewish fanaticism had caused its murder. The corpse was accordingly carried around in front of the houses of the principal Jews, and when its wounds began to bleed, no further evidence was thought necessary. In spite of the efforts of the magistrate, bought with Hebrew gold, the people forthwith set about visiting condign punishment on the guilty. All the Jews of the place were skilfully decoyed into a large stone house, and when they had been securely locked up in the upper stories a huge fire was kindled below. Those that succeeded in throwing themselves from the roof were immediately dispatched by the surrounding mob, and the rest, to the number of three hundred, were consumed by the avenging flames. The jus-

---

[1] Roger de Hoveden, ann. 1189 ; Roger of Wendover ; Benedicti Abbatis Gest. Henr. II. ann. 1189.

tice of the proceeding was satisfactorily proved by sundry miracles vouchsafed by the approbation of Heaven; and yet the godless Emperor, Louis of Bavaria, had the temerity to punish the pious townsfolk by dismantling their walls and levying a heavy fine upon them.[1]

The popular belief in this ordeal, as well as in that of fire, is well illustrated in the ballad of "Earl Richard," given by Scott in the "Minstrelsy of the Scottish Border."

> " ' Put na the wite on me,' she said ;
>   ' It was my may Catherine.'
>   Then they hae cut baith fern and thorn,
>   To burn that maiden in.
>
> " It wadna take upon her cheik,
>   Nor yet upon her chin ;
>   Nor yet upon her yellow hair,
>   To cleanse that deadly sin.
>
> " The maiden touched that clay-cauld corpse,
>   A drap it never bled ;
>   The ladye laid her hand on him,
>   And soon the ground was red."

King James I. patronized this among the other superstitions to which he gave the authority of his regal approbation ;[2] and in the notes to the above ballad, Scott quotes some curious instances of the judicial use made of the belief, even as late as the seventeenth century. In 1611, suspicion arising as to the mode by which a person had met his death, the body was exhumed, and the neighborhood summoned to touch it, according to custom. The murderer, whose rank and position placed him above suspicion, kept away; but his little daughter, attracted by curiosity, happened to approach the corpse, when it commenced bleeding, and the crime was proved. The extent

---

[1] Vitodurani Chron. ann. 1331. (Thes. Hist. Helvet)
[2] Nam ut in homicidio occulto sanguis e cadavere, tangente homicida, erumpit, quasi cælitus poscens ultionem.—Demonologiæ Lib. III. c. vi.

to which the superstition was carried is shown by a story
of a young man, who quarrelled with a companion, stabbed
him, and threw the body into a river. Fifty years passed
away, when a bone chancing to be fished up, the murderer,
then an old man, happened to touch it, and it streamed
with blood. Inquiring where it had been found, he recognized the relic of his crime, confessed it, and was duly
condemned. We may trace a more poetic form of this superstition in the touching legend of the welcome which
the bones of Abelard gave to Heloise, when, twenty years
after his death, she was consigned to the same tomb.

In the celebrated case of Philip Standsfield, tried in
1688 for the murder of his father Sir James Standsfield of
New Milnes, the dittay or indictment dramatically recounts
how, after the body had been found in a neighboring pond,
and an autopsy had been performed by a surgeon, "James
Row, merchand, having lifted the left side of Sir James,
his head and shoulder, and the said Philip the right side,
his father's body, though carefully cleaned as said is, so as
the least blood was not on it, did (according to God's
usual mode of discovering murders) blood afresh upon
him and defiled all his hands, which struck him with such
a terror, that he immediately let his father's head and body
fall with violence and fled from the body and in consternation and confusion cryed Lord have mercy upon me! and
bowed himself down over a seat in the church (where
the corp were inspected) wiping his father's innocent
blood off his own murdering hands upon his cloaths." The
defence showed that in the *post-mortem* examination an
incision had been made in the neck, where there was a
large accumulation of extravasated blood; and Mattheus
and Carpzovius were quoted to prove that such bleeding
was not even evidence sufficient to justify torture. The
accused, however, was condemned and executed, though
the circumstantial evidence against him was anything but

conclusive.[1] Somewhat remarkable, in view of the length of time which had elapsed between the death and the ordeal, is a case alluded to in the records of Accomac County, Virginia. About the middle of January, 1680, a new-born illegitimate child of "Mary, daughter of Sarah, wife of Paul Carter," died and was buried. It was nearly six weeks before suspicion was aroused, when the coroner impanelled a jury of twelve matrons, whose verdict reported that Sarah Carter was brought to touch the corpse without result, but that when Paul Carter touched it "immediately whilst he was stroaking ye childe the black and settled places above the body of the childe grew fresh and red so that blud was redy to come through ye skin of the childe." On the strength of this verdict an indictment was found against Paul Carter, but the result of the subsequent trial does not appear among the records of the county.[2]

Although there is no allusion to this custom in any of the primitive Leges Barbarorum, nor even in the German municipal codes of the thirteenth century, yet it was judicially employed there until the sixteenth century, under the name of "Bahr-recht." Thus in 1324, Reinward, a Canon of Minden, was murdered by a drunken soldier, and the crime was brought home to the perpetrator by a trial of this kind;[3] and about the year 1600, Bishop Binseld speaks of its occurrence as an indubitable fact.[4] About 1580, President Bertrand d'Argentré, in his Commentaries

[1] Cobbett's State Trials, XI. 1371.—A similar incident is recorded in the indictment of Christian Wilson, tried for witchcraft at Edinburgh in 1661. (Spottiswoode Miscellanies, II. 69.)

[2] I owe this statement to the kindness of L. S. Joynes, M.D., of Richmond, who informs me that he found it in examining the ancient records of Accomac.

[3] Swartii Chron. Ottbergens. § xlvii. (Paullini Antiq. German. Syntagma).

[4] Tract. de Confess. Maleficar. Dub. iv. Conclus. 8, Prelud. 12 (ap. Rickii § 63).

on the Customs of Bretagne, treats it as good evidence,[1] though shortly afterwards, in 1592, the learned jurisconsult Zanger, after citing numerous authorities on both sides, concludes that it is not evidence sufficient even to justify the application of torture.[2] A variation of it, known as "Schein-gehen," was practised in the Netherlands and the North, in which the hand of the corpse was cut off, and touched by all suspected persons, with protestations of innocence, and when the guilty one came, it was expected to bleed.[3]

The vitality of superstition is well illustrated by the transmission of this belief even to our own day. In 1767, the coroner's jury of Bergen County, N. J., was summoned to view the body of one Nicholas Tuers, whose murder was suspected. The attestation of Joannes Demarest, the coroner, states that he had no belief in the "bier-right," and paid no attention to the experiment, when one of the jury touched the body without result, and when Harry, a slave, who had been suspected without proof, was brought up for the same purpose. He heard an exclamation "He is the man," and was told that Tuers had bled on being touched by Harry. He then ordered the slave to place his hand on the face of the corpse, when about a tablespoonful of blood immediately flowed from each nostril, and Harry confessed the murder in all its particulars.[4] In 1833, a man named Getter was executed in Pennsylvania for the murder of his wife, and among the evidence which went to the jury on his trial was that of a female witness who deposed "If my throat was to be cut, I could tell, before God Almighty,

---

[1] "Cujus rei rationem petunt e causis naturalibus, et reddere conatur Petrus Apponensis; quæ qualescunque tandem hæ sint, constat evenisse sæpe, et magnis autoribus tradita exempla," and he proceeds to quote as authority Paris di Puteo, Hipp. Marsigli, and other eminent criminalists.— B. d'Argentré Comment. in Consuetud. Britann. p. 145. Ed. 8, Antverp. 1644.

[2] Zangeri Tract. de Quæstionibus, cap. ii. No. 160.

[3] Königswarter, op. cit. p. 183.

[4] Annual Register for 1767, pp. 144–5.

that the deceased smiled when he (the murderer) touched her. I swore this before the justice, and also that she bled considerably. I was sent for to dress her and lay her out. He touched her twice. He made no hesitation about doing it. I also swore before the justice that it was observed by other people in the house."[1] Nor is the belief even yet eradicated from the credulous minds of the uneducated. Even in 1860, the Philadelphia journals mention a case in which the relatives of a deceased person, suspecting foul play, vainly importuned the coroner, some weeks after the interment, to have the body exhumed, in order that it might be touched by a person whom they regarded as concerned in his death. In 1868, at Verdiersville, Virginia, a suspected murderer was compelled to touch the body of a woman found in a wood; and in 1869 at Lebanon, Illinois, the bodies of two murdered persons were dug up, and a crowd of two hundred persons were marched past them, each of whom was made to touch them in the hope of finding the criminals.[2]

We may even include among ordeals the ordinary purgatorial oath, when administered upon relics of peculiar sanctity, to which the superstition of the age attributed the power of punishing the perjurer. We have already seen (p. 222) Gregory the Great alluding to an oath of purgation as proving innocence by the person taking it remaining uninjured, and in one of his Homilies he assumes that perjury committed on the relics of the saints is punished by demoniacal possession.[3] When, in the tenth century, Adaulfus, Bishop of Compostella, was accused of a

---

[1] Dunglison's Human Physiology, 8th ed. II. 657.

[2] Phila. Bulletin, April 19, 1860; N. Y. World, June 5, 1868; Phila. North American, March 29, 1869.

[3] Ad extincta namque eorum corpora viventes ægri veniunt et sanantur : perjuri veniunt et a dæmonio vexantur, dæmoniaci veniunt et liberantur.— Gregor. I. Homil. xxxii. in Evangel. cap. 6.

nameless crime, and was sentenced by the hasty judgment
of the king to be gored to death by a wild bull, he had
taken the precaution, before appearing at the trial, to de-
voutly celebrate Mass in his full pontificals. The bull,
maddened with dogs and trumpets, rushed furiously at the
holy man; then, suddenly pausing, advanced gently towards him and placed its horns in his hands, nor could
any efforts of the assistants provoke it to attack him.
The king and his courtiers, awed by this divine interposition in favor of innocence, threw themselves at the feet of
the saint, who pardoned them and retired to the wildest
region of the Asturias, where he passed the rest of his
days as an anchorite. He left his chasuble behind him,
however, and this garment thenceforth possessed the miraculous power that, when worn by any one taking an oath,
it could not be removed if he committed perjury.[1] The
shrines of other saints convicted the perjurer by throwing
him down in an epileptic fit, or fixing him rigid and motionless at the moment of his invoking them to witness his
false oath.[2] The monks of Abingdon boasted a black
cross made from the nails of the crucifixion, and said to
have been given them by the Emperor Constantine, a false
oath on which was sure to cost the malefactor his life; and
the worthy chronicler assures us that the instances in
which its miraculous power had been triumphantly exhibited were too innumerable to specify.[3] In the Middle Ages,
these dangerous relics were common, and however we may
smile at the simplicity of the faith reposed in them, we
may rest assured that on many occasions they were the
means of eliciting confessions which could have been ob-

---

[1] Munionis Histor. Compostellan. Lib. i. cap. 2, § 2.

[2] Gregor. Turon. De Gloria Martyrum, cap. 58, 103.

[3] Sancta enim adeo est, ut nullus, juramento super eam præstito, impune
et sine periculo vitæ suæ possit affirmare mendacium.—Hist. Monast. Abing.
Lib. i. c. xii. (Rer. Brit. Script.)

tained by no devices of legal subtlety according to modern procedures.

Though not legally an ordeal, I may refer to a practice cognate in its origin as an appeal to Heaven to regulate the amount of punishment requisite for the expiation of a crime. One or more bands of iron were not infrequently fastened round the neck or arm of a murderer, who was banished until by pilgrimage and prayer his reconciliation and pardon should be manifested by the miraculous loosening of the fetter, showing that soul and body were each released from their bonds.[1] A case is related of a Pole thus wandering with a circlet tightly clasped to each arm. One fell before the intercession of St. Adalbert, the apostle of Prussia, but the other retained its hold until the sinner came to the shrine of St. Hidulf near Toul. There, joining in the worship of the holy monks, the remaining band flew off with such force that it bounded against the opposite wall, while the pardoned criminal fell fainting to the ground, the blood pouring from his liberated arm: a miracle gratefully recorded by the spiritual children of the saint.[2] Equally melodramatic in its details is a similar instance of an inhabitant of Prunay near Orléans, laden with three iron bands for fratricide. His weary pilgrimage was lightened of two by the intercession of St. Peter at Rome, and the third released itself in the most demonstrative manner, through the merits of St. Bertin and St. Omer.[3] If the legend of St. Emeric of Hungary be true, the Pope

---

[1] Fratricidas autem et parricidas sive sacerdotum interfectores . . . per manum et ventrem ferratos de regno ejiciat ut instar Cain jugi et profugi circueant terram.—Leg. Bracilai Bœmor. (Annal. Saxo, ann. 1039.) So also a century earlier for the murder of a chief.—Concil. Spalatens. ann. 927, can. 7 (Batthyani, I. 331).

[2] De Successoribus S. Hidulfi cap. xviii. (Patrolog. 138, p. 218.) A similar case attested the sanctity of St. Mansuetus (Vit. S. Mansueti Lib. II. c. 17—Martene et Durand. Thesaur. III. 1025).

[3] Folcardi Mirac. S. Bertin. Lib. I. c. 4.

himself did not disdain to prescribe this ordeal to the
criminal whose miraculous release caused the immediate
canonization of the saint by a synod in 1073.[1]

The spirit of the age is likewise manifested in an appeal
to Heaven which terminated a quarrel in the early part of
the twelfth century between St. Gerald, Archbishop of
Braga, and a magnate of his diocese, concerning the patronage of a church. Neither being inclined to yield, at
length the noble prayed that God would decide the cause
by not permitting the one who was in the wrong to live
beyond the year, to which St. Gerald assented; and in six
months the death of the unhappy noble showed how dangerous it was to undertake such experiments with a saint.[2]
This, indeed, may be held to have warrant of high authority, for when, in 336, Alexander Bishop of Constantinople
was about to engage in disputation with the arch-heretic
Arius, he underwent a long fast, and shut himself up for
many days and nights alone in his church praying to God,
and finally supplicating that if his faith were wrong he
might not live to see the day of contest; while if Arius
were in error he likewise might be taken off in advance;
and the orthodoxy of the Nicæan creed was confirmed
miraculously by the sudden and terrible death of the heretic
Arius within a few days.[3]

I have met with no allusion in the Middle Ages to the
poison ordeals which have been described above as in use
among the savage tribes of Africa and Madagascar. In India, however, the custom is preserved for the unfortunate

---

[1] Batthyani, Legg. Eccles. Hung. T. I. p. 413. See also Mirac. S. Swithuni,
c. ii. § 32.—Mirac. S. Yvonis c. 21 (Patrol. 155, pp. 76, 91). Various other
instances may be found in Muratori, Antiq. Med. Ævi, Diss. 23. Charlemagne seems to have considered it a deception to be restrained by law.—
Car. Mag. cap. I. ann. 789, § lxxvii.

[2] Bernald. Vit. S. Gerald. cap xv. (Baluz. et Mansi I. 134.)

[3] Socratis Hist. Eccles. Lib. I. c. 25.

caste of the Soûdras.   A specified quantity of deadly poison, varying with the activity of the article administered, is mixed with thirty times its weight of *ghee* or clarified butter.   The patient takes it with his face to the North, and if it produces no effect upon him while the bystanders can clap their hands five hundred times, he is absolved, and antidotes are at once given him.[1]

Having thus described the various forms in which the common principle of the ordeal developed itself, there are some general considerations connected with it which claim brief attention.   It was thoroughly and completely a judicial process, ordained by the law for certain cases, and carried out by the tribunals as a regular form of ordinary procedure.   From the earliest times, the accused who was ordered to undergo the trial was compelled to submit to it, as to any other decree of court.   Thus, by the Salique law, a recusant under such circumstances was summoned to the royal court; and if still contumacious, he was outlawed, and his property confiscated, as was customary in all cases of contempt.[2]   The directions of the codes, as we have seen, are generally precise, and admit of no alternative.[3]   Occasionally, however, a privilege of selection was afforded

---

[1] Ayeen Akbery, II. 497.

[2] That this was a settled practice is shown by its existence in the earliest text of the law (Tit. LVI.), as well as in the latest (L. Emend. Tit. LIX.). It is therefore difficult to understand how Montesquieu could have overlooked it, when, in order to establish his theory that the original Frankish institutions admitted no negative proofs, he asserts with regard to the ordeal that " Cette preuve étoit une chose de convention, que la loi souffroit, mais qu'elle n'ordonnoit pas" (Espr. des Loix, Lib. XXVIII. chap. 16)—a statement contradicted by all the monuments, historical and juridical, of the period. His only proof is a somewhat curious custom of the Salien Franks, to which reference is made below.

[3] Si aufugerit et ordalium vitaverit, solvat plegius compellanti captale suum et regi weram suam, vel si qui wita sua dignus erit.—L. Cnuti Sæc. cap. XXX.—See also cap. xli.

between this and other modes of compurgation, and also between the various forms of ordeal.[1]

The circumstances under which its employment was ordered varied considerably with the varying legislations of races and epochs ; and to enter minutely into the question of the power of the court to decree it, or the right to demand it by the appellant or the defendant, would require too much space, especially as it has already been discussed at some length with regard to the kindred wager of battle. Suffice it to say, that the absence of satisfactory testimony, rendering the case one not to be solved by human means alone, is frequently alluded to as a necessary element ;[2] and indeed we may almost assert that this was so, even when not specifically mentioned, as far as regards the discretion of the tribunal to order an appeal to the judgment of God. Yet there were some exceptions to this, as in the early Russian legislation, where the ordeal is prescribed for the accused in all cases in which the accusation is substantiated by testimony ;[3] and a law of King Ethelred seems

---

[1] Et eligat accusatus alterutrum quod velit, sive simplex ordalium, sive jusjurandum unius libre in tribus hundredis super XXX. den.—L. Henrici I. cap. LXV. § 3. By the municipal codes of Germany, a choice between the various forms of ordeal was sometimes allowed to the accused who was sentenced to undergo it.—Jur. Provin. Alaman. cap. XXXVII. §§ 15, 16 ; Jur. Provin. Saxon. Lib. I. Art. 39.

[2] Si certa probatio non fuerit.—L. Sal. Tit. XIV., XVI. (MS. Guelferbyt.) The same is found in the Pact. Childeberti et Chlotarii § 5—Decret. Chlotarii II. ann. 595, § 6.—Capit. Carol. Calvi, ann. 873, cap. 3, 7.—Cnuti Constit. de Foresta § 11 : "Sed purgatio ignis nullatenus admittatur nisi ubi nuda veritas nequit aliter investigari." Horne's Myrror of Justice, cap. III. Sect. 23 : "En case ou battaille ne se poit joindre ne nul tesmognage n'avoit lieu . . . . e le actor n'ad point de testmoignes a prover sa action, adonque estoit en le volunt del deffendant a purger sa fame per le miracle de Dieu." Further instances are hardly needed, as the same limitation occurs in many of the laws quoted above.

[3] Rouskaïa Prawda, art. 28. Even the evidence of a slave was sufficient to condemn the accused to the red-hot iron. If he escaped, the accuser paid him a small fine, which was not required if the witnesses had been freemen. In all cases of acquittal, however, there were fines payable to the sovereign and to the ministers of justice.

to indicate that the plaintiff might require his adversary
to submit to it,[1] while numerous examples among those
cited above authorize the conclusion that an offer on the
part of the accused was rarely refused, even when there
was strong evidence against him,[2] though this laxity of
practice was occasionally objected to stoutly.[3] When the
custom was declining, indeed, a disposition existed to
require the assent of both parties before the tribunal would
allow a case to be thus decided.[4]   In civil cases, we may
assume that absence of testimony, or the consent of both
parties, was requisite to its employment.[5] The comfort

---

[1] Et omnis accusator vel qui alium impetit, habeat optionem quid velit,
sive judicium aque vel ferri . . . et si fugiet (accusatus) ab ordalio, reddat
eum plegius wera sua."—Ethelr. Tit. III. c. vi. (Thorpe II. 516.)

[2] Thus, in the Icelandic code—" Quodsi reus ferrum candens se gerere velle
obtulerit, hoc minime rejiciatur."—Grágás, Sect. VI. c. 33.   So in the laws
of Bruges in 1190 (§ 31), we find the accused allowed to choose between the
red-hot iron and a regular inquest—" Qui de palingis inpetitur, si ad judicium
ardentis ferri venire noluerit, veritatem comitis qualem melius super hoc
inveniri poterit, accipiet" (Warnkönig, Hist. de la Fland. IV. 372)—showing that it was considered the most absolute of testimony.   And in a constitution of Frederic Barbarossa " Si miles rusticum de violata pace pulsaverit
. . . . de duobus unum rusticus eligat, an divino aut humano judicio innocentiam suam ostendat."—Feudor. Lib. II. Tit. xxvii. § 3.

[3] Thus an anonymous ecclesiastic, in an epistle quoted by Juretus (Observat. in Ivon. Carnot. Epist. 74.)—" Simoniaci non admittuntur ad judicium, si probabiles personæ, etiam laicorum, vel feminarum, pretium se ab
eis recipisse testantur ; nec aliud est pro manifestis venire ad judicium nisi
tentare Dominum."

[4] Duellum vel judicium candentis ferri, vel aquæ ferventis, vel alia canoni-
bus vel legibus improbata, nullomodo in curia Montispessulani rata sunt, nisi
utraque pars convenerit.—Statut. Montispess. ann. 1204 (Du Cange).

[5] Si accolis de neutrius jure constat, adeoque hac in re testimonium dicere
non queant, tum judicio aquæ res decidatur.—Jur. Provin. Alaman. cap.
cclxxviii. § 5.—Poterit enim alteruter eorum petere probationem per aquam
(wasser urteyll) nec Dominus nec adversarius detrectare possit ; sed non, nisi
quum per testes probatio fieri nequit.—Jur. Feud. Alaman. cap. lxxvii. § 2.

" Aut veritas reperiatur de hoc per aquaticum Dei judicium.   Tamen judicium Dei non est licitum adhiberi per ullam causam, nisi cujus veritas per
justitiam non potest aliter reperiri, hoc terminabitur judicio Dei."—Jur.
Feud. Saxon. § 100 (Senckenberg. Corp. Jur. Feud. German. p. 249) —So,

25

which the system must have afforded to indolent judges in doubtful cases is well exhibited by a rule in various ancient codes, by which a man suspected of crime, even though no accuser came forward, was thrown into prison and kept there until he could prove his innocence by the ordeal of water.[1]

We have seen above occasional instances in which the accuser or plaintiff offered to substantiate his veracity by an appeal to the ordeal. This was an established rule with regard to the wager of battle, but not as respects the other forms of the judgment of God, which were regarded rather as means of defence than of attack. I have met with but few instances of general instructions for their employment by the accusing party. In the primitive laws of Russia, an accuser who could not substantiate his case with witnesses was obliged to undergo the ordeal of red-hot iron.[2] Archbishop Hincmar directs that cases of complaint against priests for dissolute life shall be supported by seven witnesses, of whom one must submit to the ordeal to prove the truth of his companions' oaths, as a wholesome check upon perjury and subornation.[3] With a similar object, the same prelate likewise enjoins it on compurgators chosen by the accused, on his failing to obtain the support of those who had been selected for him by his judge.[4] Allied to this was a rule for its employment which was extensively adopted, allowing the accused the privilege of compur-

also, in a later text, "judicium Domini fervida aqua vel ferro non licet in causa aliqua experiri, nisi in qua modis aliis non poterit veritas indagari." —Cap. xxiv. § 19. (Ibid. p. 337.)

[1] Établissements de Normandie, Tit. de Prison (Éd. Marnier). Precisely similar to this was a regulation in the early Bohemian laws,—Bracilai Leges. (Patrol. 151, 1258-9.) And an almost identical provision is found in the Anglo-Saxon jurisprudence.—L. Cnuti Sæc. cap. xxxv.—L. Henric. I. cap. lxi. § 5.—See, also, Assises de Jerusalem, Baisse Court, cclix.

[2] Rouskaïa Prawda, Art. 28.

[3] Hincmari Capit. Synod. ann 852, ii. xxi.

[4] Hincmari Epist. xxxiv.

gation with conjurators in certain cases, only requiring
him to submit to the ordeal on his failing to procure the
requisite number of sponsors. Thus, in 794, a certain
Bishop Peter, who was condemned by the Synod of Frankfort to clear himself, with two or three conjurators, of the
suspicion of complicity in a conspiracy against Charlemagne, being unable to obtain them, one of his vassals
offered to pass through the ordeal in his behalf, and on his
success the Bishop was reinstated.[1] That this was strictly
in accordance with usage is shown by a very early text of
the Salique Law,[2] as well as by a similar provision in the
Ripuarian code.[3] Among the Anglo-Saxons it likewise obtained, from the time of the earliest allusion to the ordeal
occurring in their jurisprudence, down to the period of the
Conquest.[4] So a canon of the Council of Tribur in 895
declares that if a man is so generally suspected that he is
outsworn in compurgation, he must either confess or submit to the hot-iron ordeal.[5] Somewhat similar in tendency
was a regulation of Frederic Barbarossa, by which a slave
suspected of theft was exposed to the red-hot iron, unless
his master would release him by an oath.[6] Occasionally
it was also resorted to when the accused was outsworn,
after having endeavored to defend himself by his oath or
by conjurators. Popular belief might give to the accuser
a larger number of men willing to associate themselves in
the oath of accusation than the defendant could find to

[1] Capit. Car. Mag. ann. 794, § 7.
[2] Se juratores non potuerit invenire, aut ad ineum ambulat aut, etc.—MS.
Guelferbyt. Tit. xiv.
[3] Quod si . . . . juratores invenire non potuerit, ad ignem seu ad sortem
se excusare studeat.—L. Ripuar. Tit. xxxi. § 5.
[4] Dooms of Edward the Elder, cap. iii. So also in the laws of William the
Conqueror, Tit. i. cap. xiv.—"Si sen escundira sei duzime main. E si il
auer nes pot, si sen defende par juise." The collection known by the name
of Henry I. has a similar provision, cap. lxvi. § 3.
[5] Concil. Tribur. ann. 895, can. xxii.
[6] Radevic. de Reb. Frid. Lib. i. cap. xxvi.

join him in rebutting it, and yet his guilt might not as yet
be clear. In such cases, the ordeal was a most convenient
resort.

These regulations give to the ordeal decidedly the aspect
of punishment, as it was thus inflicted on those whose guilt
was so generally believed that they could find none to
stand up with them at the altar as partakers in their oath
of denial; and this is not the only circumstance which
leads us to believe that it was frequently so regarded. The
graduated scale of single and triple ordeals for offences of
different magnitudes is so totally at variance with the theory
of miraculous interposition to protect innocence and punish
guilt, that we can only look upon it as a mode of inflicting
graduated punishments in doubtful cases, thus holding up
a certain penalty *in terrorem* over those who would otherwise hope to escape by the secrecy of their crime—no doubt
with a comforting conviction, like that of De Monfort's
priestly adviser at the sack of Béziers, that Heaven would
know its own. This same principle is visible in a provision
of the charter of Loudun, granted by Louis-le-Gros in 1128,
by which an assault committed outside of the liberties of
the commune could be disproved by a simple sacramental
oath; but if within the limits of the commune, the accused
was obliged to undergo the ordeal.[1] Further evidence is
afforded by the principle, interwoven in various codes, by
which a first crime was defensible by conjurators, or other
means, while the " tiht-bysig" man, the "homo infamatus,"
one of evil repute, whose character had been previously
compromised, was denied this privilege, and was forced at
once to the hot iron or the water. Thus, among the Anglo-
Saxons, in the earliest allusion to the ordeal, by Edward the
Elder, it is provided that perjured persons, or those who had
once been convicted, should not be deemed thereafter oath-
worthy, but should be hurried to the ordeal; a regulation

<hr />

[1] Chart. Commun. Laudun. (Baluz. et Mansi IV. p. 39.)

repeated with some variations in the laws of Ethelred, Cnut, and Henry I.[1] The Carlovingian legislation establishes a similar principle,[2] while the canons of Burckhardt show it to be still in force in the eleventh century.[3] A hundred and fifty years later, the legislation of Flanders manifests the same tendency, the code granted to Bruges in 1190 providing that a first accusation of theft should be decided by witnesses, while a second was to be met by the cold-water ordeal.[4] In the German municipal law of the thirteenth century, the same principle is observable. An officer of the mint issuing false money was permitted the first time to swear to his ignorance, but on a second offence he had to submit to the ordeal; and it was similarly enjoined on those who had become infamous on account of a previous conviction of theft.[5] The contemporary jurisprudence of Spain has a somewhat similar provision, by which a woman accused of homicide could not be exposed to the ordeal, unless she could be proved utterly abandoned, for which a curious standard was requisite,[6] and this is the

---

[1] Ut deinceps non sint digni juramento sed ordalio.—Legg. Edwardi cap. iii.; Ethelredi cap. i. § 1; Cnuti Sæcul. cap. xxii., xxx.; Henrici I. cap. lxv. § 3.

[2] Capit. Car. Mag. I. ann. 809, cap. xxviii.—Capit. Ludov. Pii. I. ann. 819.

[3] Nobilis homo vel ingenuus . . . . cum duodecim ingenuis se expurget. Si antea deprehensus fuerit in furto vel perjurio aut falso testimonio . . . . . ferventi aqua aut candenti ferro se expurget.—Burchardi Decret. Lib. xvi. cap. 19.

[4] Keure de la Châtellenie de Bruges, § 28. (Warnkönig, Hist. de la Fland. IV. 371.)

[5] Jur. Provin. Alaman. cap. clxxxvi. §§ 4, 6, 7; cap. ccclxxiv.; Jur. Provin. Saxon. Lib. I. Art. 39. So, also, in the fourteenth century, the "vir famæ integræ" cleared himself "juramento super reliquiis sanctorum præstito," while, after a first offence "purgare se eum debere portatione ferri candentis, vel immissione brachii usque ad cubitum in aquam ferventem, vel tandem certamine singulari, pronunciatur."—Richstich Landrecht, cap. lii.

[6] Si non fuere provada por mala, que aya yazido con cinco omes.—Fuero de Baeça (Villadiego, Fuero Juzgo, fol. 317 a).

25*

more remarkable, since by the same code a procuress was forced at once to the red-hot iron to prove her innocence. In the legislation of Charlemagne there is a curious provision, by which a man convicted seven times of theft was no longer allowed to escape on payment of a fine, but was forced to undergo the ordeal of fire. If he succumbed, he was put to death; if he escaped unhurt, he was not discharged as innocent, but his lord was allowed to enter bail for his future good behavior[1]—a mode at once of administering punishment and of ascertaining whether his death would be agreeable to Heaven. When we thus regard it as a penalty on those who by misconduct had forfeited the confidence of their fellow-men, the system loses part of its absurdity, in proportion as it departs from the principle under which it was established.

There is also another aspect in which it is probable that the ordeal was viewed by those whose common sense must have shrunk from it as a simple appeal to the judgment of God. There can be little doubt that it was frequently found of material use in extorting confession or unwilling testimony. By the early codes, as in the primitive Greek and Roman law, torture could be applied only to slaves, and the ordeal was a legalized torture, applied under circumstances peculiarly provocative of truth.[2] In those ages of faith, the professing Christian, conscious of guilt, must indeed have been hardened, who could undergo the most awful rites of his religion, pledging his salvation on his innocence, and knowing under such circumstances that the direct intervention of Heaven could alone save him from having his hand boiled to rags,[3] after which he

[1] Capit. Car. Mag. III. ann. 813, cap. 46.

[2] The close relationship between some forms of the ordeal and torture is exemplified in the regulations which frequently enabled the freeman to clear himself of accusations by compurgation, while the slave was required to undergo the ordeal. See, for instance, Concil. Mogunt. ann. 847, can. xxiv.

[3] The severity of the ordeal, when the sufferer had no friends among the operators to save him, may be deduced from the description of a hand when

was to meet the full punishment of his crime, and perhaps
in addition lose a member for the perjury committed. With
such a prospect, all motives would conspire to lead him to
a prompt and frank acknowledgment in the early stages of
the proceedings against him. These views are strengthened by the fact that when, in the thirteenth century, the
judicial use of torture, as a means of obtaining testimony
and confession, was becoming systematized and generally
employed, the ordeal was falling into desuetude and rapidly
disappearing. The latter had fulfilled its mission, and the
former was a substitute better fitted for an age which
reasoned more, believed less, and at the same time was
quite as arbitrary and violent as the preceding. A further
confirmation of this supposition is afforded by the coincidence that the only primitive jurisprudence which excluded
the ordeal—that of the Wisigoths—was likewise the only
one which habitually permitted the use of torture,[1] the
only reference to the ordeal in their code being a provision
which directs its employment as a preliminary to the more
regular forms of torture.

In fact, the ordeal was practically looked upon as a torture by those whose enlightenment led them to regard as a
superstition the faith popularly reposed in it. An epistle
which is attributed both to Stephen V. and Sylvester II.
condemns the whole system on the ground that the canons
forbid the extortion of confessions by heated irons and
boiling water; and that a credulous belief could not be
allowed to sanction that which was not permitted by the
fathers.[2] When, therefore, at the Council of St. Bascul, a
priest named Adalger, in confessing the assistance he had

released from its three days' tying up after its plunge into hot water ; " in-
flatam admodum et excoriatam sanieque jam carne putrida effluentem dex-
teram invitus ostendit." (Du Cange, s. v. *Aquæ Ferv. Judicium.*) In this
case, the sufferer was the adversary of an abbey, the monks of which perhaps
had the boiling of the kettle.

[1] L. Wisig. L. vi. Tit. i. § 3.
[2] Ivon. Carnot. Epist. 74.—Can. Consuluisti. Caus. II. q. 5.

rendered to Arnoul of Rheims during Charles of Lorraine's resistance to the usurpation of Hugh Capet, offered to substantiate his testimony by undergoing the ordeal, he did it in terms which show that he expected it to be regarded as a torture giving additional weight to evidence— "If any of you doubt this and deem me unworthy of belief, let him believe the fire, the boiling water, the glowing iron. Let these tortures convince those who disbelieve my words."[1] It is observable that he omits the cold-water ordeal as not being a torture.

Some of the ordeals, however, such as that of the Eucharist, of bread and cheese, and touching the dead body, do not come within this class, but they addressed themselves powerfully to the conscience and imagination of the accused, whose callous fortitude no doubt often gave way under the trial.[2] In our own country, and almost within our own time, the latter ordeal was revived in one instance with this object, and the result did not disappoint the expectations of those who undertook it. In the case of People vs. Johnson, tried in New York in 1824, the suspected murderer was led from his cell to the hospital where lay the body of the victim, which he was required to touch. Dissimulation which had been before unshaken failed him at the awful moment; his overstrung nerves gave way, and a confession was faltered forth. The proceeding was sustained by court, and a subsequent attempt at retraction was overruled.[3] The powerful influence of such feelings

[1] Concil. Basol. cap. xi. Rainer, private secretary of Arnoul, offered to prove his statement by giving up a slave to walk the burning ploughshares in evidence of his truth. (Ibid. cap. xxx.)

[2] As regards the ordeal of bread, Boccaccio's story of Calendrino (Giorn. viii. Nov. 6), which turns upon the mixing of a quantity of aloes with the food intended for the corsnæd, perhaps throws some light on the miracles reported so freely by the honest monkish chroniclers, and on the practices by which the whole system was rendered subservient to the interests of those intrusted with its administration.

[3] Wharton and Stillé's Med. Jurisp , 2d Ed., 1860.

is shown in a custom which, as recently as 1815, was still employed at Mandeure, near Montbelliard, and which is said to be still in use in some of the remoter districts of the Ardennes. When a theft has been committed, the inhabitants are summoned to assemble after vespers on Sunday at the place of judgment. There the mayor summons the guilty person to make restitution and live in isolation for six months. If this appeal prove fruitless, recourse is had to the trial of the staff, in which two magistrates hold aloft a piece of wood, under which every one is bound to pass. No instance, it is said, is on record in which the culprit dares to do this, and he is always left alone.[1] It is easy thus to imagine how the older forms of ordeal may have conduced to the discovery of crime in ages of lively superstition. A case occurring about the commencement of the twelfth century is a fair illustration of the manner in which it frequently worked on the imagination of those whose lives or fortunes were intrusted to it. A vassal of the convent of St. Mary of Saintes, named André de Trahent, claimed certain property belonging to the convent. On the final hearing it was decreed that he must abandon his claim unless he could prove it by oath and ordeal. This he agreed to do, and on the appointed day he appeared with his men ready to undergo the trial. As there were two pieces of property in question, two ordeals were required. The caldrons of water were duly heated and André's men were prepared for the attempt, when his courage gave way; he abruptly abandoned his claim and submitted himself to the mercy of the abbess.[2]

There are two peculiarities of the system, perhaps worth alluding to, which may be thought to militate against the theory of its use as a torture. The one is the permission sometimes accorded to put forward substitutes or cham-

[1] Michelet, Origines du Droit, p. 349.—Proost, Jugements de Dieu, p. 80.
[2] Polyptichum Irminonis, App. No. 34. (Paris, 1856, p. 373.)

pions, who dared the fire or water as freely as the field of
single combat. Of this custom so many examples have
already been given incidentally, that further instances
would be superfluous, and I would only add that it is nowhere permitted as a general rule by any code, except in
the case already quoted of the ordeal of the cross, where it
was a privilege accorded to the old or infirm, and probably
only as a local custom.   That a person rich enough to
purchase a substitute, or powerful enough to force some
unhappy follower or vassal to take his place, should obtain
a favor not generally allowed, is a matter of course in the
formative periods of society; accordingly, it will be observed that all the instances of the kind mentioned above
relate to those whose dignity or station may well have
rendered them exceptional.

   This is further rendered probable by the fact that exemption from the ordeal was in some places the privilege
of freemen, who were entitled to rebut accusations by the
safer mode of procuring a definite number of compurgators
to take with them the purgatorial oath.   We find this
alluded to as early as the seventh century, in the legislation of the Ripuarian Franks, among whom the ordeal
was reserved for strangers and slaves.   In the early part
of the eleventh century, Burckhardt draws the line with
a distinctness which shows that the custom was well
established at that period.[1] I have already quoted (p. 250)

---

[1] The "nobilis homo vel ingenuus" is permitted to rebut an accusation
with twelve compurgators, but if he had previously been convicted of crime
—"sicut qui ingenuus non est, ferventi aqua aut candenti ferro se expurget."
(Burchardi Decret. Lib. xvi. cap. 19.)

   The law of William the Conqueror (Tit. ii. c. 3.—Thorpe, I. 488) by which
the duel was reserved for the Norman, and the vulgar ordeal for the Saxon,
might be supposed to arise from a similar distinction.   In reality, however,
it was only preserving the ancestral customs of the races, giving to the
defendant the privilege of his own law.   The duel was unknown to the
Anglo-Saxons, who habitually employed the ordeal, while the Normans, previous to the Conquest, according to Houard, who is good authority (Anc.
Loix Franc. I. 221–222), only appealed to the sword.

a document of 1051 giving a similar regulation in Alsace, while in 1192 the burghers of Ghent inserted it in a charter which they extorted from the Countess Matilda, widow of Philip I.[1] So when, in 1085, the Emperor Henry IV. proclaimed the Truce of God, at the Assembly of Mainz, he directed that those accused of infringing it should, if freemen, clear themselves with twelve approved compurgators, while serfs and villeins were forced to undergo the water ordeal.[2]

The other objection to our hypothesis is that to some extent the common ordeal was a plebeian process, while the patricians arrogated to themselves the wager of battle. This distinction, however, hardly existed before the rise of feudalism gave all privileges to those who were strong enough to seize them, and even then it was by no means universal. We have already seen that, although in the early part of the eleventh century the Emperor Henry II. undoubtedly promulgated such a rule, yet Glanville, a hundred and fifty years later, considers the red-hot iron as noble, and that in the thirteenth century the feudal law of Germany prescribes the *wasser-urteyll* for territorial disputes between gentlemen.   In the earlier codes the distinction is unknown, so that we are justified in assuming that no general principles can be deduced from a regulation so late in its appearance and so uncertain in its application.

The degree of confidence really inspired by the results of the ordeal is a somewhat curious subject of speculation, and one on which definite opinions are not easily reached. Judicially, the trial was conclusive; the man who had duly sunk under water, walked unharmed among the burning

---

[1] Si cui imputetur et convictus non fuerit, liber per duodecim liberos se purgabit, non liber judicio aquæ frigidæ.—Keure de Gand, §§ 7, 8, 12. (Warnkönig, Hist. de la Fland. II. 228.) We see that it is here directed to be used merely in default of other testimony, before liberating the accused who could not be otherwise convicted.

[2] Henrici IV. Constit. iv.   (Migne's Patrolog. 151, 1135.)

shares, or withdrawn an unblistered hand from a caldron
of legal temperature, stood forth among his fellows as
innocent. So, even now, the verdict of twelve fools or
knaves in a jury-box may discharge a criminal, against
the plainest dictates of common sense; but in neither case
would the sentiments of the community be changed by the
result. The reverential feelings which alone could impart
faith in the system seem scarcely compatible with the practice of compounding for ordeals, through which a man was
permitted to buy himself off, by settling the matter with his
accuser. This mode of adjustment was not extensively
introduced, but it nevertheless existed among the Anglo-
Saxons,[1] while among the Franks it was a settled custom,
permitted by all the texts of the Salique law, from the
earliest to the latest.[2] Charlemagne, at the commencement
of his reign, does not seem to have entertained much respect for the judgment of God when he prescribed the
administration of the ordeal for trifling affairs only, cases
of magnitude being reserved for the regular investigation
of the law.[3] Thirty years later, the public mind appears

---

[1] Dooms of Æthelstan, I. cap. 21.

[2] First Text, Tit. LIII. and L. Emend. Tit. LV.—A person condemned by
the court to undergo the ordeal could, by a transaction with the aggrieved
party, purchase the privilege of clearing himself by canonical compurgation,
and thus escape the severer trial. He was bound to pay his accuser only a
portion of the fine which he would incur if proved guilty—a portion varying
with different offences from one-fourth to one-sixth of the *wehr-gild*. The
interests of the tribunal were guarded by a clause which compelled him to
pay to the *grafio*, or judge, the full *fredum*, or public fine, if his conscience
impelled him to submit to an arrangement for more than the legal per-
centage. It is on this custom that Montesquieu relies to support his theory
of the absence of negative proofs in the Frankish jurisprudence. The fallacy
of the argument is however shown by the existence of a similar privilege in
the Anglo-Saxon laws, with which the learned jurist endeavors to establish
a special contrast.

[3] Quod si accusatus contendere voluerit de ipso perjurio stent ad crucem.
. . . Hoc vero de minoribus rebus. De majoribus vero, aut de statu inge-
nuitatis, secundum legem custodiant.—Capit. Car. Mag. ann. 779, § 10.

afflicted with the same doubts, for we find the monarch
endeavoring to enforce confidence in the system by his
commands.[1] How far he succeeded in this difficult attempt
we have no means of ascertaining; but a rule of English
law, nearly four hundred years later, during the expiring
struggles of the practice, would show that it was regarded
as by no means conclusive. By the assizes of Clarendon
in 1166, which directed that all malefactors indicted for
murder, robbery, and other felonies should be at once tried
by the water ordeal, it was provided that those who had
confessed or who had been found in possession of stolen
property should not be allowed the privilege of clearing
themselves by ordeal; and a still more irreverential rule
decreed that those who were pronounced innocent by the
judgment of God, if regarded as guilty by common report,
should have eight days to quit the kingdom, under pain of
outlawry.[2] In the revision of these laws, made at Northampton in 1176, it was provided that in all cases those
who passed safely through the ordeal should give bail for
their future good conduct, except in charges of murder or
aggravated felony when they were banished within forty
days, under penalty of outlawry as before.[3] St. Ivo of
Chartres, though he had no scruple in recommending and
enjoining the ordeal, and, on one occasion at least, pronounced its decisions as beyond appeal, yet has placed on
record his conviction of its insufficiency, and his experience
that the mysterious judgment of God not infrequently allowed in this manner the guilty to escape and the innocent

That this was respected as law in force, nearly a hundred years later, is
shown by its being included in the collection of Capitularies by Benedict the
Levite. (Lib. v. cap. 196)

[1] Ut omnes judicio Dei credant absque dubitatione.—Capit. Car. Mag. i.
ann. 809, § 20.

[2] Assisa facta apud Clarendune §§ 12, 13, 14 (Gesta Henrici II. T. II.
p. clii —Ed. Rer. Britann. Script.)

[3] Gesta Henrici II. T. I. p. 108.—Cf. Bracton. Lib III. Tract. ii. cap.
16, § 3.

to be punished.[1] There is also evidence that the manifest
injustice of the results obtained not infrequently tried the
faith of believers to a degree which required the most
ingenious sophistry for an explanation. When, in 1127, the
sacrilegious murder of Charles the Good, Earl of Flanders,
sent a thrill of horror throughout Europe, Lambert of Re-
denberg, whose participation in the crime was notorious,
succeeded in clearing himself by the hot iron. Shortly
afterwards he undertook the siege of Ostbourg, which he
prosecuted with great cruelty, when he was killed in a sally
of the besieged. The pious Galbert assumes that Lambert,
notwithstanding his guilt, escaped at the ordeal in consequence of his humility and repentance, and philosophically
adds: "Thus it is that in battle the unjust man is killed,
although in the ordeal of water or of fire he may escape, if
truly repentant."[2] The same doctrine was enunciated under
John Cantacuzenes, in the middle of the fourteenth century,
by a Bishop of Didymoteichos in Thrace. A frail fair one
being violently suspected by her husband, the ordeal of hot
iron was demanded by him. In this strait she applied to
the good Bishop, and he, being convinced of her repentance
and intention to sin no more, assured her that in such a
frame of mind she might safely venture on the trial, and
she accordingly carried the glowing bar triumphantly twice
around the Bishop's chair, to the entire satisfaction of her
lord and master.[3] While repentance thus enabled the criminal to escape, on the other hand the innocent were sometimes held to be liable to conviction, on account of previous
misdeeds. A striking instance of the vague notions current is afforded in the middle of the eleventh century by a

[1] Simili modo, cauterium militis nullum tibi certum præbet argumentum,
cum per examinationem ferri candentis occulto Dei judicio multos videamus
nocentes liberatos, multos innocentes sæpe damnatos.—Ivon. Carnot. Epist.
ccv.
[2] Vit. Carol. Comit. Flandren. cap. xx.
[3] Collin de Plancy, op. cit. s. v. *Fer Chaud*

case related by Othlonus, in which a man accused of horse-stealing was tried by the cold-water ordeal and found guilty. Knowing his own innocence, he appealed to the surrounding monks, and was told that it must be in consequence of some other sin not properly redeemed by penance. As he had confessed and received absolution before the trial, he denied this, till one of them pointed out that in place of allowing his beard to grow, as was meet for a layman, he had impiously carried the smooth chin reserved for ecclesiastics. Confessing his guilt, promising due penance, and vowing never to touch his beard with a razor again, he was conducted a second time to the water, and being now free from all unrepented sin, he was triumphantly acquitted.[1]

Yet, on the other hand, the ordeal sometimes was regarded as the most satisfactory kind of proof, entitled to respect beyond any other species of evidence. The age was not logical, men acted more from impulse than from reason, and the forms of jurisprudence were still in a state too chaotic for regular and invariable rules to be laid down. The confusion existing in the popular mind is well illustrated by a case occurring in the twelfth century. A serf of the Abbey of Marmoutiers married a serf who had been given by the Viscount of Blois to one of his retainers named Erbald. The husband purchased his wife's liberty, and by paying an additional sum had the deed of manumission confirmed by the Viscount and Viscountess. Years passed away, the serf and his wife died, and then also their son, when their property fell to the abbey, which enjoyed it until the heirs of Erbald and the Viscount claimed it. The monks produced the deed of manumission, and the Viscountess, then the only surviving witness to the transaction, testified to its authenticity, but to no purpose. The

---

[1] Othlon. Narrat de Mirac. quod nuper accidit, &c. (Patrol. 146, 243–4.) Lapsing again, however, into the sin of shaving, upon a quibble as to the kind of instrument employed, the anger of Heaven manifested itself by allowing him to fall into the hands of an enemy who put out his eyes.

claimants demanded the wager of battle, and the monks, in refusing this as unsuited to their calling, were obliged to produce a man who offered to undergo the ordeal of red-hot iron to prove the validity of the deed.   Then the claimants at last desisted, but still succeeded in extorting sixteen livres from the abbey as the price of appending their signatures to the controverted deed.[1]

In general, however, as the result depended mostly upon those who administered the ordeal, it conferred an irresponsible power to release or to condemn, and it would be expecting too much of human nature to suppose that men did not yield frequently to the temptation to abuse that power.   The injustice thus practised must often have shaken the most robust faith, and this cause of disbelief would receive additional strength from the fact that the result itself was not seldom in doubt, victory being equally claimed by both parties.   Of this we have already seen examples in the affairs of the lance of St. Andrew and of the Archbishop of Milan, and somewhat similar is an incident recorded by the Bollandists in the life of St. Swithin, in which, by miraculous interposition, the opposing parties beheld entirely different results from an appeal to the red-hot iron.[2]

Efforts of course were made from time to time to preserve the purity of the appeal, and to secure impartiality in its application.   Clotair II., in 595, directs that three chosen persons shall attend on each side to prevent collusion;[3] and among the Anglo-Saxons, some four hundred years later, Ethelred enjoins the presence of the prosecutor under

---

[1] Polyptichum Irminonis, App. No. 20 (Paris, 1836, p. 354).

[2] Enimvero mirum fuit ultra modum, quod fautores arsuram et inflationem conspiciebant; criminatores ita sanam ejus videbant palmam, quasi penitus fulvum non tetigisset ferrum.—Mirac. S. Swithuni c. ii. § 37.   In this case, the patient was a slave, whose master had vowed to give him to the church in case he escaped.

[3] Ad utramque partem sint ternas personas electas, ne conludius fieri possit.—Decret. Chlotharii II. cap. vii.

penalty of loss of suit and fine of twenty *ores*, apparently
for the same object, as well as to give authenticity to the
decision.[1] So in Hungary, the laws of St. Ladislas, in 1092,
direct that three sworn witnesses shall be present to attest
the innocence or guilt of the accused as demonstrated by
the result.[2] A law adopted by the Scottish Parliament
under William the Lion, in the second half of the twelfth
century, shows that corruption was not uncommon, by forbidding those concerned in the administration of ordeals
from receiving bribes to divert the course of justice,[3] and
a further precaution was taken by prohibiting the Barons
from adjudging the ordeal without the intervention of the
sheriff to see that law and justice were observed.[4] In the
trial by red-hot iron, a widely prevailing custom ordered
that for three days previous the hand should be wrapped up
to guard against its being fortified; and among the Greeks
a careful provision was made that the hand should be thoroughly washed and allowed to touch nothing afterwards,
lest there should be an opportunity of anointing it with
unguents which would enable it to resist the fire.[5] These
regulations show that evils were recognized, but we may reasonably hesitate to believe that the remedies were effectual.

The Church was not a unit in its relations to the ordeal.
During the earlier periods, indeed, scarce a question seems
to have been entertained as to the propriety of the practice;
it was sanctioned by councils, and administered by ecclesiastics, and, as we have seen, numerous formulas of prayers
and adjurations were authoritatively provided for all the
different varieties in use. This unanimity was, however,

---

[1] Ethelred, III. § 4.
[2] Synod. Zaboles, can. 27 (Batthyani, Legg. Eccles. Hung. T. I. p. 439).
[3] Statut. Wilhelmi Regis cap. 7, § 3.   (Skene II. 4.)
[4] Ibid. cap. 16.
[5] Du Cange, s. v. *Ferrum candens.*

soon disturbed. At the commencement of the sixth century, Avitus, Bishop of Vienne, remonstrated freely with
Gundobald on account of the prominence given to the
battle ordeal in the Burgundian code ; and some three centuries later, St. Agobard, Archbishop of Lyons, attacked
the whole system in two powerful treatises, which in many
points display a breadth of view and clearness of reasoning
far in advance of his age.[1] Soon after, Leo IV., about the
middle of the ninth century, condemned it in a letter to
the English bishops ; some thirty years later, Stephen V.
repeated the disapproval; in the tenth century, Sylvester II.
opposed it ; and succeeding pontiffs, such as Alexander II.
and Alexander III., in vain protested against it. In this,
the chiefs of the Church placed themselves in opposition to
their subordinates.   No ordeal could be conducted without
priestly aid, and the frequency of its employment which
has been seen above, shows how little the Papal exhorta-
tions were respected by the ministers of the Church. Nor
were they contented with simple disregard ; defenders were
not wanting to pronounce the ordeal in accordance with the
Divine law, and it was repeatedly sanctioned by provincial
synods and councils.   In 799 the Council of Salzburg prescribed the red-hot iron for the trial of witches and necro-
mancers.[2] In 853, the Synod of Soissons ordered Burchard,
Bishop of Chartres, to prove his fitness for the episcopal
office by undergoing the ordeal.[3] Hincmar, Archbishop
of Rheims, lent to it all the influence of his commanding
talents and position ; the Council of Mainz in 888, and
that of Tribur near Mainz in 895, recommended it; that
of Tours in 925 ordered it for the decision of a quarrel
between two priests respecting certain tithes ;[4] the synod

---

[1] The "Liber adversus Legem Gundobadi" and "Liber contra Judicium
Dei."

[2] Concil. Salisburg. I. can. ix. (Dalham. Concil. Salisburg. p. 35.)

[3] Capit. Carol. Calvi Tit. xi. c. iii.   (Baluze.)

[4] Concil. Turon. ann. 925 (Martene et Durand Thes. T. IV. pp. 72–3).

of the province of Mainz in 1028 authorized the hot iron in a case of murder;[1] that of Elne in 1065 recognized it; that of Auch in 1068 confirmed its use ; Burckhardt, Bishop of Worms, whose collection of canons enjoyed high authority, in 1023 assisted at the Council of Selingenstadt, which directed its employment. The Synod of Gran, in 1099, decided that the ordeal of hot iron might be administered during Lent, except in cases involving the shedding of blood.[2] In the twelfth century, we find St. Bernard alluding approvingly to the conviction and martyrdom of heretics by the cold-water process,[3] of which Guibert de Nogent gives us an instance wherein he aided the Bishop of Soissons in administering it to two backsliders with complete success.[4] Other cases, moreover, are related by Peter Cantor in which good Catholics were successfully convicted of heresy in this manner, and one instance presents a curious view of the singular confusion which existed in judicial logic at the time. A poor fellow who professed the most entire orthodoxy, and against whom there was no proof, was ordered to carry the red hot iron. This he refused unless the assembled bishops would prove that he could do so without incurring mortal sin by tempting God. This they were unable to accomplish, so all unpleasant doubts were settled by promptly having him burnt.[5]

Prelates were everywhere found granting charters containing the privilege of conducting trials in this manner. It was sometimes specially appropriated to members of the church, who claimed it, under the name of " Lex Monachorum," as a class privilege exempting them from being parties to the more barbarous and uncanonical wager of

---

[1] Annalist. Saxo. ann. 1028.

[2] Batthyani, Legg. Eccles. Hung. II. 126.

[3] Examinati judicio aquæ mendaces inventi sunt . . . . aqua eos non suscipiente.—In Cantica, Sermo 66, cap. 12.

[4] De Vita Sua, Lib. III. cap. 18.

[5] Pet. Cantor. Verb. Abbreviat. cap. lxxviii. (Patrol. CCV. 230.)

battle ;[1] and in 1061 a charter of John, Bishop of Avran-
ches, to the Abbot of Mont S. Michel, alludes to hot water
and iron as the only mode of trying priests charged with
offences of magnitude.[2] There was therefore but slender
ground for so eminent a canonist as St. Ivo of Chartres,
about the same period, to insist that ecclesiastics enjoyed
immunity from it, while admitting that the incredulity of
mankind sometimes required an appeal to the decision of
Heaven, even though such appeals were not commanded
by the Divine law.[3] Pope Calixtus II. himself, about the

---

[1] Theodericus Abbas Vice-Comitem adiit paratus aut calidi ferri judicio
secundum legem monachorum per suum hominem probare, aut scuto et
baculo secundum legem secularium deffendere.—Annal. Benedict. L. 57, No.
74, ann. 1036 (ap. Houard, Loix Anc. Franç. I. 267).

[2] Judicium ferri igniti et aquæ ferventis Abrincis portaretur, si clerici
lapsi in culpam degradationis forte invenirentur.—Chart. Joan. Abrinc.
(Patrolog. 147. 266.)

[3] Herbert, Bishop of le Mans, was accused by Henry I. of England of endeavoring to betray that city to its former master, and was ordered to prove
his innocence by the ordeal of hot iron. Ivo assured him (Epist. 74)
that no law or custom required it of an ecclesiastic, and we may presume
that churchmen knew too much of the ordeal to trust themselves willingly
to it, except when the management was in their own hands. A century
earlier, St. Abbo of Fleury had claimed the same exemption for his order—
"Ecce fama exiit, quod contra divinas humanasque leges abbas ignito ferro
se purgare voluit." (Abbon. Floriac. Epist. viii.) Ivo, however, allows it
for laymen. "Non negamus tamen quin ad divina aliquando recurrendum
sit testimonia quando, præcedente ordinaria accusatione, omnino desunt
humana testimonia : non quod lex hoc instituerit divina, sed quod exigat
incredulitas humana." (Epist. 252.) And again : "Vel, si id facere non
poterit, candentis ferri examinatione innocentiam suam comprobet. Si hæc
causa apud me ita ventilaretur, ita eam vellem tractari" (Epist. 249). And
in another instance he pronounces the result of such a trial to be a decision
beyond appeal. "Audivi enim quod vir ille de quo agitur, de objecto crimine
examinatione igniti ferri se purgaverit, et a læsione ignis illæsus repertus sit.
Quod si ita est . . . contra divinum testimonium nullum ulterius investigan-
dum intelligo esse judicium." (Epist. 232.)

The immunity claimed by ecclesiastics in England also is shown by Ecg-
behrt, Archbishop of York, who directed that when they were unable to procure compurgators, their unsupported oath on the cross was sufficient, their
punishment, if guilty, being left to God. "Pro idcirco sancimus eum cui

same period, gave his sanction to the system, in the Council of Rheims, in 1119.[1] About the same time, the learned priest Honorius of Autun specifies the benediction of the iron and water of the ordeal as part of the legitimate functions of his order;[2] and even Gratian, in 1151, hesitates to condemn the whole system, preferring to consider the canon of Stephen V. as prohibiting only the ordeals of hot water and iron.[3]

This discrepancy is easily explained. During the tenth and eleventh centuries, the chair of St. Peter was occupied too often by men whose more appropriate sphere of action was the brothel or the arena, and the influence of the Papacy was feeble in the extreme.[4] The Eternal City was civilly

crimen impingitur, ut penat super caput ejus crucem Domini, et testetur per Viventem in secula, cujus patibulum est crux, sese immunem esse a peccato hujusmodi. Et sic omnia dimittenda sunt judicio Dei."—Dialog. Ecgbert. Ebor. Interrog. III. (Thorpe, II. 88.)

About 1171, Alexander III. in an epistle to the Archbishop of Upsala stigmatizes as an intolerable abuse that throughout Sweden prelates even of the highest rank were forced to undergo the ordeal of hot iron.—Alex. PP. III. Epist. App. I. No. 19 (Hardouin. VI. ii. p. 1439.)

[1] Du Cange, s. v. *Judicium probabile.*

[2] Gemma Animæ, Lib. I. cap. 181. At least this is the only reading which will make sense of the passage—"Horum officium est . . . vel nuptias vel arma, vel peras, vel baculos vel judicia ferre et aquas vel candelas . . . benedicere," where "ferre et aquas" is evidently corrupt for "ferri et aquæ."

[3] Hoc autem utrum ad omnia genera purgationis, an ad hæc duo tantum, quæ hic prohibita esse videntur, pertineat, non immerito dubitatur propter sacrificium zelotypiæ, et illud Gregorii.—Can. Consuluisti, caus. II. Quæst. 5.

[4] In 963, a council of bishops held by Otho I. to depose John XII. pronounced that the Pope had turned his residence into a brothel—"sanctum palatium lupanar et prostibulum fecisse," and was in the habit of leading his own soldiers "incendia fecisse, ense accinctum, galea et lorica indutum esse." (Liutprandi Hist. Otton. cap. x.) Otho III. in 998, when restoring a portion of the alienated patrimony of St. Peter, alludes to the diminished influence and authority of the Papal See. "Romam caput mundi profitemur. Romanam Ecclesiam matrem omnium Ecclesiarum esse testamur ; sed incuria et inscientia Pontificum longe suæ claritatis titulos obfuscasse." (Goldast. Constit. Imp. I. 226.)

and morally a lazar-house, and the Popes had too much to do in maintaining themselves upon their tottering thrones to have leisure or inclination for combined and systematic efforts to extend their power. The Italian expeditions of the Saxon and Franconian Emperors gradually brought Italy out of the isolation into which it had fallen, and under Teutonic auspices the character of the Pontiffs improved as their circle of influence widened. At length such men as Gregory VII. and Alexander III. were able to claim supremacy over both temporal and spiritual affairs, and, after a long resistance on the part of the great body of ecclesiastics, the tiara triumphed over the mitre. During this period, the clergy found in the administration of the ordeal a source of power and profit which naturally rendered them unwilling to abandon it at the Papal mandate. Chartered privileges had accumulated around it, such as we have already seen in the case of the judicial duel, and these privileges were participated in or held exclusively by prelates and churches and monasteries. Thus in 1148 we find Thibaut the Great of Champagne making over to the church of St. Mary Magdalen the exclusive privilege of administering the oaths required on such occasions in the town of Chateaudun;[1] and in 1182 the Vicomte de Béarn conferred on the Abbey de la Seauve the revenue arising from the marble basin used for the trial by boiling water at Gavarret.[2] In the statutes of King Coloman of Hungary, collected in 1099, there is a provision prohibiting the administration of the ordeal in the smaller churches, and reserving the privilege to the cathedral seats and other important establishments.[3]

According to a grant from Péregrin de Lavedan to the monastery of Saint-Pé, in Bigorre, the fee for administering the hot-water ordeal was five crowns, of which two were paid

[1] Du Cange, s. v. *Adramire*.

[2] Revue Hist. de Droit, 1861, p. 478.

[3] Decret. Coloman. c. 11. (Batthyani T. I. p. 454.)

to the monastery, two to the cathedral at Tarbes, and one to the priest who blessed the water and stone.[1] By the laws of St. Ladislas of Hungary, in 1092, the stipend of the officiating priest for the red-hot iron was double that which he received for the water ordeal;[2] and how fiercely these rights were enforced is shown in a case related by Peter Cantor in the twelfth century. A man accused of crime was sentenced to undergo the ordeal of cold water. When stripped and bound, and seated on the edge of the tank, the prosecutor withdrew the suit, but the official of the court refused to release the accused until he should pay fees amounting to nine livres and a half. A long wrangle ensued, until the defendant declared that he would pay nothing, but would rather undergo the ordeal, and, after establishing his innocence, would give fifty sols to the poor. He was accordingly thrown in and sank satisfactorily, but on being drawn out was met with a fresh claim from the officiating priest, of five sols, for blessing the water.[3]

As these fees were paid, sometimes on conviction and sometimes on acquittal, there was danger that self-interest might lead to bringing about a given result. Thus by the acts of the Synod of Lillebonne, in 1080, a conviction by the hot iron ordeal entailed a fine for the benefit of the bishop;[4] it was apparently to prevent such influences that the Swedish laws made the successful party, whether the prosecutor or defendant, pay the fee to the officiating priest—a regulation sufficiently degrading to the sacerdotal character.[5] But besides these pecuniary advantages, the ordeal had a natural attraction to the clergy, as it afforded the means of awing the laity, by rendering the

[1] Lagrèze, Hist. du Droit dans les Pyrénées, p. 246.
[2] "Presbyter de ferro duas pensas et de aqua unam pensam accipiat." Synod. Zaboles. ann. 1092 can. 27 (Batthyani I. 439.)
[3] Pet. Cantor. Verb. Abbreviat. cap. xxiv.
[4] Orderic. Vital. Lib. v. cap. v.
[5] Leg. Scanicar. Lib. vii. cap. 15. (Du Cange, s. v. Ferrum candens.)

priest a special instrument of Divine justice, into whose
hands every man felt that he was at any moment liable to
fall; and even worse uses were sometimes made of the
irresponsible power thus intrusted to unworthy ministers.
From the decretals of Alexander III. we learn authoritatively that the extortion of money from innocent persons
by its instrumentality was a notorious fact[1]—a testimony
confirmed by Ekkehardus Junior, who, a century earlier,
makes the same accusation, and moreover inveighs bitterly
against the priests who were wont to gratify the vilest
instincts in stripping women for the purpose of exposing
them to the ordeal of cold water.[2]

At length, when the Papal authority reached its culmi-
nating point, a vigorous and sustained effort to abolish the
whole system was made by the Popes who occupied the
pontifical throne from 1159 to 1227. Nothing can be more
peremptory than the prohibition uttered by Alexander III.[3]
About the same time we find the celebrated Peter Cantor
earnestly arguing that it was a sinful tempting of God and
a most uncertain means of administering justice, which he
enforces by numerous instances of innocent persons who
within his own knowledge had been condemned by its means
and put to death; and he declares that any priest exorcis-
ing the iron or water or administering the oaths preliminary
to the judicial duel is guilty of mortal sin.[4] In 1181, Lucius

---

[1] Post Concil. Lateran. P. II. cap. 3, 11.

[2] Holophernicos . . . . Presbyteros, qui animas hominum carissime appre-
ciatas vendant; fœminas nudatas aquis immergi impudicis oculis curiose per-
spiciant, aut grandi se pretio redimere cogant.—De Casibus S. Galli, cap. xiv.

[3] Alex. PP. III. Epist. 74.

[4] Pet. Cantor. Verb. Abbreviat. cap. lxxviii.—One case fairly illustrates
how simple it rendered judicial investigations. Two friends were returning
from a pilgrimage to the Holy Land. One of them turned off to visit the
shrine of S. Jago di Compostella, while the other proceeded directly to his
home in England. The kindred of his companion accused him of murdering
their relative. He was promptly turned over to the ordeal, convicted and
executed; shortly after which the missing man turned up.

III. pronounced null and void the acquittal of a priest charged with homicide, who had undergone the water-ordeal, and ordered him to prove his innocence with compurgators,[1] and the blow was followed by his successors. Under Innocent III., the Fourth Council of Lateran, in 1215, formally forbade the employment of any ecclesiastical ceremonies in such trials;[2] and as the moral influence of the ordeal depended entirely upon its religious associations, a strict observance of this canon must speedily have swept the whole system into oblivion. Yet at this very time the inquisitor Conrad of Marburg was employing in Germany the red-hot iron as a means of condemning his unfortunate victims by wholesale, and the chronicler relates that, whether innocent or guilty, few escaped the test.[3] The canon of Lateran, however, was actively followed up by the Papal legates, and the effect was soon discernible.

Perhaps the earliest instance of secular legislation directed against the ordeal, except some charters granted to communes, is an edict of Philip Augustus in 1200, bestowing certain privileges on the scholars of the University of Paris, by which he ordered that a citizen accused of assaulting a student shall not be allowed to defend himself either by the duel or the water ordeal.[4] In England, a rescript of Henry III., dated January 27, 1219, directs the judges then starting on their circuits to employ other modes of proof—"seeing that the judgment of fire and water is forbidden by the Church of Rome."[5] A few charters and

---

[1] Can. Ex tuarum, Extra, De purgatione canonica.

[2] Nec . . . quisquam purgationi aquæ ferventis vel frigidæ, seu ferri candentis ritum cujuslibet benedictionis seu consecrationis impendat.—Concil. Lateran. can. 18. In 1227, the Council of Trèves repeated the prohibition, but only applied it to the red-hot iron ordeal. "Item, nullus sacerdos candens ferrum benedicat."—Concil. Trevirens. ann. 1227, cap. ix.

[3] Trithem. Chron. Hirsaug. ann. 1215.

[4] Fontanon, IV. 942.

[5] Rymer, Fœd. I. 228—"Cum prohibitum sit per Ecclesiam Romanam judicium ignis et aquæ."

27

confirmations, dated some years subsequently, allude to the privilege of administering it; but Matthew of Westminster, when enumerating, under date of 1250, the remarkable events of the half century, specifies its abrogation as one of the occurrences to be noted,[1] and we may conclude that thenceforth it was practically abandoned throughout the kingdom. This is confirmed by the fact that Bracton, whose treatise was written a few years later, refers only to the wager of battle as a legal procedure, and, when alluding to other forms, speaks of them as things of the past. About the same time, Alexander II. of Scotland forbade its use in cases of theft.[2] Nearly contemporary was the Neapolitan Code, promulgated in 1231, by authority of the Emperor Frederic II., in which he not only prohibits the use of the ordeal in all cases, but ridicules, in a very curious passage, the folly of those who could place confidence in it.[3] We may conclude, however, that this was not effectual in eradicating it, for, fifty years later, Charles of Anjou found it

---

[1] Prohibitum est judicium quod fieri consuevit per ignem et per aquam.— Mat. Westmon. ann. 1250.

[2] De cetero non fiat judicium per aquam vel ferrum, ut consuetum fuit antiquis temporibus.—Statut. Alex. II. cap. 7, § 3.

[3] Leges quæ a quibusdam simplicibus sunt dictæ paribiles . . . . præsentis nostri nominis sanctionis edicto in perpetuum inhibentes, omnibus regni nostri judicibus, ut nullus ipsas leges paribiles, quæ absconsæ a veritate deberent potius nuncupari, aliquibus fidelibus nostris indicet . . . . Eorum etinim sensum non tam corrigendum duximus quam ridendum, qui naturalem candentis ferri calorem tepescere, imo (quod est stultius) frigescere, nulla justa causa superveniente, confidunt; aut qui reum criminis constitutum, ob conscientiam læsam tantum asserunt ab aquæ frigidæ elemento non recipi, quem submergi potius aeris competentis retentio non permittit.—Constit. Sicular. Lib. II. Tit. 31. This last clause would seem to allude to some artifice of the operators by which the accused was prevented from sinking in the cold-water ordeal when a conviction was desired.

This common sense view of the miracles so generally believed is the more remarkable as coming from Frederic, who, a few years previously, was ferociously vindicating with fire and sword the sanctity of the Holy Seamless Coat against the aspersions of unbelieving heretics. See his Constitutions of 1221 in Goldastus, Const. Imp. I. 293–4.

necessary to repeat the injunction.[1] About the same time, Waldemar II. of Denmark, Hako Hakonsen of Iceland and Norway, and soon afterwards Birger Jarl of Sweden, followed the example.[2] In Frisia we learn that, in 1219, the inhabitants still refused to obey the Papal mandates, and insisted on retaining the red-hot iron;[3] though a century later the Laws of Upstallesboom show that ordeals of all kinds had fallen into desuetude.[4] In France, we find no formal abrogation promulgated; but the contempt into which the system had fallen is abundantly proved by the fact that in the ordinances and books of practice issued during the latter half of the century, such as the *Établissements* of St. Louis, the *Conseil* of Pierre de Fontaines, the *Coutumes du Beauvoisis* of Beaumanoir, and the *Livres de Jostice et de Plet*, its existence is not recognized even by a prohibitory allusion, the judicial duel thenceforward monopolizing the province of irregular evidence. Indeed, a Latin version of the Coutumier of Normandy, dating about the middle of the thirteenth century, or a little earlier, speaks of it as a mode of proof formerly employed in cases where one of the parties was a woman who could find no champion to undergo the wager of battle, adding that it had been forbidden by the church, and that such cases were then determined by inquests.[5]

[1] Statut. MSS. Caroli I. cap. xxii. (Du Cange, s. v. *Lex Parib.*)

[2] Königswarter, op. cit. p. 176.

[3] Emo, the contemporary Abbot of Wittewerum, instances this disobedience as one of the causes of the terrible inundation of 1219.—Emon. Chron. ann. 1219 (Matthæi Analect. III. 72).

[4] Issued in 1323.

[5] Olim mulieres criminalibus causis insecute, cum non haberent qui eas defenderent, se purgabant per aquam. . . . . Et quoniam hujusmodi ab ecclesia catholica sunt abscissa, inquisicione locorum eorum frequenter utimur et in multris.—Cod. Leg. Norman. P. II c. x. §§ 2, 3. (Ludewig, Reliq. Msctorum. VII. 292.) It is a little singular that the same phrase is retained in the authentic copy of the Coutumier, in force until the close of the sixteenth century.—Anc. Cout. de Normandie, c. 77 (Bourdot de Richebourg, IV. 32).

Germany was more tardy in yielding to the mandates of the church. The Teutonic knights who wielded their proselyting swords in the Marches of Prussia introduced the ordeal among other Christian observances, and in 1225 Honorius III., at the prayer of the Livonian converts, promulgated a decree by which he strictly interdicted its use for the future.[1] Even in 1279 we find the Council of Buda, and in 1298 that of Wurzburg, obliged to repeat the prohibition uttered by that of Lateran.[2] The independent spirit of the Empire, however, still refused obedience to the commands of the Church, and even in the fourteenth century the ancestral customs were preserved in full vigor as regular modes of procedure in a manual of legal practice still extant. An accusation of homicide could be disproved only by the judicial combat, while in other felonies a man of bad repute had no other means of escape than by undergoing the ordeal of hot water or iron.[3]

In Arragon, Don Jayme I., in 1247, prohibited it in the laws of Huesca,[4] and in 1248 in his revision of the constitution of Majorca.[5] In Castile and Leon, the Council of Palencia, in 1322, was obliged to threaten with excommunication all concerned in administering the ordeal of fire or of water,[6] which proves how little had been accomplished by the enlightened code of the " Partidas," issued about 1260 by Alfonso the Wise. In this the burden of proof is expressly thrown upon the complainant, and no negative

---

[1] Can. Dilecti, Extra, De Purgatione Vulgari.

[2] Batthyani, Legg. Eccles. Hung T. II. p. 436. Hartzheim, IV. 27.

[3] Haud secus purgare se possit imputatorum criminum ergo quam, ut supra dictum, ferro candente tacto.—Richtstich Landrecht, cap. LII. The same provisions are to be found in a French version of the Speculum Suevicum, probably made towards the close of the fourteenth century for the use of the western provinces of the Empire.—Miroir de Souabe, P. I. c. xlviii. (Éd. Matile, Neufchatel, 1843.)

[4] Du Cange, s. v. *Ferrum candens.*

[5] Du Cange, s. v. *Batalia.*

[6] Concil. Palentin. ann. 1322, can. xxvi.

proofs are demanded of the defendant, who is specially exempted from the necessity of producing them;[1] and although in obedience to the chivalrous spirit of the age, the battle ordeal is not abolished, yet it is so limited as to be practically a dead letter, while no other form of negative proof is even alluded to.

Although the ordeal was thus removed from the admitted jurisprudence of Europe, the principles of faith which had given it vitality were too deeply implanted in the popular mind to be at once eradicated, and accordingly, as we have seen above, instances of its employment continued occasionally for several centuries to disgrace the tribunals. The ordeal of battle, indeed, as shown in the preceding essay, was not legally abrogated until long afterward; and the longevity of the popular belief, upon which the whole system was founded, may be gathered from a remark of Sir William Staundford, a learned judge and respectable legal authority, who, in 1557, expresses the same confident expectation of Divine interference which had animated Hincmar or Poppo. After stating that in an accusation of felony, unsupported by evidence, the defendant had a right to wager his battle, he proceeds: "Because in that the appellant demands judgment of death against the appellee, it is more reasonable that he should hazard his life with the defendant for the trial of it, than to put it on the country . . . . and to leave it to God, to whom all things are open, to give the verdict in such case, *scilicet*, by attributing the victory or vanquishment to the one party or the other, as it pleaseth Him."[2]

Nor should we, in weighing these popular tendencies, leave out of consideration the reverent faith which the Latin church has never ceased to inculcate in the con-

---

[1] Non es tenuda la parte de probar lo que niega porque non lo podrie facer.—Las Siete Partidas, P. iii. Tit. xiv. l. 1.

[2] Plees del Corone, chap. xv. (quoted in 1 Barnewall & Alderson, 433).

tinued interference of God and the Saints in the daily
affairs of life. Not only may the sick be miraculously
healed, but the innocence of those exposed to false accusations may be proved, and even the course of human justice
be confounded. Thus, a book of devotion to the Virgin,
printed in France in the early part of the sixteenth century, piously relates a case wherein a woman guilty of incest
was condemned to be burnt, but through the interposition
of Our Lady she was saved, and the priest, who had violated the secrecy of the confessional in becoming her accuser, was put to death.[1]

The papal authority, however, was not the only element
at work to abolish this superstition. The revival of the
Roman law in the twelfth and thirteenth centuries did
much to influence the secular tribunals against all ordeals,
as has been seen in the case of the wager of battle. So,
also, a powerful assistant must be recognized in the rise
of the communes, whose sturdy common sense not infrequently rejected its absurdity. Accordingly, we find that
it is rarely comprehended in their charters, as it is in
those granted to abbeys and monasteries, while occasionally a special exemption is alluded to as a privilege.[2] The

---

[1] Heures à lusaige de Renee (Rennes). Paris, Simon Vostre. Without
date, but containing an almanac of 1507—1527.

> Une feme son filz cogneut,
> Dont elle fist confession.
> Le prestre celer ne la ceut,
> Mais en fist accusation.
> Donc fut par condamnation
> Jugee a bruler droit ou tort.
> Par la vierge eut remission.
> Et le Prestre livre a la mort.

[2] An instance of this occurs as early as 1132, in a charter granted by King
Roger of Naples to the inhabitants of Bari : " Ferrum, cacavum, pugnam,
aquam, vobis non judicabit vel judicari faciet." (Muratori, Antiq. Ital.
Dissert. 38.)

So also in the Charter of Geertsberg, confirmed by Baldwin of Constantinople, Earl of Flanders, in 1200.—" Item nemo cogatur inire duellum, vel

influence of the commercial and municipal spirit, fostered by the establishment of chartered towns, in dissipating the mists of error and prejudice, is farther shown by the fact that the early codes of commercial law make no reference whatever to the proof by ordeal, though some of those codes were drafted at a period when it was a recognized portion of ordinary jurisprudence. The Rôles d'Oléron, the laws of Wisby, and the Consulat de la Mer endeavor to regulate all questions by the reasonable rules of evidence, and offer no indication that the judgment of God was resorted to when human means were at fault. Indeed, King Amaury, who ascended the throne of Cyprus in 1194, specifically declares, in a law embodied in the Assises de Jerusalem, that maritime causes are under the jurisdiction of a special court, instead of the ordinary civic tribunal, in order to avoid the battle ordeal permitted by the latter;[1] from which we may safely assume that the other forms of ordeal were equally ignored by the maritime law dispensers. The same spirit is shown in a treaty of 1228 between Riga, a member of the Hanseatic League, and Mstislaf Davidovitch, Prince of Smolensko, which among its provisions especially exempted the Germans in the territory of the latter from all liability to the ordeal of hot iron and of battle.[2]

---

subire judicium ignis et aquæ" (Miræi Diplom. Belgic. c. lxvii.)—while, at the same time, no doubt those who desired the ordeal were not debarred from it, as is shown by the interpolation in another MS. of the words " nisi spontaneus" (Le Glay, Revue de Miræus, p. 32). It is a little singular, however, to find in the Franc de Bruges in 1190 the whole system of ordeals in full and common use. Every Saturday, a certain time was set apart for the courts to take cognizance of them—" Et tempus duellorum et bannitorum a scabinis ibi statutum observabunt, ita ut de bannitis primo, postea de duellis tractandum et de judiciis aquæ et ferri."—Keure de Bruges, § 61. (Warnkönig, Hist. de la Fland. IV. 377.)

[1] Por ce que en la cort de la mer na point de bataille por prueve ne por demande de celuy venge, et en l autre cort des borgeis deit aveir espreuves par bataille.—Baisse Court, cap. 43.

[2] Traité de 1228, art. 3. (Esneaux, Histoire de Russie, II. 272.)

Although we may hail the disappearance of the ordeal as marking an era in human progress, yet should we err in deeming it either the effect or the cause of a change in the constitution of the human mind. The mysterious attraction of the unknown and undefined, the striving for the unattainable, the yearning to connect our mortal nature with some supernal power—all these mixed motives assisted in maintaining superstitions similar to those which we have thus passed in review. The mere external manifestations were swept away, but the potent agencies which vivified them remained, not perhaps less active because they worked more secretly. Thus generation after generation of follies, strangely affiliated, waits on the successive descendants of man, and perpetuates in another shape the superstition which we had thought eradicated. In its most vulgar and abhorrent form, we recognize it in the fearful epidemic of sorcery and witchcraft which afflicted the sixteenth and seventeenth centuries; sublimed to the verge of heaven, we see it reappear in the seraphic theories of Quietism; descending again towards earth, it assumes the mad vagaries of the Convulsionnaires. In a different guise, it leads the refined scepticism of the eighteenth century to a belief in the supernatural powers of the divining-rod, which could not only trace out hidden springs and deep-buried mines, but could also discover crime, and follow the malefactor through all the doublings of his cunning flight.[1] Even at the present day, as various references in the preceding pages sufficiently attest, there is a lurking undercurrent of supersti-

---

[1] When, in 1692, Jacques Aymar attracted public attention to the miracles of the divining-rod, he was called to Lyons to assist the police in discovering the perpetrators of a mysterious murder, which had completely baffled the agents of justice. Aided by his rod, he traced the criminals, by land and water, from Lyons to Beaucaire, where he found in prison a man whom he declared to be a participant, and who finally confessed the crime. Aymar was at length proved to be merely a clever charlatan; but the mania to which he gave rise lasted through the eighteenth century, and nearly at its close his wonders were rivalled by a brother sharper, Campetti.

tion which occasionally rises into view and shows that we are not yet exempt from the weakness of the past. Each age has its own sins to answer for, its own puerilities to bewail—happiest that which best succeeds in hiding them, for it can scarce do more. Here, in our boasted nineteenth century, when the triumph of human intelligence over the forces of nature, stimulating the progress of material prosperity with the press, the steam-engine, and the telegraph, has deluded us into sacrificing our psychical to our intellectual being—even here the duality of our nature reasserts itself, and in the obscene blasphemy of Mormonism and in the fantastic mysteries of pseudo-spiritualism we see a protest against the despotism of mere reason. If we wonder at these perversions of our noblest attributes, we must remember that the intensity of the reaction measures the original strain, and in the dismal insanities of the day we thus may learn how utterly we have forgotten the Divine warning, " Man shall not live by bread alone!"

Which age shall cast the first stone? When Cicero wondered how two soothsayers could look at each other without laughing, he showed that the grosser forms of superstition were not universally shared. Such, we may be assured, has been the case at every period ; and, in our own day, can we, who proudly proclaim our disbelief in the follies which exist around us, assert individually that we have not contributed, each in his own infinitesimal degree, to the causes which have produced them ?

IV.

TORTURE.

THE preceding essays have traced the development of sacramental purgation and of the ordeal as resources devised by human ingenuity when called upon to decide questions too intricate for the impatient intellect of a rude and semi-barbarous age. There was another mode, however, of attaining the same object, which has received the sanction of the wisest lawgivers during the greater part of the world's history, and our survey of man's devious wanderings in the search of truth would be incomplete without glancing at the subject of the judicial use of torture.

In the early stages of society, when force reigns supreme and law is but an instrument for its convenient and effective exercise, the judge or the pleader would naturally seek to extort from the reluctant witness a statement of what he might desire to conceal, or from the presumed criminal a confession of his guilt. To accomplish this, the readiest means would seem to be the infliction of pain, to escape from which the witness would sacrifice his friends, and the accused would submit to the penalty of his crime. The means of administering graduated and effectual torment would thus be sought for, and the rules for its application would in time be developed into a regular system, forming part of the recognized principles of jurisprudence.

The only subject of surprise, indeed, is that torture was not more generally authorized in primitive times. To the parent stock of the Aryan family of races it would appear

to have been unknown: at least, it has left no recorded
trace in the elaborate provisions of the Hindu law as it
has existed for three thousand years.[1] Among the Semitic
nations, too, the jurisprudence of Moses is free from any
indication that such expedients were regarded as legitimate
among the Hebrews. The connection between the latter
and the Egyptians would appear to warrant the conclusion
that torture was equally unknown to the antique civilization
of the Pharaohs, and this is confirmed by the description
which Diodorus Siculus gives of the solemn and mysterious
tribunals, where written pleadings alone were allowed, lest
the judges should be swayed by the eloquence of the human
voice, and where the verdict was announced, in the unbroken
silence, by the presiding judge touching the successful suitor
with an image of the Goddess of Truth.[2]

In Greece, we find the use of torture thoroughly understood and permanently established. The oligarchical and
aristocratic tendencies, however, which were so strongly
developed in the Hellenic commonwealths, imposed upon

---

[1] In Book VIII. of the Institutes of Manu there are very minute directions
as to evidence. The testimony preferred is that of witnesses, whose comparative credibility is very carefully discussed, and when that is not procurable, the parties are ordered to be sworn or to be submitted to the ordeal.
These principles have been transmitted unchanged to the present day. See
the Ayeen Akbery, Tit. Beyhar, Vol. II. p. 494, and Halhed's Code of
Gentoo Laws, chap. xviii.

[2] Diod. Sicul. I. lxxv.—Sir Gardiner Wilkinson (Ancient Egyptians, Vol.
II.) figures several of these little images.

That torture was a customary legal procedure in Egypt has been assumed by
some writers from a passage in Ælian to the effect that Egyptians were commonly regarded as capable of dying under torture in preference to revealing
the truth—" Ægyptios aiunt patientissime ferre tormenta: et citius mori
hominem Ægyptium in quæstionibus tortum examinatumque quam veritatem
prodere." (Var. Hist. VII. xviii.) This can hardly, however, be considered
to prove anything. In the time of Ælian, the Egyptians had been for five
centuries under Greek or Roman rule, and had probably acquired ample
experience of torture. There were doubtless, also, numerous Egyptian slaves
scattered throughout the Empire, where they must have had sufficient opportunity to earn their reputation for endurance.

it a limitation characteristic of the pride and self-respect of the governing order. As a general rule, no freeman could be tortured. Even freedmen enjoyed an exemption, and it was reserved for the unfortunate class of slaves, and for strangers who formed no part of the body politic. Yet there were exceptions, as among the Rhodians, whose laws authorized the torture of free citizens; and in other states it was occasionally resorted to, in the case of flagrant political offences; while the people, acting in their supreme and irresponsible authority, could at any time decree its application to any one irrespective of privilege. Thus, when Hipparchus was assassinated by Harmodius, Aristogiton was tortured to obtain a revelation of the plot, and several similar proceedings are related by Valerius Maximus as occurring among the Hellenic nations.[1] The inhuman torments inflicted on Philotas, son of Parmenio, when accused of conspiracy against Alexander, show how little real protection existed when the safety of a despot was in question: and illustrations of torture decreed by the people are to be seen in the proceedings relative to the mutilation of the statues of Hermes, and in the proposition, on the trial of Phocion, to put him, the most eminent citizen of Athens, on the rack.

In a population consisting largely of slaves, mostly of the same race as their masters, often men of education and intelligence and employed in positions of confidence, legal proceedings must frequently have turned upon their evidence, in both civil and criminal cases. Their evidence, however, was inadmissible, except when given under torture, and then, by a singular confusion of logic, it was estimated as the most convincing kind of testimony. Consequently, the torturing of slaves formed an important portion of the administration of Athenian justice. Either party to a suit might offer his slaves to the torturer or demand those of

---

[1] Lib. iii. cap. iii.

his opponent, and a refusal to produce them was regarded as seriously compromising. When both parties tendered their slaves, the judge decided which should be received. Even without bringing a suit into court, disputants could have their slaves tortured for evidence with which to effect an amicable settlement.

In formal litigation, the defeated suitor paid whatever damages his adversary's slaves might have undergone at the hands of the professional torturer, who, as an expert in such matters, was empowered to assess the amount of depreciation they had sustained. It affords a curious commentary on the high estimation in which such testimony was held to observe that, when a man's slaves had testified against him on the rack, they were not protected from his subsequent vengeance, which might be exercised upon them without restriction.

As the laws of Greece passed away, leaving comparatively few traces on the institutions of other races, it will suffice to add that the principal modes in which torture was sanctioned by them were the wheel (τροχὸς), the ladder or rack (κλίμαξ), the comb with sharp teeth (κνάφος), the low vault (κύφων), in which the unfortunate witness was thrust and bent double, the burning tiles (πλίνθοι), the heavy hogskin whip (ὑστριχίς), and the injection of vinegar into the nostrils.[1]

In the earlier days of Rome, the general principles governing the administration of torture were the same as in Greece. Under the Republic, the free citizen was not liable

---

[1] Aristophanes (*Ranæ*, 617) recapitulates most of the processes in vogue.

Aiachos. καὶ πῶς βασανίζω;

Xanthias. πάντα τρόπον, ἐν κλίμακι
δήσας, κρεμάσας, ὑστριχίδι μαστιγῶν, δέρων,
στρεβλᾶν, ἔτι δ'εἰς τὰς ῥῖνας ὄξος ἐγχέων,
πλίνθους ἐπιτιθείς, πάντα τἄλλα—

The best summary I have met with of the Athenian laws of torture is in Eschbach's "Introduction à l'Étude du Droit," § 268.

to it, and the evidence of slaves was not received without it. With the progress of despotism, however, the safeguards which surrounded the freeman were broken down, and autocratic emperors had little scruple in sending their subjects to the rack.

Even as early as the second Triumvirate, a prætor named Q. Gallius, in saluting Octavius, chanced to have a double tablet under his toga. To the timid imagination of the future emperor, the angles of the tablet, outlined under the garment, presented the semblance of a sword, and he fancied Gallius to be the instrument of a conspiracy against his life. Dissembling his fears for the moment, he soon caused the unlucky prætor to be seized while presiding at his own tribunal, and, after torturing him like a slave without extracting a confession, put him to death.[1]

The incident was ominous of the future, when all the powers of the state were concentrated in the august person of the emperor. He was the representative and embodiment of the limitless sovereignty of the people, whose irresponsible authority was transferred to him. The rules and formularies, however, which had regulated the exercise of power, so long as it belonged to the people, were feeble barriers to the passions and fears of Cæsarism. Accordingly, a principle soon became engrafted in Roman jurisprudence that, in all cases of "crimen majestatis," or high treason, the free citizen could be tortured. In striking at the ruler he had forfeited all rights, and the safety of the state, as embodied in the Emperor, was to be preserved at every sacrifice.

The Emperors were not long in discovering and exercising their power. When the plot of Sejanus was discovered, the historian relates that Tiberius abandoned himself so entirely to the task of examining by torture the suspected

---

[1] Servilem in modum eum torsit ; ac fatentem nihil, jussit occidi.—Sueton. August. xxii.

accomplices of the conspiracy, that when an old Rhodian
friend, who had come to visit him on a special invitation,
was announced to him, the preoccupied tyrant absently
ordered him to be placed on the rack, and on discovering
the blunder had him quietly put to death, to silence all
complaints. The shuddering inhabitants pointed out a
spot at Capri where he indulged in these terrible pursuits,
and where the miserable victims of his wrath were cast into
the sea before his eyes, after having exhausted his ingenuity
in exquisite torments.[1] When the master of the world
took this fearful delight in human agony, it may readily
be imagined that law and custom offered little protection
to the defenceless subject, and Tiberius was not the only
one who relished these inhuman pleasures. The half-insane
Caligula found that the torture of criminals by the side of
his dinner-table lent a keener zest to his revels, and even
the timid and beastly Claudius made it a point to be
present on such occasions.[2]

Under the stimulus of such hideous appetites, capricious
and irresponsible cruelty was able to give a wide extension
to the law of treason. If victims were wanted to gratify
the whims of the monarch or the hate of his creatures, it
was easy to find an offender or to make a crime. Under
Tiberius, a citizen removed the head from a statue of Augustus, intending to replace it with another. Interrogated
before the Senate, he prevaricated, and was promptly put
to the torture. Encouraged by this, the most fanciful interpretation was given to violations of the respect assumed
to be due to the late Emperor. To undress one's self or to
beat a slave near his image; to carry into a *cabinet d'aisance*
or a house of ill fame a coin or a ring impressed with his
sacred features; to criticize any act or word of his became

---

[1] Sueton. Tiberius, c. lxii.
[2] Ibid. Calig. xxxii.—Claud. xxxiv.

a treasonable offence; and finally an unlucky wight was
actually put to death for allowing the slaves on his farm to
pay him honors on the anniversary which had been sacred
to Augustus.[1]

So, when it suited the waning strength of paganism to
wreak its vengeance for anticipated defeat upon the rising
energy of Christianity, it was easy to include the new religion in the convenient charge of treason, and to expose its
votaries to all the horrors of ingenious cruelty. If Nero
desired to divert from himself the odium of the conflagration of Rome, he could turn upon the Christians, and by
well-directed tortures obtain confessions involving the
whole sect, thus giving to the populace the diversion of a
persecution on a scale until then unknown, besides providing for himself the new sensation of the human torches
whose frightful agonies illuminated his unearthly orgies.[2]
Diocletian even formally promulgated in an edict the rule
that all professors of the hated religion should be deprived
of the privileges of birth and station, and be subject to the
application of torture.[3] The indiscriminate cruelty to which
the Christians were thus exposed without defence, at the
hands of those inflamed against them by all evil passions,
may, perhaps, have been exaggerated by the ecclesiastical
historians, but that frightful excesses were perpetrated
under sanction of law cannot be doubted by any one who
has traced, even in comparatively recent times and among

[1] Sueton. Tiber. lviii.
[2] Tacit. Annal. xv. xliv. Ergo abolendo rumori Nero subdidit reos, et
quæstissimis pœnis adfecit quos per flagitia invisos, vulgus Christianos appel-
labat. . . . . Igitur, primo conrepti qui fatebantur, deinde indicio eorum,
multitudo ingens, haud perinde in crimine incendii, quam odio humani
generis convicti sunt.
[3] Postridie propositum est edictum quo cavebatur ut religionis ilius
homines carerent omni honore ac dignitate, tormentis subjecti essent ex
quocumque ordine aut gradu venirent, adversus eos omnis actio caleret, etc,
—Lactant. de Mortib. Persecut. cap. xiii.

Christian nations, the progress of political and religious persecution.[1]

The torture of freemen accused of crimes against the state or the sacred person of the emperor thus became an admitted principle of Roman law. In his account of the conspiracy of Piso, under Nero, Tacitus alludes to it as a matter of course, and in describing the unexampled endurance of Epicharis, a freedwoman, who underwent the most fearful torments without compromising those who possessed little claim upon her forbearance, the annalist indignantly compares her fortitude with the cowardice of noble Romans, who betrayed their nearest relatives and dearest friends at the mere sight of the torture chamber.[2]

Under these limits, the freeman's privilege of exemption was carefully guarded, at least in theory. A slave while claiming freedom, or a man claimed as a slave, could not be exposed to torture;[3] and even if a slave, when about to be tortured, endeavored to escape by asserting his freedom, it was necessary to prove his servile condition before proceeding with the legal torments.[4] In practice, however, these privileges were continually infringed, and numerous edicts of the emperors were directed to repressing the abuses which constantly occurred. Thus we find Diocle-

---

[1] Tormentorum genera inaudita excogitabantur. (Ibid. cap. xv.)—When the Christians were accused of an attempt to burn the imperial palace, Diocletian "ira inflammatus, excarnificari omnes suos protinus præcipit. Sedebat ipse atque innocentes igne torrebat." (Ibid. cap. xiv.)—Lactantius, or whoever was the real author of the tract, addresses the priest Donatus to whom it is inscribed : "Novies etiam tormentis cruciatibusque variis subjectus, novies adversarium gloriosa confessione vicisti. . . . . Nihil adversus te verbera, nihil ungulæ, nihil ignis, nihil ferrum, nihil varia tormentorum genera valuerunt." (Ibid. cap. xvi.) Ample details may be found in Eusebius, Hist. Eccles. Lib. v. c. 1, vi. 39, 41, viii. passim, Lib. Martyrum ; and in Cyprian. Epist. x. (Ed. Oxon. 1682).

[2] Tacit. Annal. xv. lvi. lvii.

[3] In causis quoque liberalibus, non oportet per eorum tormenta, de quorum statu quæritur, veritatem requiri.—L. 10, § 6, Dig. xlviii. xviii.

[4] L. 12, Dig. xlviii. xviii. (Ulpian)

tian forbidding the application of torture to soldiers or
their children under accusation, unless they had been dismissed the service ignominiously.[1] The same emperor published anew a rescript of Marcus Aurelius declaring the
exemption of patricians and of the higher imperial officers,
with their legitimate descendants to the fourth generation;[2]
and also a dictum of Ulpian asserting the same privilege
in favor of decurions, or local town councillors, and their
children.[3] In 376, Valentinian was obliged to renew the
declaration that decurions were only liable in cases of
majestatis, and, in 399, Arcadius and Honorius found it
necessary to explicitly declare that the privilege was personal and not official, and that it remained to them after
laying down the decurionate.[4] Theodosius the Great, in
385, especially directed that priests should not be subjected
to torture in giving testimony,[5] the significance of which is
shown by the fact that no slave could be admitted into holy
orders.

The necessity of this constant renewal of the law is indicated by a rescript of Valentinian, in 369, which shows that
freemen were not infrequently tortured in contravention of
law; but that torture could legally be indiscriminately
inflicted by any tribunal in cases of treason, and that in
other accusations it could be authorized by the order of the
emperor.[6] This power was early assumed and frequently
exercised. Though Claudius at the commencement of his
reign had sworn that he would never subject a freeman to
the question, yet he allowed Messalina and Narcissus to administer torture indiscriminately, not only to free citizens.

[1] Const. 8 Cod. IX. xli. (Dioclet. et Maxim.)
[2] Const. 11 Cod. IX. xli.
[3] Ibid. § 1.
[4] Const. 16 Cod. IX. xli.
[5] Presbyteri citra injuriam quæstionis testimonium dicant.—Const. 8 Cod.
I. 3.
[6] Const. 4 Cod. IX. viii.

but even to knights and patricians.[1] So Domitian tortured
a man of prætorian rank on a doubtful charge of intrigue
with a vestal virgin,[2] and various laws were promulgated
by several emperors directing the employment of torture
irrespective of rank, in some classes of accusations. Thus,
in 217, Caracalla authorized it in cases of suspected poisoning by women.[3] Constantine decreed that unnatural
lusts should be punished by the severest torments, without
regard to the station of the offender.[4] Constantius persecuted in like manner soothsayers, sorcerers, magicians,
diviners, and augurs, who were to be tortured for confession, and then to be put to death with every refinement of
suffering.[5] So, Justinian, under certain circumstances,
ordered torture to be used on parties accused of adultery[6]
—a practice, however, which was already common in the
fourth century, if we are to believe the story related by
St. Jerome of a miracle occurring in a case of this nature.[7]
The power thus assumed by the monarch could evidently
only be limited by his discretion in its exercise.

One important safeguard, however, existed, which, if
properly maintained, must have greatly lessened the frequency of torture as applied to freemen. In bringing an
accusation the accuser was obliged to inscribe himself
formally, and was exposed to the *lex talionis* in case he
failed to prove the justice of the charge.[8] A rescript of
Constantine, in 314, decrees that in cases of *majestatis*, as
the accused was liable to the severity of torture without

---

[1] Dion. Cassius, Roman. Hist. Lib. LX. (Ed. 1592, p. 776.)

[2] Sueton. Domit. cap. viii. To Domitian the historian also ascribes the
invention of a new and infamously indecent kind of torture (Ibid. cap. x.).

[3] Ipsa quoque mulier torquebitur. Neque enim ægre feret si torqueatur,
quæ venenis suis viscera hominis extinxit.—Const. 3 Cod. IX. xli.

[4] Const. 31 Cod. IX. ix.

[5] Const. 7 Cod. IX. viii.

[6] Novell. CXVII. cap. xv. § 1.

[7] Hieron. Epist. I. ad Innocent.

[8] Const. 17 Cod. IX. ii.—Const. 10 Cod. IX. xlvi.

limitation of rank, so the accuser and his informers were to be tortured when they were unable to make good their accusation.[1] This enlightened legislation was preserved by Justinian, and must have greatly cooled the ardor of the pack of calumniators and informers, who, from the days of Sylla, had been encouraged and petted until they held in their hands the life of almost every citizen.

In all this it must be borne in mind that the freeman of the Roman law was a Roman citizen, and that, prior to the extension of citizenship generally to the subjects of the Empire, there was an enormous class deprived of the protection, such as it was, of the traditional exemption. Thus when, in Jerusalem, the Jews raised a tumult and accused St. Paul, without specifying his offence, the tribune forthwith ordered "that he should be examined by scourging, that he might know wherefore they cried so against him;" and when St. Paul proclaimed himself a Roman, the preparations for his torture were stopped forthwith, and he was examined by regular judicial process.[2] The value of this privilege is fairly exemplified by the envying remark of the tribune, "With a great sum obtained I this freedom."

All these laws relate to the extortion of confessions from the accused. In turning to the treatment of witnesses, we find that even with them torture was not confined to the servile condition. With slaves, it was not simply a consequence of slavery, but a mode of confirming and rendering admissible the testimony of those whose character was not sufficiently known to give their evidence credibility without it. Thus a legist under Constantine states that gladiators and others of similar occupation cannot be allowed to bear witness without torture;[3] and, in the same spirit, a novel

---

[1] Const. 3 Cod. IX. viii.

[2] Acts, XXII. 24 sqq.

[3] Si ea rei conditio sit ut harenarium testem vel similem personam admittere cogimur, sine tormentis testimonio ejus credendum non est.—L. 21, § 2, Dig. XXII. v.

of Justinian, in 539, directs that the rod shall be used to extract the truth from unknown persons who are suspected of bearing false witness or of being suborned.[1]

It may, therefore, readily be imagined that when the evidence of slaves was required, it was necessarily accompanied by the application of torture. Indeed, Augustus declared that while it is not to be expressly desired in trifling matters, yet in weighty and capital cases the torture of slaves is the most efficacious mode of ascertaining the truth.[2] When we consider the position occupied by slavery in the Roman world, the immense proportion of bondmen who carried on all manner of mechanical and industrial occupations for the benefit of their owners, and who, as scribes, teachers, stewards, and in other confidential positions, were privy to almost every transaction of their masters, we can readily see that scarce any suit could be decided without involving the testimony of slaves, and thus requiring the application of torture. It was not even, as among most modern nations, restricted to criminal cases. Some doubt, indeed, seems at one time to have existed as to its propriety in civil actions, but Antoninus Pius decided the question authoritatively in the affirmative, and this became a settled principle of Roman jurisprudence, even when the slaves belonged to masters who were not party to the case at issue.[3]

There was but one limitation to the universal liability of slaves. They could not be tortured to extract testimony against their masters, whether in civil or criminal cases;[4]

---

[1] Novell. xc. cap. i. § 1.

[2] Quæstiones neque semper in omni causa et persona desiderari debere arbitror: et cum capitalia et atrociora maleficia non aliter explorari et investigari possunt, quam per servorum quæstiones, efficacissimas esse ad requirendam veritatem existimo et habendas censeo.—L. 8, Dig. xlviii. xviii. (Paulus).

[2] L. 9, Dig. xlviii. xviii. (Marcianus).—Licet itaque et de servis alienis haberi quæstionem, si ita res suadeat.

[4] L. 9, § 1, Dig. xlviii. xviii.—L. 1, § 16, Dig. xlviii. xvii. (Severus).— L. 1, § 18, Dig. xlviii. xviii. (Ulpian.)

though, if a slave had been purchased by a litigant to get
his testimony out of court, the sale was pronounced void,
the price was refunded, and the slave could then be tortured.[1] This limitation arose from a careful regard for the
safety of the master, and not from any feeling of humanity
towards the slave. So great a respect, indeed, was paid to
the relationship between the master and his slave that the
principle was pushed to its fullest extent. Thus even an
employer, who was not the owner of a slave, was protected
against the testimony of the latter.[2] When a slave was
held in common by several owners, he could not be tortured in opposition to any of them, unless one were accused
of murdering his partner.[3] A slave could not be tortured
in a prosecution against the father or mother of the owner,
or even against the guardian, except in cases concerning
the guardianship;[4] though the slave of a husband could be
tortured against the wife.[5] Even the tie which bound the
freedman to his patron was sufficient to preserve the former
from being tortured against the latter;[6] whence we may
assume that, in other cases, manumission afforded no protection from the rack and scourge. This question, however,
appears doubtful. The exemption of freedmen would seem
to be proved by the rescript which provides that inconvenient testimony should not be got rid of by manumitting
slaves so as to prevent their being subjected to torture;[7]

---

[1] Qui servum ideo comparavit, ne in se torqueretur, restituto pretio, poterit
interrogari.—Pauli Lib. v. Sentt. Tit. xvi. § 7.—The same principle is involved in a rescript of the Antonines.—L. 1, § 14, Dig. xlviii. xvii. (Severus).

[2] Si servus bona fide mihi serviat, etiam si dominium in eo non habui,
potest dici, torqueri eum in caput meum non debere.—L. 1, § 7, Dig. xlviii.
xvii. The expression " in caput domini" applies as well to civil as to criminal cases.—Pauli Lib. v. Sentt. Tit. xvi. § 5.

[3] L. 3, Dig. xlviii. xviii.—Const. 13 Cod. ix. xli.

[4] L. 10, § 2, Dig. xlviii. xviii.—Const. 2 Cod. ix. xli. (Sever. et Antonin.
ann. 205).

[5] L. 1, § 11, Dig. xlviii. xvii.

[6] L. 1, § 9, Dig. xlviii. xvii.

[7] L. 1, § 13, Dig. xlviii. xvii.—Pauli Lib. v. Sentt. Tit. xvi § 9.

while, on the other hand, a decision of Diocletian directs
that, in cases of alleged fraudulent wills, the slaves and
even the freedmen of the heir could be tortured to ascertain
the truth.[1]

The policy of the law in protecting masters from the
evidence of their tortured slaves also varied at different
periods. From an expression of Tacitus, it would seem
not to have been part of the original jurisprudence of the
republic, but to have arisen from a special decree of the
Senate. In the early days of the empire, while the monarch
still endeavored to veil his irresponsible power under the
forms of law, and showed his reverence for ancient rights
by evading them rather than by boldly subverting them,
Tiberius, in prosecuting Libo and Silanus, caused their
slaves to be transferred to the public prosecutor, and was
thus able to gratify his vengeance legally by extorting the
required evidence.[2] Subsequent emperors were not reduced
to these subterfuges, for the principle became established
that in cases of *majestatis*, even as the freeman was liable
to torture, so his slaves could be tortured to convict him;[3]
and as if to show how utterly superfluous was the cunning
of Tiberius, the respect towards the master in ordinary
affairs was carried to that point that no slave could be
tortured against a former owner with regard to matters
which had occurred during his ownership.[4] On the other
hand, according to Ulpian, Trajan decided that when the
confession of a guilty slave under torture implicated his
master, the evidence could be used against the master, and

[1] Const. 10 Cod. IX. xli. (Dioclet. et Maxim.)
[2] Et quia vetere Senatusconsulto quæstio in caput domini prohibebatur,
callidus et novi juris repertor Tiberius mancipari singulos actori publico
jubet.—Tacit. Annal. II. 30. See also III. 67. Somewhat similar in spirit
was his characteristic device for eluding the law which prohibited the execution of virgins (Sueton. Tiber. lxi.).
[3] This principle is embodied in innumerable laws. It is sufficient to refer
to Constt. 6 § 2, 7 § 1, 8 § 1, Cod. IX. viii.
[4] L. 18, § 6, Dig. XLVIII. xviii. (Paulus).

this, again, was revoked by subsequent constitutions.[1]
Indeed, it became a settled principle of law to reject all
incriminations of accomplices.

Having thus broken down the protection of the citizen
against the evidence of his slaves in accusations of treason,
it was not difficult to extend the liability to other special
crimes. Accordingly we find that, in 197, Septimius Severus specified adultery, fraudulent assessment, and crimes
against the state as cases in which the evidence of slaves
against their masters was admissible.[2] The provision
respecting adultery was repeated by Caracalla in 214, and
afterwards by Maximus,[3] and the same rule was also held
to be good in cases of incest.[4] It is probable that this increasing tendency alarmed the citizens of Rome, and that
they clamored for a restitution of their immunities, for,
when Tacitus was elected emperor, in 275, he endeavored
to propitiate public favor by proposing a law to forbid the
testimony of slaves against their masters except in cases
of *majestatis*.[5] No trace of such a law, however, is found
in the imperial jurisprudence, and the collections of Justinian show that the previous regulations were in full force
in the sixth century.

Yet it is probable that the progress of Christianity produced some effect in mitigating the severity of legal procedure, and in shielding the unfortunate slave from the
cruelties to which he was exposed. Under the republic,
while the authority of the *paterfamilias* was still una-
bridged, any one could offer his slaves to the torture when
he desired to produce their evidence. In the earlier times,
this was done by the owner himself in the presence of the
family, and the testimony thus extorted was carefully

---

[1] L. 1, § 19, Dig. xlviii. xviii. (Ulpian.)
[2] Const. 1 Cod. ix. xli. (Sever. et Antonin.)
[3] Constt. 3, 32 Cod. ix. ix.—L. 17, Dig. xlviii. xviii. (Papin.)
[4] L. 5 Dig. xlviii. xviii. (Marcian.)
[5] Fl. Vopisc. Tacit. cap. ix.

29

taken down to be duly produced in court; but subsequently
the proceeding was conducted by public officers—the quæs-
tors and triumviri capitales.[1]   How great was the change
effected is seen by the declaration of Diocletian, in 286, that
masters were not permitted to bring forward their own
slaves to be tortured for evidence in cases wherein they
were personally interested.[2]   This would necessarily reduce
the production of slave testimony, save in accusations of
majestatis and other excepted crimes, to cases in which the
slaves of third parties were desired as witnesses; and even
in these, the frequency of its employment must have been
greatly reduced by the rule which bound the party calling for
it to deposit in advance the price of the slave, as estimated
by the owner, to remunerate the latter for his death, or for
his diminished value if he were maimed or crippled for life.[3]
When the slave himself was arraigned upon a false accusation and tortured, an old law provided that the master
should receive double the loss or damage sustained;[4] and
in 383, Valentinian the Younger went so far as to decree
that those who accused slaves of capital crimes should inscribe themselves, as in the case of freemen, and should be
subjected to the *lex talionis* if they failed to sustain the
charge.[5]   This was an immense step towards equalizing the
legal condition of the bondman and his master.   It was
apparently in advance of public opinion, for the law is not
reproduced in the compilations of Justinian, and probably
soon was disregarded.

There were some general limitations imposed on the application of torture, but they were hardly such as to prevent its abuse at the hands of cruel or unscrupulous judges.

---

[1] Du Boys, Hist. du Droit Crim. des Peup. Anciens. pp. 297, 331, 332.

[2] Const. 7 Cod. IX. xli. (Dioclet. et Maxim.).

[3] Pauli Lib. v. Sentt. Tit. xvi. § 3.—See also Ll. 6, 13 Dig. XLVIII. xviii.

[4] Const. 6 Cod. IX. xlvi.   This provision of the L. Julia appears to have
been revived by Diocletian.

[5] Lib. IX. Cod. Theod. i. 14.

Antoninus Pius set an example which modern jurists might
well have imitated when he directed that no one should be
tortured after confession to implicate others;[1] and a rescript
of the same enlightened emperor fixes at fourteen the minimum limit of age liable to torture, except in cases of *majestatis*, when, as we have seen, the law spared no one, for in
the imperial jurisprudence the safety of the monarch over-
rode all other considerations.[2] Women were spared during
pregnancy.[3] Moderation was enjoined upon the judges,
who were to inflict only such torture as the occasion rendered necessary, and were not to proceed further at the
will of the accuser.[4] No one was to be tortured without
the inscription of a formal accuser, who rendered himself
liable to the *lex talionis*, unless there were violent sus-
picions to justify it;[5] and Adrian reminded his magistrates
that it should be used for the investigation of truth, and
not for the infliction of punishment.[6] Adrian further
directed, in the same spirit, that the torture of slave witnesses should only be resorted to when the accused was so
nearly convicted that it alone was required to confirm his
guilt.[7] Diocletian ordered that proceedings should never
be commenced with torture, but that it might be employed
when requisite to complete the proof, if other evidence
afforded rational belief in the guilt of the accused.[8]

What was the exact value set upon evidence procured by
torture it would be difficult at this day to determine. We
have seen above that Augustus pronounced it the best form
of proof, but other legislators and jurists thought differently.

[1] L. 16, § 1, Dig. xlviii. xviii. (Modestin.)
[2] L. 10 Dig. xlviii. xviii. (Arcad.)
[2] L. 3 Dig. xlviii. xix. (Ulpian.)
[4] Tormenta autem adhibenda sunt non quanta accusator postulat ; sed ut
moderatæ rationis temperamenta desiderant.—L. 10, § 3, Dig. xlviii. xviii.
[5] L. 22 Dig. xlviii. xviii.
[6] L. 21 Dig. xlviii. xviii.
[7] L. 1, § 1, Dig. xlviii. xviii. (Ulpian.)
[8] Const. 8 Cod. ix. xli. (Dioclet. et Maxim.)

Modestinus affirms that it is only to be believed when there is no other mode of ascertaining the truth.[1] Adrian cautions his judges not to trust to the torture of a single slave, but to examine all cases by the light of reason and argument.[2] According to Ulpian, the imperial constitutions provided that it was not always to be received nor always rejected; in his own opinion it was unsafe, dangerous, and deceitful, for some men were so resolute that they would bear the extremity of torment without yielding, while others were so timid that through fear they would at once inculpate the innocent.[3] From the manner in which Cicero alternately praises and discredits it, we can safely assume that lawyers were in the habit of treating it, not on any general principle, but according as it might affect their client in any particular case; and Quintilian remarks that it was frequently objected to on the ground that under it one man's constancy makes falsehood easy to him, while another's weakness renders falsehood necessary.[4] That these views were shared by the public would appear from the often quoted maxim of Publius Syrus—"Etiam innocentes cogit mentiri dolor"—and from Valerius Maximus, who devotes his chapter "De Quæstionibus" to three cases in which it was erroneously either trusted or distrusted. A slave of M. Agrius was accused of the murder of Alexander, a slave of C. Fannius. Agrius tortured him, and, on his confessing the crime, handed him over to Fannius, who put him to death. Shortly afterwards, the missing slave returned home. This same Alexander was made of sterner stuff, for when he was subsequently suspected of being privy to the murder of C. Flavius, a Roman knight, he was tortured six times and persistently denied his guilt, though he subsequently confessed it and was duly crucified.

[1] L. 7, Dig. xx. v.   [2] L. 1, § 4, Dig. xlviii. xviii. (Ulpian.)
[3] L. 1, § 23, Dig. xlviii. xviii.—Res est fragilis et periculosa et quæ veritatem fallat.
[4] Altera sæpe etiam causam falsa dicendi, quod aliis patientia facile mendacium faciat, aliis infirmitas necessarium.—M. F. Quintil. Inst. Orat. v. iv.

A curious instance, moreover, of the little real weight attached to such evidence is furnished by the case of Fulvius Flaccus, in which the whole question turned upon the evidence of his slave Philip. This man was actually tortured eight times, and refused through it all to criminate his master, who was nevertheless condemned.[1] The same conclusion is to be drawn from the story told by St. Jerome of a woman of Vercelli repeatedly tortured on an accusation of adultery, and finally condemned to death in spite of her constancy in asserting her innocence, the only evidence against her being that of her presumed accomplice, extorted under torment.[2] Quintus Curtius probably reflects the popular feeling on the subject, in his pathetic narrative of the torture of Philotas on a charge of conspiracy against Alexander. After enduring in silence the extremity of hideous torment, he promised to confess if it were stopped, and when the torturers were removed he addressed his brother-in-law Craterus, who was conducting the investigation: " Tell me what you wish me to say." Curtius adds that no one knew whether or not to believe his final confession, for torture is as apt to bring forth lies as truth.[3]

From the instances given by Valerius Maximus, it may be inferred that there was no limit set upon the application of torture. The extent to which it might be carried appears to have rested with the discretion of the tribunals, for, with the exception of the general injunctions of moderation alluded to above, no instructions for its administration are to be found in the Roman laws which have been preserved to us, unless it be the rule that when several persons were accused as accomplices, the judges were directed to commence with the youngest and weakest.[4]

[1] Valer. Maxim. Lib. VIII. c. iv.
[2] Hieron. Epist. I. ad Innocentium.
[3] Q. Curt. Ruf. Hist. VI. xi.   Anceps conjectura est quoniam et vera confessis et falsa dicentibus idem doloris finis ostenditur.
[4] Pauli Lib. v. Sentt. Tit. xiv. § 2.—L. 18 Dig. XLVIII. xviii.

Since the time of Sigonius, much antiquarian research has been directed to investigating the various forms of torture employed by the Romans. They illustrate no principles, however, and it is sufficient to enumerate the rack, the scourge, fire in its various forms, and hooks for tearing the flesh, as the modes generally authorized by law. The Christian historians, in their narratives of the fearful persecutions to which their religion was exposed, give us a more extended idea of the resources of the Roman torture chamber. Thus Prudentius, in his description of the martyrdom of St. Vincent, alludes to a number of varieties, among which we recognize some that became widely used in after times, showing that little was left for modern ingenuity to invent.

    " Vinctum retortis brachiis,
Sursum ac deorsum extendite,
Compago donec ossium
Divulsa membratim crepet.
    Post hinc hiulcis ictibus
Nudate costarum abdita
Ut per lacunas vulnerum
Jecur retectum palpitet.
       *   *   *   *
    Tunc deinde cunctatus diu
Decernit extrema omnium :
Igni, grabato, et laminis
Exerceatur quæstio.
       *   *   *   *
    In hoc barathrum conjicit

Truculentus hostis martyrem
Lignoque plantas inserit,
Divaricatis cruribus.
    Quin addit et pœnam novam
Crucis peritus artifex,
Nulla tyranno cognitam
Nec fando compertam retro.
    Fragmenta testarum jubet
Hirta impolitis angulis
Acuminata, informia,
Tergo jacentis sternere.
    Totum cubile spiculis
Armant dolores anxii :
Insomne qui subter latus
Mucrone pulsent obvio." etc.[1]

I have dwelt thus at length on the details of the Roman law of torture because, as will be seen hereafter, it was the basis of all modern legislation on the subject, and has left its impress on the far less humane administration of criminal justice in Europe almost to our own day. Yet at first it seemed destined to disappear utterly from human sight with the downfall of the Roman power.

---

[1] Aurel. Prudent. de Vincent. Hymn. v.

In turning from the nicely poised and elaborate provisions of the Imperial laws to the crude jurisprudence of the Barbarian hordes who gradually-inherited the crumbling remains of the Empire of the West, we enter into social and political conditions so different that we are naturally led to expect a corresponding contrast in every detail of legislation. For the cringing suppliant of the audience chamber, abjectly prostrating himself before a monarch who combines in his own person every legislative and executive function, we have the freeman of the German forests, who sits in council with his chief, who frames the laws which both are bound to respect, and who pays to that chief only the amount of obedience which superior vigor and intellect may be able to enforce. The structure of such a society is fairly illustrated by the incident which Gregory of Tours selects to prove the kingly qualities of Clovis. During his conquest of Gaul, and before his conversion, his wild followers pillaged the churches with little ceremony. A bishop, whose cathedral had suffered largely, sent to the king to request that a certain vase of unusual size and beauty might be restored to him. Clovis could only promise that if the messenger would accompany him to Soissons, where the spoils were to be divided, and if the vase should chance to fall to his share, it should be restored. When the time came for allotting the plunder, he addressed his men, requesting as a special favor that the vase might be given to him before the division, but a sturdy soldier, brandishing his axe, dashed it against the coveted article, exclaiming, "Thou shalt take nothing but what the lot assigns to thee." For a year, Clovis dissembled his resentment at this rebuff, but at length, when opportunity offered, he was prompt to gratify it. While reviewing and inspecting his troops, he took occasion to bitterly reproach the uncourtly Frank with the condition of his weapons, which he pronounced unserviceable. The battle-axe excited his especial displeasure. He threw it angrily to the ground, and as the owner stooped to pick it up, Clovis drove his own into the soldier's head, with the remark, "It was thus you served the vase at Soissons."[1]

This personal independence of the freeman is one of the distinguishing characteristics of all the Teutonic institutions of that age. Corporal punishments for him were unknown to the laws. The principal resource for the repression of crime was by giving free scope to the vengeance of the injured party, and by providing fixed rates of composition by which he could be bought off. As the criminal could defend himself with the sword against the *faida* or feud of his adversary, or could compound for his guilt with money, the suggestion of torturing him to extort a confession would seem an absurd violation of all his rights. Crimes were regarded solely as injuries to individuals, and the idea that society at large was interested in their discovery, punishment, and prevention, was entirely too abstract to have any influence on the legislation of so barbarous an age.

Accordingly, the codes of the Feini, the Ripuarians, the Alamanni, the Angli and Werini, the Frisians, the Saxons, and the Lombards contain no allusion to the employment of torture under any circumstances; and such few directions for its use as occur in the laws of the Salien Franks, of the Burgundians, and of the Baioarians, do not conflict with the general principle.

The personal inviolability which shielded the freeman cast no protection over the slave. He was merely a piece of property, and if he were suspected of a crime, the readiest and speediest way to convict him was naturally adopted. His denial could not be received as satisfactory, and the machinery of sacramental purgation or the judicial duel was not for him. If he were charged with a theft at home, his master would undoubtedly tie him up and flog him until

---

[1] Greg. Turon. Hist. Franc. Lib. ii. c. xxvii.

he confessed, and if the offence were committed against a third party, the same process would necessarily be adopted by the court. Barbarian logic could arrive at no other mode of discovering and repressing crime among the friendless and unprotected, whose position seemed to absolve them from all moral responsibility.

The little that we know of the institutions of the ancient Gauls presents us with an illustration of the same principle developed in a somewhat different direction. Cæsar states that, when a man of rank died, his relatives assembled and investigated the circumstances of his death. If suspicion alighted upon his wives, they were tortured like slaves, and if found guilty they were executed with all the refinements of torment.[1]

In accordance with this tendency of legislation, therefore, we find that among the Barbarians the legal regulations for the torture of slaves are intended to protect the interests of the owner alone. When a slave was accused of crime the master, indeed, could not refuse to hand him over to the torturer, unless he were willing to pay for him the full *wehrgild* of a freeman, and if the slave confessed under the torture, the master had no claim for compensation arising either from the punishment or crippling of his bondman.[2] When, however, the slave could not be forced to confess and was acquitted, the owner had a claim for damages, though no compensation was made to the unfortunate sufferer himself. The original law of the Burgundians, promulgated in 471, is the earliest of the Teutonic codes extant, and in that we find that the accuser who failed to extract a confession was obliged to give to the owner

---

[1] De Bell. Gall. vi. xix.

[2] These provisions are specified only in the Salique Law (First Text of Pardessus, Tit. xl. §§ 6, 7, 8, 9, 10.—L. Emend. Tit. xlii. §§ 8, 9, 10, 11, 12, 13), but they were doubtless embodied in the practice of the other tribes.

another slave, or to pay his value.[1]　The Baioarian law is
equally careful of the rights of ownership, but seems in
addition to attach some criminality to the excess of torture by the further provision that, if the slave die under
the torment without confession, the prosecutor shall pay
to the owner two slaves of like value, and if unable to do
so, that he shall himself be delivered up as a slave.[2]　The
Salique law, on the other hand, only guards the interests
of the owner by limiting the torture to 120 blows with a
rod of the thickness of the little finger.　If this does not
extort a confession, and the accuser is still unsatisfied, he
can deposit the value of the slave with the owner, and
then proceed to torture him at his own risk and pleasure.[3]

It will be observed that all these regulations provide
merely for extracting confessions from accused slaves, and
not testimony from witnesses.　Indeed, the system of evidence adopted by all the Barbarian laws for freemen was
of so different a character, that no thought seems to have
been entertained of procuring proof by the torture of witnesses.　The only allusion, indeed, to such a possibility
shows how utterly repugnant it was to the Barbarian
modes of thought.　In some MSS. of the Salique law there

---

[1] L. Burgund. Tit. VII.—The other allusions to torture in this code, Tit.
XXXIX. §§ 1, 2, and Tit. LXXVII. §§ 1, 2, also refer only to slaves, *coloni*,
and *originarii*.　Persons suspected of being fugitive slaves were always tortured to ascertain the fact, which is in direct contradiction to the principles
of the Roman law.

[2] L. Baioar. Tit. VIII. c. xviii. §§ 1, 2, 3.

[3] L. Salic. First Text, Tit. XL. §§ 1, 2, 3, 4.—L. Emend. Tit. XLII. §§ 1,
2, 3, 4, 5.—In a treaty between Childebert and Clotair, about the year 593,
there is, however, a clause which would appear to indicate that in doubtful
cases slaves were subjected, not to torture, but to the ordeal of chance. "Si
servus in furto fuerit inculpatus, requiratur a domino ut ad viginti noctes
ipsum in mallum præsentet. Et si dubietas est, ad sortem ponatur." (Pact.
pro Tenore Pacis cap. v.—Baluz.)　This was probably only a temporary international regulation to prevent frontier quarrels and reprisals.　That it
had no permanent force of law is evident from the retention of the procedures of torture in all the texts of the Salique law, including the revision
by Charlemagne.

occurs the incidental remark that when a slave accused is under the torture, if his confession implicates his master, the charge is not to be believed.[1]

Such was the primitive legislation of the Barbarians, but though in principle it was long retained, in practice it was speedily disregarded by those whom irresponsible power elevated above the law. The Roman populations of the conquered territories were universally allowed to live under their old institutions; in fact, law everywhere was personal and not territorial, every race and tribe, however intermingled on the same soil, being subjected to its own system of jurisprudence. The summary process of extracting confessions and testimony which the Roman practice thus daily brought under the notice of the Barbarians could not but be attractive to their violent and untutored passions. Their political system was too loose and undefined to maintain the freedom of the Sicambrian forests in the wealthy plains of Gaul, and the monarch, who, beyond the Rhine, had scarce been more than a military chief, speedily became a despot, whose power over those immediately around him was limited only by the fear of assassination, and over his more distant subjects by the facility of revolution.

When all thus was violence, and the law of the strongest was scarcely tempered by written codes, it is easy to imagine that the personal inviolability of the freeman speedily ceased to guarantee protection. In the long and deadly struggle between Fredegonda and Brunhilda, for example, the fierce passions of the adversaries led them to employ without scruple the most cruel tortures in the endeavor to fathom each other's plots.[2] A single case may be worth recounting

---

[1] First Text, Tit. XL. § 4.—MSS. Monaster. Tit. XL. § 3.—L. Emend. Tit. XLII. § 6.

[2] Greg. Turon. Hist. Franc. Lib. VII. c. XX. ; Lib. VIII. cap. XXXI. Also, Lib. V. cap. XXXVII.—Aimoin. Lib. III. c. XXX. XLII. li. lxiv. lxvii.—Flodoard. Hist. Remens. Lib. II. c. ii.—Greg. Turon. Miraculorum Lib. I. cap. 73.

to show how completely torture had become a matter of
course as the first resource in the investigation of doubtful
questions. When Leudastes, about the year 580, desired
to ruin the pious Bishop Gregory of Tours, he accused him
to Chilperic I. of slandering the fair fame of Queen Fredegonda, and suggested that full proof for condemnation
could be had by torturing Plato and Gallienus, friends of
the bishop. He evidently felt that nothing further was
required to substantiate the charge, nor does Gregory himself, in narrating the affair, seem to think that there was
anything irregular in the proposition. Gallienus and Plato
were seized, but from some cause were discharged unhurt.
Then a certain Riculfus, an accomplice of Leudastes, was
reproached for his wickedness by a man named Modestus,
whereupon he accused Modestus to Fredegonda, who
promptly caused the unhappy wretch to be severely tortured without extracting any information from him, and
he was imprisoned until released by the miraculous aid of
St. Medard. Finally, Gregory cleared himself canonically
of the imputation, and the tables were turned. Leudastes
sought safety in flight. Riculfus was not so fortunate.
Gregory begged his life, but could not save him from being
tortured for confession. For six hours the wretched man
was hung up with his hands tied behind his back, after
which, stretched upon the rack, he was beaten with clubs,
rods, and thongs, by as many as could get at him, until,
as Gregory naïvely remarks, no piece of iron could have
borne it. At last, when nearly dead, his resolution gave
way, and he confessed the whole plot by which it had been
proposed to get rid of Chilperic and Fredegonda, and to
place Clovis on the throne.[1] Now, Plato, Gallienus, and
Modestus were probably of Gallo-Roman origin, but Riculfus was evidently of Teutonic stock; moreover, he was a
priest, and Plato an archdeacon, and the whole transaction

---

[1] Gregor. Turon. Hist. Franc. Lib. v. c. xlix.

shows that Roman law and Frankish law were of little avail against the unbridled passions of the Merovingian.

Of all the Barbarian tribes, none showed themselves so amenable to the influences of Roman civilization as the Goths. Their comparatively settled habits, their early conversion to Christianity, and their position as allies of the empire long before they became its conquerors, rendered them far less savage under Alaric than were the Franks in the time of Clovis. The permanent occupation of Septimania and Catalonia by the Wisigoths, also, took place at a period when Rome was not as yet utterly sunk, and when the power of her name still possessed something of its ancient influence, which could not but modify the institutions of the new-comers as they strove to adapt their primitive customs to the altered circumstances under which they found themselves. It is not to be wondered at, therefore, if their laws reflect a condition of higher civilization than those of kindred races, and if the Roman jurisprudence has left in them traces of the appreciation of that wonderful work of the human intellect which the Goths were sufficiently enlightened to entertain.

The Ostrogoths, allowing for the short duration of their nationality, were even more exposed to the influences of Rome. Their leader, Theodoric, had been educated in Constantinople, and was fully as much a Roman as many of the Barbarian soldiers who had risen to high station under the emperors, or even to the throne itself. All his efforts were directed to harmonizing the institutions of his different subjects, and he was too sagacious not to see the manifest superiority of the Roman polity.

His kingdom was too evanescent to consolidate and perfect its institutions or to accumulate any extended body of jurisprudence. What little exists, however, manifests a compromise between the spirit of the Barbarian tribes of the period and that of the conquered mistress of the world.

30

The Edict of Theodoric does not allude to the torture of
freemen, and it is probable that the free Ostrogoth could
not legally be subjected to it.   With respect to slaves, its
provisions seem mainly borrowed from the Roman law.
No slave could be tortured against a third party for evidence
unless the informer or accuser was prepared to indemnify
the owner at his own valuation of the slave.   No slave
could be tortured against his master, but the purchase of a
slave to render his testimony illegal was pronounced null
and void; the purchase money was returned, and the slave
was tortured.   The immunity of freedmen is likewise shown
by the cancelling of any manumission conferred for the
purpose of preventing torture for evidence.[1]   Theodoric,
however, allowed his Roman subjects to be governed by
their ancient laws, and he apparently had no repugnance
to the use of torture when it could legally be inflicted.
Thus he seems particularly anxious to ferret out and
punish sorcerers, and in writing to the Prefect and Count
of Rome he urges them to apprehend certain suspected
parties, and try them by the regular legal process, which,
as we have seen, by the edicts of Constantius and his
successors, was particularly severe in enjoining torture in
such cases, both as a means of investigation and of punishment.[2]

On the other hand, the Wisigoths founded a permanent
state, and as they were the only race whose use of torture
was uninterrupted from the period of their settlement until
modern times, and as their legislation on the subject was
to a great extent a model for that of other nations, it may
be worth while to examine it somewhat closely.

The earliest code of the Wisigoths is supposed to have
been compiled by Eurik, in the middle of the fifth century,
but it was subsequently much modified by recensions and
additions.   It was remoulded by Chindaswind and Recas-

---

[1] Edict. Theodor. cap. c. ci. cii.   [2] Cassiodor. Variar. IV. xxii. xxiii.

wind about the middle of the seventh century, and it has
reached us only in this latest condition, while the MSS.
vary so much in assigning the authorship of the various
laws, that but little reliance can be placed upon the
assumed dates of most of them. Chindaswind, moreover,
in issuing his revised code, prohibited for the future the
use of the Roman law, which had previously been in force
among the subject populations, under codes specially prepared for them by order of Alaric II. Thus the Wisigothic
laws, as we have them, are not laws of race, like the other
Barbarian codes, but territorial laws carefully digested for
a whole nation by men conversant alike with the Roman
and with their own ancestral jurisprudence.

It is therefore not surprising to find in them the use of
torture legalized somewhat after the fashion of the imperial constitutions, and yet with some humane modifications
and restrictions. Slaves were liable to torture under accusation, but the accuser had first to make oath that he was
actuated by neither fraud nor malice in preferring the
charge; and he was further obliged to give security that he
would deliver to the owner another slave of equal value if
the accused were acquitted. If an innocent slave were
crippled in the torture, the accuser was bound to give two
of like value to the owner, and the sufferer received his
freedom. If the accused died under the torture, the judge
who had manifested so little feeling and discretion in permitting it was also fined in a slave of like value, making
three enuring to the owner, and careful measures were prescribed to insure that a proper valuation was made. If the
accuser were unable to meet the responsibility thus incurred,
he was himself forfeited as a slave. Moreover, the owner
was always at liberty to save his slave from the torture by
proving his innocence otherwise if possible; and if he succeeded, the accuser forfeited to him a slave of equal value,
and was obliged to pay all the costs of the proceedings.[1]

[1] L. Wisigoth. Lib. vi. Tit. i. l. 5.

Freedmen were even better protected. They could only be tortured for crimes of which the penalties exceeded a certain amount, varying with the nature of the freedom enjoyed by the accused. If no confession were extorted, and the accused were crippled in the torture, the judge and the accuser were both heavily fined for his benefit, and if he died, the fines were paid to his family.[1]

There could have been little torturing of slaves as witnesses, for in general their evidence was not admissible, even under torture, against any freeman, including their masters. The slaves of the royal palace, however, could give testimony as though they were freemen,[2] and, as in the Roman law, there were certain excepted crimes, such as treason, adultery, homicide, sorcery, and coining, in accusations of which slaves could be tortured against their masters, nor could they be preserved by manumission against this liability.[3]

As regards freemen, the provisions of different portions of the code do not seem precisely in harmony, but all of them throw considerable difficulties in the way of procedures by torture. An early law directs that, in cases of theft or fraud, no one shall be subjected to torture unless the accuser bring forward the informer, or inscribe himself with three sureties to undergo the *lex talionis* in case the accused prove innocent. Moreover, if no confession were extorted, the informer was to be produced. If the accuser could not do this, he was bound to name him to the judge, who was then to seize him, unless he were protected by some one too powerful for the judicial authority to control. In this event it was the duty of the judge to summon the authorities to his aid, and in default of so doing he was liable for all the damages arising from the case. The informer, when thus brought within control of the court,

---

[1] L. Wisigoth. Lib. vi. Tit. i. l. 5.　　　[2] Ibid. ii. iv. 4.

[3] Ibid. vi. i. 4; vii. vi. 1; viii. iv. 10, 11.

was, if a freeman, declared infamous, and obliged to pay ninefold the value of the matter in dispute; if a slave, sixfold, and to receive a hundred lashes. If the freeman were too poor to pay the fine, he was adjudged as a slave in common to the accuser and the accused.[1]

A later law, issued by Chindaswind, is even more careful in its very curious provisions. No accuser could force to the torture a man higher in station or rank than himself. The only cases in which it was permitted for nobles were those of treason, homicide, and adultery, while for freemen of humbler position the crime must be rated at a fine of 500 solidi at least. In these cases, an open trial was first prescribed. If this were fruitless, the accuser who desired to push the matter bound himself in case of failure to deliver himself up as a slave to the accused, who could maltreat him at pleasure, short of taking his life, or compound with him at his own valuation of his sufferings. The torture then might last for three days; the accuser himself was the torturer, subject to the supervision of the judge, and might inflict torment to any extent that his ingenuity could suggest, short of producing permanent injury or death. If death resulted, the accuser was delivered to the relatives of the deceased to be likewise put to death; the judge who had permitted it through collusion or corruption was exposed to the same fate, but if he could swear that he had not been bribed by the accuser, he was allowed to escape with a fine of 500 solidi. A very remarkable regulation, moreover, provided against false confessions extorted by torment. The accuser was obliged to draw up his accusation in all its details, and submit it secretly to the judge. Any confession under torture which did not agree substantially with this was set aside, and neither convicted the accused nor released the accuser from the penalties to which he was liable.[2]

[1] L. Wisigoth. vi. i. 1.   [2] Ibid. vi. i. 2.

Under such a system, strictly enforced, few persons
would be found hardy enough to incur the dangers of subjecting an adversary to the rack. As with the Franks,
however, so among the Wisigoths, the laws were not powerful enough to secure their own observance. The authority
of the kings grew gradually weaker and less able to repress
the assumptions of ambitious prelates and unruly grandees,
and it is easy to imagine that in the continual struggle all
parties sought to maintain and strengthen their position
by an habitual disregard of law. At the Thirteenth Council of Toledo, in 683, King Erwig, in his opening address,
alludes to the frequent abuse of torture in contravention of
the law, and promises a reform. The council, in turn, de-
plores the constantly recurring cases of wrong and suffering
wrought "regiæ subtilitatis astu vel profanæ potestatis
instinctu," and proceeds to decree that in future no freeman,
noble, or priest shall be tortured unless regularly accused
or indicted, and properly tried in public; and this decree
duly received the royal confirmation.[1]

As the Goths emerge again into the light of history
after the Saracenic conquest, we find these ancient laws
still in force among the descendants of the refugees who
had gathered around Don Pelayo. The use of the Latin
tongue gradually faded out among them, and about the
twelfth or thirteenth century the Wisigothic code was
translated into the popular language, and this Romance
version, known as the *Fuero Juzgo*, long continued the
source of law in the Peninsula. In this, the provisions of
the early Gothic monarchs respecting torture are textually
preserved, with two trifling exceptions, which may reasonably be regarded as scarcely more than mere errors of
copyists.[2] Torture was thus maintained in Spain as an

[1] Concil. Toletan. XIII. ann. 683, can. ii.

[2] See the Fuero Juzgo, Lib. i. Tit. iii. 1. 4 ; Tit. iv. 1. 4.—Lib. iii. Tit. iv.
ll. 10, 11.—Lib. vi. Tit. i. ll. 2, 4, 5.—Lib. vii. Tit. i. 1. 1 ; Tit vi. l. 1.
The only points in which these vary from the ancient laws are that in Lib.

unbroken ancestral custom, and when Alfonso the Wise, about the middle of the thirteenth century, attempted to revise the jurisprudence of his dominions, in the code known as *Las Siete Partidas* which he promulgated, he only simplified and modified the proceedings, and did not remove the practice. Although he proclaimed that the person of man is the noblest thing of earth—" La persona del home es la mas noble cosa del mundo"[1]—he held that stripes and other torture inflicted judicially were no dishonor even to Spanish sensitiveness.[2] Asserting that torture was frequently requisite for the discovery of hidden crimes,[3] he found himself confronted by the church which taught, as we shall see hereafter, that confessions extorted under torture were invalid. To this doctrine he gave his full assent,[4] and then, to reconcile these apparently incompatible necessities, he adopted an expedient partially suggested not long before by Frederic II., which subsequently became almost universal throughout Europe, whereby the prohibition of conviction on extorted confessions was eluded. After confession under torture, the prisoner was remanded to his prison. On being subsequently brought before the judge, he was again interrogated, when, if he persisted in his confession, he was condemned. If he re-

---

VI. Tit. i. 1. 2, adultery is not included among the crimes for suspicion of which nobles can be tortured, and that the accuser is not directed to conduct the torture. In Lib. VII. Tit. i. 1. 1, also, the informer who fails to convict is condemned only in a single fine, and not ninefold ; he is, however, as in the original, declared infamous, as a *ladro ;* if a slave, the penalty is the same as with the Wisigoths.

[1] Partidas, P. VII. Tit. i. 1. 26.   [2] Ibid. P. VII. Tit. ix. 1. 16.

[3] Ca por los tormentos saben los judgadores muchas veces la verdad de los malos fechos encubiertos, que non se podrian saber dotra guisa.—Ibid. P. VII. Tit. xxx. 1. 1.

[4] Por premia de tormentos ó de feridas, ó por miedo de muerte ó de deshonra que quieren facer á los homes, conoscen á las vegadas algunas cosas que de su grado non las conoscerien : e por ende decimos que la conoscencia que fuere fecha en alguna destas maneras que non debe valer nin empesce al que la face.—Ibid. P. III. Tit. xiii. 1. 5.

canted, he was again tortured ; and, if the crime was grave, the process could be repeated a third time : but, throughout all, he could not be convicted unless he made a free confession apart from the torture. Even after conviction, moreover, if the judge found reason to believe that the confession was the result of fear of the torture, or of rage at being tortured, or of insanity, the prisoner was entitled to an acquittal.[1] The humane interference of the church thus resulted only in a redoublement of cruelty; and the system once introduced speedily tended to break down the limits imposed on it. In little more than half a century after the death of Alfonso, judges were in the habit of not contenting themselves with three inflictions, but continued the torture as long as the prisoner confessed on the rack and retracted his confession subsequently.[2]

Alfonso's admiration of the Roman law led him to borrow much from it rather than from the Gothic code, though both are represented in the provisions which he established. Thus, except in accusations of treason, no one of noble blood could be tortured, nor a doctor of laws or other learning, nor a member of the king's council, or that of any city or town, except for official forgery, nor a pregnant woman, nor a child under fourteen years of age.[3] So, when several accomplices were on trial, the torturer was directed to commence with the youngest and worst trained, as the truth might probably be more readily extracted from him.[4] The provision, also, that when a master, or mistress, or

[1] Partidas, P. vii. Tit. xxx. l. 4.—Porque la conoscencia que es fecha en el tormento, si non fuere confirmada despues sin premia, non es valedera.

[2] Alvari Pelagii de Planctu Ecclesiæ, Lib. ii. Art. xli.

[3] Partidas, P. vii. Tit. xxx. l. 2. Except the favor shown to the learned professions, "por honra de la esciencia," which afterwards became general throughout Europe, these provisions may all be found in the Roman law.— Const. 4 Cod. ix. viii. ; L. 3, Dig. xlviii. xix. ; L. 10, Dig. xlviii. xviii. ; Const. 11 Cod. ix. xli.

[4] Partidas, P. vii. Tit. xxx. l. 5.—Imitated from L. 18, Dig. xlviii. xviii.

one of their children was found dead at home, all the household slaves were liable to torture in the search for the murderer, bears a strong resemblance to the cruel law of the Romans, which condemned them to death in case the murderer remained undiscovered.[1]

The regulations concerning the torture of slaves are founded, with little variation, on the Roman laws. Thus, the evidence of a slave was only admissible under torture, and no slave could be tortured to prove the guilt of a present or former owner, nor could a freedman, in a case concerning his patron, subject to the usual exceptions which we have already seen. The excepted crimes enumerated by Alfonso are seven, viz: adultery, embezzlement of the royal revenues by tax collectors, high treason, murder of a husband or wife by the other, murder of a joint owner of a slave by his partner, murder of a testator by a legatee, and coining. With the slave, as with the freeman, all testimony under torture required subsequent confirmation.[2]

There is one noteworthy innovation, however, in the Partidas, which was subsequently introduced widely into the torture codes of Europe, and which, in theory at least, greatly extended their sphere of action. This was the liability of freemen as witnesses. When a man's evidence was vacillating and contradictory, so as to afford reasonable suspicion that he was committing perjury, all criminal judges were empowered to subject him to torture, so as to ascertain the truth, provided always that he was of low condition, and did not belong to the excepted classes.[3]

With all this, there are indications that Alfonso designed rather to restrict than to extend the use of torture, and, if his general instructions could have been enforced, there must have been little occasion for its employment

---

[1] Partidas, P. VII. Tit. xxx. 1. 7. Cf. Tacit. Annal. XIV. xliii.-xlv.

[2] Ibid. P. VII. Tit. xxx. 1. 16.

[3] Ibid. P. III. Tit. xvi. 1. 43.—P. VII. Tit. xxx. 1. 8.

under his code. In one passage, he directs that when the evidence is insufficient to prove a charge, the accused, if of good character, must be acquitted; and in another, he orders its application only when common report is adverse to a prisoner, and he is shown to be a man of bad repute.[1] Besides, an accuser who failed to prove his charge was always liable to the *lex talionis*, unless he were prosecuting for an offence committed on his own person, or for the murder of a relative not more distant than a brother or sister's child.[2] The judge, moreover, was strictly enjoined not to exceed the strict rules of the law, nor to carry the torture to a point imperilling life or limb. If he deviated from these limits, or acted through malice or favoritism, he was liable to a similar infliction on his own person, or to a penalty greater than if he were a private individual.[3] The liability of witnesses was further circumscribed by the fact that in cases involving corporal punishment, no one could be forced to bear testimony who was related to either of the parties as far as the fourth degree of consanguinity, in either the direct or collateral lines, nor even when nearly connected by marriage, as in the case of fathers-in-law, step-children, &c.[4] Orders to inflict torture, moreover, were one of the few procedures which could be appealed from in advance.[5] Several of these limitations became generally adopted throughout Europe. We shall see, however, that they afforded little real protection to the accused, and it is more than probable that they received as little respect in Spain as elsewhere.

There were many varieties of torture in use at the period, but Alfonso informs us that only two were commonly

[1] Partidas, P. VII. Tit. i. l. 26, "Home mal enfamado."—P. VII. Tit. XXX. l. 3, "Et si fuere home de mala fame ò vil."

[2] Ibid. P. VII. Tit. i. l. 26.

[3] Ibid. P. VII. Tit. XXX. l. 4; Tit. ix. l. 16.

[4] Ibid. P. VII. Tit. XXX. l. 9.

[5] Ibid. P. III. Tit. xxiii. l. 13.

employed, the scourge and the strappado, or hanging the
prisoner by the arms while his back and legs were loaded
with heavy weights.[1] The former of these, however, seems
to be the only one alluded to throughout the code.

As a whole, the Partidas were too elaborate and too
much in advance of the wants of the age to be successful
as a work of legislation. With the death of Alfonso they
became discredited, but still retained a certain amount of
authority, and, a hundred years later, in the Ordenamiento
di Alcalà of Alfonso XI., issued in 1348, they are referred
to as supplying all omissions in subsequent codes.[2]

It is probable that in his system of torture, Alfonso the
Wise merely regulated and put into shape the customs
prevalent in his territories, for the changes in it which
occurred during the succeeding three or four centuries are
merely such as can be readily explained by the increasing
influence of the revived Roman jurisprudence, and the introduction of the doctrines of the Inquisition with respect to
criminal procedures. In the final shape which the administration of torture assumed in Spain, as described by Villadiego, an eminent legist writing about the year 1600, it
was only employed when the proof was strong, and yet not
sufficient for conviction. No allusion is made to the torture of witnesses, and Villadiego condemns the cruelty of
some judges who divide the torture into three days in
order to render it more effective, since, after a certain pro-
longation of torment, the limbs begin to lose their sensi-
bility, which is recovered after an interval, and on the
second and third days they are more sensitive than at first.
This he pronounces rather a repetition than a continuation
of torture, and repetition was illegal unless rendered ne-

---

[1] Partidas, P. vii. Tit. xxx. l. 1.
[2] Ordenamiento di Alcalà, Tit. xxviii. l. 1. The Partidas are quoted as
an authority on the subject of torture by Simancas, Bishop of Badajos, in
the latter half of the sixteenth century. (De Cathol. Instit. Tit. lxv. No.
24, 37.)

cessary by the introduction of new testimony.[1] As in the
thirteenth century, nobles, doctors of laws, pregnant women, and children under fourteen were not liable, except
in cases of high treason and some other heinous offences.
The clergy also were now exempted, unless previously condemned as infamous, and advocates engaged in pleading
enjoyed a similar privilege. With the growth of the Inquisition, however, heresy had now advanced to the dignity
of a crime which extinguished all prerogatives, for it was
held to be a far more serious offence to be false to Divine
than to human majesty.[2] The Partidas allow torture in
the investigation of comparatively trivial offences, but
Villadiego states that it should only be employed in the
case of serious crimes, entailing bodily punishment more
severe than the torture itself, and torture was worse than
the loss of the hands. Thus, when only banishment, fines,
or imprisonment were involved, it could not be used. The
penalties incurred by judges for its excessive or improper
application were almost identical with those prescribed by
Alfonso, and the limitation that it should not be allowed
to endanger life or limb was only to be exceeded in the
case of treason, when the utmost severity was permissible.
Many varieties were in use, but the most common were the
strappado and pouring water down the throat; but when
the accused was so weak as to render these dangerous, fire
was applied to the soles of the feet; and the use of the
scourge was not unusual. As in the ancient laws, the
owner of slaves was entitled to compensation when his
bondmen were unjustly tortured. If there was no justification for it, he was reimbursed in double the estimated
value; if the judge exceeded the proper measure of torment,
he made it good to the owner with another slave.[3]

---

[1] Simancas, however, states that a single repetition of the torture was
allowable.—De Cathol. Instit. Tit. LXV. No. 76.

[2] Ibid. Tit. LXV. No. 44–48.

[3] Villadiego, Gloss. ad Fuero Juzgo, Lib. VI. Tit. i. 1. 2, Gloss. c, d, e, f,
g.—Lib. VI. Tit. i. 1. 5, Gloss. b, c.

Whatever limitations may theoretically have been assigned to the application of torture, however, it is probable that they received litle respect in practice. Simancas, Bishop of Badajos, who was a little anterior to Villadiego, speaks of it as a generally received axiom that scarcely any criminal accusation could be satisfactorily tried without torture.[1] This is confirmed by the account recently discovered by Bergenroth of the secret history of the execution of Don Carlos, for whether it be authentic or not, it shows how thoroughly the use of torture had interpenetrated the judicial system of Spain. It states that when Philip II. determined to try his wretched son for the crime of encouraging the rebellious movements in the Netherlands, and the prince denied the offence, torture was applied until he fainted, and on recovering his senses consented to confess in order to escape the repetition which was about to be applied. It is hardly to be believed that even a Spanish imagination could conceive the dark and terrible details of this dismal story; and even if it be not true, its author must have felt that such an incident was too probable to destroy its vraisemblance.

In turning to the other barbarian races which inherited the fragments of the Roman empire, we find that the introduction of torture as a recognized and legal mode of investigation was long delayed. Under the Merovingians, as we have seen, its employment, though not infrequent, was exceptional and without warrant of law. When the slow reconstruction of society at length began, the first faint trace of torture is to be found in a provision respecting the crimes of sorcery and magic. These were looked upon with peculiar detestation, as unpardonable offences against both God and man. It is no wonder then if the safeguards which the freeman enjoyed under the ordinary modes of

<hr />

[1] Simancæ de Cathol. Instit. Lib. Tit. LXV. No. 8.

judicial procedure were disregarded in the case of those who violated every law, human and divine. The legislation of Charlemagne, indeed, was by no means merciful in its general character. His mission was to civilize, if possible, the savage and turbulent races composing his empire, and he was not over nice in the methods selected to accomplish the task. Still, he did not venture, even if he desired, to prescribe torture as a means of investigation, except in the case of suspected sorcerers, for whom, moreover, it is ordered indirectly rather than openly.[1] Yet, by this time, the personal inviolability of the freeman was gone. The infliction of stripes and of hideous mutilations is frequently directed in the Capitularies, and even torture and banishment for life are prescribed as a punishment for insulting bishops and priests in church.[2]

This apparent inconsistency is easily explicable. Though there was no theoretical objection to torture as a process of investigation, yet there was no necessity for its employment as a means of evidence. That the idea of thus using it in matters of great moment was not unfamiliar to the men of that age is evident when we find it officially stated that the accomplices of Bernard, King of Italy, in his rebellion against Louis-le-Débonnaire, in 817, on their capture confessed the whole plot without being put to the torture.[3] Such instances, however, were purely exceptional. In ordinary matters, there was a complete system of attack and defence which supplemented all deficiencies of testimony in doubtful cases. Sacramental purgation, the wager of battle, and the various forms of vulgar ordeals were not only primeval customs suited to the feelings and modes of

[1] Capit. Carol. Mag. II. ann. 805, § xxv. (Baluz.). No other interpretation can well be given of the direction "diligentissime examinatione constringantur si forte confiteantur malorum quæ gesserunt. Sed tali moderatione fiat eadem districtio ne vitam perdant."

[2] Capitul. Lib. VI. cap. cxxix.

[3] Non solum se tradunt sed ultro etiam non admoti quæstionibus omnem technam hujus rebellionis detegunt.—Goldast. Constit. Imp. I. 151.

thought of the race, but they were also much more in
harmony with the credulous faith inculcated by the church,
and the church had by this time entered on the career of
temporal supremacy which gave it so potential a voice in
fashioning the institutions of European society. For all
these, the ministrations of the ecclesiastic were requisite,
and in many of them his unseen agency might prove
decisive. On the other hand, the humane precepts which
forbade the churchman from intervening in any manner
in judgments involving blood precluded his interference
with the torture chamber; and in fact, while torture was
yet frequent under the Merovingians, the canons of various
councils prohibited the presence of any ecclesiastic in places
where it was administered.[1] Every consideration, therefore, would lead the church in the ninth century to prefer
the milder forms of investigation, and to use its all-powerful
influence in maintaining the popular belief in them. The
time had not yet come when, as we shall see hereafter, the
church, as the spiritual head of feudal Christendom, would
find the ordeal unnecessary and torture the most practicable instrumentality to preserve the purity of faith and
the steadfastness of implicit obedience.

In the ninth century, moreover, torture was incompatible
with the forms of judicial procedure handed down as relics
of the time when every freeman bore his share in the public
business of his sept. Criminal proceedings as yet were
open and public. The secret inquisitions which afterwards
became so favorite a system with lawyers did not then
exist. The *mallum*, or court, was perhaps no longer held
in the open air,[2] nor were the freemen of the district con-

---

[1] Non licet presbytero nec diacono ad trepalium ubi rei torquentur stare.
—Concil. Autissiodor. ann. 578, can. xxxiii.

Ad locum examinationis reorum nullus clericorum accedat.—Concil. Ma-
tiscon. II. ann. 585, can. xix.

[2] Under Charlemagne and Louis-le-Débonnaire seems to have commenced
the usage of holding the court under shelter. Thus Charlemagne, " Ut in locis
ubi mallus publicus haberi solet, tectum tale constituatur quod in hiberno

strained as of old to be present,[1] but it was still free to
every one. The accuser and his witnesses were confronted
with the accused, and the criminal must be present when
his sentence was pronounced.[2] The purgatorial oath was
administered at the altar of the parish church; the ordeal
was a public spectacle; and the judicial duel drew thousands
of witnesses as eager for the sight of blood as the Roman
plebs. These were all ancestral customs, inspiring implicit reverence, and forming part of the public life of the
community. To substitute for them the gloomy dungeon
through whose walls no echo of the victim's screams could
filter, where impassible judges coldly compared the inco-
herent confession wrung out by insufferable torment with
the anonymous accusation or the depositions of secret
witnesses, required a total change in the constitution of
society.

The change was long in coming. Feudalism arose and
consolidated its forces on the ruins of the Carlovingian em-

---

et in æstate observandus esse possit."—(Capit. Carol. Mag. II. ann. 809,
§ xiii.) See also Capit. I. eod. ann. § xxv. Louis-le-Débonnaire prohibits
the holding of courts in churches, and adds, "Volumus utique ut domus a
comite in locum ubi mallum tenere debet construatur, ut propter calorem
solis et pluviam publica utilitas non remaneat."—(Capit. Ludov. Pii. I. ann.
819, § xiv.)

[1] In 769, we find Charlemagne commanding the presence of all freemen in
the general judicial assembly held twice a year, "Ut ad mallum venire nemo
tardet, unum circa æstatem et alterum circa autumnum." At others of less
importance, they were only bound to attend when summoned, "Ad alia vero,
si necessitas fuerit, vel denunciatio regis urgeat, vocatus venire nemo tardet."
—(Capit. Carol. Mag. ann. 769, § xii.)

In 809, he desired that none should be forced to attend unless he had business, "Ut nullus ad placitum venire cogatur, nisi qui caussam habet ad
quærendam."—(Capit. I. ann. 809, § xiii.)

In 819, Louis ordered that the freemen should attend at least three courts
a year, "et nullus eos amplius placita observare compellat, nisi forte quilibet
aut accusatus fuerit, aut alium accusaverit, aut ad testimonium perhibendum
vocatus fuerit."—(Capit. Ludov. Pii. v. ann. 819, § xiv.)

[2] Placuit ut adversus absentes non judicetur. Quod si factus fuerit pro-
lata sententia non valebit.—Capitul. Lib. v. § cccxi.

pire without altering the principles upon which the earlier
procedures of criminal jurisdiction had been based. As
the local dignitaries seized upon their fiefs and made them
hereditary, so they arrogated to themselves the dispensa-
tion of justice which had formerly belonged to the central
power, but their courts were still open to all. Trials were
conducted in public upon well-known rules of local law
and custom; the fullest opportunities were given for the
defence; and a denial of justice authorized the vassal to
renounce the jurisdiction of his feudal lord and seek a
superior court.[1]

Still, as under the Merovingians, torture, though un-
recognized by law, was occasionally employed as an extraordinary element of judicial investigation, as well as a
means of punishment to gratify the vengeance of the irresponsible and cruel tyrants who ruled with absolute sway
over their petty lordships. A few such instances occur in
the documents and chronicles of the period, but the terms
in which they are alluded to show that they were regarded
as irregular.

Thus, it is related of Wenceslas, Duke of Bohemia, in
the early part of the tenth century, that he destroyed the
gibbets and fearful implements of torture wherewith the
cruelty of his judges had been exercised, and that he never
allowed them to be restored.[2] An individual case of torture
which occurred in 1017 has chanced to be preserved to us
by its ending in a miracle, and being the occasion of the
canonization of a saint. A pious pilgrim, reputed to belong
to the royal blood of Scotland, while wandering on the

---

[1] This right of appeal was not relished by the seigneurs, who apparently
foresaw that it might eventually become the instrument of their destruction.
It was long in establishing itself, and was resisted energetically. Thus the
Kings of England who were Dukes of Aquitaine, sometimes discouraged the
appeals of their French subjects to the courts of the King of France by
hanging the notaries who undertook to draw up the requisite papers.—Meyer,
Instit. Judiciaires, I. 461.

[2] Annalist. Saxo ann. 928.

marches between the Bavarians and the Moravians, was
seized by the inhabitants on suspicion of being a spy, and,
to extort a confession, was exposed to a succession of torments which ended in hanging him on a withered tree until
he died. The falsity of the accusation and the sanctity of
the victim were manifested by the uninterrupted growth of
his hair and nails and the constant flowing of blood from a
wound, while the dead tree suddenly put forth leaves and
flowers. Margrave Henry of Bavaria had him reverently
buried, and he was duly enrolled in the catalogue of saints.[1]
A letter of Gerard, Bishop of Cambrai, in 1025, relating
how certain suspected heretics could not be forced by torment to confession, shows that ecclesiastics already were
prepared, in spite of the received dogmas of the church, to
have recourse to such means when no others could be found
to protect the purity of the faith.[2] In the celebrated case,
also, of the robbery of the church of Laon, about the year
1100, the suspected thief, after conviction by the cold water
ordeal, was tortured by command of the bishop in order
to make him surrender the sacred vessels which he had
concealed. Basting with hot lard was tried unsuccessfully;
he was then hanged by the neck and let down at intervals
for nearly a whole day, and when life was almost extinct
his resolution gave way and he agreed to discover the place
where the valuables were hidden.[3]

These are evidently rather sporadic and exceptional cases
than indications of any systematic introduction of the practice. A more significant allusion, however, is found in the
reproof administered, about 1125, by Hildebert, Bishop of
le Mans, to one of his priests, who had been concerned in
the torture of a suspected thief, for the purpose of extract-

---

[1] Dithmari Chron. Lib. VII. ad. fin.

[2] Multa dissimulatione renitebant, adeo ut nullis suppliciis possent cogi
ad confessionem.—Synod. Atrebatens. ann. 1025 (Hartzheim III. 68).

[3] Hermannus de S. Mariæ Lauden. Mirac. Cf. Guibert. Noviogent. de
Vita Sua, cap. xvi.

ing a confession. Hildebert argues that the infliction of torture for confession is a matter for judicial decision and not of church discipline, and therefore not fit for a clerk to be engaged in.[1] This would seem to show that it occasionally was a recognized means of proof in the lay tribunals of the period, though as yet not favored by the church. If so, no record of its introduction or evidence of its customary use has been preserved to us, though there is abundant evidence of its employment as a punishment and for the extortion of money.

As a punishment legally inflicted, we find it prescribed, in 1168, by Frederic Barbarossa in cases of petty thefts,[2] and in the next century by Frederic II. as a penalty for high treason.[3] Special cases, too, may be instanced, where its infliction on a large scale shows that the minds of men were not unfamiliar with its use. Thus when, in 1125, the inhabitants of Erfurt were guilty of some outrages on the imperial authority, and the town was besieged and captured by the Emperor Lothair, the chronicler relates that large numbers of the citizens were either killed, blinded, or tortured in various ways by the vindictive conqueror,[4] and in 1129 he treated the citizens of Halle in the same manner.[5]

So summary and effective a mode of forcing the weak and unprotected to ransom themselves was not likely to be overlooked in those ages of violence, and though the extra-judicial use of torture is foreign to our purpose, yet, as

[1] Reos tormentis afficere vel suppliciis extorquere confessionem censura curiæ est non ecclesiæ disciplina. Unde et ab ejus animadversione abstinere debuisti quem pecuniam tuam furto suspicaris asportasse; neque enim carnifex es sed sacrifex.—Hildebert. Cenoman. Epist. xxx.

[2] Si quis quinque solidos valens aut plus fuerit furatus laqueo suspendatur: si minus, scopis et forcipe excorietur et tundatur.—Feudor. Lib. ii. Tit. xxvii. § 8.

[3] Fred. II. Lib. Rescript. II. §§ 1, 6. (Goldast. Constit. Imp. II. 54.)

[4] Trucidatis aliis, aliis cæcatis, nonnullis diversis tormentorum generibus excruciatis, multisque per diversis fugientibus.—Erphurdianus Variloquus ann. 1125.

[5] Annal. Bosovienses, ann. 1129.

showing how men educated themselves in its employment,
it may be worth while to allude briefly to this aspect of
the subject.   Thus, Duke Swantopluck of Bohemia, in a
marauding expedition into Hungary in 1108, caused to be
racked or put to death all prisoners who could not purchase
escape by heavy ransoms.[1]   At the same period, Germany
is described to us by an eye witness as covered with feudal
chieftains who lived a life of luxury by torturing the miserable wretches that could scarce obtain bread and water
for their own existence.[2]   In Spain, the same means were
understood and employed by the savage nobles of that
barbarous period.[3]   In England, the fearful anarchy which
prevailed under King Stephen encouraged a similar condition of affairs.   The baronial castles which then multiplied
so rapidly became mere dens of robbers who ransacked
the country for all who had the unfortunate reputation of
wealth.   From these they extracted the last penny by tortures ;   and the chronicler expatiates on the multiplicity
and horrid ingenuity of the torments devised—suspension
by the feet over slow fires ; hanging by the thumbs ; knot-
ted ropes twisted around the head ; crucet-houses, or chests
filled with sharp stones, in which the victim was crushed ;
sachentages, or frames with a sharp iron collar preventing
the wearer from sitting, lying, or sleeping ; dungeons filled
with toads and adders ; slow starvation, &c. &c.[4]   Such

---

[1] Alios interfeci jussit, alios in eculeo suspensos, paucis vero, accepta
magna pecunia, vitam concessit—Cosmæ Pragens. Lib. III. ann. 1108.

[2] Ab his qui pane sole et aqua victitare solebant, delicias sibi ministrari
tormentis exigebant.—Annalist. Saxo ann. 1123.

[3] A contemporary chronicler, writing in 1126, alludes to a case—"F. Jo-
hannides S. Pelagii de Luto dominus . . . . Compostellanæ civitatis bur-
genses nefanda proditione captioni mancipavit et eos in carcere retrusos
diversorum tormentorum illatione ad redemptionem inhumanitus et intoler-
abiliter cogere cœpit."—Gerardi Hist. Compostellan. Lib. II. cap. 80.

[4] Anglo-Saxon Chronicle, ann. 1137.   Even in the more settled times
towards the close of the century there is an epistle of Clement III. respecting a knight who confessed that " W. Bricet presbyterum variis tormentis
afflictum compulisset ad redemptionem non modicam."   (Jaffé Regesta,
p. 884.)

experiments were a fitting education for the times that were to come.

In all this, however, there is no evidence of the revival of torture as a means of legal investigation. The community was satisfied with the old barbaric forms of trial, and the church, still true to its humanizing instincts, lost no opportunity of placing the seal of its disapprobation on the whole theory of extorting confessions. At an early period, it had even been a matter of dispute whether a Christian magistrate, after baptism, was at liberty to inflict torment and pronounce sentence of death. The synod of Rome in 384 had declared that no Christian could exercise secular power without sin, because he was obliged to contravene the teachings of the church by ordering the application of torture in judicial pleadings;[1] and if Innocent I., in 405, had decided that such proceedings were lawful, it was only on the ground that the church had no right to resist the laws or to oppose the powers ordained of God.[2] About the same time St. Augustine had exposed the cruel absurdity of torture with a cogent terseness that has rarely been excelled, and had stamped it with the infamy which it deserved.[3] The great name of Gregory I. was on record in the sixth century, denouncing as worthless a confession extorted by incarceration and hunger.[4] When Nicholas I., who did so much to build up ecclesiastical power and influence, addressed, in 866, his well-known epistle to the Bulgarians to aid and direct them in their conversion to orthodoxy, he recites that he is told that in cases of suspected theft, their courts endeavor to extort confession by stripes, and by pricking with a pointed iron. This he pronounces to be contrary to all law, human and divine, for confessions to be valid should be spontaneous; and he

---

[1] Synod. Roman. ann. 384, can. 10.
[2] Innocent PP. I. Epist. III. cap. iii.
[3] De Civ. Dei Lib. XIX. cap. vi.
[4] Gregor. PP. I. Lib. VIII. Epist. xxx.

argues at some length on the uncertainty of the system of torture, and the injustice to which it leads, concluding with a peremptory prohibition of its continuance.[1]

In the first half of the same century, the manufacturers of the False Decretals had attributed to Alexander I. an epistle designed to protect the church from pillage and oppression, in which that pontiff is made to threaten with infamy and excommunication those who extort confessions or other writings from ecclesiastics by force or fear, and to lay down the general rule that confessions must be voluntary and not compulsory.[2]   On the authority of this, Ivo of Chartres, at the commencement of the twelfth century, declares that men in holy orders cannot be forced to confess;[3] and half a century later, Gratian lays down the more general as well as more explicit rule that no confession is to be extorted by the instrumentality of torture.[4] This position was consistently maintained until the revival of the Roman law familiarized the minds of men with the procedures of the imperial jurispru   nce, when the policy of the church altered, and it yielded to the temptation of obtaining so useful a means of reaching and proving the otherwise impalpable crime of heresy.

The latter half of the twelfth century saw the study of the civil law prosecuted with intense ardor, and, in the beginning of the thirteenth, Innocent III. struck a fatal blow at the barbaric systems of the ordeal and sacramental compurgation by forbidding the rites of the church to the one and altering the form of oath customary to the other.

---

[1] Nicolai PP. I. Epist xcvii. § 86.

[2] Pseudo-Alexand. decret. "Omnibus orthodoxis"—Confessio vero in talibus non compulsa sed spontanea fieri debet. . . . Confessio enim non extorqueri debet in talibus, sed potius sponte profiteri, pessimum est enim de suspicione aut extorta confessione quemquam judicare.

[3] Ministrorum confessio non sit extorta sed spontanea.—Ivon. Panorm. IV. cxviii.

[4] Quod vero confessio cruciatibus extorquenda non est.—Decreti Caus. xv. q. 6, can. 1.

The unreasoning faith which had reposed confidence in the boiling caldron, or the burning ploughshare, or the trained champion as the special vehicle of Divine judgment, was fading before the Aristotelian logic of the schools, and dialectical skill could not but note the absurdity of acquitting a culprit because he could beg or buy two, or five, or eleven men to swear to their belief in his oath of denial.

Yet with all these influences at work, the ancestral customs maintained their ground long and stubbornly. It is not until the latter half of the thirteenth century that the first faint traces of legalized torture are to be found in France, at whose University of Paris for more than a hundred years the study of the Pandects had become the absorbing topic, and where the constantly increasing power of the crown found its most valuable instruments in the civil lawyers, and its surest weapon against feudalism in the extension of the royal jurisdiction. In Germany, the progress was even slower. The decline of the central authority, after the death of Frederic Barbarossa, rendered any general change impossible, and made the absolutist principles of the imperial jurisprudence especially distasteful to the crowd of feudal sovereigns, whose privileges were best supported by perpetuating organized anarchy. The early codes, therefore, the Sachsenspiegel, the Schwabenspiegel, the Kayser-Recht, and the Richstich Landrecht, which regulated the judicial proceedings of the Teutonic nations from the thirteenth to the fifteenth centuries, seem to know no other mode of deciding doubtful questions than sacramental purgation and the various forms of ordeal. During the latter portion of this period, it is true, torture begins to appear, but it is an innovation.

The first indications of the modern use of torture show distinctly that its origin is derived from the civil law. In the Latin kingdoms of the East, the Teutonic races were brought into contact with the remains of the old civilization, impressive even in its decrepitude. It was natural that, in governing the motley collection of Greeks, Syrians, and Franks, for whom they had to legislate, they should adopt some of the institutions which they found in force amid their new possessions, and it is only surprising that torture did not form a more prominent feature in their code. The earliest extant text of the *Assises de Jerusalem* is not older than the thirteenth century, and the blundering and hesitating way in which it recognizes, in a single instance, the use of torture shows how novel was the idea of such procedure to the feudal barons, and how little they understood the principles governing its application. When a murderer was caught in the act by two witnesses, he could be promptly hanged on their testimony, if they were strangers to the victim. If, however, they were relatives, their testimony was held suspect, and the confession of the accused was requisite to his conviction. To obtain this, he was subjected to torture for three days; if he confessed, he was hanged; if obdurate, he was imprisoned for a year and a day, with the privilege of clearing himself during that period by the ordeal of the red-hot iron. If he declined this, and if during his confinement no additional evidence was procured, he was acquitted, and could not be again appealed for the murder.[1]

This shows the transition state of the question. The criminal is caught with the red hand and the evidence of guilt is complete, save that the witnesses may be interested; confession thus becomes requisite, yet the failure to extort it by the most prolonged torment does not clear the accused; the ordeal is resorted to in order to supplement the torture, and solve the doubts which the latter could not remove; and finally, the criminal is absolved, though he dare not trust the judgment of God, and though the uncertainties in which torture had left the case are not removed.

Italy was the centre from which radiated the influences

---

[1] Assises de Jerusalem, Baisse Court, cap. cclix.

of the Roman law throughout Western Europe, and, as might be expected, it is to Italy that we must look for the earliest incorporation of torture in the procedures of modern criminal jurisprudence. The Veronese laws in force in 1228 already show a mixture of proceedings suggestive, like the Assises de Jerusalem, of the impending change. In doubtful cases, the Podestá was empowered to ascertain the truth of testimony by either inquest, torture or the duel.[1] This shows that the employment of torture was by this time recognized to some extent, though as the code is a very full one and this is the only allusion to it, it evidently had not yet grown into one of the regular legal processes. So in the legislation of Frederic II. for his Neapolitan provinces, promulgated in 1231, the mode in which it is prescribed shows that it was as yet but sparingly employed. As Frederic was one of the earliest secular legislators who discountenanced and restricted the various forms of the ordeal, it was natural that, with his education and temperament, he should seek to replace them with the system of the Roman codes which he so much admired.

When a secret murder or other heinous crime was committed, and the most stringent investigation could not convict the perpetrators, if the weight of suspicion fell on persons of humble station and little consequence, they could be tortured for confession.* If no torment could wring from them an acknowledgment of guilt, or if, as often happened ("prout accidere novimus in plerisque"), their resolution gave way under insufferable torment and they subsequently recanted, then the punishment, in the shape of a fine, was inflicted on the district where the crime had occurred.[2] From this it is evident that torture was not exactly a novelty, but that as yet it was only ventured

[1] Lib. Juris Civilis Veronæ cap. 75 (p. 61).
[2] Constit. Sicular. Lib. I. Tit. xxvii.

upon with the lowest and most unprotected class of society, and that confession during its infliction was not regarded as sufficient for conviction, unless subsequently persisted in.

During the remainder of the century, the statutes of many of the Italian cities show the gradual introduction of torture to replace the barbarian processes which were not indigenous,[1] and which the traditional hate of the Italian States for the Tedeschi was not likely to render popular. That by the middle of the century, indeed, the practical applications of torture had been profoundly studied and were thoroughly understood in all their most inhuman ramifications is sufficiently evident from the accounts which we possess of the fearful cruelties habitually practised by petty despots such as Eccelino di Romano.[2]

The manner in which the use of torture thus in time was superimposed upon the existing customs of Europe is clearly shown in the law of Lubeck. The mercantile law of the Middle Ages disregarded, as we have seen, all the irregular forms of evidence, such as the ordeal, the judicial duel, &c., and it naturally was not favorable to torture. As the chief of the Hanse-towns Lubeck, therefore, in its legislation preserved the principles of the mercantile law, but in time this came to be expounded by a race of lawyers imbued with the ideas of the imperial jurisprudence, and little was left of the primitive simplicity of the original code. Thus the latter, when treating of adultery, simply provides that the accused must clear himself by oath, or be held guilty of the charge; but a commentary on it, written in 1664, assumes that as the crime is a peculiarly

---

[1] Du Boys, Droit Criminel des Peup. Mod. II. 405.

[2] Monach. Paduan. Chron. Lib. ii. ann. 1252-3 (Urstisii Script. Rer. German. pp. 594-5).—Quotidie diversis generibus tormentorum indifferenter tam majores quam minores a carnificibus necabuntur. Voces terribiles clamantum in tormentis die noctuque audiebantur de altis palatiis. . . . Quotidie sine labore, sine conscientiæ remorsione magna tormenta et inexcogitata corporibus hominum infligebat, etc.

secret one recourse must be at once had to torture where there is colorable ground for suspicion.[1]

About this time we also find, in the increasing rigor and gradual systematizing of the Inquisition, an evidence of the growing disposition to resort to torture, and a powerful element in extending and facilitating its introduction. The church had been actively engaged in discountenancing and extirpating the ordeal, and it now threw the immense weight of its authority in favor of the new process of extorting confessions. When Frederic II., in 1221, published at Padua his three constitutions directed against heresy, cruel and unsparing as they were, they contained no indication that torture was even contemplated as a mode of investigation. In fact, suspected parties, against whom insufficient evidence was brought, were directed to prove their innocence by some fitting mode of purgation,[2] and the same process is indicated in the instructions of Gregory IX. in 1235.[3] In 1252, however, when Innocent IV. issued his elaborate instructions for the guidance of the Inquisition in Tuscany and Lombardy, he ordered the civil magistrates to extort from all heretics by torture not merely a confession of their own guilt, but an accusation of all who might be their accomplices; and this derives significance from his reference to similar proceedings as customary in trials of thieves and robbers.[4] It shows the progress made during the quarter of the century, and the

[1] Mevii Comment. in Jus Lubecense, Lib. IV. Tit. VI. Art. 4 (Francofurt. 1664).

[2] Congrua purgatione.—Goldast. Constit. Imp. I. 293–5.

[3] Harduin. Concil. VII. 164.

[4] Teneatur praeterea potestas seu rector omnes haereticos quos captos habuerit, cogere citra membri diminutionem et mortis periculum, tanquam vere latrones et homicidas animarum et fures sacramentorum Dei et fidei Christianae, errores suos expresse fateri et accusare alios haereticos quos sciunt, et bona eorum, et credentes et receptatores et defensores eorum, sicut coguntur fures et latrones rerum temporalium accusare suos complices et fateri maleficia quae fecerunt.—Innocent. IV. Leg. et Const. contra Haeret. § 26.

high appreciation entertained by the church for the convenience of the new system.

As yet, however, this did not extend beyond Italy. There is extant a tract, written not long after this time, containing very minute instructions as to the established mode of dealing with the Waldensian sectaries known as the "Poor Men of Lyons." It gives directions to break down their strength and overcome their fortitude by solitary confinement, starvation, and terror, but it abstains from recommending the infliction of absolute and direct torture, while its details are so full that the omission is tolerable evidence that such measures were not then customary.[1]

The whole system of the Inquisition, however, was such as to render the resort to torture inevitable. Its proceedings were secret; the prisoner was carefully kept in ignorance of the exact charges against him, and of the evidence upon which they were based.   He was presumed to be guilty, and his judges bent all their energies to force him to confess. To accomplish this, no means were too base or too cruel. According to the tract just quoted, pretended sympathizers were to be let into his dungeon, whose affected friendship might entrap him into an unwary admission; officials armed with fictitious evidence were directed to frighten him with assertions of the testimony obtained against him from supposititious witnesses; and no resources of fraud or guile were to be spared in overcoming the caution and resolution of the poor wretch whose mind, as we have seen, had been carefully weakened by solitude, suffering, hunger, and terror. From this to the rack and estrapade the step was easily taken, and was not long delayed. In 1301, we find even

---

[1] Tract. de Hæres. Paup. de Ludg. (Martene Thesaur. V. 1787).   In the tract, Frederic II., who died in 1250, is spoken of as "quondam imperator."

I have, however, met with a letter of St. Dominic, dated April 7th, 1217, which if genuine would show that the various kinds of torture, the rack, the pincers, the wheel, &c. were employed against the heretic Albigenses as early as that date.—See the *Fra Paolo Sarpi*, Venezia, Ottob. 27, 1869.

Philippe-le-Bel protesting against the cruelty of the Inquisition, and interfering to protect his subjects from the
refinements of torture to which, on simple suspicion of
heresy, unfortunate victims were habitually exposed.[1] Yet
when, a few years later, the same monarch resolved upon
the destruction of the Templars, he made the Inquisition
the facile instrument to which he resorted, as a matter of
course, to extort from De Molay and his knights, with
endless repetition of torments, the confessions which were
to recruit his exhausted treasury with their broad lands
and accumulated riches.[2]

The history of the Inquisition, however, is too large a
subject to be treated here in detail, and it can only be
alluded to for the purpose of indicating its influence upon
secular law. That influence was immense. The legists who
were endeavoring to eradicate the feudal customs could not
expect the community to share their admiration of the
Roman law, and naturally grasped with eagerness the advantage offered them in adducing the example of ecclesiastical institutions. In founding their new system, they
could thus hardly avoid copying that which presented itself
under all the authority of an infallible church, and which
had been found to work so successfully in unveiling the
most secret of hidden crimes, those of faith and belief.[3]

[1] Clamor validus et insinuatio luctuosa fidelium subditorum . . . processus
suos in inquisitionis negotio a captionibus, quæstionibus et excogitatis tormentis incipiens personas quas pro libito asserit hæretica labe notatas, abne-
gasse Christum . . . . vi vel metu tormentorum fateri compellit.—Lit. Philip.
Pulchri, *ap.* Raynouard, Monuments Historiques relatifs à la Condamnation
des Chevaliers du Temple, pp. 37-8.

[2] The fearful details of torture collected by Raynouard (op. cit.) show that
the Inquisition by this time was fully experienced in such work.

[3] Simancæ de Christ. Instit. Tit. LXV. No. 19.—To the Inquisition is
likewise attributable another of the monstrous iniquities of criminal justice—
the denial to the accused of the assistance of counsel. Under the customary law of the feudal courts, the avocat or "avantparlier" was freely
admitted, but such privilege was incompatible with the arbitrary process
of which the sole object was to condemn for a crime scarce susceptible of

When, therefore, men were taught that in these cases the ordinary forms and safeguards of the law were not to stand in the way of the public good, a principle was enunciated capable of illimitable development.

About the time when Innocent IV. was prescribing torture in Italy, we find the first evidence of its authoritative use in France as an ordinary legal procedure. In December, 1254, an assembly of the nobles of the realm at Paris adopted an ordonnance regulating many points in the administration of justice. Among these occurs an order that persons of good reputation, even though poor, shall not be put to the torture on the evidence of one witness, lest, on the one hand, they may be forced to convict themselves falsely, or, on the other, to buy themselves off from the infliction.[1]

This would seem to indicate that the system of judicial torture was so completely established that its evils and abuses had begun to render themselves apparent and to require restrictive legislation. Yet the contemporaneous remains of jurisprudence show no trace of the custom, and some of them are of a nature to render their silence a negative proof of no little weight. To this period, for instance, belongs the earliest extant coutumier of Normandy, published by Ludewig, and it contains no allusion to torture. The same may be said of the *For de Béarn*, granted

---

proof. The decretal against heretics issued in 1235 by Gregory IX. forbids all judges, advocates and notaries from helping the suspected heretic under pain of perpetual deprivation of function—"Item, judices, advocati, et notarii nulli eorum officium suum impendant; alioquin eodem officio perpetuo sint privati" (Harduin. Concil. VII. 164); and the same rule was enjoined "ne Inquisitionis negotium per advocatorum strepitum retardetur" by the Council of Valence (can. xi.) in 1248 and that of Alby (can. xxiii.) in 1254. (Harduin. VII. 426, 461.)

[1] Personas autem honestas vel bonæ famæ, etiam si sint pauperes, ad dictum testis unici, tormentis seu quæstionibus inhibemus, ne ob metum falsum confiteri, vel suam vexationem redimere compellantur.—Fontanon, Edicts et Ordonn. I. 701. A somewhat different reading is given by Isambert, Anciennes Lois Françaises I. 270.

in 1288, and recently printed by MM. Mazure and Hatoulet, which is very full in its details of judicial procedure. The collection of the laws of St. Louis, known as the *Établisse- ments*, is likewise free from any instructions or directions as to its application, though it could scarcely have been omitted, had it formed part of the admitted jurisprudence of the age. It may be argued, indeed, that these codes and laws assume the existence of torture, and therefore make no reference to it, but such an argument would not hold good with respect to the books of practice which shrewd and experienced lawyers commenced at that time to draw up for the guidance of courts in the unsettled period of conflict between the ancient feudal customs and the invading civil law. For instance, no text-book can well be more minute than the "Livres de Jostice et de Plet," written about the year 1260, by a lawyer of the school of Orléans, then celebrated as the headquarters of the study of the Imperial jurisprudence. He manifests upon almost every page his familiar acquaintance with the civil and canon law, and he could not possibly have avoided some reference to torture, if it had been even an occasional resource in the tribunals in which he pleaded, and yet he does not in any way allude to it.

The same conclusion is derivable from the "Coutumes du Beauvoisis," written about 1270 by Philippe de Beau- manoir. In his position as royal bailli, Beaumanoir had obtained the fullest possible familiarity with all the prac- tical secular jurisprudence of his day, and his tendencies were naturally in favor of the new system with which St. Louis was endeavoring to break down the feudal customs. Yet, while he details at much length every step in all the cases, civil and criminal, that could be brought into court, he makes no allusion to torture as a means of obtaining evidence. In one passage, it is true, he seems to indicate that a prisoner could be forced, while in prison, to criminate himself, but the terms employed prove clearly that this

was not intended to include the administration of torment.[1]
In another place, moreover, when treating of robberies, he
directs that all suspected parties should be long and closely
confined, but that, if they cannot be convicted by external
evidence, they must at last be discharged.[2] All this is
clearly incompatible with the theory of torture.

The "Conseil" of Pierre de Fontaines, which was probably written about the year 1260, affords the same negative evidence in its full instructions for all the legal proceedings then in use. In these three works, notwithstanding the reforms attempted by St. Louis, the wager of battle
is still the recognized resource for the settlement of doubtful cases, wherein testimony is insufficient, and the legist
seems to imagine no other solution. The form of trial
is still public, in the feudal or royal courts, and every
opportunity is given both for the attack and the defence.
The work of De Fontaines, moreover, happens to furnish
another proof that he wrote at the commencement of a
transition period, during which the use of torture was introduced. In the oldest MSS. of his work, which are considered to date from 1260 to 1280, there is a passage to the
effect that a man convicted of crime may appeal, if he has
not confessed, or, when he has confessed, if it has been in
consequence of some understanding (*covent*). In later MSS.,
transcribed in the early part of the fourteenth century, the

---

[1] Cil qui est pris et mis en prison, soit por meffet ou por dete, tant comme
il est en prison il n'est tenus à respondre à riens c'on li demande fors es
cas tant solement por quoi il fu pris. Et s'on li fet respondre autre coze
contre se volenté, et sor ce qu'il allige qu'il ne veut pas respondre tant
comme il soit en prison ; tout ce qui est fait contre li est de nule valeur, car
il pot tout rapeler quand il est hors de prison —Beaumanoir, cap. LII. § xix.

[2] Quant tel larrecin sunt fet, le justice doit penre toz les souspeçonneus
et fere moult de demandes, por savoir s'il porra fere cler ce qui est orbe.
Et bien les doit en longe prison tenir et destroite, et toz cex qu'il arn
souspechonneus par malvese renommée. El s'il ne pot en nule maniere
savoir le verité du fet, il les doit delivrer, se nus ne vient avant qui partie
se voille fere d'aus acuser droitement du larrecin.—Ibid. cap. XXXI. § vi.

word "covent" is replaced by "tourmenz,"[1] thus showing not only the introduction of torture during the interval, but also that a conviction obtained by it was not final.

The Ordonnance of 1254, indeed, as far as it relates to torture, is asserted by modern criticism to have been applicable only to the bailliages of Beauvais and Cahors.[2] I do not know upon what facts this opinion is based, but the omission of Beaumanoir to allude to any such custom would seem to render doubtful its application to Beauvais. That it was limited to a great extent is more than probable; for in the ordonnance as registered in the council of Béziers in 1255, the section respecting torture is omitted,[3] and this would explain the silence preserved on the subject by all contemporary legal authorities.

While giving due weight, however, to all this, we must not lose sight of the fact that the laws and regulations prescribed in royal ordonnances and legal text-books were practically applicable only to a portion of the population. All non-nobles, who had not succeeded in extorting special privileges by charter from their feudal superiors, were exposed to the caprices of barbarous and irresponsible power. It was a maxim of feudal law that God alone could intervene between the lord and his villein—"Mès par notre usage n'a-il, entre toi et ton vilein, juge fors Deu"[4]—the villein being by no means necessarily a serf; and another rule prohibited absolutely the villein from appealing from the judgment of his lord.[5] Outside of law, and unauthorized by coutumiers and ordonnances, there must, under such institutions, have been habitually vast numbers of cases in

---

[1] Si li hons n'est connoissans de son mesfet, ou s'il l'a coneu et ce a esté par covent, s'en li fait jugement, apeler en puet.—Conseil, ch. xxii. art. 28. (Édition Marnier, Paris, 1846.)

[2] L'Oiseleur, Les Crimes et les Peines, p. 113 (Paris, 1863).

[3] Baluz. Concil. Gall. Narbon. p. 75.

[4] Conseil ch. xxi. art. 8.

[5] Ibid. art. 14. Et encor ne puisse li vileins fausser le jugement son seignor.

which the impatient temper of the lord would seek a solution of doubtful matters in the potent cogency of the rack
or scourge, rather than waste time or dignity in endeavoring
to cross-question the truth out of a quick-witted criminal.

Still, as an admitted legal procedure, the introduction of
torture was very gradual. The "Olim," or register of
cases decided by the Parlement of Paris, extends, with
some intervals, from 1255 to 1318, and the paucity of affairs
in which torture was used shows that it could not have
been habitually resorted to during this period. The first
instance, indeed, only occurs in 1283, when the Bishop of
Amiens complains of the bailli of that town for having
tried and tortured three clerks in defiance of the benefit of
clergy which entitled them to exemption from secular jurisdiction. The bailli pleaded ignorance of their ecclesiastical character, and his plea was admitted as sufficient.[1] The
next instance of the use of torture is found in 1299, when
the royal bailli of Senlis cites the mayor and jurats of that
town before the Parlement, because in a case of theft they
had applied the question to a suspected criminal; and
though theft was within their competence, the bailli argued
that torture was an incident of "haute justice" which the
town did not possess. The decision was in favor of the
municipality.[2] The next year (1300), we find a clerk,
wearing habit and tonsure, complaining that the royal
officials of the town of Villeneuve in Rouergue had tortured him in divers ways, with ropes and heavy weights,
heated eggs and fire, so that he was crippled, and had been
forced to expend three hundred livres Tournois in medi-
cines and physicians. This, with other proper damages,
he prays may be made good to him by the perpetrators,
and the arrêt of the Parlement orders their persons and
property to be seized, and their possessions valued, in

---

[1] Actes du Parlement de Paris, I. 382 (Paris, 1863).

[2] Olim. T. II. p. 451.

order that the amount may be properly assessed among them.[1] Philippe-le-Bel, notwithstanding his mortal quarrel with the papacy—or perhaps in consequence of it—was ever careful of the rights and privileges of the clergy, among which the immunity from secular jurisdiction and consequently from torture was prominent. The case evidently turned upon that point.

The fourth case does not present itself until 1306. Two Jews, under accusation of larceny by their brethren, complain that they had been illegally tortured by the bailli of Bourges, and though one of them under the infliction had confessed to complicity, the confession is retracted and damages of three thousand livres Tournois are demanded. On the other hand, the bailli maintains that his proceedings are legal, and asks to have the complainants punished in accordance with the confession. The Parlement adopts a middle course; it acquits the Jews and awards no damages, showing that the torture was legal and a retracted confession valueless.[2]

The fifth case, which occurs in 1307, is interesting as having for its reporter no less a personage than Guillaume de Nogaret, the captor of Boniface VIII. A certain Guillot de Ferrières, on a charge of robbery, had been tried by the judge of Villelongue and Nicolas Bourges, royal chatelain of Mont-Ogier. The latter had tortured him repeatedly and cruelly, so that he was permanently crippled, and his uncle, Etienne de Ferrières, Chatelain of Montauban, claims damages. The decision condemns Nicolas Bourges in a mulct of one thousand livres Tournois, half to Guillot for his sufferings and half to Stephen for his expenses, besides a fine to the crown.[3] It is evident that judges were not allowed to inflict unlimited torment at their pleasure.

The sixth case, occurring in 1310, may be passed over, as

---

[1] Olim. III. 49–50.   [2] Ibid. III. 185–6.   [3] Ibid. III. 221–2.

the torture was not judicial, but merely a brutal outrage
by a knight on a noble damsel who resisted his importuni-
ties: though it may be mentioned that of the fine inflicted
on him, fifteen hundred livres Tournois enured to the crown,
and only one hundred to the victim.[1]

The seventh case took place in 1312, when Michael de
Poolay, accused of stealing a sum of money from Nicolas
Loquetier, of Rouen, was subjected to long imprisonment
and torture at Château-Neuf de Lincourt, and was then
brought to the Châtelet at Paris, where he was again examined without confession or conviction. Meanwhile, the
real criminal confessed the theft, and Nicolas applies to
the Parlement for the liberation of Michael, which is duly
granted.[2]

A long interval then occurs, and we do not hear of torture again until 1318, when Guillaume Nivard, a money-
changer of Paris, was accused of coining, and was tortured
by the Prevôt of the Châtelet. He contends that it was illegal, while the Prevôt asserts that his jurisdiction empowered him to administer it. The Parlement investigates
the case, and acquits the prisoner, but awards him no
damages.[3]

The essentially commonplace and trivial character of
these cases has its interest in showing that the practice of
appealing to the Parlement was not confined to weighty

---

[1] Olim, III. 505–6.   [2] Ibid. III. 751–2.

[3] Ibid. III. 1299.—It is somewhat singular that torture does not appear
to have been used in the trial of Enguerrand de Marigny, the principal
minister of Philippe-le-Bel, sacrificed after his death to the hatred of Charles
de Valois. The long endeavor of the young king to protect him, and the
final resort of his enemies to the charge of sorcery, with the production of his
miserable accomplices, would seem to render the case one particularly suited
to the use of torture. See the detailed account of the trial in the " Grandes
Chroniques de France" V. 212–220 (Paris, 1837). In 1315, Raoul de Presles,
accused of causing the death of Philippe, was tortured. " Mais après moult
de paines et de tormens qu'il ot souffert, ne pot on riens traire de sa bouche
fors que bien, si fu franchement laissié aler, et ot moult de ses biens gastés
et perdus." Ibid. p. 221.

matters, and therefore that the few instances in which torture was involved in such appeals afford a fair index of the rarity of its use during this period. These cases, too, have seemed to me worth reciting, as they illustrate the principles upon which its application was based in the new jurisprudence, and the tentative and uncertain character of the progress by which the primitive customs of the European races were gradually becoming supplanted by the resuscitated Roman law.

This progress had not been allowed to continue uninterrupted by protest and resistance. In the closing days of the reign of Philippe-le-Bel, the feudal powers of France awoke to the danger with which they were menaced by the extension of the royal prerogative during the preceding half-century. A league was formed, which seemed to threaten the existence of the institutions so carefully nurtured by St. Louis and his successors. It was too late, however, and though the storm broke on the new and untried royalty of Louis Hutin, the crown lawyers were already too powerful for the united seigneurie of the kingdom. When the various provinces presented their complaints and their demands for the restoration of the old order of things, they were met with a little skilful evasion, a few artful promises, some concessions which were readily withdrawn, and negatives carefully couched in language which seemed to imply assent.

Among the complaints, we find the introduction of torture enumerated as an innovation upon the established rights of the subject, but the lawyers who drew up the replies of the king took care to infringe as little as they could upon a system which their legal training led them to regard as an immense improvement in procedure, especially as it enabled them to supersede the wager of battle, which they justly regarded as the most significant emblem of feudal independence.

The movement of the nobles resulted in obtaining from
33

the king a series of charters for the several provinces, by
which he defined, as vaguely, indeed, as he could, the
extent of royal jurisdiction claimed, and in which he promised to relieve them from certain grievances. In some
of these charters, as in those granted to Britanny, to Burgundy, and to Amiens and Vermandois, there is no allusion
made to torture.[1] In the two latter, the right to the wager
of battle is conceded, which may explain why the nobles
of those provinces were careless to protect themselves from
a process which they could so easily avoid by an appeal to
the sword. In the charter of Languedoc, all that Louis
would consent to grant was a special exemption to those
who had enjoyed the dignity of capitoul, consul, or decurion
of Toulouse and to their children, and even this trifling
concession did not hold good in cases of " lèse-majesté" or
other matters particularly provided for by law.[2] Normandy
only obtained a vague promise that no freeman should be
subjected to torture unless he were the object of violent
presumptions in a capital offence, and that the torture
should be so regulated as not to imperil life or limb; and
though the Normans were dissatisfied with this charter,
and succeeded in getting a second one some months later,
they gained nothing on this point.[3]

The official documents concerning Champagne have been
preserved to us more in detail. The nobles of that province
complained that the royal prevôts and serjeants entered
upon their lands to arrest their men and private persons,
whom they then tortured in defiance of their customs and
privileges ("contre leurs coustumes et libertez"). To this

---

[1] Isambert, Anciennes Lois Françaises, III. 131, 60, 65.

[2] Ordonnance, 1ᵉʳ Avril, 1315, art. xix. (Ibid. III. 58). The whole
clause is borrowed from the Roman law, which may have reconciled Louis's
legal advisers to it. It is noteworthy as containing the first introduction of
the crime of *lèse-majesté* into French jurisprudence, thus marking the triumph
of civil over feudal law.

[3] Cart. Norman i. Mar. 1315, cap. xi. Cart. ii. Jul. 1315, cap. xv. ('bid.
51, 109).

Louis promised to put an end. The nobles further alleged that, in contravention of the ancient usages and customs of Champagne ("contre les us et coustumes enciens de Champagne"), the royal officers presumed to torture nobles on suspicion of crime, even though not caught in the act, and without confession. To this, Louis vaguely replied, that for the future no nobles should be tortured, except under such presumptions as might render it proper, in law and reason, to prevent crime from remaining unpunished; and that no one should be convicted unless confession were persevered in for a sufficient time after torture.[1] This, of course, was anything but satisfactory, and the Champenois were not disposed to accept it, but all that they could obtain after another remonstrance was a simple repetition of the promise that no nobles should be tortured except under capital accusations.[2] The struggle apparently continued, for, in 1319, we find Philippe-le-Long, in a charter granted to Périgord and Quercy, promising that the proceedings preliminary to torture should be had in the presence of both parties, doubtless to silence complaints as to the secret character which criminal investigations were assuming.[3]

The use of torture was thus permanently established in the judicial machinery of France, as one of the incidents in the great revolution which destroyed the feudal power. Even yet, however, it was not universal, especially where communes had the ability to preserve their franchises. Count Beugnot has published, as an appendix to the "Olim," a collection known as the "Tout Lieu de St. Disier," consisting of 314 decisions of doubtful cases referred by the magistrates of St. Dizier to the city of Ypres

[1] Ordonn. Mai 1315, art. v. xiv. (Bourdot de Richebourg, III. 233–4).
[2] Ordonn. Mars 1315, art ix. (Ibid. p. 235.) This ordonnance is incorrectly dated. It was issued towards the end of May, subsequently to the above.
[3] Ordonn. Jul. 1319, art. xxii. (Isambert, III. 227).

for solution, as they were bound to do by their charter.
The cases date mostly from the middle third of the fourteenth century, and were selected as a series of established
precedents.   The fact that, throughout the whole series,
torture is not alluded to in a single instance shows that it
was a form of procedure unknown to the court of the
eschevins of St. Dizier, and even to the superior jurisdiction of the bailli of their suzerain, the Seignieur of Dam-
pierre.   Many of these cases seem peculiarly adapted to
the new inquisitorial system.   Thus, in 1335, a man was
attacked and wounded in the street at night.   A crowd
collected at his cries, and he named the assailant.   No rule
was more firmly established than the necessity of two impartial witnesses to justify condemnation, and the authorities of St. Dizier, not knowing what course to take, applied
as usual for instructions to the magistrates of Ypres.   The
latter defined the law to be that the court should visit the
wounded man on his sick-bed and adjure him by his salvation to tell the truth.   If on this he named any one and subsequently died, the accused should be pronounced guilty;
if, on the other hand, he recovered, then the accused should
be treated according to his reputation; that is, if of good
fame, he should be acquitted; if of evil repute, he should
be banished.[1]   No case more inviting to the theory of torture could well be imagined, and yet neither the honest
burghers of St. Dizier nor the powerful magnates of Ypres
seem to have entertained the idea of its application.   So,
again, when the former inquire what proof is sufficient
when a man accuses another of stealing, the answer is that

---

[1] Tout Lieu de Saint Disier, cap. cclxxii. (Olim. T. II. Append. p. 856.)
The charter of St. Dizier directs that all cases not therein specially provided
for shall be decided according to the customs of Ypres.   For two hundred
and fifty years, therefore, whenever the eschevins of the little town of Champagne felt at a loss, they referred the matter to their lordly neighbors of
Flanders, as to a court of last appeal.

no evidence will convict, unless the goods alleged to be stolen are found in the possession of the accused.[1] The wealthy city of Lille equally rejected the process of torture. The laws there in force, about the year 1350, prescribe that in cases of homicide conviction ought to be based upon absolute evidence, but where this is unattainable, then the judges are allowed to decide on mere opinion and belief, for uncertain matters cannot be rendered certain.[2] In such a scheme of legislation, the extortion of a confession as a condition precedent to condemnation can evidently find no place.

Attempts to introduce torture in Aquitaine were apparently made, but they seem to have been resisted. In the Coutumier of Bordeaux during the fourteenth century there is a significant declaration that the sages of old did not wish to deprive men of their liberties and privileges. Torture, therefore, was prohibited in the case of all citizens except those of evil repute and declared to be infamous. The nearest approach to it that was permitted was tying the hands behind the back, without using pulleys to lift the accused from the ground.[3]

By this time, however, places where torture was not used were exceptional. By a document of 1359, it appears that it was the custom to torture all malefactors brought to the Châtelet of Paris,[4] and though privileged persons constantly endeavored to exempt themselves from it, as the consuls of

[1] Ibid. cap. cclxxiii.
[2] Roisin, Franchises, Lois et Coutumes de Lille, p. 119. Thus, "on puet et doit demander de veir et de oir," but when this is impossible, "on doit et puet bien demander et enquerre de croire et cuidier. Et sour croire et sour cuidier avoec un veritet aparent de veir et d'oir, et avoec l'omechide aparant, on puet bien jugier, lonc l'usage anchyen, car d'oscure fait oscure veritet."
[3] Rabanis, Revue Hist. de Droit, 1861, p. 515.—No volgoren les savis antiquament qu'om pergossa sa franquessa ni sa libertat.
[4] Du Cange s. v. *Quæstionarius*.

Villeneuve in 1371,[1] and the Seigneur d'Argenton in 1385,[2] other privileged persons as constantly sought to obtain the power of inflicting it, as shown in the charter of Milhaud, granted in 1369, wherein the consuls of that town are honored with the special grace that no torture shall be administered except in their presence, if they desire to attend.[3] At the end of the century, indeed, the right to administer torture in cases wherein the accused denied the charge was regularly established as incident to the possession of haute justice.[4]

The recent publication of the records of the Châtelet of Paris from 1389 to 1392,[5] enables us to form a tolerably distinct idea of the part assigned to torture in the criminal procedure of this period. It had virtually become the rule and the main reliance of the tribunal, for the cases in which it was not employed appear to be simply exceptional. Noble blood afforded no exemption, for gentlemen were placed on the rack for petty crimes as freely as roturiers.[6] No avenue of escape was open to the miserable culprit. If he denied the alleged offence, he was tortured at once for a confession, and no settled rules seem to have existed as to the amount of evidence requisite to justify it. Thus, in one case, a man on the "tresteau" relating the misdeeds of his evil life chanced to mention the name of another as a professional thief. The latter was immediately arrested, and

---

[1] Letters granting exemption from torture to the consuls of Villeneuve for any crimes committed by them were issued in 1371 (Isambert, V. 352). These favors generally excepted the case of high treason.

[2] He pleaded his rank as baron as an exemption from the torture, but was overruled. Dumoulin, however, admits that persons of noble blood are not to be as readily exposed to it as those of lower station.—Desmaze, Les Pénalités Anciennes, d'apris des Textes inédits, p. 39 (Paris, 1866).

[3] Du Cange s. v *Quæstio* No. 3.

[4] Pour denier mettre à question et tourment.—Jean Desmarres, Décisions, Art. 295 (Du Boys, Droit Criminel II. 48).

[5] Registre Criminel du Châtelet de Paris. Publié pour la première fois par la Société des Bibliophiles Français. 2 tom. 8vo. Paris, 1864.

[6] Ibid. I. 9, 14.

though there was no specific crime charged against him, he was tortured repeatedly until sufficient confession was extracted from him to justify his execution.[1] If, on the other hand, the prisoner persistently denied his guilt there was no limit to the repetition of the torture, and yet, even when ho confession could be thus extracted, the failure did not always exempt the prisoner from punishment.[2] If he retracted the confession extorted from him, he was tortured again and again until he ceased to assert his innocence, for it was a positive necessity for conviction that the confession under torture should be confirmed by the prisoner without constraint—"sans aucune force, paour ou contrainte de gehayne"—when sentence came to be passed upon him outside of the torture-chamber.

If, again, the luckless prisoner freely confessed the crime of which he stood accused, he was likewise promptly tortured to find out what other offences he might at some previous time have committed. This was so universally the received practice that it is scarcely worth while to cite particular examples, but I may however refer to the case of Gervaise Caussois on account of its quaintness. Arrested for stealing some iron tools, he promptly confessed the crime. Among the reasons on record for proceeding to torture him in order to elicit an account of his other

[1] Ibid. I. 143. See also the similar case of Raoulin du Pré (p. 149) who recanted on the scaffold and protested his innocence "sur la mort qu'il atendoit à avoir et recevoir presentement," but who nevertheless was executed. Also that of Perrin du Quesnoy (p. 164).

[2] See the case of Berthaut Lestalon (Ibid. p. 501) accused of sundry petty thefts and tortured unsuccessfully. The court decided that in view of the little value of the articles stolen and of their having been recovered by the owners, the prisoner should be tortured again, when, if he confessed, he should be hanged, and if he still denied, he should have his right ear cropped and be banished from Paris. This logical verdict was carried out. No confession was obtained, and he was punished accordingly. Somewhat similar was the case of Jehan de Warlus (Ibid. p. 157), who was punished after being tortured five times without confession, and that of Jaquet de Dun (Ibid. p. 494).

presumed misdemeanors, is included the excellent one, "attendu qu'il est scabieux." Under the torment, the poor wretch accused himself of some other petty thefts, but even this did not satisfy his examiners, for the next day he was again brought before them and bound to the *tresteau*, when he confessed a few more trifling larcenies. Having apparently thus obtained enough evidence to satisfy their consciences, his judges mercifully hanged him without further infliction.[1] In fact, the whole matter apparently was left very much to the discretion of the judges, who seem to have been bound by no troublesome limitations to their curiosity in investigating the past career of the miserable beings brought before them.

How that discretion was habitually exercised may be judged from the case of a certain Fleurant de Saint-Leu, who was brought up for examination, Jan. 4, 1390, on a charge of stealing a silver buckle. Denying the accusation, he was twice tortured with increasing severity, until he confessed the alleged crime, but asserted it to be a first offence. On Jan. 8th the court decided that as the petty theft was insufficient to merit death, he should be tortured repeatedly to ascertain whether he had not been guilty of something else worthy of capital punishment. On that day he was therefore thrice exposed to the question, in an ascending scale of severity, but without success. On the 13th he was again twice tortured, when the only admission that rewarded the examiners was that three years before he had married a prostitute at Senlis. This uncommon obduracy seems to have staggered the court, for he was then kept in his dungeon until April 9th, when his case was carefully considered, and though nothing had been extorted from him since his first confession, he was condemned, and was hanged the same day—thus proving how purely gratuitous were the fearful sufferings to which he

[1] Registre Criminel du Châtelet de Paris, I. 36.

had been exposed in order to gratify the curiosity or satisfy the consciences of his remorseless judges.[1]

Few criminals, however, gave so much trouble as Fleurant. The "petit et grand tresteaux," on which the torture was customarily administered, were a sword which cut many a Gordian knot, and, by rendering the justice of the Châtelet sharp and speedy, saved the court a world of trouble. It was by no means unusual for the accused to be arraigned, tortured, condemned and executed all on the same day,[2] and not a few of the confessions read as though they were fictions composed by the accused in order to escape by death from the interminable suffering to which they were exposed.[3] In one case, indeed, the prisoner stated that he had known a person tortured at the Châtelet with such severity that he died in the hands of his tortur-

[1] Ibid. I. 201–209.—Somewhat similar was the case of Marguerite de la Pinele (Ibid. p. 322), accused of stealing a ring, which she confessed under torture. As she did not, however, give a satisfactory account of some money found upon her, though her story was partially confirmed by other evidence, she was again twice tortured. This was apparently done to gratify the curiosity of her judges, for though no further confession was extracted from her, she was duly buried alive.

Crimes for which a man was hanged or decapitated were punished in a woman by burying or burning. Jews were executed by being hanged by the heels between two large dogs suspended by the hind legs—a frightful death, the fear of which sometimes produced conversion and baptism on the gallows. (Ibid. II. 43.)

[2] Ibid. I. pp. 1, 268, 289; II. 66, etc.

[3] The sameness frequently visible in a long catalogue of crimes seems to indicate this, but it is especially visible in some singular cases of parties accused of poisoning wells throughout the north of France, when there was an evident necessity for the authorities to satisfy the excited people by procuring them some victims, and the unfortunate wretches who were arrested on suspicion were tortured until they were ready to accuse themselves of anything (Ibid. I. 419–475). The same result is evident in a very curious case in which an old sorceress and a young "fille de vie" were accused of bewitching a bride and groom, the latter of whom had been madly loved by the girl. The incantations confessed by her, after six tortures, on being threatened with the seventh, afford an instructive insight into the superstitions of the period. (Ibid. I. 327.)

ers, and for himself he declared, after one or two inflictions, that he would confess anything that would relieve him from a repetition of what he had endured.[1]

Yet, with all this reckless disregard of the plainest principles of justice, the inquisitorial process had not yet entirely obliterated the memory of the old customary law. The prisoner was not, as we shall see practised hereafter, kept in ignorance of the charges against him and of the adverse testimony. The accusation was always made known to him, and when witnesses were examined, the record is careful to specify that it was done in his presence.[2] The court deliberated in private, but the prisoner was brought before it to receive condemnation either to torture or to death. Facilities were likewise afforded him to procure evidence in his favor, when the swift justice of the Châtelet might allow him leisure for such defence, for his friends were allowed to see him in prison during the intervals of his trial.[3]

Thus, in the capital, the royal power aided by the civil lawyers, was fast encroaching upon all the liberties of the subject, but in the provinces a more stubborn resistance was maintained. It was some little time after the period under consideration that the ancient Coutumier of Britanny was compiled, and in it we find the use of torture, though fully established as a judicial expedient, yet subjected to much greater restrictions. A prisoner, accused of a capital crime and denying the charge, was liable to torture only if positive evidence was unattainable, and then only if he had been under accusation within the previous five years. Moreover, if he endured its application three times without confession, he was discharged acquitted as one in whose

---

[1] Registre Criminel du Châtelet de Paris, I. 516.
[2] Ibid. I. 151, 163, 164, 173–77, 211, 269, 285, 306, 350, etc.
[3] See, for instance, the case of Pierre Fournet (Ibid. I. 516).

favor God had worked a miracle[1]—thus showing how torture was assimilated in the popular mind to the ordeal
which it had supplanted. Such escape indeed might well
be regarded as a miracle, for the reckless barbarity of the
age had little scruple in pushing the administration of the
question to the utmost rigor. About this same time, the
Council of Rheims, in 1408, drew up a series of instructions
for the bishops of the province in visiting their dioceses;
and among the abuses enumerated for investigation was
whether the judges were in the habit of torturing prisoners
to death on feast days.[2] It was not the cruelty, but the
sacrilege to which the church took exception.

Even in Germany, the citadel of feudalism, the progress
of the new ideas and the influence of the Roman law had
spread to such an extent that in the Golden Bull of Charles
IV., in 1356, there is a provision allowing the torture of
slaves to incriminate their masters in cases of sedition
against any prince of the empire;[3] and the form of expression employed shows that this was an innovation.

In Corsica, at the same period, we find the use of torture
fully established, though subject to careful restrictions.
In ordinary cases, it could only be employed by authority
of the governor, to whom the judge desiring to use it
transmitted all the facts of the case; the governor then
issued an order, at his pleasure, prescribing the mode and
degree to which it might be applied.[4] In cases of treason,
however, these limitations were not observed, and the

---

[1] Très Ancienne Cout. de Bretagne, cap. ci. (Bourdot de Richebourg IV.
224-5)—"Et s'il se peut passer sans faire confession en la gehenne, ou les
jons, il se sauveroit, et il apparestroit bien que Dieu montreroit miracles
pour luy."

[2] Concil. Remens. ann 1408, cap. 49 (Martene Ampliss. Collect. VII. 420).

[3] In hac causa in caput domini servos torqueri statuimus, id est, propter
causam factionis.—Bull. Aur. cap. xxiv. § 9 (Goldast. I. 365).

[4] Statut. Criminali cap. xiv. (Gregorj, Statuti di Corsica p. 101).

accused was liable to its infliction as far and as often as
might be found requisite to effect a purpose.[1]

The peculiar character of Venetian civilization made torture almost a necessity. The atmosphere of suspicion and
secrecy which surrounded every movement of that republi-
can despotism, the mystery in which it delighted to shroud
itself, and the pitiless nature of its legislation conspired
to render torture an indispensable resource. How freely
it was administered, especially in political affairs, is well
illustrated in the statutes of the State Inquisition, where
the merest suspicion is sufficient to authórize its application. Thus, if a senatorial secretary were observed to be
more lavish in his expenditures than his salary would
appear to justify, he was at once suspected of being in the
pay of some foreign minister, and spies were ordered on
his track. If he were then simply found to be absent from
his house at undue hours, he was immediately to be seized
and put to the torture. So, if any one of the innumerable
secret spies employed by the inquisitors were insulted by
being called a spy, the offender was arrested and tortured
to ascertain how he had guessed the character of the
emissary.[2] Human life and human suffering were of little
account in the eyes of the cold and subtle spirits who
moulded the policy of the mistress of the Adriatic.

Other races adopted the new system less readily. In
Hungary, for instance, the first formal embodiment of
torture in the law occurs in 1514, and though the terms
employed show that it had been previously used to some
extent, yet the restrictions laid down manifest an extreme
jealousy of its abuse. Mere suspicion was not sufficient.
To justify its application, a degree of proof was requisite
which was almost competent for condemnation, and the
nature of this evidence is well exemplified in the direction
that if a judge himself witnessed a murder, he could not

---

[1] Statut. Criminali cap. lx. (p. 163).
[2] Statuts de l'Inquisition d'État, 1 Supp. §§ 20, 21 (Daru).

order the homicide to be tortured unless there was other testimony sufficient, for he could not be both witness and judge, and his knowledge of the crime belonged to his private and not to his judicial capacity.[1] With such refinements, there would seem to be little danger of the extension of the custom.

In Poland, torture does not make its appearance until the fifteenth century, and then it was introduced gradually, with strict instructions to the tribunals to use the most careful discretion in its administration.[2] In Russia, the first formal allusion to it is to be found in the Oulagenié Zakonoff, a code promulgated in 1497, by Ivan III., which merely orders that persons accused of robbery, if of evil repute, may be tortured to supply deficiencies of evidence; but as the duel was still freely allowed to the accused, the use of torture must have been merely incidental.[3] From another source, dating about 1530, we learn that it was customary to extort confessions from witches by pouring upon them from a height a small stream of cold water; and in cases of contumacious and stubborn criminals, the finger-nails were wrenched off with little wooden wedges.[4]

[1] Synod. Reg. ann. 1514, Proœm. (Batthyani Legg. Eccles. Hung. I. 574.) According to some authorities, this was a general rule—"Judex quamvis viderit committi delictum non tamen potest sine aliis probationibus reum torquere, ut per Specul. etc."—Jo. Emerici a Rosbach Process. Criminal. Tit. v. cap. v. No. 13 (Francof. 1645).

[2] Du Boys, Droit Criminel, I. 650.

[3] Esneaux, Hist. de Russie, III. 236.

[4] Pauli Jovii Moschovia.—This is a brief account of Russia, compiled about the year 1530, by Paulus Jovius, from his conversations with Dmitri, ambassador to Clement VII. from Vasili V., first Emperor of Russia. Olaus Magnus, in the pride of his Northern blood, looks upon this as a slander on the hardihood of the rugged Russ—"hoc scilicet pro terribili tormento in ea durissima gente reputari, quæ flammis et eculeis adhibitis, vix, ut acta revelet, tantillulum commovetur"—and he broadly hints that the wily ambassador amused himself by hoaxing the soft Italian : "Sed revera vel ludibriose bonus præsul a versuto Muscovitici principis nuntio Demetrio dicto, tempore Clementis VII. informatus est Romæ." (Gent. Septent. Hist. Brev. Lib. xi. c. xxvi.) The worthy archbishop doubtless spoke of his own know-

34

Still, torture makes but little show in the subsequent codes,
such as the Soudebtnick, issued in 1550, and the Sobornoié
Oulagenié, promulgated in 1648.[1]

In fact, these regions were still too barbarous for so
civilized a process. Returning to Central and Western
Europe, which during this period had advanced with such
rapid strides of enlightenment, we find the inquisitorial
process of torture attaining a portentous importance as the
groundwork of all criminal procedure, and its administration prescribed with the most careful and minute precision.

Allusion has already been made to the influence of the
Inquisition in introducing the use of torture. Its influence
did not cease there, for with torture there gradually arose
the denial to the accused of all fair opportunity of defending himself, accompanied by the system of secret procedure
which formed so important a portion of the inquisitorial

ledge with respect to the use of the rack and fire in Russia, but the contempt
he displays for the torture of a stream of water is ill-founded. In our prisons
the punishment of the shower-bath is found to bring the most refractory
characters to obedience in an incredibly short time, and its unjustifiable
severity in a civilized age like this may be estimated from the fact that it
has occasionally resulted in the death of the patient. Thus, at the New
York State Prison at Auburn, in December, 1858, a strong, healthy man,
named Samuel Moore, was kept in the shower-bath from a half to three-
quarters of an hour, and died almost immediately after being taken out. A
less inhumane mode of administering the punishment is to wrap the patient
in a blanket, lay him on his back, and, from a height of about six feet, pour
upon his forehead a stream from an ordinary watering-pot without the rose.
According to experts, this will make the stoutest criminal beg for his life in
a few seconds.

During the later period of our recent war, when the prevalence of exaggerated bounties for recruits led to an organized system of desertion, the magnitude of the evil seemed to justify the adoption of almost any means to
arrest a practice which threatened to rapidly exhaust the resources of the
country. Accordingly, the shower-bath was occasionally put into requisition
by the military authorities to extort confession from suspected deserters,
when legal evidence was not attainable, and it was found exceedingly efficacious.

[1] Du Boys, op. cit. I. 618.

practice. In the old feudal courts, the prosecutor and the
defendant appeared in person. Each produced his witnesses; the case was argued on both sides, and unless the
wager of battle intervened, a verdict was given in accordance with the law after duly weighing the evidence, while
both parties were at liberty to employ counsel and to appeal
to the suzerain. When St. Louis endeavored to abolish
the duel and to substitute a system of inquests, which were
necessarily to some extent *ex parte*, he did not desire to
withdraw from the accused the legitimate means of defence,
and in the Ordonnance of 1254 he expressly instructs his
officers not to imprison the defendant without absolute
necessity, while all the proceedings of the inquest are to be
communicated freely to him.[1] All this changed with time
and the authoritative adoption of torture. The theory of
the Inquisition, that the suspected man was to be hunted
down and entrapped like a wild beast, that his guilt was to
be assumed, and that the efforts of his judges were to be
directed solely to obtaining against him sufficient evidence
to warrant the extortion of a confession without allowing
him the means of defence—this theory became the admitted
basis of criminal jurisprudence. The secrecy of these inquisitorial proceedings, moreover, deprived the accused of
one of the great safeguards accorded to him under the
Roman law of torture. That law, as we have seen, required
the formality of inscription, by which the accuser who failed
to prove his charge was liable to the *lex talionis*, and in
crimes which involved torture in the investigation, he was
duly tortured. This was imitated by the Wisigoths, and
its principle was admitted and enforced by the Church
before the introduction of the Inquisition had changed its

---

[1] Statut. S. Ludov. ann. 1254, §§ 20, 21 (Isambert, I. 270)—Et quia in
dictis senescalliis secundum jura et terre consuetudinem fit inquisitio in
criminibus, volumus et mandamus quod reo petenti acta inquisitionis tra-
dantur ex integro.

policy;[1] but modern Europe, in borrowing from Rome the use of torture, combined it with the inquisitorial process, and thus in civilized Christendom it speedily came to be used more recklessly and cruelly than ever it had been in pagan antiquity.

In 1498, an assembly of notables at Blois drew up an elaborate ordonnance for the reformation of justice in France. In this, the secrecy of the inquisitorial process is dwelt upon with peculiar insistence as of the first importance in all criminal cases. The whole investigation was in the hands of the government official, who examined every witness by himself, and secretly, the prisoner having no knowledge of what was done, and no opportunity of arranging a defence. After all the testimony procurable in this one-sided manner had been obtained, it was discussed by the judges, in council with other persons named for the purpose, who decided whether the accused should be tortured. He could be tortured but once, unless fresh evidence meanwhile was collected against him, and his confession was read over to him the next day, in order that he might affirm or deny it. A secret deliberation was then held by the same council, who decided as to his fate.[2]

---

[1] Thus Gratian, in the middle of the twelfth century—"Qui calumniam illatam non probat pœnam debet incurrere quam si probasset reus utique sustineret."—Decreti P. II. caus. v. quæst. 6, c. 2.

[2] Ordonnance, Mars 1498, §§ 110–116 (Isambert, XI. 365.—Fontanon, I. 710). It would seem that the only torture contemplated by this ordonnance was that of water, as the clerk is directed to record "la quantité de l'eau qu'on aura baillée audit prisonnier." This was administered by gagging the patient, and pouring water down his throat until he was enormously distended. It was sometimes diversified by making him eject the water violently, by forcible blows on the stomach (Fortescue de Laudibus Legg. Angliæ, cap. xxii.). Sometimes a piece of cloth was used to conduct the water down his throat. To this, allusion is made in the "Appel de Villon :"

"Se fusse des hoirs Hue Capel
Qui fut extraict de boucherie,
On ne m'eust, parmy ce drapel,
Faict boyre à celle escorcherie."
Œuvres de Villon, p. 310, Ed. Prompsault, Paris, 1834.

This cruel system was still further perfected by Francis
I., who, in an ordonnance of 1539, expressly abolished the
inconvenient privilege assured to the accused by St. Louis,
which was apparently still occasionally claimed, and directed that in no case should he be informed of the accusation against him, or of the facts on which it was based,
nor be heard in his defence.   Upon examination of the *ex
parte* testimony, without listening to the prisoner, the
judges ordered torture proportioned to the gravity of the
accusation, and it was applied at once, unless the prisoner
appealed, in which case his appeal was forthwith to be
decided by the superior court of the locality.[1] The whole
process was apparently based upon the conviction that it
was better that a hundred innocent persons should suffer
than that one culprit should escape, and it would not be
easy to devise a course of procedure better fitted to render
the use of torture universal.   There was some protection
indeed, theoretically at least, in the provision which held
the judge responsible when an innocent prisoner was tortured without sufficient preliminary proof to justify it;
but this salutary regulation, from the very nature of things,
could not often be enforced, and it was so contrary to the
general spirit of the age, that it soon became obsolete.
Thus, in Britanny, perhaps the most independent of the
French provinces, the Coutumier, as revised in 1539, retains
such a provision,[2] but it disappears in the revision of 1580.

[1] Ordonn. de Villers-Cotterets, Août 1539, §§ 162–164 (Isambert, XIII.
633–4).   "Ostant et abolissant tous styles, usances ou coutumes par les-
quels les accusés aveient accoutumés d'être ouïs en jugement pour sçavoir
s'ils devoient être accusés, et à cette fin avoir communication des faits et
articles concernant les crimes et délits dont ils étoient accusés."

[2] Qui met aucun en torture sans avoir charge, per presumptions ou en-
queste du fait, ou de commune renommée, le doit amender à la suseraine
justice et desdommager la partie.—Anc. Cout. de Bretagne, Tit. I. art. xli.
—D'Argentré's labored commentary on this article is a lamentable exhibition of the utter confusion which existed as to the nature of preliminary proof
justifying torture.   Comment. pp. 139, sqq.

34*

But even this was not all. Torture, as thus employed
to convict the accused, became known as the *question préparatoire;* and, in defiance of the old rule that it could be
applied but once, a second application, known as the *question définitive* or *préalable*, became customary, by which,
after condemnation, the prisoner was again subjected to
the extremity of torment in order to discover whether he
had any accomplices, and, if so, to identify them. In this
detestable practice we find another instance of the unfortunate influence of the Inquisition in modifying the Roman
law. The latter expressly and wisely provided that no
one who had confessed should be examined as to the guilt
of another;[1] and in the ninth century the authors of the
False Decretals had emphatically adopted the principle,
which thus became embodied in ecclesiastical law,[2] until
the ardor of the Inquisition in hunting down heretics
caused it to regard the conviction of the accused as a
worthless triumph unless he could be forced to incriminate
his possible associates; and the lawyers followed eagerly
in its footsteps.

Torture was also generically divided into the *question ordinaire* and *extraordinaire*—a rough classification to proportion the severity of the infliction to the gravity of the
crime or the urgency of the case. Thus, in the most usual
kind of torment, the strappado, popularly known as the
Moine de Caen, the ordinary form was to tie the prisoner's
hands behind his back with a piece of iron between them ;
a cord was then fastened to his wrists by which, with the
aid of a pulley, he was hoisted from the ground with a
weight of one hundred and twenty-five pounds attached to

---

[1] Nemo igitur de proprio crimine confitentem super conscientia scrutetur
aliena—Const. 17 Cod. IX. ii. (Honor. 423).

[2] Nemini de se confesso credi potest super crimen alienum, quoniam ejus
atque omnis rei professio periculosa est, et admitti adversus quemlibet non
debet.—Pseudo-Julii Epist. II. cap. xviii.—Gratian. Decret. P. II. caus. v.
quæst. 3, can. 5.

his feet. In the extraordinary torture, the weight was increased to two hundred and fifty pounds, and when the victim was raised to a sufficient height, he was dropped with a jerk that dislocated his joints, the operation being thrice repeated.[1]

Thus, in 1549, we see the system in full operation in the case of Jacques de Coucy, who, in 1544, had surrendered Boulogne to the English. This was deemed an act of treachery, but he was pardoned in 1547; yet, notwithstanding his pardon, he was subsequently tried, convicted, condemned to decapitation and quartering, and also to the *question extraordinaire* to obtain a denunciation of his accomplices.[2]

When Louis XIV., under the inspiration of Colbert, remoulded the jurisprudence of France, various reforms were introduced into the criminal law, and changes both for better and worse were made in the administration of torture. The Ordonnance of 1670 was drawn up by a committee of the ablest and most enlightened jurists of the day, and it is a melancholy exhibition of human wisdom

[1] Chéruel, Dict. Hist. des Institutions, etc. de la France, p. 1220 (Paris, 1855).

[2] Isambert, XIV. 88. Beccaria comments on the absurdity of this proceeding, as though a man who had accused himself would make any difficulty in accusing others.—"Quasi che l'uomo che accusa sè stesso, non acusi più facilmente gli altri. E egli giusto il tormentare gli uomini per l'altrui delitto?"—Dei Delitte e delle Pene, § XII. A curious illustration of its useless cruelty when applied to prisoners of another stamp is afforded by the record of a trial which occurred at Rouen in 1647. A certain Jehan Lemarinier, condemned to death for murder, was subjected to the *question définitive*. Cords twisted around the fingers, scourging with rods, the strappado with fifty pounds attached to each foot, the thumb-screw were applied in succession and together, without eliciting anything but fervent protestations of innocence. The officials at last wearied out remanded the convict to prison, when he sent for them and quietly detailed all the particulars of his crime, committed by himself alone, requesting especially that they should record his confession as having been spontaneous, for the relief of his conscience, and not extorted by torment.—Desmaze, Les Pénalités Anciennes, p. 159, Paris. 1866.

when regarded as the production of such men as Lamoignon, Talon, and Pussort. The cruel mockery of the *question préalable* was retained; and in the principal proceedings all the chances were thrown against the prisoner. All
preliminary testimony was still *ex parte*. The accused was
heard, but he was still examined in secret. Lamoignon
vainly endeavored to obtain for him the advantage of
counsel, but Colbert obstinately refused this concession,
and the utmost privilege allowed the defence was the permission accorded to the judge, at his discretion, to con-
front the accused with the adverse witnesses. In the *question préliminaire*, torture was reserved for capital cases,
when the proof was strong and yet not enough for conviction. During its application it could be stopped and re-
sumed at the pleasure of the judge, but if the accused
were once unbound and removed from the rack, it could not
be repeated, even though additional evidence were subsequently obtained.[1]

It was well to prescribe limitations, slender as these
were, but in practice it was found impossible to enforce
them, and they afforded little real protection to the accused,
when judges bent upon procuring conviction chose to evade
them. A contemporary whose judicial position gave him
every opportunity of knowing the truth, remarks : " They
have discovered a jugglery of words, and pretend that
though it may not be permissible to *repeat* the torture, still
they have a right to *continue* it, though there may have
been an interval of three whole days. Then, if the sufferer,
through good luck or by a miracle, survives this reduplica-
tion of agony, they have discovered the notable resource
of *nouveaux indices survenus*, to subject him to it again
without end. In this way they elude the intention of the
law, which sets some bounds to these cruelties and re-

---

[1] Ordonnance Criminel d'Août 1670, Tit. xiv. xix. (Isambert, XIX. 398,
412).

quires the discharge of the accused who has endured the
question without confession, or without confirming his
confession after torture."[1] Nor were these the only modes
by which the scanty privileges allowed the prisoner were
curtailed in practice. In 1681, a royal Declaration sets
forth that, in the jurisdiction of Grenoble, judges were in
the habit of refusing to listen to the accused, and of condemning him unheard, an abuse which was prohibited for
the future. Yet other courts subsequently assumed that
this prohibition was only applicable to the Parlement of
Grenoble, and in 1703 another Declaration was necessary
to enforce the rule throughout the kingdom.[2]

The Ordonnance of 1670, moreover, gave formal expression to another abuse which was equally brutal and illogical—the employment of torture *avec réserve des preuves.*
When the judge resolved on this, the silence of the accused
under torment did not acquit him, though the whole theory
of the question lay in the necessity of confession. He
simply escaped the death penalty, and could be condemned
to any other punishment which the discretion of the judge
might impose, thus presenting the anomaly of a man
neither guilty nor innocent, relieved from the punishment
assigned by the law to the crime for which he had been
arraigned, and condemned to some other penalty without
having been convicted of any offence. This punishing for
suspicion was no new thing. Before torture came fully
into vogue, in the early part of the fourteenth century, a
certain Estevenes li Barbiers of Abbeville was banished
under pain of death for suspicion of breach of the peace,
and was subsequently tried, acquitted, and allowed to
return.[3] So in the records of the Parlement of Paris there
is a sentence rendered in 1402, against Jehan Dubos, a

[1] Nicolas, Dissertation Morale et Juridique sur la Torture, p. 111. (Am-
sterd. 1682).
[2] Déclaration du 13 Avril, 1703 (Ordonnances d'Alsace, I. 340).
[3] Coutumier de Picardie, Éd. Marnier, p. 88.

procureur of the Parlement, and Ysabelet his wife, for
suspicion of the poisoning of another procureur, Jeñan le
Charron, the first husband of Ysabelet, and Dubos was
accordingly hanged, while his wife was burnt.[1] The application to the torture-process of this determination not to
allow a man to escape unless his innocence was proved led
to the illogical system of the *réserve des preuves*. The cruel
absurdities which it produced in practice are well illustrated
by a case occurring in Naples in the sixteenth century.
Marc Antonio Maresca of Sorrento was tried by the Admiralty Court for the murder of a peasant of Miani, in the
market place. The evidence was strong against him, but
there were no eye-witnesses, and he endured the torture
without confession. The court asserted that it had reserved
the evidence, and condemned him to the galleys for seven
years. He appealed to the High Court of the royal council,
and the case was referred to a distinguished jurisconsult,
Thomaso Grammatico, a member of the council. The latter
reported that he must be considered as innocent, after having passed through torture without confession, and denied
the right of the court to reserve the evidence. Then, with an
exhibition of the peculiar logic characteristic of the criminal jurisprudence of the time, he concluded that Maresca
might be relegated to the islands for five years. The only
thing necessary to complete this tissue of legal wisdom
was afforded by the council, which set aside the judgment
of the Admiralty Court, rejected the report of their col-
league, and condemned the prisoner to the galleys for three
years.[2] Somewhat less complicated in its folly, but more
inexcusable from its date, was the sentence of the court of
Orléans in 1740, by which a man named Barberousse, from
whom no confession had been extorted, was condemned to

[1] Desmaze, Pénalités Anciennes, p. 204.
[2] Thomæ Grammatici Decisiones Neapolitanæ, pp. 1275-6. (Venetiis,
1582.)

the galleys for life, because, as the sentence declared, he was *strongly suspected* of premeditated murder.[1]

The same tendency to elude all restrictions on the use of torture was manifested in the Netherlands, where it was scarcely known until the sixteenth century, and where it was only administered systematically by the ordonnance on criminal justice of Philip II. in 1570. It rapidly extended until it became almost universal, both in the provinces which threw off the yoke of Spain, and in those which remained subject to their sovereign. The limits which Philip had imposed on it were soon transcended. He had forbidden its employment in all cases " où il n'y a plaine, demye preuve, ou bien où la preuve est certaine et indubitable," thus restricting it to those where there was very strong presumption without absolute certainty. In transcription and translation, however, the wording of the ordonnance became changed to " plaine ou demye preuve, ou bien où la preuve est incertaine ou doutense," thus allowing it in all cases where the judge might have a doubt not of the guilt but of the innocence of the accused ; and by the time these errors were discovered by a zealous legal antiquarian, the customs of the tribunals had become so fixed that the attempt to reform them was vain.[2]

In Germany, torture had been reduced to a system, in 1532, by the Emperor Charles V., whose "Caroline Constitutions" contain a more complete code on the subject than had previously existed, except in the records of the Inquisition. Inconsistent and illogical, it quotes Ulpian to prove the deceptive nature of the evidence thence derivable ; it pronounces torture to be "res dira, corporibus hominum admodum noxia et quandoque lethalis, cui et mors ipsa

[1] L'Oiseleur, Les Crimes et les Peines, pp. 206–7.
[2] Meyer, Institutions Judiciaires, IV. 285, 293.

prope proponenda;"[1] in some of its provisions it manifests
extreme care and tenderness to guard against abuses, and
yet practically it is merciless to the last degree. Confession
made during torture was not to be believed, nor could a
conviction be based upon it;[2] yet what the accused might
confess after being removed from torture was to be received
as the deposition of a dying man, and was full evidence.[3]
In practice, however, this only held good when adverse to
the accused, for he was brought before his judge after an
interval of a day or two, when, if he confirmed the confession, he was condemned, while if he retracted it, he was
at once thrust again upon the rack. In confession under
torture, moreover, he was to be closely cross-questioned,
and if any inconsistency was observable in his self-con-
demnation, the torture was at once to be redoubled in
severity.[4] The legislator thus makes the victim expiate
the sins of his own vicious system; the victim's sufferings
increase with the deficiency of the evidence against him,
and the legislator consoles himself with the remark that
the victim has only himself to thank for it, "de se tantum
non de alio quæratur." To complete the inconsistency of
the code, it provided that confession was not requisite for
conviction; irrefragable external evidence was sufficient;
and yet even when such evidence was had, the judge was
empowered to torture in mere surplusage.[5] Yet there was
a great show of tender consideration for the accused.
When the weight of conflicting evidence inclined to the
side of the prisoner, torture was not to be applied.[6] Two
adverse witnesses, or one unexceptionable one, were a
condition precedent, and the legislator shows that he was
in advance of his age by ruling out all evidence resting
on the assertions of magicians and sorcerers.[7] To guard

---

[1] Legg. Capital. Caroli V. c. lx., lviii.
[2] Ibid. c. xx.
[3] Ibid. c. lviii.
[4] Ibid. c. lv., lvi., lvii.
[5] Ibid. c. xxii., lxix.
[6] Ibid. c. xxviii.
[7] Ibid. c. xxiii., xxi.

against abuse, the impossible effort was made to define strictly the exact quality and amount of evidence requisite to justify torture, and the most elaborate and minute directions were given with respect to all the various classes of crime, such as homicide, child-murder, robbery, theft, receiving stolen goods, poisoning, arson, treason, sorcery, and the like;[1] while the judge administering torture to an innocent man on insufficient grounds was liable to make good all damage or suffering thereby inflicted.[2] The amount of torment, moreover, was to be proportioned to the age, sex, and strength of the patient; women during pregnancy were never to be subjected to it; and in no case was it to be carried to such a point as to cause permanent injury or death.[3]

Charles V. was too astute a ruler not to recognize the aid derivable from the doctrines of the Roman law in his scheme of restoring the preponderance of the Kaisership, and he lost no opportunity of engrafting them on the jurisprudence of Germany. In his Criminal Constitutions, however, he took care to embody largely the legislation of his predecessors and contemporaries, and though protests were uttered by many of the Teutonic princes, the code, adopted by the Diet of Ratisbon in 1532, became part and parcel of the common law of Germany.[4] A fair idea of the shape assumed, under these influences, by the criminal law in its relations with torture, can be obtained by examining some

---

[1] Legg. Capital. Carol. V. c. xxxiii.–xliv. [2] Ibid. c. xx., lxi.

[3] Ibid. c. lviii., lix. Accusatus, si periculum sit, ne inter vel post tormenta ob vulnera expiret, ea arte torquendus est, ne quid damni accipiat.

[4] Heineccii Hist. Jur. Civ. Lib. ii. §§ cv. sqq.—Meyer (Instit. Judiciaires, Liv. vi. chap. xi.) gives a very interesting sketch of the causes which led to the overthrow of the old system of jurisprudence throughout Germany. He attributes it to the influence of the emperors and the municipalities, each equally jealous of the authority of the feudal nobles, aided by the lawyers, now becoming a recognized profession. These latter of course favored a jurisprudence which required long and special training, thus conferring upon them as a class peculiar weight and influence.

35

of the legal text-books which were current as manuals of
practice from the sixteenth to the eighteenth century.[1] As
the several authors of these works all appear to condemn
the principle or to lament the necessity of torture, their
instructions as to its employment may safely be assumed
to represent the most humane and enlightened views current
during the period.[2] It is easy to see from them, however,
that though the provisions of the Caroline Constitutions
were still mostly in force, yet the practice had greatly
extended itself, and that the limitations prescribed for the
protection of innocence and helplessness had become of
little real effect.

Upon the theory of the Roman law, nobles and the

[1] My principal authorities are four :—

I. "Rerum Criminalium Praxis," by Jodocus Damhouder, a lawyer and
statesman of repute in Flanders, where he held a distinguished position
under Charles V. and Philip II. His work was received as an authority
throughout Europe for two centuries, having passed through numerous edi-
tions, from that of Louvain, in 1554, to that of Antwerp, in 1750. My edition
is of Antwerp, 1601.

II. "Tractatus de Quæstionibus seu Torturis Reorum," published in 1592
by Johann Zanger, of Wittemberg, a celebrated jurisconsult of the time, and
frequently reprinted. My edition is that of 1730, with notes by the learned
Baron Senckenberg, and there is still a later one, published at Francfort
in 1763.

III. "Practica Criminalis, seu Processus Judiciarius ad usum et consuetudinem judiciorum in Germania hoc tempore frequentiorem," by Johann
Emerich von Rosbach, published in 1645 at Frankfort-on-the-Mayn.

IV. "Tractatio Juridica, de Usu et Abusu Torturæ," by Heinrich von
Boden, a dissertation read at Halle in 1697, and reprinted by Senckenberg
in 1730, in conjunction with the treatise of Zanger.

[2] Cum nihil tam severum, tam crudele et inhumanum videatur quam
hominem conditum ad imaginem Dei . . . tormentis lacerare et quasi excar-
nificare, etc.—Zangeri Tract. de Quæstion. cap. i. No. 1.

Tormentis humanitatis et religionis, necnon jurisconsultorum argumenta
repugnant.—Jo. Emerici a Rosbach Process. Crimin. Tit. v. c. ix. No. 1.

Saltem horrendus torturæ abusus ostendit, quo miseri, de facinore aliquo
suspecti, fere infernalibus, et si fieri possit, plusquam diabolicis cruciatibus
exponuntur, ut qui nullo legitimo probandi modo convinci poterant, atroci-
tate cruciatuum contra propriam salutem confiteri, seque ita destruere sive
jure sive injuria, cogantur.—Henr. de Boden Tract. Præfat.

learned professions had claimed immunity from torture, and the Roman law inspired too sincere a respect to permit a denial of the claim,[1] yet the ingenuity of lawyers reduced the privilege to such narrow proportions that it was practically almost valueless. For certain crimes, of course, such as *majestas*, adultery, and incest, the authority of the Roman law admitted of no exceptions, and to these were speedily added a number of other offences, classed as *crimina excepta* or *nefanda*, which were made to embrace almost all offences of a capital nature, in which alone torture was at any time allowable. Thus, parricide, uxoricide, fratricide, witchcraft, sorcery, counterfeiting, theft, sacrilege, rape, arson, repeated homicide, etc., came to be included in the exceptional cases, and the only privileges extended in them to nobles were that they should not be subjected to "plebeian" tortures.[2] As early as 1514, I find an instance which shows how little advantage these prerogatives afforded in practice. A certain Dr. Bobenzan, a citizen of good repute and syndic of Erfurt, who both by position and profession belonged to the excepted class, when brought up for sentence on a charge of conspiring to betray the city, and warned that he could retract his confession, extracted under torture, pathetically replied—"During my examination, I was at one time stretched upon the rack for six hours, and at another I was slowly burned for eight hours. If I retract, I shall be exposed to these torments

---

[1] Zangeri, cap. i. Nos. 49–58.

[2] Zangeri, cap. i. Nos. 59–88.—Knipschild, in his voluminous "Tract. de Nobilitate" (Campodun. 1693), while endeavoring to exalt to the utmost the privileges of the nobility, both of the sword and robe, is obliged to admit their liability to torture for these crimes, and only urges that the preliminary proof should be stronger than in the case of plebeians (Lib. ii. cap. iv. No. 108–120); though, in other accusations, a judge subjecting a noble to torture should be put to death, and his attempt to commit such an outrage could be resisted by force of arms (Ibid. No. 103). He adds, however, that no special privileges existed in France, Lombardy, Venice, Italy, and Saxony (Ibid. Nos. 105–7).

again and again. I had rather die"—and he was duly hanged.[1]

In Catholic countries, of course, the clergy were specially favored, but the immunity claimed for them by the canon law was practically reduced to nearly the same as that accorded to nobles.[2] The torture inflicted on them, however, was lighter than in the case of laymen, and proof of a much more decided character was required to justify their being exposed to torment. As an illustration of this von Rosbach remarks that if a layman is found in the house of a pretty woman, most authors consider the fact sufficient to justify torture on the charge of adultery, but that this is not the case with priests, who if they are caught embracing a woman are presumed to be merely blessing her.[3] They moreover had the privilege of being tortured only at the hands of clerical executioners, if such were to be had.[4] In Protestant territories respect for the cloth was manifested by degrading them prior to administering the rack or strappado.[5]

Slight as were the safeguards with which legislators endeavored to surround the employment of torture, they became almost nugatory in practice under a system which, in the endeavor to reduce doubts into certainties, ended by leaving everything to the discretion of the judge. It is instructive to see the parade of insisting upon the necessity of strong preliminary evidence,[6] and to read the elaborate details as to the exact kind and amount of testimony severally requisite in each description of crime, and

[1] Erphurdianus Variloquus, ann. 1514.

[2] Damhouder. Rer. Crimin. Praxis, cap. xxxvii. Nos. 23, 24. Cf. Passerini Regulare Tribunal, Quæst. xv. Art. ix. No. 117.

[3] Emer. a Rosbach Process. Crimin. Tit. v. cap. xiv.

[4] Simancæ de Cathol. Instit. Tit. LXV. No. 50.

[5] Willenbergii Tract. de Excess. et Pœnis Cleric. 4to. Jenæ, 1740, p. 41.

[6] Even this, however, was not deemed necessary in cases of conspiracy and treason " qui fiunt secreto, propter probationis difficultatem devenitur ad torturam sine indiciis." (Emer. a Rosb. Tit. v. cap. x. No. 20.)

then to find that common report was held sufficient to
justify torture, or unexplained absence before accusation,
prevarication under examination, and even silence; and it
is significant of fearful cruelty when we see judges solemnly
warned that an evil countenance, though it may argue de-
pravity in general, does not warrant the presumption of
actual guilt in individual cases;[1] though pallor, under many
circumstances, was considered to sanction the application
of torture.[2] Subtle lawyers thus exhausted their ingenuity
in discussing all possible varieties of indications, and there
grew up a mass of confused rules wherein, on many points,
each authority contradicted the other. In a system which
thus waxed so complex, the discretion of the judge at last
became the only practical guide, and the legal writers themselves acknowledge the worthlessness of the rules so labo-
riously constructed when they admit that it is left for his
decision to determine whether the indications are sufficient
to warrant the infliction of torture.[3] How absolute was

[1] Fama frequens et vehemens facit indicium ad torturam. (Zanger. c. II.
No. 80.) Reus ante accusationem vel inquisitionem fugiens et citatus con-
tumaciter absens, se suspectum reddit ut torqueri possit. (Ibid. No. 91.
Cf. Simancæ Cathol. Instit. Tit. LXV. Nos. 28–30.) Inconstantia sermonis
facit indicium ad torturam. (Ibid. Nos. 96–99.) Ex taciturnitate oritur
indicium ad torturam. (Ibid. No. 103.) Physiognomia malam naturam
arguit, non autem delictum. (Ibid. No. 85.) How exceedingly lax was the
application of these rules may be guessed from a remark of Damhouder's,
that although rumor was sufficient to justify torture, yet a contrary rumor
neutralized the first and rendered torture improper.—Damhouder. Rer.
Crimin. Praxis cap. xxxv. Nos. 14, 15.

[2] Deinde a pallore et similibus oritur indicium ad torturam secundum
Bartol. (Emer. a Rosbach Tit. v. c. vii. Nos. 28–31.) Whereupon von Rosbach enters into a long dissertation as to the causes of paleness.

[3] Judicis arbitrio relinquitur an indicia sint sufficientia ad torturam.
(Zanger. cap. II. Nos. 16–20.) An indicia sufficiant ad torturam judicis
arbitrio relictum est. . . . Indicia ad torturam sufficientia reliquuntur officio
judicis. (Emer. a Rosbach Tit. v. c. ii. p. 529.) Damhouder, indeed, states
that no rules can be framed—"neque ea ullis innituntur regulis : sed uni-
versum id negotium geritur penes arbitrium, discretionem ac conscientiam
judicis."—Rer. Crimin. Praxis cap. xxxvi. Nos. 1, 2.

this discretion, and how it was exercised, is manifest when Damhouder declares that in his day bloodthirsty judges were in the habit of employing the severest torture without sufficient proof or investigation, boasting that by its means they could extract a confession of everything;[1] and von Rosbach tells us that the magistrates of his time, in the absence of all evidence, sometimes resorted to divination or the lot in order to obtain proof on which they could employ the rack or strappado.[2]

Such a system tends of necessity to its own extension, and it is therefore not surprising to find that the aid of torture was increasingly invoked. The prisoner who refused to plead, whether there was any evidence against him or not, could be tortured until his obstinacy gave way.[3] Even witnesses were not spared, whether in civil suits or criminal prosecutions.[4] It was discretionary with the judge to inflict moderate torture on them, when the truth could not otherwise be ascertained. Infamous witnesses could always be tortured; those not infamous, only when they prevaricated, or when they were apparently committing perjury; but, as this was necessarily left with the judge to determine, the instructions for him to guide his decision by observing their appearance and manner show how completely the whole case was in his power, and how readily he could extort evidence to justify the torture of the prisoner, and then extract from the latter a confession by the same means. In prosecutions for treason, all witnesses,

---

[1] Sunt tamen nonnulli prætores et judices sanguine fraterno adeo inexsaturabiles ut illico quemvis malæ famæ virum, citra ulla certa argumenta aut indicia, corripiant ad sævissimam torturam, inclementer dicentes, cruciatum facile ab illis extorturum rerum omnuim confessionem.—Damhouder. Rer. Crimin. Praxis, cap. xxxv. No. 13.

[2] Emer. a Rosbach Tit. v. c. x. No. 25. Sed aliqui judices quando desunt indicia, procedunt per sortilegia et similia.

[3] Ibid. Tit. v. cap. x. No. 2.

[4] Ibid. Tit. v. cap. xiv. No. 16.

irrespective of their rank, were liable to torture,[1] so that when Pius IV., in 1560, was determined to ruin Cardinal Charles Caraffa, no scruple was felt, during his trial, as to torturing his friends and retainers to obtain the evidence upon which he was executed.[2]

An ingenious plan was also adopted by which, when two witnesses gave testimony irreconcilable with each other, their comparative credibility was tested by torturing both simultaneously in each other's presence.[3] Some jurists indeed, held, that no witness of low or vile condition could be heard without torture, but others maintained that poverty alone was not sufficient to render it necessary. Evidence given under torture was esteemed the best kind, and yet with the perpetually recurring inconsistency which marks this branch of criminal law it was admitted that the spontaneous testimony of a man of good character could outweigh that of a disreputable person under torment.[4] Witnesses, however, could not be tortured more than three times;[5] and indeed it was a question between jurists whether their evidence thus given required, like the confession of an accused person, to be subsequently ratified by them.[6] A reminiscence of Roman law, moreover, is visible in the rule that no witness could be tortured against his kindred to the seventh degree, nor his near connections by marriage, his feudal superiors, nor other similar persons.[7]

Some limitations were imposed as to age and strength. Children under fourteen could not be tortured, nor the aged whose vigor was unequal to the endurance, though

[1] Passerini Regulare Tribunal, Quæst. xv. Art. ix. No. 115. Colon. Agripp. 1695.

[2] Process. contr. Card. de Carrafa (Hoffman. Collect. Script. I. 632).

[3] Damhouder, op. cit. cap. xlvii. No. 3.

[4] Passerini, loc. cit. Nos. 122-3.

[5] Ibid. No. 118.

[6] Simancæ de Cathol. Instit. Tit. LXV. No. 73.

[7] Zangeri, op. cit. cap. I. No. 8-25.

they could be tied to the rack, and menanced to the last
extremity. Insanity was likewise a safeguard, and much
discussion was had as to whether the deaf, dumb, and blind
were liable or not.   Zanger decides in the affirmative,
whenever, whether as principals or witnesses, good evidence was to be expected from them.[1] The Roman rule
was followed that, whenever several parties were on trial
under the same accusation, the torturer should commence
with the weakest and tenderest; while a refinement of
cruelty prescribed that if a husband and wife were arraigned together, the wife should be tortured first, and in the
presence of her husband; and if a father and son, the son
before his father's face.[2]

Some facilities for defence were allowed to the accused,
but in practice they were almost hopelessly slender. He
was permitted to employ counsel, and if unable to do so,
it was the duty of the judge to look up testimony for the
defence.[3] After all the adverse evidence had been taken,
and the prisoner had been interrogated, he could demand
to see a copy of the proceedings, in order to frame a defence; but the demand could be refused, in which case, the
judge was bound to sift the evidence himself, and to investigate the probable innocence or guilt of the accused. The
recognized tendency of such a system to result in an un-
favorable conclusion is shown by Zanger's elaborate instructions on this point, and his warning that, however
justifiable torture may seem, it ought not to be resorted to
without at least looking at the evidence which may be
attainable in favor of innocence;[4] while von Rosbach cha-
racterizes as the greatest fault of the tribunals of his day,
their neglect to obtain and consider testimony for the
prisoner as well as that against him;[5] and the earnest

---

[1] Zangeri, op. cit. cap. i. Nos. 34–48.
[2] Ibid. cap. iv. Nos. 25–30.—Damhouder, op. cit. cap. xxxvii. Nos. 15, 16.
[3] Zangeri, op. cit. cap. iii. No. 3.   [4] Ibid. cap. iii. Nos. 1, 4, 5–43.
[5] Process. Crim. Tit. v. cap. xi. No. 6.

arguments of Simancas to prove that no one should be
tortured without first being heard in his defence show that
even this last refinement of cruelty and injustice could not
have been uncommon.[1] In some special and extraordinary
cases, the judge might allow the accused to be confronted
with the accuser, but this was so contrary to the secrecy
required by the inquisitorial system, that he was cautioned
that it was a very unusual course, and one not lightly to
be allowed, as it was odious, unnecessary, and not perti-
nent to the trial.[2] Theoretically, there was a right of appeal against an order to inflict torture, but this, even when
permitted, could usually avail the accused but little, for
the *ex parte* testimony, which had satisfied the lower judge,
could, of course, in most instances, be so presented to the
higher court as to insure the affirmation of the order, and
prisoners, in their helplessness, would doubtless feel that
by the attempt to appeal they would probably only increase the severity of their inevitable sufferings.[3]

Slender as were these safeguards in principle, they were
reduced in practice almost to a nullity. That the discretion
lodged in the tribunals was habitually and frightfully
abused is only too evident, when von Rosbach deems it
necessary to reprove, as a common error of the judges of
his time, the idea that the use of torture was a matter altogether dependent upon their pleasure, " as though nature
had created the bodies of prisoners for them to lacerate at
will."[4] Thus it was an acknowledged rule that when guilt
could be sufficiently proved by witnesses, torture was not
admissible ;[5] yet Damhouder feels it necessary to condemn
the practice of some judges, who, after conviction by suffi-

[1] De Cathol. Instit. Tit. LXV. No. 17.

[2] Zangeri, cap. II. Nos. 49–50.—Cum enim confrontatio odiosa sit et species
suggestionis, et remedium extraordinarium ad substantiam processus non
pertinens, et propterea non necessaria.

[3] Ibid. cap. IV. Nos. 1–6.

[4] Process. Crimin. Tit. V. cap. IX. No. 10.

[5] Zangeri, cap I. No. 37.

cient evidence were in the habit of torturing the convict,
and boasted that they never pronounced sentence of death
without having first extorted a confession.[1] Moreover, a
practice grew up whereby, after a man had been duly convicted of a capital crime, he was tortured to extract confessions of any other offences of which he might be guilty.[2]
Martin Bernhardi, writing in 1705, asserts that this was
resorted to in order to prevent the convict from appealing
from the sentence;[3] and as late as 1764, Beccaria lifts his
voice against it as a still existing abuse, which he well
qualifies as senseless curiosity, impertinent in the wanton-
ness of its cruelty.[4] So, although a man who freely confessed a crime could not be tortured, according to the
general principle of the law, still, if he were suspected of
having accomplices and refused to name them, he could be
tortured as in the *question préalable* of the French courts.[5]
Yet the accusation thus obtained was held to be of so little
value that it only warranted the arrest of the parties in-
criminated, who could not legally be tortured without
further evidence.[6]

Another positive rule was that torture could only be
applied in accusations invoking life or limb;[7] but Senckenberg assures us that he had known it to be resorted to

[1] Rer. Crimin. Praxis cap. xxxviii. Nos. 6, 7.

[2] Boden de Usu et Abusu Torturæ Th. xii. Damhouder declares this
practice to be unjustifiable, though not infrequent.—Rer. Crimin. Praxis
cap. xxxvii. No. 12. See the cases tried in the châtelet of Paris, as related
above, pp. 390–4.

[3] Martini Bernhardi Diss. Inaug. de Tortura cap. i. § 4.

[4] He represents the judge as addressing his victim "Tu sei il reo di un
delitto, dunque è possibile che lo sii di cent' altri delitti : questo dubbio mi
pesa, voglio accertarmene col mio criterio di verità : le leggi ti tormentano,
perche sei reo, perche puoi esser reo, perche voglio che tu sii reo."—Dei
Delitti e delle Pene, § xii.

[5] Damhouder. Rer. Crimin. Prax. cap. xxxv. No. 9, cap. xxxviii. No. 14.

[6] Ejusd. cap. xxxix. No. 6.   [7] Zangeri Præfat. No. 31.

in mercantile matters, where money only was at stake.[1]
Equally absolute was the maxim that torture could not
be employed unless there was positive proof that crime of
some sort had been committed, for its object was to ascertain the criminal and not the crime ;[2] yet von Rosbach
remarks that as soon as any one claimed to have lost anything by theft, the judges of his day hastened to torture
all suspect, without waiting to determine whether or not
the theft had really been committed as alleged ;[3] and von
Boden declares that many tribunals were in the habit of
resorting to it in cases wherein subsequent developments
showed that the alleged crime had really not taken place,
and he quotes a brother lawyer, who jocosely characterized
such proceedings as putting the cart before the horse, and
bridling him by the tail.[4] The history of criminal jurisprudence is full of such proceedings. Boyvin du Villars
relates that during the war in Piedmont, in 1559, he released from the dungeons of the Marquis of Masserano an
unfortunate gentleman who had been secretly kept there
for eighteen years, in consequence of having attempted to
serve a process from the Duke of Savoy on the marquis.
His disappearance having naturally been attributed to foul
play, his kindred prosecuted an enemy of the family, who,
under stress of torture, duly confessed to having committed the murder, and was accordingly executed in a town
where Masserano himself was residing.[5]

We have seen above that the prisoner was entitled to

---

[1] Zangeri Tract. Not. ad p. 903. Bernhardi states that in cases of presumed
fraudulent bankruptcy, not only the accused, but also the witnesses, if suspected of concealing the truth, could be tortured.—Diss. Inaug. de Tort.
cap. I. § iv.

[2] Zangeri Præfat. No. 32.—Tortura enim datur non ad liquidandum factum sed personam.—Damhouder. Rer. Crimin. Prax. cap. xxxv. No. 7.

[3] Process. Criminal. Tit. v. cap. ix. No. 17.

[4] De Usu et Ab. Tort. Th. IX.—Qui aliter procedit judex, equum cauda
frenat et post quadrigas caballum jungit.

[5] Boyvin du Villars, Mémoires, Liv. VII.

see a copy of the evidence taken in secret against him; yet
von Rosbach states that judges were not in the habit of
permitting it, though no authority justified them in the
refusal;[1] and half a century later this is confirmed by Bernhardi, who gives as a reason that by withholding the proceedings from the accused they saved themselves trouble.[2]
Even the inalienable privilege of being heard in his defence
was habitually refused by many tribunals, which proceeded
at once to torture after hearing the adverse evidence, and
von Rosbach actually feels it necessary to argue at some
length the propriety of hearing what the accused may
have to say.[3] In the same way, the right to appeal from
an order to torture was evaded by judges, who sent the
prisoner to the rack without a preliminary formal order,
thus depriving him of the opportunity of appealing.[4] Indeed, in time it was admitted by many jurists that the
judge at his pleasure could refuse to allow an appeal; and
that in no case was he to wait more than ten days for the
decision of the superior tribunal.[5]

---

[1] Process. Criminal. Tit. v. cap. x. No. 7.—Hodie vero judices reis captis
non exhibent indiciorum exemplum, et procedunt ad torturam. Sed hæc
opinio in jure undique refellitur, et ego senio confectus nunquam inveni
aliquam legem seu rationem pro tali observantia.

We have already seen (p. 401) that in France the accused was not allowed
to see the evidence against him; and the same rule was in force in Flanders
—"Toutes depositions de tesmoins en causes criminelles demeureront
secrétes à l'égard de l'accusé."—Coutume d'Audenarde, Stile de la Procedure, Art. 10. (Le Grand, Coutumes de Flandre, Cambrai, 1719, p. 103.)

[2] Diss. Inaug. cap. I. § xii.

[3] Process. Criminal. Tit. v. cap. x. Nos. 8-16.

[4] Bernhardi, loc. cit. The difference between the practice and principles of the law is shown by the rules laid down in 1647 by Brunnemann,
coexisting with the above. He directs that the proceedings are to be exhibited
to the accused or his friends, and then submitted to a college of jurists who
are to decide as to the necessity of torture, and he warns the latter that they
can have no graver question placed before them—"Et sane nullam gravi-
orem puto esse deliberationem in Collegiis Juridicis quam ubi de tortura
infligenda agitur."—Brunneman de Inquisitionis Processu cap. VIII. Memb.
iv. No 10; Memb. v. No 1.

[5] Passerini Regulare Tribunal ; Praxis, cap. viii. No. 170.

If the irresponsible power which the secret inquisitorial
process lodged in the hands of the judges was thus fearfully abused in destroying all the safeguards provided for
the prisoner by law, it was none the less so in disregarding
the limitations provided against excessive torture. A universal prescription existed that the torment should not be
so severe or so prolongɩ l as to endanger life or limb, or to
permanently injure the patient; but Senckenberg assures
us that he was personally cognizant of cases in which innocent persons had been crippled for life by torture under
false accusations;[1] and the meek Jesuit Del Rio, in his
instructions to inquisitors, quietly observes that the flesh
should not be wounded nor the bones broken, but that torture could scarce be properly administered without more
or less dislocation of the joints.[2] There is indeed something
very suggestive in the direction which Simancas gives to
judges, that they should warn the accused when brought
into the torture-chamber, that if he is crippled or dies
under the torture he must hold himself accountable for it
in not spontaneously confessing the truth.[3] Von Boden,
moreover, very justly points out the impossibility of establishing any rules or limitations of practical utility, when
the capacity of endurance varies so greatly in different
constitutions, and the executioners had so many devices
for heightening or lessening, within the established bounds,
the agony inflicted by the various modes of torture allowed
by law. Indeed, he does not hesitate to exclaim that human ingenuity could not invent suffering more terrible

[1] Not. ad p. 907 Zangeri, op. cit.
[2] Del Rio Magicar. Disquisit. Lib. v. sect. ix.—Ut corpus rei maneat vel
illæsum vel modice læsum, salvum innocentiæ vel supplicio : illæsum, dico,
quod ad carnis lacerationem aut ossium vel nervorum fracturam, nam quoad
discompaginationem, sive disjunctionem juncturarum et ossium non immode-
ratum vix in tormentis ea potest evitari.
[3] Simancæ de Cathol. Instit. Tit. lxv. No. 56.
36

than was constantly and legally employed, and that Satan himself would be unable to increase its refinements.[1]

It is true that the old rules which subjected the judge to some responsibility were still nominally in force. When torture was ordered without a preliminary examination, or when it was excessive and caused permanent injury, the judge was held by all authorities to have acted through malice, and his office was no protection against reclamation for damages.[2] Zanger also quotes the Roman law as still in force, to the effect that if the accused dies under the torture, and the judge has been either bribed or led away by passion, his offence is capital, while if there had been insufficient preliminary evidence, he is punishable at discretion.[3] The secrecy of criminal trials, however, offered an almost impenetrable shield to the judge, and, according to Damhouder, he could clear himself by his own declaration that he had acted in accordance with the law, and without fraud or malice.[4] We are therefore quite prepared to believe the assertion of Senckenberg that the rules protecting the prisoner had become obsolete, and that he had seen not a few instances of their violation without there being any idea of holding the judge to accountability.[5]

Not the least of the evils of the system, indeed, was its inevitable influence upon the judge himself. He was required by his office to be present during the infliction of torture, and to conduct the interrogatory personally. Callousness to human suffering, whether natural or acquired, thus became a necessity, and the delicate conscientiousness which should be the moving principle of every Christian

---

[1] De Usu et Abusu Tort. Th. XIII.

It must not be supposed from this and the preceding extracts that von Boden was an opponent of torture on principle. Within certain bounds, he advocated its use, and he only deplored the excessive abuse of it by the tribunals of the day.

[2] Zangeri, op. cit. cap. I. No. 42–44.   [3] Ibid. cap. III. No. 20–22.
[4] Chap. xxxviii. No. 18.   [5] Zangeri, cap III. No. 20–22.

tribunal was well-nigh an impossibility.[1] Nor was this all,
for when even a conscientious judge had once taken upon
himself the responsibility of ordering a fellow-being to the
torture, every motive would lead him to desire the justification of the act by the extortion of a confession;[2] and the
very idea that he might be possibly held to accountability,
instead of being a safeguard for the prisoner, became a
cause of subjecting him to additional agony.   Indeed, the
prudence of persevering in torture until a confession was
reached was at least recognized, if not advised, by jurists,
and in such a matter to suggest the idea was practically
to recommend it.[3]   Both the good and the evil impulses of
the judge were thus enlisted against the unfortunate being
at his mercy.   Human nature was not meant to face such
temptations, and the fearful ingenuity, which multiplied
the endless refinements of torment, testifies how utterly
humanity yielded to the thirst of wringing conviction from
the weaker party to the unequal conflict, where he who
should have been a passionless arbiter was made necessarily
a combatant.   How completely the prisoner thus became
a quarry to be hunted to the death is shown by the jocular
remark of Farinacci, a celebrated authority in criminal law,

---

[1] So thoroughly was this recognized, that in 1668 Racine represents a
judge, desirous of ingratiating himself with a young girl, as offering to
exhibit to her the spectacle of the question as an agreeable pastime.

> "DANDIN. N'avez vous jamais vu donner la question?
> ISABELLE. Non, et ne le verrai, que je crois de ma vie.
> DANDIN. Venez, je vous en veux faire passer l'envie.
> ISABELLE. Hé! Monsieur, peut-on voir souffrir les malhereux?
> DANDIN. Bon! cela fait toujours passer une heure ou deux."
>   *Les Plaideurs*, Acte III. Sc. dernière.

[2] Fortescue, in his arguments against the use of torture, does not fail to
recognize that the acquittal of a tortured prisoner is the condemnation of
the judge—"qui judex eum pronuntiet innocentem, nonne eodem judicio
judex ille seipsum reum judicat omnis sævitiæ et pœnarum quibus innocentem afflixit?" (De Laud. Legg. Angl. cap. xxii.)

[3] Occurrit hic cautela Bruni dicentis, si judex indebite torserit aliquem,
facit reum confiteri quod fuit legitime tortus, de qua confessione faciat nota-
rium rogatum.—Jo. Em. a Rosb. Process. Crim. Tit. v. cap. xv. No. 6.

that the torture of sleeplessness, invented by Marsiglio, was most excellent, for out of a hundred martyrs exposed to it not two could endure it without becoming confessors as well.[1] Few, when once engaged in such a pursuit, could be expected to follow the example of the Milanese judge, who resolved his doubts as to the efficacy of torture in evidence by killing a favorite mule, and allowing the accusation to fall upon one of his servants. The man of course denied the offence, was duly tortured, confessed, and persisted in his confession after torture. The judge, thus convinced by experiment of the fallacy of the system, resigned the office whose duties he could no longer conscientiously discharge, and in his subsequent career rose to the cardinalate.[2]

---

[1] Quoted by Nicolas, Diss. Mor. et Jurid. sur la Torture, p. 21. This mode of torture consisted in placing the accused between two jailers, who pummelled him whenever he began to doze, and thus, with proper relays, deprived him of sleep for forty hours. Its inventor considered it humane, as it endangered neither life nor limb, but the extremity of suffering to which it reduced the prisoner is shown by its efficaciousness.

I have purposely abstained from entering into the details of the various forms of torture. They may be interesting to the antiquarian, but they illustrate no principle, and little would be gained by describing these melancholy monuments of human error. Those who may be curious in such matters will find ample material in Grupen Observat. Jur. Crim. de Applicat. Torment., 4to., Hanov. 1754; Zangeri, op. cit. cap. IV. No. 9, 10; Hieron. Magius de Equuleo cum Appendd. Amstelod. 1664, etc. According to Bernhardi, Johann Graefe enumerates no less than six hundred different instruments invented for the purpose. Damhouder (op. cit. cap. xxxvii. No. 17–23) declares that torture can legally be inflicted only with ropes, and then proceeds to describe a number of ingenious devices. One of these, which he states to produce insufferable torment without risk, is bathing the feet with brine and then setting a goat to lick the soles.

[2] I give this anecdote on the authority of Nicolas (op. cit. p. 169), who quotes it as a well-known circumstance, without furnishing either name or date. He also relates (p. 178) a somewhat similar case which was told to him at Amsterdam in explanation of the fact that the city was obliged to borrow a headsman from the neighboring towns whenever the services of one were required for an execution. It appears that a young man of Amsterdam, returning home late at night from a revel, sank upon a door-step in a

In theory, the accused could be tortured only once, but this, like all other attempts to humanize the law, amounted to but little. A repetition of torture could be justified on the ground that the first application had been light or insufficient; the production of fresh evidence authorized a second and even a third infliction; a failure to persevere in confession after torture rendered a repetition requisite, and even a variation in the confession required confirmation by the rack or strappado.[1] In fact, some authorities go so far as to place it entirely at the discretion of the judge whether the accused shall be subjected or not to repeated torment without fresh evidence,[2] and Del Rio mentions a case occurring in Westphalia wherein a man accused of lycanthropy was tortured twenty times;[3] while Damhouder finds it necessary to reprove the excessive zeal of some judges who were in the habit of exposing obstinate prisoners to prolonged and excessive hunger and thirst, in the determination to extract a confession from them.[4]

The frequency with which torture was used is manifested in the low rate which was paid for its application. In the municipal accounts of Valenciennes, between 1538 and 1573, the legal fee paid to the executioner for each tor-

---

drunken sleep. A thief emptied his pockets, securing, among other things, a dirk, with which, a few minutes later, he stabbed a man in a quarrel. Returning to the sleeper, he slipped the bloody weapon back to its place. The young man awoke, but, before he had taken many steps, he was seized by the watch, who had just discovered the murder. Appearances were against him; he was tortured, confessed, persisted in confession after torture, and was duly hanged. Soon after, the real criminal was condemned for another crime, and revealed the history of the preceding one, whereupon the States General of the United Provinces, using the ordinary logic of the criminal law, deprived the city of Amsterdam of its executioner, as a punishment for a result that was inevitable under the system.

[1] Zangeri, cap. v. No. 73–83.

[2] Damhouder. op. cit. cap. xxxviii. No. 3, 4.—Rosbach. Tit. v. cap. xv. No. 14.—Simancas, however, declares that only two applications of torture are allowable (De Cathol. Instit. Tit. LXV. No. 76, 81).

[3] Lib. v. sect. ix.   [4] Cap. xxxviii. No. 13.

turing of a criminal is only two sous and a half, while he
is allowed the same sum for the white gloves worn at an
execution, and ten sous are given him for such light jobs as
piercing the tongue.[1]

With all this hideous accumulation of cruelty which
shrank from nothing in the effort to wring a confession
from the wretched victim, that confession, when thus so
dearly obtained, was estimated at its true worthlessness.
It was insufficient for conviction unless confirmed by the
accused in a subsequent examination beyond the confines
of the torture-chamber. If then retracted, the accused was
again tortured, when a second confession and retraction
made an exceedingly awkward dilemma for the subtle jurisconsults. They agree that he should not be allowed to
escape after giving so much trouble. Some advocated the
regular punishment of his crime, others demanded for him
an extraordinary penalty; some, again, were in favor of
incarcerating him;[2] others assumed that he should be tortured a third time, when a confession, followed as before
by a recantation, released him from further torment, for
the admirable reason that nature and justice alike abhorred
infinity.[3] This was too metaphysical for some jurists, who
referred the whole question to the discretion of the judge,
with power to prolong the series of alternate confession
and retraction indefinitely.[4] The magistrates in some
places were in the habit of imprisoning or banishing such
persons, thus punishing them without conviction, and inflicting a penalty unsuited to the crime of which they were

[1] Louïse, Sorcellerie et Justice Criminelle à Valenciennes. Valenciennes,
1861, pp. 121–125.

[2] Zangeri, cap. v. No. 79–81.

[3] Bernhardi, Diss. Inaug. cap. i. § xi.

[4] Emer. a Rosbach, op. cit. Tit. v. cap. xviii. No. 13. So Beccaria (Delitt
e Pene, § xii.)—"Alcuni dottori ed alcune nazioni non permettono questa
infame petizione di principio che per tre volte; altre nazioni ed altri dottori
la lasciano ad arbitrio del giudice,"

accused.[1] Others solved the knotty problem by judiciously
advising that in the uncertainty of doubt as to his guilt,
the prisoner should be soundly scourged and turned loose,
after taking an oath not to bring an action for false imprisonment against his tormentors;[2] but, according to some
authorities, this kind of oath, or *urpheda* as it was called,
was of no legal value.[3]

There were other curious inconsistencies in the system
which manifest still more clearly the real estimate placed
on confessions under torture. If the torture had been
inflicted by an over-zealous judge without proper preliminary evidence, confession amounted legally to nothing,
even though proof were subsequently discovered.[4] If, on
the other hand, absolute and incontrovertible proof of guilt
were had, and the over-zealous judge tortured in surplusage
without extracting a confession, the offender was absolved.[5]
According to law, indeed, torture without confession was
a full acquittal; but here, again, practice intervened to
destroy what little humanity was admitted by jurists, and
the accused under such circumstances was still held suspect, and was liable at any moment to be tried again for
the same offence.[6] If, again, a man and woman were tor-

---

[1] This was especially the case at Amsterdam. Meyer (Institutions Judiciaires, IV. 295) states that the registers there afford scarcely an instance
of a prisoner discharged after enduring torture without conviction.

[2] Zangeri, loc. cit.

[3] Bernhardi, cap. I. § xii. Cf. Caroli V. Const. Crim. cap. xx. § 1.

[4] Zangeri, cap. II. No. 9-10; cap. v. No. 19-28.—Damhouder. op. cit. cap.
xxxvi. No. 36.

[5] Zangeri, cap. v. No. 1-18.

[6] Damhouder. op. cit. cap. xl. No. 3.—Bigotry and superstition, especially,
did not allow their victims to escape so easily. In accusations of sorcery,
if appearances were against the prisoner—that is, if he were of evil repute,
if he shed no tears during the torture, and if he recovered speedily after
each application—he was not to be liberated because no confession could be
wrung from him, but was to be kept for at least a year, "squaloribus car-
ceris mancipandus et cruciandus, sæpissime etiam examinandus, præcipue
sacratioribus diebus."—Rickii Defens. Aq. Probæ cap. I. No. 22.

tured on an accusation of adultery committed with each
other, and if one confessed while the other did not, both
were acquitted.[1] Nothing more contradictory and illogical
can well be imagined, and, as if to crown the absurdity of
the whole, torture after conviction was allowed in order to
prevent appeals; and if the unfortunate, at the place of
execution, chanced to assert his innocence, he was often
hurried from the scaffold to the rack in obedience to the
theory that the confession must remain unretracted.[2] One
can scarcely repress a grim smile at finding that this series
of horrors had pious defenders who urged that a merciful
consideration for the offender's soul required that he should
be brought to confess his iniquities in order to secure his
eternal salvation.[3]

The atrocity of this whole system of so-called criminal
justice is forcibly described by the honest indignation of
Augustin Nicolas, who, in his judicial capacity under Louis
XIV., had ample opportunities of observing its practical
working and results. "The strappado, so common in Italy,
and which yet is forbidden under the Roman law . . . the
vigils of Spain, which oblige a man to support himself by
sheer muscular effort for seven hours, to avoid sitting on a
pointed iron, which pierces him with insufferable pain; the
vigils of Florence, or of Marsiglio, which have been described above; our iron stools heated to redness, on which
we place poor half-witted women accused of witchcraft,
exhausted by frightful imprisonment, rotting from their
dark and filthy dungeons, loaded with chains, fleshless,
and half dead; and we pretend that the human frame can
resist these devilish practices, and that the confessions
which our wretched victims make of everything that may
be charged against them are true."[4] Under such a scheme
of jurisprudence, it is easy to understand and appreciate

[1] Zangeri, cap. v. No. 53–61.
[2] Boden, op cit. Th. v. vi.   [3] Ibid.
[4] Dissert. Mor. et Jurid sur la Torture, pp. 36–7.

the case of the unfortunate peasant, sentenced for witch-craft, who, in his dying confession to the priest, admitted that he was a sorcerer, and humbly welcomed death as the fitting retribution for the enormous crimes of which he had been found guilty, but pitifully inquired of the shuddering confessor whether one could not be a sorcerer without knowing it.[1]

If anything were wanting to show how completely the inquisitorial process turned all the chances against the accused it is to be found in the quaint advice given by Damhouder. He counsels the prisoner, when required to plead, to prevent his judge from taking advantage of any adverse points that might occur, as, for instance, in a charge of homicide to assert his innocence, but to add that, if he were proved to have committed the crime, he then declares it to have been done in self-defence.[2]

We have seen above how great was the part of the In-quisition in introducing and moulding the whole system of torture on the ruins of the Roman law. Even so, in the reconstruction of European jurisprudence, during the six-teenth and seventeenth centuries, the ardor of the inquisi-torial proceedings against witchcraft, and the panic on the subject which long pervaded Christendom, had a powerful influence in familiarizing the minds of men with the use of torture as a necessary instrument of justice, and in autho-rizing its employment to an extent which now is almost inconceivable.

From a very early period, torture was recognized as in-dispensable in all trials for sorcery and magic. In 358, an edict of Constantius decreed that no dignity of birth or station should protect those accused of such offences from its application in the severest form.[3] How universal its

---

[1] Nicolas, p. 169.

[2] Damhoud. Rer. Criminal. Prax. cap. 34, § 7.

[3] Const. 7 Cod. IX. xviii.

employment thus became is evident from a canon of the
council of Merida, in 666, declaring that priests, when
sick, sometimes accused the slaves of their churches of
bewitching them, and impiously tortured them against all
ecclesiastical rules.[1] That all such crimes should be regarded as peculiarly subjecting to the last extremity of
torture all suspected of them is therefore natural, and its
use in the trials of witches and sorcerers came to be regarded as indispensable.

The necessity which all men felt that these crimes should
be extirpated with merciless severity, and the impalpable
nature of the testimony on which the tribunals had mostly
to depend, added to this traditional belief in the fitness of
torture. Witchcraft was considered as peculiarly difficult
of proof, and torture consequently became an unfailing
resource to the puzzled tribunal, although every legal safeguard was refused to the wretched criminal, and the widest
latitude of evidence was allowed. Bodin expressly declares that in so fearful a crime no rules of procedure were
to be observed.[2] Sons were admitted to testify against their
fathers, and young girls were regarded as the best of witnesses against their mothers; the disrepute of a witness
was no bar to the reception of his testimony, and even
children of irresponsible age were allowed to swear before
they rightly knew the nature of the oath on which hung
the life of a fellow creature.[3] Even advocates and counsel

---

[1] Concil. Emeritan, ann. 666, can. xv.

In the middle of the thirteenth century, the Emperor Theodore Lascaris invented a novel mode of torture in a case of this kind. When a noble lady of
his court was accused of sorcery, he caused her to be inclosed naked in a
sack with a number of cats. The suffering, though severe, failed to extort
a confession.—Georg. Pachymeri Hist. Mich. Palæol. Lib. i. cap. xii.

[2] Bodini de Magorum Dæmonoman. Lib. iv. cap. 2.

[3] Boguet, Code des Sorciers, A. D. 1601 (*Ap.* Louïse, La Sorcellerie et la
Justice Criminelle à Valenciennes. Valenciennes, 1861, p. 91)—Louïse prints
(pp. 133–164) the records of a trial in 1662, wherein Philippe Polus is condemned on the evidence of his daughter, a child in her ninth year. There

could be forced to give evidence against their clients.[1] Notwithstanding the ample resources thus afforded for conviction, Jacob Rickius, who, as a magistrate during an epidemic of witchcraft, at the close of the sixteenth century, had the fullest practical experience on the subject, complains that no reliance could be placed on legal witnesses to procure conviction;[2] and Del Rio only expresses the general opinion when he avers that torture is to be more readily resorted to in witchcraft than in other crimes, in consequence of the extreme difficulty of its proof.[3]

Even the wide-spread belief that Satan aided his worshippers in their extremity by rendering them insensible to pain did not serve to relax the efforts of the extirpators of witchcraft, though they could hardly avoid the conclusion that they were punishing only the innocent, and allowing the guilty to escape. Boguet, indeed, in his *Code des Sorciers*, recognizes the practical contradiction of it with the current belief, and advises the judge not to have recourse to torture, because of its inutility, though it is permissible to use it even during church festivals.[4] How impossible it was for the accused to escape the question is shown in the charter of Hainault of 1619 where in these cases the tribunal is authorized to employ it to ascertain the truth of the charge, or to discover accomplices, or *for*

appears to have been no other testimony against him, and according to her confession the girl had herself been a sorcerer since her fourth year.—For other instances see Bodin Lib. iv. cap. 1, 2.

[1] Bodin. Lib. i. cap. 2.

[2] Per legales testes hujus rei ad convincendum fides certa haberi non potest.—Rickii Defens. Aquæ Probæ cap. iii. No. 117.

[3] Idque facilius in excepto et occulto difficilisque probationis crimine nostro sortilegii admiserim quam in aliis.—Disquisit. Magicar. Lib. v. Sect. iii. No. 8.

[4] Le juge doit éviter la torture pour le prévenu, puisqu'il ne fait rien sur le sorcier; neanmois il est permis d'en faire usage, même un jour de fête. (Louïse, p. 91.)

any other purpose.[1] In this dilemma, various means were
resorted to to circumvent the arch-enemy, of which the one
most generally adopted was that of shaving the whole person carefully before applying the torture;[2] but notwithstanding all the precautions of the most experienced exor-
cists, we find in the bloody farce of Urbain Grandier that
the fiercest torments left him in capital spirits and good
humor.[3] Damhouder relates at much length a curious
case which occurred under his own eyes while member of
the council of Bruges, when he assisted at the torture of
a reputed witch who had exercised her power only in good
works. During three examinations, she bore the severest
torture without shrinking, sometimes sleeping and sometimes defiantly snapping her fingers at her judges. At
length, during the process of shaving, a slip of parchment
covered with cabalistic characters was found concealed in

[1] Soit pour ne trouver les délitz suffisament vérifiez, ou pour savoir tcus
les complices, *ou autrement.*—Chart. nouv. du Haynau, chap. 135, art.
xxvi. (Louïse, p. 94).

[2] Nicolas (p. 145) inveighs with honest indignation at the frightfully indecent outrages to which female prisoners were subjected in obedience to
this superstition. The curious reader will find in Del Rio (Lib. v. Sect. ix.)
ample details as to the arts of the Evil One to sustain his followers against
the pious efforts of the Inquisition. There was so general a belief among
enlightened men that criminals of all kinds had secrets to deaden the sufferings of torture, that it is quite likely the unfortunates were sometimes able
to strengthen their endurance with some anæsthetic. Damhouder states
that professional malefactors were in the habit of torturing each other in
turn for the purpose of hardening themselves when brought to justice, and
he advises the judges to inquire into the antecedents of criminals in order
to proportion the severity of torment in such cases.—Cap. xxxviii. No. 19.

[3] "Q'après qu'on eut lavé ses jambes, qui avoient été déchirées par la
torture, et qu'on les eut présentées au feu pour y rapeller quelque peu d'esprits
et de vigueur, il ne cessa pas de s'entretenir avec ses Gardes, par des discours peu sérieux et pleins de railleries ; qu'il mangea avec apétit et but
avec plaisir trois ou quatre coups ; et qu'il ne répandit aucuns larmes en souf-
frant la question, ni après l'avoir soufferte, lors même qu'on l'exorcisa de
l'exorcisme des Magiciens, et que l'Exorciste lui dit à plus de cinquante re-
prises ' præcipio ut si sis innocens effundas lachrymas.' "—Hist. des Diables
de Loudon, pp. 157-8.

her person, and on its removal she was speedily brought
to acknowledge her pact with the Evil One.[1]   The tender-
hearted Rickius was so convinced of this source of uncertainty that he was accustomed to administer the cold
water ordeal to all the miserable old women brought before him on such charges, but he is careful to inform us
that this was only preparatory proof, to enable him with a
safer conscience to torture those who were so ill-advised
as to float instead of sinking.[2]

When the concentrated energies of these ingenious and
determined law dispensers failed to extort by such means
a confession from the wretched clowns and gossips thus
placed at their mercy, they were even yet not wholly at
fault.   The primitive teachings of the Inquisition of the
thirteenth century were not yet obsolete, and they were
instructed to treat the prisoner kindly; to introduce into
his dungeon some prepossessing agent who should make
friends with him and induce him to confess what was wanted
of him, promising to influence the judge to pardon; at that
moment the judge is to enter the cell and to promise mercy,
with the mental reservation that his mercy should be
shown to the community and not to the prisoner.[3]   Or, still
following the ancient traditions, spies were to be confined
with him who should profess to be likewise sorcerers and
lead him to incriminate himself, or else the unhappy wretch
was to be told that his associate prisoners had borne testimony against him, in order to induce him to revenge him-

---

[1] Rerum Crimin. Praxis Cap. xxxvii. No. 21, 22.   Cf. Brunnemann. de
Inquisit. Process. Cap. viii. Memb. v. No. 70.

[2] Tunc non quæstioni subjiciebantur statim, sed pro confortatione præ-
cidentium indiciorum, probam aquæ adhibebamus primitus, non ad convin-
cendam eam per hinc, sed præparandum et muniendum torturæ viam.—
Rickii op. cit. cap. i. No. 24.

[3] "Judex . . . promittet facere gratiam, subintelligendi sibi vel reipub.
in cujus conservationem totum quod sit est gratiosum."   The pun upon the
word "gratia," on which a human life is made to depend, is scarcely trans-
latable.   Sprenger. Mall. Maleficar. P. iii. q. xvi.

self by turning witness against them.[1] Boguet, indeed, does not consider it correct to mislead the accused with promises of pardon, and though it was practised by many judges, he stigmatizes it as barbarous,[2] and Simancas considers such artifices to be illegal, and that a confession thus procured could be retracted.[3] Del Rio, on the other hand, while loftily condemning the outspoken trickery recommended by Bodin and Sprenger, proceeds to draw a careful distinction between *dolum bonum* and *dolum malum*. He forbids absolute lying, but advises equivocation and ambiguous promises, and then, if the prisoner is deceived, he has only himself to thank for it.[4] In fact, these men conceived that they were engaged in a direct and personal struggle with the Evil One, and that Satan could only be overcome with his own arts.

When the law thus pitilessly turned all the chances against the victim, it is easy to understand that few escaped. In the existing condition of popular frenzy on the subject, there was no one but could feel that he might at any moment be brought under accusation by personal enemies or by unfortunates compelled on the rack to declare the names of all whom they might have seen congregated at the witches' sabbat. We can thus readily comprehend the feelings of those who, living under such uncertainties, coolly and deliberately made up their minds in advance that, if chance should expose them to suspicion, they would at once admit everything that the inquisitors might desire of them, preferring a speedy death to one more lingering and scarcely less certain.[5] The evil fostered with such careful exaggeration grew to so great proportions that Father Tanner speaks of the multitude of witches who

[1] Bodin. Lib. IV. cap. 1. [2] Louïse, loc. cit.
[2] De Cathol. Instit. Tit. XIII. No. 12.
[4] Disquisit. Magicar. Lib. V. Sect. x.
[5] Father Tanner states that he had this from learned and experienced men.—Tanneri Tract. de Proc. adv. Veneficas, Quæst. II. Assert. iii. § 2.

were daily convicted through torture;[1] and that this was no mere form of speech is evident when one judge, in a treatise on the subject, boasted of his zeal and experience in having dispatched within his single district nine hundred wretches in the space of fifteen years, and another trustworthy authority relates with pride that in the diocess of Como alone as many as a thousand had been burnt in a twelvemonth, while the annual average was over a hundred.[2]

Were it not for the steady patronage bestowed on the system by the church, it would seem strange that torture should invade the quiet and holy retirement of the cloister. Its use, however, in monasteries was, if possible, even more arbitrary than in secular tribunals. Monks and nuns were exempt from the jurisdiction of the civil authorities, and were bound by vows of blind obedience to their superiors. The head of each convent thus was an autocrat, and when investigating the delinquencies of any of his flock, he was subjected to no limitations. Not only could he order the accused to be tortured at will, but the witnesses, whether male or female, were liable to the same treatment, with the exception that in the case of nuns it was recommended that the tortures employed should not be indecent or too severe for the fragility of the sex. As elsewhere, it was customary to commence the torment with the weakest of the witnesses or criminals.[3]

In this long history of legalized cruelty and wrong, the races of northern Europe are mostly exceptional. Yet it is somewhat remarkable that the first regular mediæval code in which torture is admitted as a means of investigation is the one of all others in which it would be least expected. The earliest extant law of Iceland, the Grágás, which dates from 1119, has one or two indications of its existence,

---

[1] Ibid. loc. cit.   [2] Nicolas, p. 164.
[3] Chabot, Encyclopédie Monastique, p. 426 (Paris, 1827).

which are interesting as being purely autochthonic, and in
no sense derivable, as in the rest of Europe, from the
Roman law. The character of the people, indeed, and of
their institutions would seem to be peculiarly incompatible
with the use of torture, for almost all cases were submitted
to inquests or juries of the vicinage, and, when this was
unsuitable, resort was had to the ordeal. The indigenous
origin of the custom, however, is shown by the fact that
while it was used in but few matters, the most prominent
class subjected to it was that of pregnant women, who have
elsewhere been spared by the common consent of even the
most pitiless legislators. An unmarried woman with child,
who refused to name her seducer, could be forced to do so
by moderate torments which should not break or discolor
the skin.[1] The object of this was to enable the family to
obtain the fine from the seducer, and to save themselves
the expense of supporting the child. When the mother
confessed, however, additional evidence was required to
convict the putative father. When the inhabitants of a
district, also, refused to deliver up a man claimed as an
outlaw by another district, they were bound to torture him
to ascertain the truth of the charge[2]—a provision doubtless
explicable by the important part occupied by outlawry in
all the schemes of Scandinavian legislation. These are
the only instances in which it is permitted, while its occasional abuse is shown by a section providing punishment
for its illegal employment.[3] Slaves, moreover, under the
Icelandic, as under other codes, had no protection at law,
and were at the mercy of their masters.[4] These few indications of the liability of freemen, however, disappear
about the time when the rest of Europe was commencing

---

[1] "Ita torquatur ut nec plagam referat nec color cutis livescat."—Grágás,
Festathattr cap. xxxiii.

[2] Ibid. Vigslothi cap. cxi.

[3] Ibid. Vigslothi cap. lxxxviii.

[4] Schlegel, Comment. ad Grágás, § xxix.

to adopt the use of torture. In the " Jarnsida," or code compiled for Iceland by Hako Hakonsen of Norway, in 1258, there is no allusion whatever to its use.

The Scandinavian nations, as a whole, did not admit torture into their systems of jurisprudence. The institution of the jury in various forms was common to all, and where proof upon open trial was deficient, they allowed, until a comparatively recent date, the accused to clear himself by sacramental purgation. Thus, in the Danish laws of Waldemar II., to which the date of 1240 is generally assigned, there is a species of permanent jury, *sandemend*, as well as a temporary one, *nefninge*, and torture seems to have formed no part of judicial proceedings.[1] This code was in force until 1683, when that of Christiern V. was promulgated. It is probable that the employment of torture may have crept in from Germany, without being regularly sanctioned, for we find Christiern forbidding its use except in cases of high treason, where the magnitude of the offence seems to him to justify the infraction of the general rule. He, however, encouraged one of its greatest abuses in permitting it on criminals condemned to death.[2]

So, in Sweden, the code of Raguald, compiled in 1441 and in force until 1614, during a period in which torture flourished in almost every European state, has no place for it. Trials are conducted before twelve *nempdarii*, or jury-

---

[1] Leg. Cimbric. Woldemari Lib. II. cap. i., xl. (Ed. Ancher, Hafniæ, 1783).

[2] Christiani V. Jur. Danic. Lib. I. cap. xx. (Ed. Weghorst, Hafniæ, 1698).

Senckenberg (Corp. Jur. German. T. I. Præf. p. lxxxvi.) gives the chapter heads of a code in Danish, the *Keyser Retenn*, furnished to him by Ancher, in which cap. iv. and v. contain directions as to the administration of torture. The code is a mixture of German, civil, and local law, and probably was in force in some of the Germanic provinces of Denmark.

The Frisian code of 1323 is a faithful transcript of the primitive Barbarian jurisprudence. It contains no allusion to torture, and as all crimes, except theft, were still compounded by wehr-gilds, it may safely be assumed that extorted confession was unknown (Leges Opstalbomicæ ann. 1323, published by Gärtner, Saxonum leges tres, Lipsiæ, 1730).

men, and in doubtful cases the accused is directed to clear
himself by oath or by conjurators. For atrocious crimes
the punishments are severe, such as the wheel or the stake,
but inflictions like these are reserved for the condemned.[1]
Into these distant regions the Roman jurisprudence pene-
trated slowly, and the jury trial was an elastic institution
which adapted itself to all cases.

To the same causes may be attributed the absence of
torture from the Common Law of England. In common
with the other Barbarian races, the Anglo-Saxons solved
all doubtful questions by the ordeal and wager of law, and
in the collection known as the laws of Henry I. a principle is laid down which is incompatible with the whole
theory of torture, whether used to extract confession or
evidence. A confession obtained by fear or fraud is pronounced invalid, and no one who has confessed his own
crime is to be believed with respect to that of another.[2]
Such a principle, combined with the gradual growth of
the trial by jury, doubtless preserved the law from the
contamination of inquisitorial procedure, though, as we
have seen, torture was extensively employed for purposes
of extortion by marauders and lawless nobles during periods of civil commotion. Glanville makes no allusion to
it, and though Bracton shows a wide acquaintance with the
revived Roman jurisprudence, and makes extensive use of
it in all matters where it could be advantageously har-
monized with existing institutions, he is careful to abstain

---

[1] Raguald. Ingermund. Leg. Suecor., Stockholmiæ, 1623.

[2] Ll. Henrici I. cap. v. § 16.

A curious exception to this principle occurs in the Welsh laws, which provide that when a thief is at the gallows, with the certainty of being hanged,
his testimony as to his accomplices is to be received as sufficient without
requiring it to be sworn to on a relic--the inseparable condition of all other
evidence. By a singular inconsistency, however, the accomplice thus convicted was not to be hanged but to be sold as a slave.—Dimetian Code, Bk.
II. ch. v. § 9. (Owen I. 425).

from introducing torture into criminal procedure.[1] A clause in Magna Charta, indeed, has been held by high authority to inhibit the employment of torture, but it has no direct allusion to the subject, which was not a living question at the time, and was probably not thought of by any of the parties to that transaction.[2] In fact, the whole spirit of English law was irreconcilable with the fundamental principles of the inquisitorial process. When the accused was brought before court, he was, it is true, required to appear ungirdled, without boots, or cap, or cloak, to show his humility, but it is expressly directed that he shall not be chained, lest his fetters should embarrass his self-possession in his defence, and he was not to be forced in any way to state anything but of his own free will.[3] Men who

---

[1] Many interesting details on the influence of the Roman law upon that of England will be found in the learned work of Carl Güterbock, "Bracton and his Relation to the Roman Law," recently translated by Brinton Coxe (Philadelphia, 1866). The subject is one which well deserves a more thorough consideration than it is likely to receive at the hands of English writers.

It is curious to observe that the *crimen læsæ majestatis* makes its appearance in Bracton (Lib. III. Tract. ii. cap. 3, § 1) about the middle of the thirteenth century, earlier than in France, where, as we have seen, the first allusion to it occurs in 1315. This was hardly to be expected, when we consider the widely different influences exerted upon the jurisprudence of the two countries by the Roman law.

[2] The passage which has been relied on by lawyers is chap xxx.: "Nullus liber homo capiatur, vel imprisoneter, aut dissaisiatur, aut utlagetur, aut aliquo modo destruatur; nec super eum ibimus, nec super eum mittemus, nisi per legale judicium parium suorum, vel per legem terræ." If the law just above quoted from the collection of Henry I. could be supposed to be still in force under John, then this might possibly be imagined to bear some reference to it; but it is evident that had torture been an existing grievance, such as outlawry, seizure, and imprisonment, the barons would have been careful to include it in their enumeration of restrictions. Moreover, Magna Charta was specially directed to curtail the royal prerogative, and at a later period it was not held by any one to interfere with that prerogative whenever the king desired to test with the rack the endurance of his loving subjects.

[3] Et come ascuns felons viendrount en Jugement respondre de lour felonie, volons que ils viegnent dechausses et descients sauns coiffe, et a teste des-

could frame legal maxims so honorable to their sense of
justice and so far in advance of the received notions of
their age could evidently have nothing in common with
the principles which placed the main reliance of the law
on confession to be wrung from the lips of an unfortunate
wretch who was systematically deprived of all support and
assistance. To do so, in fact, is classed with homicide by
a legal writer of the period;[1] but that it was occasionally
practised is shown by his giving a form for the appeal of
homicide against judges guilty of it.[2]

Under the common law, therefore, torture had properly
no existence in England, and in spite of occasional efforts on
the part of the Plantagenets the character of the national
institutions kept at bay the absorbing and centralizing
influences of the Roman law.[3] Yet their wide acceptance
in France, and their attractiveness to those who desired
to wield absolute authority, gradually accustomed the
crown and the crown lawyers to the idea that torture
could be administered by order of the sovereign. Sir John
Fortescue, who was Lord Chancellor under Henry VI.,
inveighs at great length against the French law for its
cruel procedures, and with much satisfaction contrasts it

couverte, en pure lour cote hors de fers et de chescun manere de liens, issint
que la peine ne lour toille nule manere de reson, selon par force ne lour
estouva mye respondre forsque lour fraunche volunte.—Britton, chap. v.

[1] Per volunté aussi se fait ceste pesché [homicide] si come per ceux qui
painent home tant que il est gehist pur avouer pesché mortelment.—Horne,
The Myrror of Justice, cap. I. sect. viii.—See also Fleta, Lib. I. cap. xxvi.
§ 5.

[2] Ou faussement judgea Raginald . . . . ou issint; tant luy penia pur
luy faire conoistre, approver que il se conoist faussement aver pesché ou
nient ne pescha.—Horne, cap. II. sect. xv.

[3] See Fortescue de Laud. Legg. Angliæ. cap. xxxiii.—The jealousy with
which all attempted encroachments of the Roman law were repelled is manifested in a declaration of Parliament in 1388. "Que ce royalme d'Engle-
terre n'estait devant ces heures, ne à l'entent du roy nostre dit seignior et
seigniors du parlement unque ne serra rulé ne governé par la ley civill."—
Rot. Parl., 11 Ric. II. (Selden's Note to Fortescue, loc. cit.)

with the English practice,[1] and yet he does not deny that torture was occasionally used in England. Indeed, his fervent arguments against the system, addressed to Prince Edward, indicate an anxiety to combat and resist the spread of civil law doctrines on the subject, which doubtless were favored by the influence of Margaret of Anjou. An instance of its application in 1468 has, in fact, been recorded, which resulted in the execution of Sir Thomas Coke, Lord Mayor of London ;[2] and in 1485, Innocent VIII. remonstrated with Henry VII. respecting some proceedings against ecclesiastics who were scourged, tortured, and hanged.[3]

Under Henry VIII. and his children, the power of the crown was largely extended, and the doctrine became fashionable that, though no one could be tortured for confession or evidence by the law, yet outside and above the law the royal prerogative was supreme, and that a warrant from the King in Privy Council fully justified the use of the rack and the introduction of the secret inquisitorial process, with all its attendant cruelty and injustice. It is difficult to conceive the subserviency which could reconcile men, bred in the open and manly justice of the common law, to a system so subversive of all the principles in which they had been trained. Yet the loftiest names of the profession were concerned in transactions which they knew to be in contravention of the laws of the land.

Sir Thomas Smith, one of the ornaments of the Elizabethan bar, condemned the practice as not only illegal, but illogical. "Torment or question, which is used by order of the civile law and custome of other countries, ... is

---

[1] De Laudibus Legum Angliæ, cap. xxii.

[2] See Jardine's "Reading on the Use of Torture in the Criminal Law of England," p. 7 (London, 1837), a condensed and sufficiently complete account of the subject under the Tudors and Stuarts.

[3] Partim tormentis subjecti, partim crudelissime laniati, et partim etiam furca suspensi fuerant.—Wilkins Concil. III. 617.

not used in England. . . . . The nature of Englishmen is
to neglect death, to abide no torment; and therefore hee
will confesse rather to have done anything, yea, to have
killed his owne father, than to suffer torment." And yet,
a few years later, we find the same Sir Thomas writing to
Lord Burghley, in 1571, respecting two miserable wretches
whom he was engaged in racking under a warrant from
Queen Elizabeth.[1]

In like manner, Sir Edward Coke, in his Institutes, declares—"So, as there is no law to warrant tortures in this
land, nor can they be justified by any prescription, being
so lately brought in." Yet, in 1603, there is a warrant
addressed to Coke and Fleming, as Attorney and Solicitor
General, directing them to apply torture to a servant of
Lord Hundsdon, who had been guilty of some idle speeches
respecting King James, and the resultant confession is in
Coke's handwriting, showing that he personally superintended the examination.[2]

Coke's great rival, Lord Bacon, was as subservient as
his contemporaries. In 1619, while Chancellor, we find
him writing to King James concerning a prisoner confined
in the Tower on suspicion of treason—"If it may not be
done otherwise, it is fit Peacock be put to torture. He
deserveth it as well as Peacham did."[3]

As in other countries, so in England, when torture was
once introduced, it rapidly broke the bounds which the

[1] Jardine, op. cit. pp. 8–9, 24–5. It is due to Sir Thomas to add that he
earnestly begs Lord Burghley to release him from so uncongenial an employment.   [2] Ibid. pp. 8, 47.

[3] Works, Philadelphia, 1846, III. 126. Peacham was an unfortunate clergyman in whose desk was found a MS. sermon, never preached, containing
some unpalatable reflections on the royal prerogative, and the prerogative
asserted itself by putting him on the rack. How elastic was the definition
of treason was shown by the torture, in 1553, of one Stonyng, a prisoner in
the Marshalsea, who had transcribed for the amusement of his fellow-cap-
tives a satirical description of Philip of Spain, whose marriage with Queen
Mary was then under contemplation.—Strype's Eccles. Memorials III. 101.

prudence of the Roman lawgivers had established for it. Thus, it was not only in cases of high treason that the royal prerogative was allowed to transgress the limits of the law. Matters of religion, indeed, in those times of perennial change, when dynasties depended on dogmas, might come under the comprehensive head of constructive treason, and be considered to justify the torture even of women, as in the instance of Ann Askew in 1546;[1] and of monks guilty of no greater crime than the endeavor to preserve their monasteries by pretended miracles;[2] but numerous cases of its use are on record, which no ingenuity can remove from the sphere of the most ordinary criminal business. Suspicion of theft, murder, horse-stealing, embezzlement, and other similar offences was sufficient to consign the unfortunate accused to the tender mercies of the rack, the Scavenger's Daughter,[3] and the manacles, when the aggrieved person had influence enough to procure a royal warrant; nor were these proceedings confined to the secret dungeons of the Tower, for the records show that torture began to be habitually applied in the Bridewell. Jardine, however, states that this especially danger-

[1] Burnet, Hist. Reform. Bk. III. pp. 341–2.

[2] According to Nicander Nucius (Travels, Camden Soc. 1841, pp. 58, 62,) the investigation of these deceptions with the severest tortures, βασάνοις ἀφορήτοις, was apparently the ordinary mode of procedure.

[3] Sir William Skevington, a lieutenant of the Tower, under Henry VIII., immortalized himself by reviving an old implement of torture, consisting of an iron hoop, in which the prisoner was bent, heels to hams and chest to knees, and was thus crushed together unmercifully. It obtained the nickname of Skevington's daughter, corrupted in time to Scavenger's Daughter. Among other sufferers from its embraces was an unlucky Irishman, named Myagh, whose plaint, engraved on the wall of his dungeon, is still among the curiosities of the Tower:—

> " Thomas Miagh, which liethe here alone,
> That fayne wold from hens begon :
> By torture straunge mi truth was tryed,
> Yet of my libertie denied.
>   1581. Thomas Myagh."—Jardine, op. cit. pp. 15, 30.

ous extension of the abuse appears to have ceased with
the death of Elizabeth, and that no trace of the torture
even of political prisoners can be found later than the
year 1640.[1] The royal prerogative had begun to be too
severely questioned to render such manifestations of it
prudent, and the Great Rebellion finally settled the constitutional rights of the subject on too secure a basis for even
the time-serving statesmen of the Restoration to venture
on a renewal of the former practices. Yet how nearly, at
one time, it had come to be engrafted on the law of the
land is evident from its being sufficiently recognized as a
legal procedure for persons of noble blood to claim immunity from it, and for the judges to admit that claim as a
special privilege. In the Countess of Shrewsbury's case,
the judges, among whom was Sir Edward Coke, declared
that there was a " privilege which the law gives for the
honor and reverence of the nobility, that their bodies are
not subject to torture *in causa criminis læsæ majestatis;*"
and no instance is on record to disprove the assertion.[2]

In one class of offences, however, torture was frequently
used to a later date, and without requiring the royal intervention. As on the Continent, sorcery and witchcraft
were regarded as crimes of such peculiar atrocity, and the
aversion they excited was so universal and intense, that
those accused of them were practically placed beyond the
pale of the law, and no means were considered too severe
to secure the conviction which in many cases could only be
obtained by confession. We have seen that among the
refinements of Italian torture, the deprivation of sleep for
forty hours was considered by the most experienced authorities on the subject to be second to none in severity and
effectiveness. It neither lacerated the flesh, dislocated the
joints, nor broke the bones, and yet few things could be
conceived as more likely to cloud the intellect, break down

---

[1] Jardine, pp. 53, 57–8.   [2] Op. cit. p. 65.

the will, and reduce the prisoner into a frame of mind in which he would be ready to admit anything that the questions of his examiners might suggest to him. In English witch trials, this method of torture was not infrequently resorted to, without the limitation of time to which it was restricted by the more experienced jurists of Italy.[1]

Another form of torture used in Great Britain, which doubtless proved exceedingly efficacious, was the "pricking" adopted to discover the insensible spot, which, according to popular belief, was one of the invariable signs of a witch. There were even professional "prickers" who were called in as experts in the witch-trials, and who thrust long pins into the body of the accused until some result, either negative or positive, was obtained.[2] Thus at the prosecution of Janet Barker, in Edinburgh, in 1643, it is recorded that "she had the usual mark on the left shoulder, which enabled one James Scober, a skilful pricker of witches, to find her out by putting a large pin into it, which she never felt."[3] One witch pricker, named Kincaid, used to strip his victims, bind them hand and foot, and then thrust his pins into every part of their bodies, until, exhausted and rendered speechless by the torture, they failed to scream, when he would triumphantly proclaim that he had found the witch-mark. Another pricker confessed on the gallows that he had illegally caused the

---

[1] Lecky, Hist. of Rationalism, Am. ed. I. 122.—In his very interesting work, Mr. Lecky mentions a case, occurring under the Commonwealth, of an aged clergyman named Lowes, who, after an irreproachable pastorate of fifty years, fell under suspicion. "The unhappy old man was kept awake for several successive nights, and persecuted 'till he was weary of his life, and was scarcely sensible of what he said or did.' He was then thrown into the water, condemned, and hung."—Ibid. p. 126.

[2] Cobbett's State Trials, VI. 686.—Although ostensibly not used to extort confession, this pricking was practically regarded as a torture. Thus in 1677 the Privy Council of Scotland "found that they (i. e., the inferior magistracy) might not use any torture by pricking or by withholding them from sleep." (loc. cit.)

[3] Spottiswoode Miscellany, Edinburgh, 1845, II. 67.

death of a hundred and twenty women whom he had thus
pricked for witchcraft.[1]

In Scotland, torture, as a regular form of judicial investigation, was of late introduction. In the various codes
collected by Skene, extending from an early period to the
commencement of the fifteenth century, there is no allusion
whatever to it. In the last of these codes, adopted under
Robert III., by the Parliament of Scotland in 1400, the
provisions respecting the wager of battle show that torture
would have been superfluous as a means of supplementing
deficient evidence.[2] The influence of the Roman law, however, though late in appearing, was eventually much more
deeply felt in Scotland than in the sister kingdom, and
consequently torture at length came to be regarded as an
ordinary resource in doubtful cases. In the witch persecutions, especially, which in Scotland rivalled the worst
excesses of the Inquisition of Germany and Spain, it was
carried to a pitch of frightful cruelty which far transcended
the limits assigned to it elsewhere.[3] Indeed, it is difficult
to believe that the accounts which have been preserved to
us of these terrible scenes are not exaggerated. No cruelty
is too great for the conscientious persecutor who believes
that he is avenging his God, but the limitless capacity of
human nature for inflicting is not complemented by a
limitless capacity of endurance on the part of the victim;
and well authenticated as the accounts of the Scottish

---

[1] Rogers' Scotland, Social and Domestic, p. 266.

[2] Statut. Roberti III. cap. xvi. (Skene).

[3] Thus the vigils, which elsewhere consisted simply in keeping the accused awake for forty hours by the simplest modes, in Scotland were fearfully aggravated by a witch-bridle, a band of iron fastened around the face,
with four diverging points thrust into the mouth. With this the accused
was secured immovably to a wall, and cases are on record in which this insupportable torment was prolonged for five and even for nine days.—(Lecky,
op. cit. I. 145–6.)—In other cases an enormous weight of iron hoops and
chains, amounting to twenty-five or thirty stone, would be accumulated on
the body of the patient. (Rogers, op. cit. pp. 267–300.)

witch-trials may be, they seem to transcend the possibility of human strength.[1] In another respect these witch-trials were marked with a peculiar atrocity. Elsewhere, as we have seen, confession was requisite for condemnation, thus affording some color of excuse for torture. In Scotland, however, the testimony of the pricker was sufficient, and torture thus became a wanton and cruel surplusage, rendered the less defensible in that the poor wretch who yielded to the torment and confessed was rewarded by being mercifully strangled before being burnt, while those who held out under torture were condemned and burnt alive.[2]

Torture thus maintained its place in the law of Scotland as long as the kingdom preserved the right of self-legislation, though an attempt seems to have been made to repress it during the temporary union with England under the Commonwealth. In 1652, when the English Commissioners for the administration of justice sat in Edinburgh, among other criminals brought before them were two

---

[1] I quote from Mr. Lecky (p. 147), who gives as his authority "Pitcairn's Criminal Trials of Scotland."

"But others and perhaps worse trials were in reserve. The three principal that were habitually applied were the penniwinkis, the boots, and the caschielawis. The first was a kind of thumbscrew; the second was a frame in which the leg was inserted, and in which it was broken by wedges driven in by a hammer; the third was also an iron frame for the leg, which was from time to time heated over a brazier. Fire matches were sometimes applied to the body of the victim. We read, in a contemporary legal register, of one man who was kept for forty-eight hours in 'vehement tortour' in the caschielawis; and of another who remained in the same frightful machine for eleven days and eleven nights, whose legs were broken daily for fourteen days in the boots, and who was so scourged that the whole skin was torn from his body." These cases occurred in 1596.

These horrors are almost equalled by those of another trial in which a Dr. Fian was accused of having caused the storms which endangered the voyage of James I. from Denmark in 1590. James personally superintended the torturing of the unhappy wretch, and after exhausting all the torments known to the skill and experience of the executioners, he invented new ones. All were vain, however, and the victim was finally burnt without confessing his ill-deeds. (*Ibid.* p. 123.)

[2] Rogers, op. cit. p. 307.

witches who had confessed their guilt before the Kirk They were the remains of a party of six, four of whom had died under the tortures employed to procure confession—such as hanging by the thumbs tied behind the back, scourging, burning the feet and head and putting lighted candles into their mouths, clothing them in haircloth soaked in vinegar "to fetch off the skin," &c. Another woman was stripped naked, laid on a cold stone with a hair-cloth over her, and thus kept for twenty-eight days and nights, being fed on bread and water. The diarist who records this adds that "The judges are resolved to inquire into the business, and have appointed the sheriff, ministers and tormentors to be found out, and to have an account of the ground of this cruelty."[1] What result their humane efforts obtained in this particular instance I have not been able to ascertain, but the legal administration of torture was not abolished until after the Union, when, in 1709, the United Parliament made haste, at its second session, to pass an act for "improving the Union," by which it was done away with.[2] Yet the spirit which had led to its abuses could not be repressed by Act of Parliament, and a case is on record, occurring in 1722, when a poor old

[1] Diurnal of Occurrences in Scotland. (Spottiswoode Miscellany, II. 90–91.)

[2] 7 Anne c. 21.—While thus legislating for the enlightenment of Scotland, the English majority took care to retain the equally barbarous practice of the *peine forte et dure* which had been introduced under the Stuarts, in defiance of the principles of the Common Law (See Fleta, Lib. I. cap. xxxii. § 33, also, Horne's Myrror of Justice, cap. I. sect. viii.). This was not strictly a torture for investigation, but a punishment, which was inflicted on those who refused to plead either guilty or not guilty. After its commencement, the unfortunate wretch was not allowed to plead, but was kept under the press until death, "donec oneris, frigoris atque famis cruciatu extinguitur."—See Hale, Placit. Coron. c. xliii. This relic of modern barbarism was not abolished until 1772, by 12 Geo. III. c. 20. The only case of its employment in America is said to have been that of Giles Cory, in 1692, during the witchcraft epidemic. Knowing the hopelessness of the trials, he refused to plead, and was duly pressed to death. (Cobbett's State Trials, VI. 680.)

woman in her dotage, condemned to be burnt as a witch, actually warmed her withered hands at the stake lighted for her destruction, and mumbled out her gladness at enjoying the unaccustomed warmth.[1]

A system of procedure which entailed results so deplorable as those which we have seen accompany it everywhere, could scarcely fail to arouse the opposition of independent men who were not swayed by reverence for precedent or carried away by popular impulses. Accordingly, an occasional voice was raised in denunciation of the use of torture. The Spaniard, Juan Luis Vives, one of the profoundest scholars of the sixteenth century, condemned it as useless and inhuman.[2] The sceptic of the period, Montaigne, was too cool and clear-headed not to appreciate the vicious principle on which it was based, and he did not hesitate to stamp it with his reprobation. "To tell the truth, it is a means full of uncertainty and danger; what would we not say, what would we not do to escape suffering so poignant? whence it happens that when a judge tortures a prisoner for the purpose of not putting an innocent man to death, he puts him to death both innocent and tortured. . . . . Are you not unjust when, to save him from being killed, you do worse than kill him?"[3] In 1624, the learned Johann Graefe, in his "Tribunal Reformatum," argued forcibly in favor of its abolition. When the French Ordonnance of 1670 was in preparation, various magistrates of the highest character and largest experience gave it as

[1] Rogers, op. cit. p. 301.

[2] His arguments are quoted and controverted by Simancas, Bishop of Badajos, in his Cathol. Institut. Tit. LXV. No. 7, 8.

[3] Essais, Liv. II. chap. v.—This passage is little more than a plagiarism on St. Augustine, de Civ. Dei, Liv. XIX. cap. vi.—Montaigne further illustrates his position by a story from Froissart (Liv. IV. ch. lviii.), who relates that an old woman complained to Bajazet that a soldier had foraged on her. The Turk summarily disposed of the soldier's denial by causing his stomach to be opened. He proved guilty—but what had he been found innocent?

38*

their fixed opinion that torture was useless, that it rarely succeeded in eliciting the truth from the accused, and that it ought to be abolished.[1] Towards the close of the century, various writers took up the question. The best known of these was perhaps Augustin Nicolas, who has been frequently referred to above, and who argued with more zeal and learning than skill against the whole system, but especially against it as applied by the Inquisition in cases of witchcraft.[2] In 1692, von Boden, in a work alluded to in the preceding pages, inveighed against its abuses, while admitting its utility in many classes of crimes. In 1705, at the University of Halle, Martin Bernhardi of Pomerania, a candidate for the doctorate, in his inaugural thesis, argued with much vigor in favor of abolishing it, and the dean of the faculty, Christian Thomas, acknowledged the validity of his reasoning, though expressing doubts as to the practicability of a sudden reform. Bernhardi states that in his time it was no longer employed in Holland, and its disuse in Utrecht he attributes to a case in which a thief procured the execution, after due torture and confession, of a shoemaker, against whom he had brought a false charge in revenge for the refusal of a pair of boots.[3] His assertion, however, is too general, for it was not until the

[1] Des magistrats recommendables par une grande capacité et par une expérience consommée, s'étant expliqués sur ce genre de question, auroient déclaré qu'elle leur avoit toujours semblé inutile, qu'il étoit rare que la question préparatoire eût tiré la vérité de la bouche d'un accusé, et qu'il y avoit de fortes raisons pour en supprimer l'usage.—Déclaration du 24 Août, 1780 (Isambert, XXVII. 374).

[2] Nicolas is careful to assert his entire belief in the existence of sorcery and his sincere desire for its punishment, and he is indignant at the popular feeling which stigmatized those who wished for a reform in procedure as "avocats des sorciers."

[3] Bernhardi Diss. Inaug. cap. II. §§ iv., x.—Bernhardi ventured on the use of very decided language in denunciation of the system.—"Injustam, iniquam, fallacem, insignium malorum promotricem, et denique omni divini testimonii specie destitutam esse hanc violentam torturam et proinde ex foris Christianorum rejiciendam intrepide assero." (Ibid. cap. I. § I.)

formation of the Republic of the Netherlands, in 1798, that it was formally abolished.[1]

These efforts had little effect, but they manifest the progress of enlightenment, and doubtless paved the way for change, especially in the Prussian territories. Yet, in 1730, we find the learned Baron Senckenberg reproducing Zanger's treatise, not as an archæological curiosity, but as a practical text-book for the guidance of lawyers and judges, and in 1740 a legal tract published at Jena speaks of its being administered only by order of the highest courts.[2] It was at this time, however, that the process of reform began in earnest. Frederic the Great succeeded to the throne of Prussia, May 31, 1740. Few of his projects of universal philanthropy and philosophical regeneration of human nature survived the hardening experiences of royal ambition, but, while his power was yet in its first bloom, he made haste to get rid of this relic of mediæval barbarism. It was almost his earliest official act, for the cabinet order abolishing torture is dated June 3d.[3] Yet even Frederic could not absolutely shake off the traditional belief in its necessity when the safety of the State or of the head of the State was concerned. Treason and rebellion and some other atrocious crimes were excepted from the reform; and in 1752, at the instance of his high chancellor, Cocceji, by a special rescript, he ordered two citizens of Oschersleben to be tortured on suspicion of robbery.[4] With singular inconsistency, moreover, torture

[1] Meyer, Institutions Judiciaires, IV. 297. Even then, however, the inquisitorial process was not abolished, and criminal procedure continued to be secret. For the rack and strappado were substituted prolonged imprisonment and other expedients to extort confession; and in 1803 direct torture was used in the case of Hendrik Janssen, executed in Amsterdam on the strength of a confession extracted from him with the aid of a bull's pizzle.

[2] Willenbergii Tract. de Excess. et Pœnis Cleric. 4to. Jenæ, 1740, p. 42.

[3] Carlyle, Hist. Friedrich II. Book xi. ch. i.

[4] I find this statement in an account by G. F. Günther (Lipsiæ, 1838) of the abolition of torture in Saxony.

in a modified form was long permitted in Prussia, not precisely as a means of investigation, but as a sort of punishment for obdurate prisoners who would not confess, and
as a means of marking them for subsequent recognition.[1]
It is evident that the abrogation of torture did not carry
with it the removal of the evils of the inquisitorial process.

When the royal philosopher of Europe thus halted in
the reform, it is not singular that the more conservative
monarchs around him should have paused before committing themselves to so great an innovation. Yet it came
at last. From 1770 to 1783, Saxony was engaged in a
thorough remodelling of her system of criminal jurisprudence, in which the whole apparatus of torture was swept
away; and in Switzerland and Austria it shared a like
fate about the same time. In Russia, the Empress Catherine, in 1762, removed it from the jurisdiction of the inferior courts, where it had been greatly abused; in 1767, by
a secret order, it was restricted to cases in which the confession of the accused proved actually indispensable, and
even in these it was only permitted under the special command of governors of provinces.[2] In the singularly enlightened instructions which she drew up for the framing
of a new code in 1767 the use of torture was earnestly
argued against in a manner which betrays the influence of
Beccaria.[3] Under these auspices it soon became almost
obsolete, and it was finally abolished in 1801. Yet, in
some of the states of central Europe, the progress of enlightenment was wonderfully slow. Torture continued to

[1] Günther, op. cit.—It appears that the authorities of Leipzig, in 1769,
when asked their opinion on the subject, reported their approval of the plan
then followed in the Prussian dominions —"In terris Borussicis tormenta
non plane esse abrogata, sed interdum adhuc adhiberi, non tantum ut re-
facinora commissa confiteri cogantur, sed etiam ne, qui pertinaciter nega-
rent, plane impunes evaderent; imo interdum torqueri quasi memoriæ causa,
videlicet ut nefarii homines, si rursus deliquerent, facilius cognoscerentur."
[2] Du Boys, Droit Criminel des Peuples Modernes, I. 620.
[3] Grand Instructions of Catherine II.—London, 1768, pp. 113-8.

disgrace the jurisprudence of Wirtemberg and Bavaria until 1806 and 1807. Though the wars of Napoleon abolished it temporarily in other states, on his fall in 1814 it was actually restored. In 1819, however, George IV. consented, at the request of his subjects, to dispense with it in Hanover; while in Baden it continued to exist until 1831. Yet legists who had been trained in the old school could not admit the soundness of modern ideas, and in the greater part of Germany the theories which resulted in the use of torture continued to prevail. The secret inquisitorial process was retained and the principle that the confession of the accused was requisite to his condemnation. Torture of some kind is necessary to render the practical application of this system efficacious, and accordingly though the rack and strappado were abolished their place was taken by other modes, in reality not less cruel. When appearances were against the prisoner, he was confined for an indefinite period and subjected to all the hard usage to be expected from officials provoked by his criminal obstinacy. He was brought up repeatedly before his judge and exposed to the most searching interrogatories and terrified with threats. Legists, unwilling to abandon the powerful weapon which had placed every accused person at their mercy, imagined a new expedient for its revival. It was held that every criminal owed to society a full and free confession. His refusal to do this was a crime, so that if his answers were unsatisfactory to the judge, the latter could punish him on the spot for contumacy. As this punishment was usually administered with the scourge, it will be seen that the abolition of torture was illusory, and that the worst abuses to which it gave rise have been carefully retained.[1]

Even France had maintained a conservatism which may seem surprising in that centre of the philosophic specula-

[1] Jardine, Use of Torture in England, p. 3.—Meyer, Institutions Judiciaires, T. I. p. xlvi.—T. II. p. 262.

tion of the eighteenth century. Her leading writers had
not hesitated to condemn it. In the "Esprit des Lois,"
published in 1748, Montesquieu stamped his reprobation
on the system with a quiet significance which showed that
he had on his side all the great thinkers of the age, and that
he felt argument to be mere surplusage.[1] Voltaire did not
allow its absurdities and incongruities to escape, and in
1777 he addressed an earnest request to Louis XVI. to
include it among the subjects of the reforms which marked
the opening of his reign.[2] In 1761 the celebrated *affaire
Calas*, which attracted the attention of all Europe, had demonstrated the utterly useless cruelty of the system. In
that year, at midnight of Oct. 13th, at Toulouse, the body
of Marc-Antoine Calas was found strangled in the back
shop of his father. The family were Protestants and the
murdered man had given signs of conversion to Catholi-
cism, in imitation of his younger brother. A minute investigation left scarcely a doubt that the murder had been
committed by the father, from religious motives, and he
was condemned to death. He appealed to the Parlement
of Toulouse, which after a patient hearing sentenced him
to the wheel, and to the *question ordinaire et extraordinaire*, to extract a confession. He underwent the extremity of torture and the hideous punishment of being broken
alive without varying from his protestations of innocence.

[1] Tant d'habiles gens et tant de beaux génies ont écrit contre cette pra-
tique que je n'ose parler après eux. J'allois dire qu'elle pourroit convenir
dans les gouvernements despotiques ; où tout qui inspire la crainte entre
plus dans les ressorts du gouvernement : j'allois dire que les esclaves, chez
les Grecs et chez les Romains —— Mais j'entends la voix de la nature qui
crie contre moi.—Liv. vi. ch. xvii.

[2] Chéruel, Dict. Hist. des Institutions de la France, P. II. p. 1220 (Paris,
1855). Voltaire had already, in 1765, endeavored to arouse public opinion
on the case of the Chevalier de la Barre, a youthful officer only 20 years of
age, who was tortured and executed on an accusation of having recited a
song insulting to Mary Magdalene and of having mutilated with his sword
a wooden crucifix on the bridge of Abbeville —Desmaze, Pénalités Anciennes, Pièces Justificatives, p. 423.

Though both trials appear to have been conducted with rigorous impartiality, the protestantism of Europe saw in the affair the evidence of religious persecution, and a fearful outcry was raised. Voltaire, ever on the watch for means to promote toleration and freedom of thought, seized hold of it with tireless energy, and created so strong an agitation on the subject that in 1764 the supreme tribunal at Paris reversed the sentence, discharged the other members of the family, who had been subjected to various punishments, and rehabilitated the memory of Calas.[1] It would be difficult to conceive of a more striking exemplification of the worse than uselessness of torture as a judicial expedient. Yet it was not until 1780 that the *question préparatoire* was abolished by a royal edict which, in a few weighty lines, indicated that only the reverence for traditional usage had preserved it so long.[2] This edict, however, was not strictly obeyed, and cases of the use of torture still occasionally occurred, as that of Marie Tison at Rouen, in 1788, accused of the murder of her husband;[3] and in the same year, 1788, another ordonnance was requisite to insure the observance of the previous one.[4] In fact, when the States-General was convened in 1789, the *cahier des doléances* of Valenciennes contained a prayer for the abolition of torture, showing that it had not as yet been dis-

[1] Mary Lafon, Histoire du Midi de la France, T. IV. pp. 325–355.—The theory of the defence was that the murdered man had committed suicide; but this is incompatible with the testimony, much of which is given at length by Mary Lafon, a writer who cannot be accused of any leanings against protestantism.

[2] Déclaration du 24 Août 1780 (Isambert, XXVII. 373).

[3] Thumb-screws were applied to both thumbs and at the same time she was hoisted in the strappado, in which she was allowed to hang for an hour after the executioner had reported that her shoulders were out of joint. All these inhuman cruelties were insufficient to extort a confession.—Desmaze, Pénalités Anciennes, pp. 176–77.

[4] Déclaration du 3 Mai 1788, art. 8. "Nôtre déclaration du 24 Août sera exécutée" (Isambert, XXIX. 532).

continued there.[1] The *question définitive* or *préalable*, by
which the prisoner after condemnation was again tortured
to discover his accomplices, still remained until 1788, when
it, too, was abolished, at least temporarily. It was pronounced uncertain, cruel to the convict and perplexing to
the judge, and, above all, dangerous to the innocent
whom the prisoner might name in the extremity of his
agony to procure its cessation, and whom he would per-
sist in accusing to preserve himself from its repetition.
Yet, with strange inconsistency, the abolition of this cruel
wrong was only provisional, and its restoration was threatened in a few years, if the tribunals should deem it necessary.[2] When those few short years came around they
dawned on a new France, from which the old systems had
been swept away as by the besom of destruction; and torture as an element of criminal jurisprudence was a thing
of the past. By the decree of October 9th, 1789, it was
abolished forever.

In Italy, Beccaria, in 1764, took occasion to devote a few
pages of his treatise on crimes and punishments to the subject of torture, and its illogical cruelty could not well be
exposed with more terseness and force.[3] It was probably

---

[1] Louïse, Sorcellerie et Justice Criminelle à Valenciennes, p. 96.

[2] Isambert, XXIX. 529.—It is noteworthy, as a sign of the temper of
the times, on the eve of the last convocation of the Notables, that this edict,
which introduced various ameliorations in criminal procedure, and promised
a more thorough reform, invites from the community at large suggestions on
the subject, in order that the reform may embody the results of public
opinion—"Nous élèverons ainsi au rang des lois les résultats de l'opinion
publique." This was pure democratic republicanism in an irregular form.

The edict also indicates an intention to remove another of the blots on the
criminal procedure of the age, in a vague promise to allow the prisoner the
privilege of counsel.

[3] Dei Delitti e delle Pene § xii.—The fundamental error in the prevalent
system of criminal procedure was well exposed in Beccaria's remark that a
mathematician would be better than a legist for the solution of the essential
problem in criminal trials—"Data la forza dei muscoli e la sensibilitá delle
fibre di un innocente, trovare il grado di dolore che lo farà confessar reo di
un dato delitto."

due to the movement excited by this work that in 1786 torture was formally abolished in Tuscany. Yet Italy, which
was the first to revive its use in the Middle Ages, was not
disposed wholly to abandon it. Unless we may disbelieve
all that is told of the means adopted to preserve legitimacy
against revolutionism during the interval between Napoleon and Garibaldi, the dungeons of Naples and Palermo
were the last places where this relic of brutal and unreasoning force was habitually resorted to.

Yet so long as human nature retains its imperfections
the baffled impatience of the strong will be apt to wreak
its vengeance on the weak and defenceless. As recently
as 1867, in Texas, the Jefferson *Times* records a case in
which, under the auspices of the military authorities, torture was applied to two negroes suspected of purloining a
considerable amount of money which had been lost by a
revenue collector. More recently still, in September 1868,
the London journals report fearful barbarities perpetrated
by the Postmaster-General of Roumania to trace the authors of a mail robbery. A woman was hung to a beam
with hot eggs under the armpits; others were burned
with grease and petroleum, while others again were tied
by the hair to horses' tails and dragged through thorn
bushes. It must be added that the offending officials were
promptly dismissed and committed for trial. The most
recent case, however, is one which has lately been the subject of legislative discussion in Switzerland, where it appears that in the Canton of Zug, under order of court, a
man suspected of theft was put on bread and water from
Oct. 26th to Nov. 10th, 1869, to extort confession, and
when this failed he was subjected to thumb-screws and
beaten with rods. It is to be hoped that the scandal caused
by the development of this barbarism may render its repetition impossible.

In casting a retrospective glance over this long history
39

of cruelty and injustice, it is curious to observe that Christian communities, where the truths of the Gospel were
received with unquestioning veneration, systematized the
administration of torture with a cold-blooded ferocity
unknown to the legislation of the heathen nations whence
they derived it.   The careful restrictions and safeguards,
with which the Roman jurisprudence sought to protect
the interests of the accused, contrast strangely with the
reckless disregard of every principle of justice which sullies
the criminal procedure of Europe from the thirteenth
almost to the nineteenth century.   From this no race or
religion was exempt.   What the Calvinist suffered in Flanders, he inflicted in Scotland; what the Catholic enforced
in Italy, he endured in England; nor did either of them
deem that he was forfeiting his share in the Divine Evangel
of peace on earth and goodwill to men.

The mysteries of the human conscience and of human
motives are well nigh inscrutable, and it may seem shocking
to assert that these centuries of unmitigated wrong are
indirectly traceable to that religion of which the second
great commandment was that man should love his neighbor
as himself.   Yet so it was.   The first commandment, to
love God with all our heart, when perverted by superstition, gave a strange direction to the teachings of Christ.
For ages, the assumptions of an infallible church had led
men to believe that the interpreter was superior to Scrip-
ture.   Every expounder of the holy text felt in his inmost
heart that he alone, with his fellows, worshipped God as
God desired to be worshipped, and that every ritual but
his own was an insult to the Divine nature.   Outside of his
own communion there was no escape from eternal perdition,
and the fervor of religious conviction thus made persecution a duty to God and man.   This led the Inquisition, as
we have seen, to perfect a system of which the iniquity was
complete.   Thus commended, that system became part and
parcel of secular law, and when the Reformation arose the

habits of thought which ages had consolidated were universal. The boldest Reformers who shook off the yoke of
Rome, as soon as they had attained power, had as little
scruple as Rome itself in rendering obligatory their interpretation of divine truth, and in applying to secular as
well as to religious affairs the cruel maxims in which they
had been educated.

Yet, in the general enlightenment which caused and
accompanied the Reformation, there passed away gradually
the necessity which had created the rigid institutions of
the Middle Ages. Those institutions had fulfilled their
mission, and the savage tribes that had broken down the
worn-out civilization of Rome were at last becoming fitted
for a higher civilization than the world had yet seen, wherein
the precepts of the Gospel might at length find practical
expression and realization. For the first time in the history of man the universal love and charity which lie at
the foundation of Christianity are recognized as the elements on which human society should be based. Weak
and erring as we are, and still far distant from the ideal of
the Saviour, yet are we approaching it, even if our steps
are painful and hesitating. In the slow evolution of the
centuries, it may only be by comparing distant periods that
we can mark our progress; but progress nevertheless
exists, and future generations, perhaps, may be able to
emancipate themselves wholly from the cruel and arbitrary
domination of superstition and force.

INDEX.